I0093982

Diagnosing Corruption in Ethiopia

Diagnosing Corruption in Ethiopia

Perceptions, Realities, and the
Way Forward for Key Sectors

Janelle Plummer, Editor

Canadian International
Development Agency

Agence canadienne de
développement international

THE WORLD BANK
Washington, D.C.

Kingdom of the Netherlands

UKaid
from the Department for International Development

© 2012 International Bank for Reconstruction and Development / The World Bank
1818 H Street NW, Washington DC 20433
Telephone: 202-473-1000; Internet: www.worldbank.org

Some rights reserved

1 2 3 4 15 14 13 12

This work is a product of the staff of The World Bank with external contributions. Note that The World Bank does not necessarily own each component of the content included in the work. The World Bank therefore does not warrant that the use of the content contained in the work will not infringe on the rights of third parties. The risk of claims resulting from such infringement rests solely with you.

The findings, interpretations, and conclusions expressed in this work do not necessarily reflect the views of The World Bank, its Board of Executive Directors, or the governments they represent. The World Bank does not guarantee the accuracy of the data included in this work. The boundaries, colors, denominations, and other information shown on any map in this work do not imply any judgment on the part of The World Bank concerning the legal status of any territory or the endorsement or acceptance of such boundaries.

Nothing herein shall constitute or be considered to be a limitation upon or waiver of the privileges and immunities of The World Bank, all of which are specifically reserved.

Rights and Permissions

This work is available under the Creative Commons Attribution 3.0 Unported license (CC BY 3.0) **http://creativecommons.org/licenses/by/3.0.** Under the Creative Commons Attribution license, you are free to copy, distribute, transmit, and adapt this work, including for commercial purposes, under the following conditions:

Attribution—Please cite the work as follows: Plummer, Janelle. 2012. *Diagnosing Corruption in Ethiopia: Perceptions, Realities, and the Way Forward.* Washington, DC: World Bank. DOI 10.1596/978-0-8213-9531-8. License: Creative Commons Attribution CC BY 3.0

Translations—If you create a translation of this work, please add the following disclaimer along with the attribution: *This translation was not created by The World Bank and should not be considered an official World Bank translation. The World Bank shall not be liable for any content or error in this translation.*

All queries on rights and licenses should be addressed to the Office of the Publisher, The World Bank, 1818 H Street NW, Washington, DC 20433, USA; fax: 202-522-2625; e-mail: pubrights@worldbank.org.

ISBN: 978-0-8213-9531-8
ISBN (electronic): 978-0-8213-9532-5
DOI: 10.1596/978-0-8213-9531-8
Cover design: Debra Naylor, Washington, D.C.

Library of Congress Cataloging-in-Publication Data
Diagnosing corruption in Ethiopia : perceptions, realities, and the way forward for key sectors/
edited by Janelle Plummer.
    p. cm.
  Includes bibliographical references.
  ISBN 978-0-8213-9531-8 — ISBN 978-0-8213-9532-5 (electronic)
1. Corruption—Ethiopia. 2. Public administration—Corrupt practices—Ethiopia. I. Plummer, Janelle.
  JQ3759.5.C6D53 2012
  364.13230963—dc23   2012011962

Contents

Map

Figures

Tables

Foreword

The government of the Federal Democratic Republic of Ethiopia (FDRE) clearly recognizes that corruption hinders development, democratization, and good governance endeavors. Hence, it has been striving to prevent and combat this socioeconomic evil by designing various strategies. Encouraging results have been registered. Nevertheless, it is the strong conviction of the government that the anticorruption struggle should continue in a strengthened manner to attain better results.

The Ethiopian government believes that anti-corruption activities should be supported by studies to make them fruitful. However—apart from the Corruption Perception Index by Transparency International (which we do not believe accurately indicates the level of corruption in the country) and the National Corruption Perception Survey conducted by Addis Ababa University in 2001—no study was conducted that gave full information about the reality on the ground.

In recent years, diagnostic studies aiming at assessing the level of corruption in Ethiopia have been conducted with the financial support of our development partners. The findings of the first phase of study, which focused on the construction sector, indicated a high perception of corruption but a low reality. We found it important to expand the scope of the study to include corruption in health, education, water, land management, justice, telecommunications, and the mining sectors, all relevant to the achievement of the Millennium Development Goals (MDGs). As the government allocates substantial budgets to these sectors, conducting diagnostic studies and finding out the reality will contribute significantly to ensuring that the country's financial resources are deployed to the desired objectives, and to filling an information gap in this area.

The diagnostic studies and the recommendations forwarded play a pivotal role in accelerating the ongoing struggle against corruption by ensuring transparency and accountability in our country. They will also create the opportunity to base comments on concrete information. The studies have achieved their objective in this respect.

I would like to assure you that the Federal Ethics and Anti-Corruption Commission of Ethiopia (FEACC) is committed to the follow-up and implementation of recommendations put forward in the same way that it cooperated during the execution of the studies. We will also do our best to make the diagnostic studies accessible to stakeholders.

The Ethiopian government wishes to support similar studies in the future to reinvigorate the nationwide struggle against corruption. As long as our partners support the anti-corruption endeavor, we will be willing to conduct similar studies, and the door is open for those who would like to support us in such efforts. Finally, on behalf of the Commission, I would like to express my sincere gratitude to U.K. Department for International Development (DFID), the Canadian International Development Agency (CIDA), the Royal Netherlands Embassy, and the World Bank, which have taken part in and financed the studies.

Ali Sulaiman
Commissioner
Federal Ethics and Anti-Corruption
Commission of Ethiopia

Preface

Although many would argue that opaque decision making, control over the flows of information, and a lack of open debate have constrained development and governance processes in Ethiopia for decades, the situation with regard to corruption is different in many respects. Corruption is an area of governance where a significant number of government stakeholders would like to see a detailed story told; there is a greater openness to the assessment of corruption than to the assessment of other areas of governance. Moreover, it is an area of governance where the government of Ethiopia is, potentially, on strong ground.

Unraveling the story of corruption in Ethiopia is complex and presents a different picture at every turn. On the one hand, there is a general sense that the story is somehow different, that—at least in some key areas—corruption is just not experienced at the same levels as in other African and low-income countries. Many private stakeholders argue that corruption in Ethiopia is comparatively controlled; first-hand experience is that it is much lower than elsewhere. This is not to say that corruption is not increasing or emerging as an issue for serious consideration, but when international observers apply a direct cross-country comparison, Ethiopia tends to come out well. On the other hand, many domestic stakeholders argue that corruption is highly problematic. The global indicators measuring corruption are also inconsistent.

The drive for this study arose from this set of conflicting and unresolved perspectives as to the nature and scope of corruption in Ethiopia. In early consultations, the World Bank country team in Ethiopia and many key development partners argued that they needed to know more about the nature, scope, causes, impacts, and costs of corruption so that development decisions were not based on assumptions. In late 2008, the World Bank approached the Federal Ethics and Anti-Corruption Commission (FEACC) to propose an independent diagnostic to unravel the story of corruption in Ethiopia.

With the full support of the government of Ethiopia, the World Bank then commissioned an independent set of sector-level diagnostics. With the benefit of hindsight, the sector approach was a hugely ambitious undertaking that has been achieved but has been significantly delayed. Although the studies themselves were completed by January 2010, the process of checking, review, and agreement for publication was slow and finally brought to conclusion only in 2011. Nevertheless, the funding development partners and the FEACC consider the story worth telling, and the disaggregated framework for each sector facilitates ongoing comparison and assessment. The chapters in this book are put forward with this caveat—that this was a long process and information is bound to have changed in the process.

The process and outputs are nevertheless revealing, opening the path for further assessment work to be undertaken in hitherto unreported areas. For this purpose, the Joint Governance Assessment and Measurement (J-GAM) Initiative has been established in Ethiopia with the support of the World Bank, Canadian International Development Agency (CIDA), U.K. Department for International Development (DFID), and the Royal Netherlands Embassy. This joint fund aims to enable better measurement, promote dialogue, and improve harmonization of governance interventions.

We would like to thank all those whose engagement and commitment to this effort has led to these diagnostics and to those who will take forward this first stage into more detailed assessment efforts that will help to improve the efficiency of public resources. In particular, we are very grateful to the FEACC Commissioner, Ato Ali Sulaiman; the World Bank Country Director, Guang Zhe Chen; as well as the former Country Director, Ken Ohashi, for their support throughout; the excellent team of consultants that has worked diligently to explore new ground—Hamish

Goldie-Scot, Piers Cross and Roger Callow, Linn Hammergren, Bill Savedoff and Karen Grepin, Michael Latham, Neill Stansbury, and Tony Burns—all the local consultants who took part in the survey work, including Imeru Tamrat; all the peer reviewers; and Nathaniel Myers for excellent coordination during the field work.

Considerable thanks are also due to Rupert Bladon, Senior Public Sector/Governance Specialist, for finalizing the study and preparing it for publication.

Finally, thanks are due to Greg Toulmin, Jean Edillon, Parveen Moses, and Senper Shimeles for their support throughout the process.

About the Editor and Authors

Janelle Plummer is the World Bank's senior governance specialist in the Cambodia Country Office. Previously, she was the Department for International Development-funded Governance Adviser in the Ethiopia Country Office and led the development of the Joint Governance Assessment Initiative, of which this corruption diagnostics work is a central part. She has worked on corruption in sectors since the tsunami in Aceh in 2004, was a founding member of the Water Integrity Network, and has pursued a risk-mapping approach to anticorruption action. The author of numerous policy and capacity building publications on good governance, she received her master's degree from the School of Oriental and African Studies at the University of London.

Tony Burns is a land administration specialist with extensive experience in designing, managing, and evaluating systematic registration and land administration projects. He is the managing director of Land Equity International, a company focused on supporting land administration projects worldwide. He has more than 25 years of experience in land sector projects, including serving as a team leader and project director supervising large-scale, long-term, multidisciplinary projects. He has also undertaken numerous short-term consultancies for a range of multilateral and bilateral development partners. His technical expertise includes land policy, cadastral survey and mapping, systematic registration, land administration, and spatial information systems.

Roger Calow is head of the Water Policy Programme of the Overseas Development Institute and an honorary research associate at the British Geological Survey. He has over 20 years of experience leading international research and development projects in Africa, Asia, and the Middle East, including two years as director of the RiPPLE program in Ethiopia, building local capacity for the design, implementation, and management of rural water supply and sanitation services. He leads an interdisciplinary team of eight staff members working on water supply and sanitation, climate change and water security, water resources management, and the political economy of sector reform.

Piers Cross is a leading international spokesperson and strategist in water supply and sanitation. A South African with a background in social anthropology and public health, he worked for the World Bank Water and Sanitation Program for over 20 years, holding the positions of Global Program Manager and Principal Regional Team Leaders for South Asia and Africa. He was the founding chief executive officer of the Mvula Trust and cofounder of the Water Integrity Network, and he is now a leading voice in the Sanitation and Water for All alliance. He advises leading sector agencies.

Kate Dalrymple is a land administration specialist with extensive research and consultancy experience in land policy, community engagement, and program implementation of land reform projects. After completing her Ph.D. in tenure security for poverty alleviation, she joined Land Equity International as a senior land consultant. She has experience in Asia, Africa, and the Pacific, where she worked on assignments in land titling, regularization, institutional modernization, land policy, and program design. In addition, she played a key role in managing and contributing to the pilot and ongoing implementation of the Land Governance Assessment Framework.

Hamish Goldie-Scot is a cofounder of the U.K. Anti-Corruption Forum and author of the paper "Corruption in Construction in Developing Countries," published in 2008 by the U.K. Institution of Civil Engineers. A former volunteer teacher, he has since 1980 worked as a civil engineer and planner in 25 developing countries. His professional and voluntary work combines technical, environmental, socioeconomic, and institutional considerations in optimizing the sustainable benefits of infrastructure provision. This process includes identifying and pursuing fresh collaborative approaches to understanding and addressing the drivers of corruption in a constructive manner that learns from the perspective of those still engaged in corrupt practices.

Karen Grépin is an assistant professor of Global Health Policy at New York University's Robert F. Wagner Graduate School of Public Service. She holds a S.M. in health policy and management from the Harvard School of Public Health and a Ph.D. in health policy (economics) from Harvard University. Her research focuses on the economics and politics of health service delivery in developing countries, with a focus on Sub-Saharan Africa. In particular, her work focuses on health systems, development assistance for health, and maternal health issues.

Linn Hammergren is an independent consultant specializing in rule of law, anticorruption policies, and general governance issues. She has a doctorate in political science. Before 2008, she spent 10 years with the World Bank and 12 years as an internal consultant for the United States Agency for International Development, where she managed Administration of Justice projects. Her research and publications focus on judicial politics and reform, judicial corruption, citizen security, and the politics of foreign assistance. She is a consultant to the World Bank, Inter-American Development Bank (IADB), U.S. Agency for International Development (USAID), New Zealand AID (MFAT), and the Mexican judiciary system, among others.

Michael Latham has worked with the CfBT Education Trust since 1982. Over the past two decades, he has worked in Africa, Asia, and the United States and Caribbean area. One of his key areas of work is in the role of the non-state sector in partnerships in education. He has presented papers and conducted training on behalf of the United Nations Institute for Training and Research, the Institute for Development Studies, the World Bank Institute, and Harvard University. He has been involved in the education sector in Hyderabad, India, since 2003 and has resided in the city since 2009.

Alan MacDonald is a principal hydrogeologist at the British Geological Survey where he divides his work between U.K. and international groundwater issues. He has published more than 40 scientific papers and is author of the book *Developing Groundwater: A Guide to Rural Water Supply* (Practical Action, 2005) and editor of *Applied Groundwater Studies in Africa* (Taylor and Francis, 2008). Much of his work focuses on the science base for sustainable development and management of groundwater, with a particular interest in climate resilience and poverty reduction. He has a B.S. in geophysics from Edinburgh University and an M.S. and Ph.D. in hydrogeology from University College London.

William D. Savedoff is a senior fellow at the Center for Global Development (CGD), where he works on aid effectiveness, corruption, and health policy. Before joining CGD, he prepared and advised projects in Africa, Asia, and Latin America for the Inter-American Development Bank and World Health Organization. As a consultant, he has worked for the National Institutes of Health, Transparency International, and the World Bank, and he helped establish the International Initiative for Impact Evaluation. His publications include *Cash on Delivery* (Center for Global Development, 2011), *Governing Mandatory Health Insurance* (World Bank, 2008), and *Diagnosis Corruption* (Inter-American Development Bank, 2001). He received his Ph.D. in economics from Boston University.

Abbreviations

ASC	Audit Services Corporation
BOFED	Bureaus of Finance and Economic Development (regional)
BPR	business process reengineering
CCTV	closed-circuit television
CMS	case management system
DACA	Drug Administration and Control Authority
DBST	double bitumen surface treatment (roads)
EPRDF	Ethiopian People's Revolutionary Democratic Front (ruling coalition)
ERA	Ethiopian Roads Authority
ERPA	Ethiopian Radiation Protection Authority
ESDP	Education Sector Development Program
ETA	Ethiopian Telecommunications Agency
ETC	Ethiopian Telecommunications Corporation
ETP	Education and Training Policy
FBO	faith-based organization
FEACC	Federal Ethics and Anti-Corruption Commission
FMOH	Federal Ministry of Health

GAC	Governance and Anticorruption (World Bank program)
GAVI Alliance	formerly the "Global Alliance for Vaccinations and Immunisations"
GEQIP	General Education Quality Improvement Program
GER	gross enrollment rate
GFATM	Global Fund to Fight AIDS, Tuberculosis and Malaria
GPS	global positioning system
HIV/AIDS	human immunodeficiency virus and acquired immune deficiency syndrome
HSDP	Health Sector Development Program
ICB	International Competitive Bidding
ICT	information and communication technology
LGAF	Land Governance Assessment Framework
MDG	Millennium Development Goal
MDTF	Multi-Donor Trust Fund
MOE	Ministry of Education
MOFCOMM	Ministry of Commerce (China)
MOFED	Ministry of Finance and Economic Development (Ethiopia)
MOME	Ministry of Mines and Energy (2005–09)
MOM	Ministry of Mines (2002–04 and 2010–present)
MOWR	Ministry of Water Resources
MSF	multistakeholder forum
NCB	National Competitive Bidding
NGO	nongovernmental organization
NMSG	national multistakeholder group
NSP	nonstate provider (education)
OECD	Organisation for Economic Co-operation and Development
OFAG	Office of the Federal Auditor General
O&M	operation and maintenance
PACS	Project Anti-Corruption System
PASDEP	Plan for Accelerated and Sustained Development to End Poverty
PBS	Protection of Basic Services (program)
PEPFAR	(U.S.) President's Emergency Plan for AIDS Relief
PFSA	Pharmaceutical Fund and Supply Agency
PPA	Public Procurement Agency
PTA	parent-teacher association

RHB	Regional Health Bureau
RRA	regional road authority
RSDP	Road Sector Development Program
SNNPR	Southern Nations, Nationalities and People's Region
SOE	state-owned enterprise
TTC	technical training college
TVET	technical and vocational education and training
UAP	Universal Access Program (water)
UCBP	University Capacity Building Program
UN	United Nations
UNICEF	United Nations Children's Fund
UNFPA	United Nations Population Fund
WASH	water, sanitation, and hygiene
WEO	Woreda Education Office
WHO	World Health Organization
WOFED	Woreda Offices of Finance and Economic Development
WoHO	Woreda Health Office
WTO	World Trade Organization
WUA	Water User Association

CHAPTER 1

Overview

Janelle Plummer

Introduction

For decades, corruption in Ethiopia has been discussed only at the margins. Perhaps because many have not experienced corruption as a significant constraint to their lives and businesses, or perhaps because a culture of circumspection has dampened open dialogue, Ethiopia has seen neither the information flows nor the debate on corruption that most other countries have seen in recent years.

To address this information gap, the World Bank agreed with the government of Ethiopia and its Federal Ethics and Anti-Corruption Commission (FEACC) to undertake research and produce an independent overview of corruption, identify follow-up actions to these diagnostics, and articulate the proposed approach in an Anti-Corruption Strategy and Action Plan for Ethiopia (World Bank 2007).

Although this chapter results from studies completed by January 2010, the process of checking, reviewing, and securing agreement for publication was finally brought to conclusion only in late 2011. The chapter is therefore put forward with the caveat that while it reflects the situation at the time of the study, some details will have understandably changed.

This publication fulfills the first stage of the process through a set of preliminary studies that map the nature of corruption in eight Ethiopian sectors, focusing on three key objectives:

- Develop sector frameworks that enable mapping of the potential areas of corruption on a sector-by-sector basis.
- Map the different forms and types of corrupt practices in the selected sectors.
- Consider the higher-risk areas and identify appropriate sector or cross-cutting responses for government and other stakeholders.

Unraveling the Issues and Challenges

Corruption is widely seen as one of the biggest impediments to economic growth, investment, and poverty reduction in developing contexts. The World Bank defines corruption as "the use of public office for private gain" (Campos and Pradhan 2007) and elaborates that corruption has a number of faces: bureaucratic corruption, nepotism and patronage, and state capture (often equated with political corruption).

Transparency International defines corruption as "the abuse of entrusted power for private gain" and also differentiates between "according to rule" corruption (where bribes might be given to receive preferential treatment for services to which users are entitled by law) and "against the rule" corruption (where the service provider is not entitled to provide that service by law.")[1]

Sector-Based Corruption Assessment

The body of literature on corruption has expanded in recent years, filling gaps and systematically building knowledge and understanding. *The Many Faces of Corruption: Tracking Vulnerabilities at the Sector Level* (Campos and Pradhan 2007) introduced an approach to corruption assessment that prioritized sector-level efforts within the World Bank Governance and Anticorruption (GAC) agenda. The sector-based approach allows for a more tangible and easily understandable approach to corruption analysis and action. Those working in a particular sector often know what the issues and challenges are. Furthermore, by breaking the problem down sector-by-sector, it is possible both to determine what can be done to meet challenges and to produce an overview of which institutions in a given country context seem prone to corruption—and which do not.

Focusing on Ethiopia, this book builds on the fundamental premise of *The Many Faces of Corruption* and attempts (within the limitations set out below) to consider the forms that corruption takes and identify the risks of corruption in eight sectors. The compilation enables the reader to observe the commonalities and differences among the selected sectors and to construct a broad picture of corruption risks in Ethiopia.

Mapping Corruption along a Sector Value Chain

The mapping of corrupt practices and risks can be structured in a number of ways: by government jurisdiction; by actor (public, private, civil society); or by stage along the sector value chain—the chain of actions or transactions that occur within the sector.

In service delivery, for example, the value chain approach might mean consideration of corrupt practices in policy making, planning and budgeting, procurement, and so on. The chain moves through the process of service delivery to the final payment at the point of service delivery, as shown in figure 1.1. The corruption maps identify the corrupt transactions that occur at each point in the value chain.

This type of sector corruption map improves understanding of which risks dominate the sector, how risks are linked across the sector, and which actors are involved in the transactions identified. It also provides pointers for further diagnosis. Although the results can vary significantly by region, sector, and institution, the mapping approach can highlight the factors and incentives that determine the areas of high and low corruption risk. Where the sectors show commonalities, cross-cutting anticorruption mechanisms can be developed.

Methodologies for Sector Diagnostics

Although the sector experts designed the diagnostic methodologies most suited to their respective sector and stakeholder contexts, they also applied a number of universal principles.

Figure 1.1   A Value Chain Approach to Mapping Corrupt Practices in Service Delivery

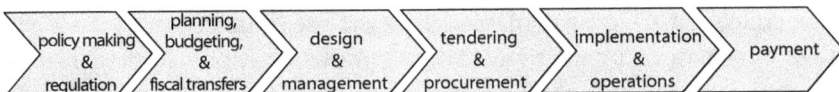

policy making & regulation → planning, budgeting, & fiscal transfers → design & management → tendering & procurement → implementation & operations → payment

Source: Author.

Comprehensive Stakeholder Inclusion

One commonality in the methodology was the effort to tap into the perceptions and knowledge of *all* stakeholders, be they politicians, senior government officials, private sector businessmen, civil society advocates, or consumers of services. In each case, a validation workshop was held at the end of the process to test and expose any lack of consensus around the findings.

Broad Mapping Approach

The sector experts were also asked to consider a broad approach to the sectors selected rather than a focused one. This approach enabled the development of a comprehensive sector map for each sector. It also facilitated a constructive approach that mapped not only the areas where corrupt practices seemed to exist but also those where corruption was not found at all. This distinction is critical to considering how Ethiopia compares with other countries, both regionally and globally. For example, the education sector across many countries frequently uses narrow tools to focus on particular areas of concern (such as teacher absenteeism or Public Expenditure Tracking Surveys).

Although these sorts of studies can be useful if the overall framework of sector corruption is already known and understood, and can also help track the progress of reform, the studies' singular focus can also create a biased picture of the extent of the corruption. The approach taken in this set of diagnostics aimed to reveal, or uncover, the overall picture of corruption in the sector, expose the high and lows, examine the interrelations of different corrupt practices, and finally identify the detailed diagnostic instruments that would increase understanding of the sector as a whole.

Sector-Specific Information Collection

To meet the overall diagnostic objective, each sector expert also adopted specific information collection techniques over four to six months: document analysis, on-site investigations, surveys, perception surveys, semistructured interviews with a range of stakeholders, focus group discussions, ranking exercises, and multistakeholder validation workshops.

As in any other approach to studying corruption, the sector overview approach clearly has both strengths and weaknesses regarding information collection. One particular caveat is the use of perception surveys: by their very nature, perception surveys capture what people perceive but do not provide an absolute, empirical measure. Nevertheless, the approach used here supplemented expert interviews with significant document analysis by the independent sector experts, who were selected for their knowledge of corruption in the sector in a range of countries. This mixture of approaches for the various sector-based surveys has attempted to get as unbiased and representative a view of each sector as possible, given the obvious resource constraints under which such an exercise must operate.

Contributions of This Volume

The book is structured along the lines of the sector experts' diagnostic work and divided into eight chapters, one for each sector studied.

Chapter 2: Health Sector Corruption in Ethiopia

William D. Savedoff and Karen Grépin identify and map the most common forms of corruption across the health sector through interviews and analyses of public documentation and previously conducted surveys. Their analysis suggests that corruption in Ethiopia's health sector is not as pervasive as in other countries or sectors. However, it also notes that recent developments, including the sector's expansion and rising expenditures, could increase the risk of corruption in the future, particularly in the following subsectors:

- *Public financial management.* Limited oversight of the public procurement system, as well as weak compliance with audits and reporting requirements among both public and private institutions, has opened the sector to significant risk of corrupt practices.
- *Human resources.* The civil service employees who are responsible for regulating and inspecting health care providers are poorly paid and trained and thus tempted to request or accept bribes.
- *Pharmaceuticals.* Dual practice (in both public and private facilities or practices) by pharmacists and other health care workers is another significant concern, based on reports that health care workers take advantage of the public health care system by referring patients or diverting supplies to more lucrative private practices.

To address these risks, Savedoff and Grépin recommend that the government improve oversight institutions and mechanisms by systematizing audits, adequately resourcing regulatory institutions, and ensuring oversight and support of the Pharmaceutical Fund and Supply Agency.

In addition, the authors recommend that the government regulate the relationship between the private and public health sectors by first delineating acceptable and unacceptable ways for providers to combine their public and private practices and then enacting systems to ensure compliance. These recommendations aim to mitigate the risks of corruption as the sector continues to expand and develop in both public and private domains.

Chapter 3: Education Sector Corruption in Ethiopia

Michael Latham presents the findings and recommendations from a perception-based field study, interviews, and workshops in the education sector. The analysis divides risks into two categories: upstream (at the "high end" of the value chain) and downstream (at the "low end"). Latham concludes that corruption risks in the education sector are lower than those typically encountered in many developing countries but that high-risk areas in certain downstream functions warrant attention and further study—particularly concerning teacher management, recruitment, and service delivery (for example, within teaching services, the selection and assessment of students).

Of particular concern are the widespread perceptions of fraud in examinations, falsification of qualifications, teacher absenteeism, and favoritism toward members of the ruling party both in teacher recruitment and in student selection and assessment. Corruption risks in the management, procurement, and delivery of capital stock (buildings, equipment, and so on) are also highlighted because of the sector's vulnerability should investments increase in the future. Those few risks along the upstream functions center on the perception by a minority of survey respondents that political appointees unduly influence policy development and implementation through planning and budget allocations.

To address these issues, the author recommends using the risk map to develop a range of tools and review mechanisms to deepen understanding of risks along the value chain, beginning with those high-risk areas— especially in teacher management and recruitment. Specifically, Latham recommends that a working group comprising key stakeholders be established to take up the challenge of corruption, review the findings of this preliminary study, and agree on achievable actions to mitigate the identified corruption risks.

Chapter 4: Rural Water Supply Corruption in Ethiopia

Roger Calow, Alan MacDonald, and Piers Cross review the evidence and perception of corruption in the provision of rural water supplies, following a delivery chain from policy making and budgeting to water point commissioning and construction. Their approach combined interviews and group discussion with a field survey of shallow boreholes using a submersible camera—lowered down the borehole—to ascertain whether construction standards matched design specifications and invoices.

In terms of policy making and regulation, the chapter notes that few opportunities for rent seeking appear to exist for politicians because funding mechanisms and prioritization is systematized, reasonably transparent, and rules-based. In addition to recommendations for improving sector governance and efficiency, the authors propose (a) that the position of state-owned drilling companies be clarified to reduce perceptions of malpractice or unfair competition, and (b) that licensing procedures for drilling contractors be relaxed somewhat to lower entry barriers and encourage competition.

In terms of planning, budgeting, and financial transfers, corruption risk is viewed as low despite the speed of program development, investment, and decentralization. In tendering and procurement, the study highlights major variations in stakeholder perceptions of corruption risk but does not uncover concrete evidence of malpractice. Recommendations focus on the need to strengthen record keeping and ensure greater transparency and access to information about tender processes.

In borehole construction and management, the postconstruction survey of 26 shallow drinking water boreholes in the Oromia region and the Southern Nations, Nationalities, and People's Region (SNNPR) highlighted corrupt practice in the form of short-drilling in 10 percent of the sample and concerns about a further 20 percent. Calow, MacDonald, and Cross suggest that spot checks on construction (using the approach piloted) and improvements in site supervision of drilling contractors by government staff, combined with stronger community oversight and monitoring of headwork construction, would help improve construction standards and reduce corruption risk.

Chapter 5: Justice Sector Corruption in Ethiopia

Linn A. Hammergren assesses the levels of corruption in the justice sector as being relatively low. Mixing informant interviews, focus groups, performance statistics provided from the agencies covered, and document analysis, her study finds that corruption risks center primarily on political interference in high-profile cases and payments or solicitation of bribes to change decisions or pretrial actions in both criminal and civil cases.

Of the two types of risks, the latter—payment or solicitation of bribes to alter preliminary actions (for example, arrests, witness summonses, and

traffic citations)—is the most common, particularly among police officers. Other forms of bribes, such as those offered or solicited for the
performance of standard duties by courtroom staff, appear to be decreasing because of an ongoing modernization program that makes such
actions more difficult to conduct without detection.

The study also revealed that political interference in the judicial process appears to be decreasing, contributing to the overall assessment of
low actual corruption in the sector. But it also reveals significant variations in system actors' perceptions about the frequency of corruption.
These differences, and the gap between the perception and the likely
real incidence of corruption, appear to be a function of limited transparency in personnel policies and the weakness of internal mechanisms such
as complaint-handling and disciplinary offices.

To address these issues, Hammergren recommends that the organizational complaint-handling and disciplinary offices as well as the FEACC
improve transparency by explaining their criteria for accepting and
deciding on cases and by making the record of their decisions and
actions more accessible. One suggestion is to improve (or in some cases,
create) databases that track the processing of complaints about official
malfeasance (both corruption and other abuses of office), thereby
facilitating more systematic analyses of corruption risks and the identification of misperceptions and unfounded claims. Such analyses and
identification would enable a more targeted response to problem areas
and provide an informed basis on which to engage the civil sector and
disseminate information.

Hammergren also recommends (a) that independent bar associations
be made responsible for monitoring members rather than (or at least in
conjunction with) the government and (b) that the police and prosecutors improve their internal monitoring systems to decrease the risk of
bribe solicitation and acceptance.

Overall, the study notes that the Ethiopian government has made
important strides toward discouraging, and reducing the incentives for,
corruption in the justice sector. The author contends it is now time to
develop more proactive responses to identified problem areas as well as
more effective civic outreach.

Chapter 6: Construction Sector Corruption in Ethiopia
Hamish Goldie-Scot provides an initial scoping of corruption in
Ethiopia's construction sector. Using data from expert interviews,
confidential questionnaires, closed-door workshops, and document

analysis, Goldie-Scot generated a map of corruption risk at each stage of the value chain, based on both perceptions and reported nonspecific examples.

The resulting picture is complex but plausible. Ethiopia's construction sector exhibits most of the classic warning signs of corruption risk, including instances of poor-quality construction, inflated costs, and delays in implementation. In some cases, these instances may have resulted from corruption driven by unequal contractual relationships, poor enforcement of professional standards, low public sector pay, wide-ranging discretionary powers exercised by government, a lack of transparency, and a widespread perception of hidden barriers to market entry. These factors notwithstanding, corrupt practices at the operational level appear to be largely opportunistic, relatively minor, and capable of being controlled through professionally managed systems and procedures.

The impression of favoritism and controls on market entry appears to be fueled by (a) the perceived hidden influence of the ruling party on the sector; (b) a tendency toward top-down development planning; and (c) the government's dominant role as client, regulator, and upholder of professional standards. A small case study of unit costs of federal roads tentatively supports the view that limited competition may be playing a role in driving up unit output costs.

The study concludes that, without corrective action, both the perception and the reality of corruption in the sector are likely to increase. Ethiopia's recent bold decision to join the international Construction Sector Transparency will not in itself suffice to address the growing risk of corruption as spending levels continue to outstrip management capacity.

At the strategic level, Goldie-Scot recommends the following:

- *Strengthen accountability* by increasing performance audits and allowing independent bodies to set, monitor, and enforce professional standards.
- *Strengthen client capacity*, not only through civil service reform but also through the extended use of proven management systems and procedures and related training.
- *Restore trust* through specific confidence-building measures, including a fairer allocation of risk in contracts and more openness about the practical application of rules limiting the commercial interests of officials involved within the sector.

The author also recommends a further stage of this diagnostic to consolidate and validate the findings to date and to fill gaps in the scope, particularly those relating to cross-sectoral issues, the power sector, and large-scale community roads initiatives.

Chapter 7: Land Sector Corruption in Ethiopia

Tony Burns and Kate Dalrymple focus on corruption in the rural and urban land sector. Using the Land Governance Assessment Framework they developed, the authors find that corruption risks in Ethiopia are increasing because of a weak policy and regulatory framework surrounding land allocation, titling, and management.

In rural areas, only five out of nine regions have implemented laws for land registration, and land is held by citizens' entitlement through perpetual use right and made available to foreign and domestic investors through a lease system. In urban areas, land is administered through a lease or perpetual permit system and through separate legislation for condominiums. However, the procedures for recording transactions are unclear, the systems inefficient and ineffective, and an estimated 90 percent of housing units lack formal tenure.

In conjunction with weaknesses in the legal framework, this informal environment has facilitated opportunities for asset capture by elite and senior officials as well as corruption in the implementation of existing land policy and laws. Instances of such corruption include the institutionalization of informal fees, officials' allocation of land to themselves or developers, and issuance of forged land documents.

Burns and Dalrymple recommend the following short-term and long-term actions to address these issues and decrease the sector's vulnerability to corruption:

- *Improve land governance* by developing a more comprehensive legal and policy framework.
- *Strengthen institutions and systems* throughout the land sector.
- *Formally review the government's pilot to improve land allocation systems* in four subcities in Addis Ababa (following the FEACC investigation) to deepen understanding and best practice, and then expand the pilot to other urban centers.
- *Conduct similar FEACC investigations* in rural areas and urban centers outside of Addis Ababa, given the government's positive reform following the previous FEACC investigation.
- *Establish a regulatory body* to address complaints and improve responsiveness to reduce corruption, perceived or actual, in Ethiopia's land sector.

Chapter 8: Telecommunications Sector Corruption in Ethiopia

The telecommunications sector is examined; of all the sectors studied, it appears to be at the highest risk of corruption. Despite a strong policy and regulatory framework, a high perceived level of corruption has resulted from weak accountability mechanisms and the monopolization of the sector by a state-owned enterprise: the Ethiopian Telecommunications Corporation (ETC).

To examine this perception, document analysis, stakeholder interviews, and workshops are used to map seven areas of perceived risk, which are ranked in terms of the *value* of the perceived corruption in the sector. The results identify the appointment of equipment suppliers, delivery and installation of equipment, and construction of telecom facilities as the areas most vulnerable to corruption. Of these, the supply of equipment to the ETC is considered the area at highest risk.

Despite a strong framework of procedural safeguards around ETC procurement, apparent breaches in regulating equipment supplies (where most of the spending occurs) has contributed to the deterioration of public and market confidence in the sector. If market confidence is to improve, corrective actions in the telecom sector must address both the risks and the perceptions of corruption.

To help restore trust, it is recommended that the government take the following actions:

- *Commission an independent audit and public inquiry* into the ETC's largest agreement (in 2006, worth US$1.5 billion) to address issues surrounding the supply of telecom equipment and facilitate the development and implementation of targeted reforms.
- *Apply standards to the ETC* that are equivalent to those established under Ethiopia's Public Procurement Proclamation, which regulates other government agencies.
- *Establish a working group* to assess the ETC's current procedures.
- *Establish an ETC-supplier forum* to improve communication, understanding, and trust among stakeholders.

Chapter 9: Mining Sector Corruption in Ethiopia

The mining sector is examined; although corruption appears to be low, the ongoing rapid expansions in the sector could increase both the risk of corruption and the amounts of money potentially lost. The analysis maps corruption risks across the sector value chain based on data from surveys, workshops, and interviews with senior government and private sector representatives of mining operations.

The analysis finds that license issuing, license operation, and mining revenue are the three areas at significant risk of corruption. Corruption risks also arise in the relationships between mining operations and local communities, between contractors and suppliers, and in the quality of the operation.

Although the government has enacted effective anticorruption measures in the mining sector—including a new computer database to improve access to information and a business process review to make license issuing more efficient—the recommendation is to take several actions to strengthen existing mechanisms to mitigate corruption in high-risk areas:

- *Increase the number and capacity of qualified officials and staff* in federal, regional, and city licensing departments.
- *Improve transparency* through public disclosure of all relevant documents related to license issuing and mining operations.
- *Establish a forum* comprising Ministry of Mines members, regional and city licensing authorities, FEACC officials, and representatives of mining companies to facilitate improvements in license issuing and management and in anticorruption mechanisms in general.

The Overall Picture

Although each chapter provides a starting point for discussing corruption with the FEACC and the sectors' respective line ministries, when viewed together, the findings point toward an emerging pattern in sector-level corruption, and a number of similar or collective responses can be identified.

Wide Variations in Corruption across Sectors

Perhaps one of the primary cross-cutting findings of this multisector study in Ethiopia is the variation—the marked highs and lows—in the levels of corruption across three groups of sectors: (a) basic services (health, education, water, and justice); (b) "old" sectors (construction, land, and mining); and (c) "new" sectors (telecommunications and the HIV/AIDS and pharmaceutical subsectors of health).

Basic service sectors. The diagnostics strongly suggest that, in Ethiopia, corruption in the delivery of basic services (primary health, basic education, rural water supply, and justice) is comparatively limited and potentially much lower than in other low-income countries. This finding might be explained by the lack of any significant capital investment, but the corrupt practices identified in relation to recurrent costs also appear to be relatively limited. Whereas the standard practices in Kenya, Nigeria, and Uganda might reveal problems with textbook procurement and distribution, widespread absenteeism in primary health clinics, or undercutting in specifications of rural boreholes, in Ethiopia these practices seem to be under control and subject to either self- or community regulation.

Old sectors. The studies found a relatively higher risk of corruption in the "old" investment sectors (such as construction, land, and mining), but the risk was still not at the levels the sector experts saw in other contexts. In construction (mostly roads), land, and mining, the studies found that the trends and risks of corrupt practices typically found elsewhere are indeed occurring in Ethiopia, albeit to a lesser extent than elsewhere. The types and levels of corruption identified were often specific to the Ethiopian context and to flashpoints of change and opportunity. Nevertheless, in late 2009, risks in the construction, land, and mining sectors were on an upward trajectory.

New sectors. Finally, a third group of sectors appeared to be set on a trajectory similar to highly corrupt countries. We have grouped these as the "new" investment sectors: those where there are new flows of funds, less history, and fewer stakeholder experiences. They include, for instance, telecommunications as well as HIV/AIDS and pharmaceuticals. In these sectors or subsectors, the research identified significant levels of corruption at the most vulnerable parts of the value chain, raising concerns that new levels of corruption could take hold in the Ethiopian context.

Overall, similar value chain profiles. The overall "profile" of corruption along the value chain is not dissimilar for each of these three sectoral categories. In the basic service sectors, only a few instances of corruption were identified in policy making and regulation or in planning and budgeting (at the national level); some instances were noted in management; more were found in procurement processes; and petty corruption was found at the point of service delivery.

This profile also describes the risks of corruption in the construction, land, and mining sectors—albeit with increased risk in policy making and regulation (market entry in construction, licensing risks in mining) and significantly higher risks in the procurement and construction stages.

This profile flattens, however, and levels at a much higher risk for the telecommunications sector as well as the HIV/AIDS and pharmaceuticals health care subsectors, indicating that in these "new investment sectors," the opportunity for and risk of corruption is seized at all stages in the sector investment and service delivery value chain.

An Overarching Concern:

A specific finding that spans a number of sectors points toward widely held concerns about members of the ruling political party. Survey respondents in the following sectors cited particular examples:

- *In the education sector*, there were widespread perceptions that a ruling-party affiliation resulted in the lack of fairness, most notably in the selection of teachers for employment and in selection and grading of students.
- *In the justice sector*, there is a perception of an increasing tendency to select the judiciary from party members, sometimes resulting in more-able candidates being passed over in a professional culture marked by an eagerness to please those in government.
- *In the construction sector*, there is a perception that favoritism determines market entry, exacerbated by a further perception that top-down planning processes and the government's dual role as both client and regulator also results in hidden party influence. As a result, many feel that the construction industry lacks genuine competition in some areas.
- *In the water sector*, there is a perception that state-owned drilling companies benefit from favoritism, in part resulting from the relatively high entry barriers that seem to exist for private drilling concerns.

Although the sector studies acknowledge the initiatives to reduce this apparent favoritism—some also making specific recommendations toward this end—it is nevertheless noteworthy that this issue appears to be an overarching concern.

It would seem remiss in a country-specific publication to ignore the issue of culture in corruption. Ethiopia is a country steeped in custom and cultural norms. A devout, mainly religious people (both Christian Orthodox and Muslim), Ethiopians live with an overwhelming sense of honor and pride. In most regions, but not all, corruption is not acceptable culturally, is not considered to be "the way things are," and does not typify the way that most people expect to obtain services.

The perceptions of corruption within Ethiopia *by Ethiopians* are therefore high but do not reflect the perceptions of corruption in Ethiopia *by non-Ethiopians*. It is worth recalling the Korean businessman who, when asked about the comparison in the countries where he had worked, replied that "Ethiopia is a paradise" (relatively free of the burden corruption places on business).

Cross-Sector Recommendations

Although the recommendations of the study are preliminary and mostly specific to each of the eight sectors studied in this volume, some common threads emerge:

- *Additional study and analysis* is needed to deepen knowledge and understanding (perhaps unsurprising, given that this diagnostic represents the first effort to unpack corruption in each of the sectors). In particular, all of the authors favor more study to consolidate and validate findings, expand study to areas not yet researched (construction), and step up investigations (land). Further information could also be developed by reviewing pilot initiatives in place (land). This preliminary mapping, however, provides clear pointers to the higher-risk areas where in-depth study might be useful.
- *Enhanced oversight* in the form of systematic and better auditing was recommended across the board, including performance audits (construction), spot checks and community monitoring (water supply), internal monitoring (justice agencies), and an independent audit and public inquiry (telecommunications).
- *Enhanced transparency, public disclosure, and access to information* (justice, license issuing, and mining operations) are also recommended, including complaint-handling mechanisms that could inform as well as address public concerns (justice).
- *Procurement standards, procedures, and frameworks* should be equivalent to those established under the nation's Public Procurement Proclamation (especially in the telecommunications sector).
- *Stronger regulatory institutions* are needed, in particular a regulatory body to examine land issues; a licensing authority for the mining sector; and independent bodies to set, monitor, and enforce professional standards for the justice sector and construction.
- *Capacity building* is needed across the board to address the chronic lack of capacity noted in all sectors and to clarify the gray area between weak capacity and corrupt practice. Recommendations to build

capacity included further development and reform of the civil service, increased numbers of qualified professionals (particularly for licensing of mines), and adoption of proven management systems and procedural improvements (particularly in construction).

- *Promotion of trust*, which emerged as a critical recommendation in a number of sectors, could be addressed through (a) procedural changes to remove conflict of interest and make decision making and procurement more transparent and rules-based (construction); (b) civic outreach (justice); and (c) establishment of professional and multistakeholder forums (the ETC-supplier forum in telecom or the education working group) that promote dialogue and improve communication among stakeholders.

A Basis for Dialogue, A Time to Circumvent Corruption

To the World Bank and other development partners, the study offers lessons in how to promote dialogue on corruption in a transparent and relatively unthreatening way. Although the Bank's GAC strategy and support has been in place for three years, many donors (including the Bank) are still reticent to discuss corruption. All too often, the discussions are left until misdoings are discovered and sanctions are being applied.

The mapping approach used in this multisector corruption diagnostic proved that in most instances (all but one of the eight sectors), all stakeholders (both state and nonstate) are willing and able to discuss corruption when given the appropriate forum(s) to do so. It showed, in all cases, that disaggregating the sector into clearly defined parts, and discussing each in turn, systematizes the discussion and enables more methodical and objective reporting. It also showed that stakeholders involved in corruption transactions are often willing to discuss what happens (when and why) in some detail, many of them underlining to outsiders the reasons why they engage. It is notable, too, that discussions in the workshops were significantly more open and productive when facilitated by people experienced in "talking corruption." These are all critical lessons for analysis in other countries in the region and elsewhere.

Finally, readers are urged to consider this document as a start to a process of uncovering and tackling corruption. The limitations of the diagnostics notwithstanding, this multisector effort has provided useful information for discussion, validation, or triangulation in new sector-level forums for dialogue.

Given the Ethiopian government's stated zero tolerance of corruption, its challenge now is to acknowledge, not dismiss, the possible risks and to put in place a rigorous campaign of efforts to celebrate and protect the areas of low corruption risk—and investigate and tackle the apparent high-risk areas—directly and transparently. In this way, the country can guard against those practices that might otherwise take Ethiopia down the high-risk path of so many other countries in the region.

Note

1. TI (Transparency International). 2010. Definition of "corruption" in frequently asked questions (FAQ) on TI website. http://www.transparency.org /news_room/faq/corruption_faq.

References

Campos, J. Edgardo, and Sanjay Pradhan, eds. 2007. *The Many Faces of Corruption: Tracking Vulnerabilities at the Sector Level.* Washington, DC: World Bank.

World Bank. 2008. Country Assistance Strategy. World Bank, Washington, DC, April 2.

CHAPTER 2

Health Sector Corruption in Ethiopia

William D. Savedoff and Karen Grépin

Introduction

All health systems, no matter how well resourced by either public or private sources, are vulnerable to corruption. Health sector corruption drains limited public resources and can compromise population health by limiting access to care, lowering the quality of services, or even directly

This report was completed and submitted to the World Bank in October 2009 on the basis of research conducted in 2008 and 2009; all information and figures that do not specify a particular year refer to conditions in Ethiopia at that time. The authors would like to acknowledge the support provided by Janelle Plummer in commissioning the work, providing contacts, and guiding the research. Special thanks go to the many Ethiopians who gave their time and courageously agreed to share their information regarding this sensitive and difficult topic. We would also like to acknowledge the Ethiopian government's support of this study— particularly the efforts of Ato Solomon Mebratu and Ato Omar Ali Seid, who explained the workings of the Ministry of Health and helped us to obtain interviews with numerous federal and regional officials. We would also like to thank Senper Shimeles and Kefale Diress for excellent logistical support, advice, insights, and encouragement. Two anonymous reviewers also provided challenging and helpful comments.

Although this chapter results from studies completed by January 2010, the process of checking, reviewing, and securing agreement for publication was finally brought to conclusion only in late 2011. The chapter is therefore put forward with the caveat that while it reflects the situation at the time of the study, some details will have understandably changed.

harming individuals. Ethiopia's health sector has many problems—including limited resources, a high burden of disease, and weak institutions—but corruption also plays a role.

Corruption in Ethiopia's health sector has been relatively minor compared to that in other countries and sectors. Low public health spending and limited job options for public health staff workers may explain why the health sector has been less prone to fraud and abuse. However, rapidly rising expenditures, a growing private health sector, concentrated procurement, and new financing arrangements could increase the sector's vulnerability to corruption in the future.

This study assesses the nature and extent of corruption within Ethiopia's health sector. It relies primarily on interviews to map the flow of resources in Ethiopia's health sector and to assess whether resources are being diverted from their intended uses. The interviews were supplemented by analysis of documentation, including internal and external audits and previously collected survey data.

Overview of Findings

In summary, the study identified the following key areas of concern:

- *Financial management.* Although the Ethiopian health sector has implemented and improved its financial management system, compliance is still weak in critical areas such as record keeping, performance audits, and follow-up on audits.
- *Procurement.* Although the public procurement system has been greatly strengthened in recent years, significant challenges remain such as poorly functioning reporting systems and weak oversight.
- *Pharmaceutical management.* Concerns involve the licensing, selection, and sale of medicines; pharmacists' opportunities to exploit patients; and a growing black market for pharmaceuticals.
- *Regulation.* Several agencies regulate, license, and inspect health care providers, facilities, and associated institutions. The inspectors who enforce these regulations, however, are poorly paid and vulnerable to requesting and accepting bribes.
- *Unequal patient treatment.* Although illegal payments do not appear to be a major issue in Ethiopia's front-line service delivery, many interviewees reported complaints that providers give preferential services to friends and colleagues. In addition, the practice of dual job holding in both the public and private sector has opened up opportunities for providers to take advantage of patients.

- *Rising foreign and other donor aid.* New aid modalities and rapidly increasing aid flows have introduced both new opportunities and new challenges to control corruption. Increased coordination among core donors has simplified financial and administrative control functions and likely strengthened the public financial management and procurement systems. However, the influx of funds outside of the public system and the sheer size of these new funds have also increased the risk of corruption.

Chapter Structure

The chapter is organized as follows:

- "Context for Analysis" describes the Ethiopian health care system and the characteristics that make it prone to corruption.
- "Framework for Analysis" describes the study's methods and sources and maps the Ethiopian health sector's major funding flows.
- "Findings" compares corruption within Ethiopia's health care system with that of other countries and sectors and analyzes its vulnerabilities in the areas of budget allocations, procurement, drug supplies, regulation and inspections, facility-level interactions between staff members and patients, and foreign aid.
- "Next Steps," the concluding section, analyzes the trends in Ethiopia's rapidly changing health sector and recommends actions that could reduce vulnerabilities to corruption and head off problems in the future.

Context for Analysis

All health systems, no matter how well financed by either public or private sources, are vulnerable to corruption. However, corruption varies across contexts in as many ways as health sector institutions vary from place to place. In most countries, the health sector is more prone to corruption than other sectors because it often involves large amounts of money; highly dispersed locations; large numbers of people and transactions; highly specialized services that are specific to particular clients; and outcomes that are hard to observe, measure, and report.

Corruption in health care can have dire consequences because it does more than drain public resources; it also compromises the population's health by limiting access to care, compromising quality, or even directly harming individuals. Corruption's impact on population health is insidious because it is so dispersed and hidden. When a substandard building collapses, the headlines focus on resulting deaths and any allegations of corruption. But when substandard drugs are prescribed, the press rarely reports on the resulting deaths, let alone links those deaths to potential corruption.

Difficulty of Detecting Health Sector Corruption

Health care services have specific features that make corruption difficult to detect and even more difficult to prove:

- *Health care services are delivered in highly dispersed locations by large numbers of people engaged in numerous transactions.* In Ethiopia, for example, public funds are used to provide health care services in 143 hospitals, 690 health centers, and more than 10,000 health posts for a population of 82 million with a public sector staff of more than 50,000.
- *Health care services are highly varied and patient specific.* Individuals do not go to a health facility to buy a particular service. Instead, health professionals diagnose the individuals and tell them what treatment they need. Patients are rarely equipped to question the health professional's judgment or to assess diagnoses from alternative practitioners. In any country, people can be manipulated about what to buy, how much they should pay, and what their rights are in terms of public service provision. In Ethiopia, widespread illiteracy and low school enrollment exacerbate this susceptibility to manipulation.
- *Health care provision is inherently uncertain.* No diagnosis is perfect, and no treatment is foolproof. If an individual's health fails to improve after treatment, it is not clear whether the diagnosis was mistaken, drugs were substandard, or the individual's particular condition was unresponsive. People sometimes regain their health even without treatment, just as those who receive treatment might not recover.

Impact of Health Sector Corruption

Corruption, when it occurs, creates serious problems in health systems, especially in low-income countries like Ethiopia. As in other sectors, health sector corruption diverts resources from their intended uses. Ethiopia spends about US$8 per person[1] on health each year, among the lowest amounts in the world, and every penny stolen cuts further into limited health care resources.

In addition to stealing from limited resources, corruption in the health care sector directly affects people's health, causing situations in which health facilities lack supplies and staff, substandard and dangerous substances are peddled as life-saving medications, or people go without care because they cannot pay a bribe.

Corruption also erodes trust in the public sector concerning not only provision of care but also drug regulation, practitioner licensure, and equity. In Ethiopia, where foreign aid accounts for more than half of all health spending, corruption could seriously undermine the country's ability to continue attracting these resources from wealthier countries.

Finally, corruption encompasses more actors and practices in the health sector than in other sectors. Although corruption is often associated exclusively with public officials, it occurs whenever someone entrusted by the public abuses his or her position of power. The health sector includes many private actors who hold such positions of trust. Societies generally invest medical practitioners with status and privileges in the expectation that they will put their clients' health and needs above their pecuniary interests. Health is considered so important that even pharmaceutical companies and medical equipment suppliers suffer particular disapproval when they breach social norms regarding the appropriate balance between self-interest and clients' well-being. Therefore, an assessment of health sector corruption often requires consideration of not only public sector employees but also a range of private actors.

The Ethiopian Health System
Ethiopia's health sector has a number of features that make it susceptible to corruption:

- A highly dispersed and weakly supervised system of service delivery
- Accounting systems that overlap between governmental levels and external aid agencies
- A weakly regulated relationship between public and private provision.

Decentralization, programs address lagging health indicators. After the Derg (the ruling military junta, formally known as the Provisional Military Government of Socialist Ethiopia) was overthrown in 1991, the new government replaced the highly centralized health delivery system with one that is highly decentralized: sharing responsibility among federal, regional, and woreda (district) governments; allowing private health care provision; and welcoming increasing flows of foreign aid.

Health financing in Ethiopia can be broken into four major funding categories: federal and regional governments, bilateral and multilateral funders, nongovernmental organizations, and households' out-of-pocket expenditures. Government policies have increased the share of government expenditures for social programs, including health, during the past decade. Health as a share of government expenditures rose from approximately 4 percent in 2004 to about 9 percent in 2007, but a large share of this was financed by donors. The government spent an estimated US$230 million on health in 2007, about two-thirds of which came from international aid, as shown in table 2.1.

The increased government health expenditures have been accompanied by fiscal decentralization and broad reforms in the administration and management of public finance. Despite the increased expenditures, total annual expenditures on health in Ethiopia amount to only about US$8 per person, among the lowest in the world. By contrast, average spending on health in Sub-Saharan Africa (excluding South Africa) is about US$58 per person, according to the World Health Organization (WHOSIS 2009).

Although Ethiopia has made significant progress in the past two decades, health indicators in Ethiopia remain some of the poorest in the world. World Health Organization (WHO) statistics show that life expectancy at birth was 56 years of age and the under-5 child mortality rate was 123 per 1,000 live births in 2006 (WHOSIS 2009). Only about half of pregnant woman receive any form of prenatal care, and trained medical personnel supervise only 16 percent of births. Coverage rates of standard Expanded Programme on Immunization vaccines are low—anywhere from 53 percent to 73 percent, depending on the data source. The country's ratios of health human resources to population also are among the lowest in the world.

The Federal Ministry of Health's (FMOH) sector policy has been structured around a series of Health Sector Development Programs (HSDPs), the first of which ran from 1997 to 2005, followed by HSDP-II (2002–05) and HSDP-III (2005–10). These programs address the government's commitment to achieving numerous international health objectives, including the Millennium Development Goals (MDGs), and domestic health objectives such as

- expanding physical access to health care services
- raising immunization coverage

Table 2.1 Estimated Health Expenditures in Ethiopia, by Source and Control Mechanism, 2006[a]

Funding sources	Primary financial agents	Procurement agents	Control mechanisms	Main uses of funds	Amount (US$, millions)	Share (%)
Taxpayers	MOFED, block grants	Regions, zones, woredas	FDRE, PPA	Salaries, local purchases	100	13
Patients	Health facilities	Woreda	FDRE, PPA	Drugs, supplies	25	3
Taxpayers	MOE	MOE	FDRE, PPA	Educational services	30	4
GAVI	FMOH, MDG fund	PFSA	FDRE, PPA	Commodities, training, infrastructure	110	15
Donors, WB	Regions, PBS II Component A	Woreda	FDRE, WB agreement	Salaries, local purchases	30	4
Donors, WB (Multi-Donor Trust Fund)	FMOH, PBSII Component B	PFSA	FDRE, WB agreement	Imported commodities	60	8
GFATM	HAPCO	Various	FDRE, local financing agent	Commodities, special activities	54	7
GFATM	FMOH	UNICEF, UNFPA	UN system	Commodities	64	9
U.S. PEPFAR	Various	Various	United States	Commodities, special activities	123	16
"Channel 3" donors[b]	Donor (largest is USAID)	Donor	Donor	Commodities, special activities	25	3
Patients	Private facilities, pharmacies	Private facility	n.a.	Salaries, drugs, supplies, facilities	130	17
Total	n.a.	n.a.	n.a.	n.a.	751	100[c]

Sources: Authors' calculations based on Alemu 2009; HCFT 2006; FMOH 2008; GAVI 2005, 2006, 2007; GFATM website (http://www.theglobalfund.org); PEPFAR website (http://www.pepfar.gov); and interviews (for a list of individuals interviewed, see the annex).

Note: MOFED = Ministry of Finance and Economic Development. FDRE = Federal Democratic Republic of Ethiopia. PPA = Public Procurement Agency. MOE = Ministry of Education. GAVI = GAVI Alliance (formerly the Global Alliance for Vaccines and Immunisation). FMOH = Federal Ministry of Health. MDG = Millennium Development Goal. PFSA = Pharmaceutical Fund and Supply Agency. WB = World Bank. PBS = Protection of Basic Services (program). GFATM = Global Fund to Fight AIDS, Tuberculosis and Malaria. HAPCO = HIV/AIDS Prevention and Control Office. UNICEF = United Nations Children's Fund. UNFPA = United Nations Population Fund. U.S. PEPFAR = U.S. President's Emergency Plan for AIDS Relief. USAID = U.S. Agency for International Development. n.a. = not applicable.

a. At the time this study was completed, the only National Health Accounts data available were from 2005. National Health Accounts for 2007–08 were subsequently published in 2010 (FDRE 2010).

b. International aid flows directly through MOFED (Channel 1), FMOH (Channel 2), or outside of the government's oversight and information systems (Channel 3).

c. Column total is rounded to 100.

- combating major infectious diseases (AIDS, tuberculosis, and malaria)
- promoting health with a new cadre of health extension workers.

The health sector program is moving forward within a national context of modernization and reform that includes substantial efforts to improve public sector capacity through training (implemented by the Ministry of Capacity Building) and business process reengineering (BPR), reform of procurement (administered by the Public Procurement Agency [PPA]), and substantial decentralization of most public services to local governments (FMOH 2005, 2008; Independent Review Team 2008).

Responsibilities for the planning and implementation of public sector health activities are shared by FMOH, Regional Health Bureaus (RHBs), Zonal Health Bureaus (ZHBs), and Woreda Health Offices (WoHOs), as table 2.2 illustrates.

Under the decentralization strategy, the FMOH, RHBs, and ZHBs have become increasingly focused on policy development, technical assistance, and regulatory oversight, while the WoHOs are assuming greater responsibility for managing and coordinating the implementation of health activities, particularly the delivery of primary health services. Tertiary health services are mainly the responsibility of the RHBs. Increasingly, the

Table 2.2   Public Health Sector Structure and Responsibilities in Ethiopia

Federal Ministry of Health (FMOH)	Regional Health Bureau (RHB)[a]	Woreda Health Office (WoHO)
National health policy and planning	Regional health policy and planning	Local budget planning and financial controls
Regulation of suppliers, drugs, and providers	Supervision and support of WoHOs	Health clinics
Specialized hospitals	Regional hospitals	Health posts[b]
Issuance of block grants	Administration of block grants	Health Services Extension Program
Health Management Information System	Health worker training	
Special programs		
Donor coordination		

Sources: FMOH 2005, 2008.
a. Some regions are further divided into administrative levels called "zones," which have some planning and oversight functions as well as responsibilities for service provision. Ethiopia has nine regions and two city administrations (Addis Ababa and Dire Dawa).
b. Health posts are small-scale public facilities, staffed by health extension workers, that provide the most basic of health services.

WoHOs are also assuming responsibilities for local budget planning by means of the Marginal Budgeting for Bottlenecks planning software.[2]

One of the FMOH's major strategic priorities is to improve physical access to health services and health care providers across the country. It has expanded access to basic health care services by training and deploying additional health care workers; investing in construction of new facilities; and increasing spending on supplies, drugs, and commodities. The Health Services Extension Program is a key part of this strategy and involves training and deploying two health extension workers to each village in the country. In the past three years, the government has trained and deployed more than 24,000 of these workers, with a target of 30,000.

Role of international donors. International donor contributions to the health sector have increased dramatically over the past decade from both bilateral and multilateral sources. When the last National Health Accounts were reported in 2005, households and government each accounted for about 30 percent of total health spending while donors accounted for almost 40 percent. Today, the donor share is likely to be substantially larger because of the disbursements of major initiatives such as the Global Fund to Fight AIDS, Tuberculosis and Malaria (GFATM); the U.S. President's Emergency Plan for AIDS Relief (PEPFAR); and the GAVI Alliance (formerly the Global Alliance for Vaccinations and Immunisations). GFATM increased its disbursements from US$118 million in 2006 to US$630 million in 2007; PEPFAR, from US$123 million in 2006 to US$242 million in 2007; and the GAVI Alliance, from US$4.6 million in 2006 to US$110 million in 2007.

These amounts far surpass domestic government spending and represent an enormous influx of resources over a short time. Substantial shares of these funds procure pharmaceuticals (for example, antiretrovirals, antimalarials, and vaccines) and commodities (such as contraceptives and bednets) through international competitive bidding managed by (a) firms contracted by bilateral agencies (for example, Management Sciences for Health procures for the U.S. Agency for International Development) or (b) United Nations (UN) agencies (such as the UN Children's Fund [UNICEF] and UN Population Fund [UNFPA]). Still, much of the foreign aid money goes to the Ethiopian government to cover recurrent costs through block grants (for example, the Protection of Basic Services [PBS] program) or to pay for specific programs; other funds go directly to nongovernmental organizations (NGOs) and service providers outside of governmental channels.

Ethiopia has a particularly large number of international donors: 10 multilateral institutions, 22 bilateral agencies, and 50 international NGOs. However, it has been reasonably successful in fostering coordination among most of its donors. For example, Ethiopia was the first country to sign an International Health Partnership for donor coordination, and donors are pooling their contributions into a Multi-Donor Trust Fund (MDTF) and the PBS program (managed by the World Bank) as well as an MDG Fund managed by the FMOH. As a result of this coordination, a substantial amount of international aid flows directly through the Federal Ministry of Finance and Economic Development (MOFED) (Channel 1) and FMOH (Channel 2), with the rest remaining outside of the government's oversight and information systems (Channel 3).

Using a variety of information sources, as shown in figure 2.1, we estimate the share of total health expenditures supported by taxpayers has fallen to about 17 percent, out-of-pocket expenses for private care and user fees is approximately 20 percent, and donors account for 63 percent.[3]

The public-private conundrum. In addition to the highly dispersed nature of the public health system and the overlapping flows of funds from

Figure 2.1   Share of Total Health Expenditures by Source

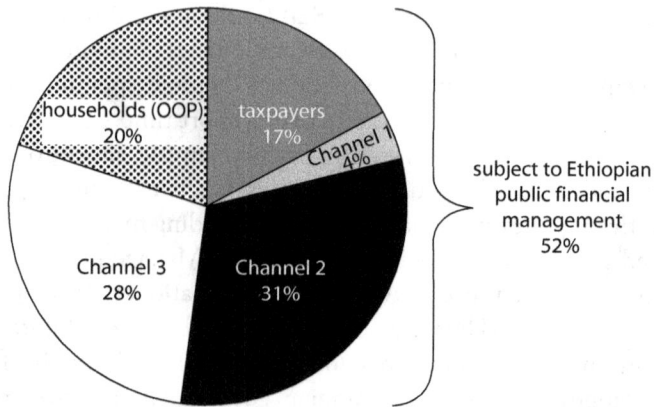

Sources: Authors' calculations based on Alemu 2009; HCFT 2006; FMOH 2008; GAVI 2005, 2006, 2007; GFATM website (http://www.theglobalfund.org); PEPFAR website (http://www.pepfar.gov); and interviews (for a list of individuals interviewed, see the annex).
Note: Channel 1 = donor funding directed through MOFED. Channel 2 = donor funding directed through FMOH. Channel 3 = donor funding through nongovernmental channels. OOP = out-of-pocket.

external agencies, the expansion of private health care provision is creating challenges for controlling corruption in Ethiopia.

Until the mid-1990s, following the Derg's collapse, private health care provision was illegal. Today, it is legal and expanding. Currently, about 30 percent of households that seek health care services do so at a private facility (authors' calculation from FDRE 2008). The overall share of people seeking care is higher in urban areas than in rural areas, as is the private share. Although private health care is formally most extensive in the major cities (such as Addis Ababa and Dire Dawa), it appears to be expanding informally throughout the country. Average household spending on health care is about US$2.20 per person per year, accounting for 20 percent of total health expenditures in the country. Although this amount includes user fees in public facilities, most of it (at least two-thirds) pays for medications and consultations in the private sector.

Ethiopia's regulations and oversight system does not appear to have kept pace with the expansion of private practice. In 2003, individuals and public health workers described how common it was for public sector health workers to redirect patients from public facilities to private consultations or particular pharmacies (Lindelow, Serneels, and Lemma 2005). Our interviews show that this phenomenon continues today: individuals commonly attribute absenteeism and theft of supplies to health sector workers who shirk their public duties and see patients in private, using the justification that they are too poorly paid in their public sector jobs.

Although private providers play a positive role in the provision of health care services in many countries, the relationship between private and public provision needs to be carefully delineated if corruption is to be limited.

Framework for Analysis

Accurately measuring the extent and forms of corruption in such a large health sector would require extensive resources. This study aimed to establish the most common forms of corruption in Ethiopia's health sector, the most vulnerable aspects of the system, and potential remedial actions to limit future opportunities for corruption.

Methods and Approach

The research was primarily qualitative, interviewing 66 people at the woreda, regional, and national levels between May and June 2009 and reviewing primary and secondary documents (audit reports and disbursement records, for example). The interviewees included the following:

- federal officials (from the Ministry of Health [FMOH], Federal Ethics and Anti-Corruption Commission [FEACC], and Office of the Auditor General, among others)
- regional officials from Amhara and Tigray (the Bureaus of Finance, Regional Auditors General, and Regional Health Bureaus, among others)
- woreda health officials from a rural woreda in the Amhara region;
- public sector health workers such as pharmacists, nurses, doctors, and technicians
- nongovernmental representatives such as journalists, NGO staff, foreign agency staff, and patients at visited facilities.

We also extracted useful quantitative information from the Woreda and City Administrations Benchmarking Survey (FDRE 2008), the Financial Transparency and Accountability Perception Survey (Urban Institute 2009), and Demographic and Health Surveys (Central Statistical Agency [Ethiopia] and ORC Macro 2001, 2006).

The findings presented here represent our informed judgments based on this information and our experiences in other countries. We cross-checked the information from interviews with alternative sources whenever possible and gave more credence to views that were based on firsthand experience. In terms of geographic coverage, a number of interviewees said that conditions in Amhara and Tigray were better with respect to corruption than in other regions, particularly in remote rural areas. The informants told us that these two regions had better systems for managing finances, personnel, and supplies than other regions where capacities were weaker and oversight more limited. These comments suggest that the findings here should be interpreted as a conservative estimate of the extent of corruption experienced at the regional and local levels.

Public reforms and changes in foreign aid are proceeding so quickly that many of the findings here may also be outdated and should be interpreted accordingly. Ethiopia has been implementing a new public procurement law since 2005 and is implementing

- civil service reforms (such as BPR)
- a new health management information system

- a new budget planning system
- a new procurement and distribution process
- extensive capacity building and training.

For example, responsibilities and procedures for drug procurement have changed completely since the creation of the Pharmaceutical Fund and Supply Agency (PFSA) in 2007, so earlier evidence of corruption may not be relevant for judging future prospects.

Mapping of Resources and Activities

As noted above, health sectors are vulnerable to numerous corrupt practices. Using a value chain framework, we can see the full range of potential abuses, from distortions in policy and budget decisions to illegal charges at public health facilities, as listed in figure 2.2.

Some of these practices cannot occur in the Ethiopian health sector today because of its structure. For example, fraudulent billing is a regular problem in countries where public insurance agencies reimburse providers, but Ethiopia does not yet have such an insurer. Similarly, federal officials' ability to distort budget allocations is limited because most federal health funds are distributed in block grants to regions, and these allocations are calculated based on population and other measures of need.

An alternative way of mapping health sector corruption is to focus on the different actors. As figure 2.3 illustrates, the public health sector is vulnerable to the following types of corruption:

A. Manipulating bureaucratic procedures for personal gain or political goals; favoritism in employment
B. Fraud, kickbacks, and bribing inspectors
C. Absenteeism, theft of supplies, and misuse of funds
D. Diverting patients to private practice
E. Charging illicit fees
F. Embezzlement, fraud, kickbacks, and theft

Finally, the opportunities for health sector corruption can be mapped in terms of the applicable control mechanisms, as table 2.1 previously laid out. In this regard, Ethiopia has made some important advances relative to other countries that rely so heavily on foreign aid. In particular, the efforts of government and external agencies to bring significant amounts of funding into a single or few channels of financial management has been quite successful.

Figure 2.2   Value Chain Framework of Potential Health Sector Abuses

	Corruption type	Evidence or allegations in Ethiopia
Policy and budgets	• policy capture (restricting competition and protecting monopolies) • allocating funds to favored groups or regions • allocating funds to specific projects to facilitate kickbacks, embezzlement, or theft	• allegations of favoritism in awarding major consulting contracts
Foreign aid	• establishment of fraudulent implementing organizations • siphoning of funds away from intended purpose • leakage of donated drugs or commodity for resale	• evidence of commodities being stolen or diverted in major campaigns • lax financial reporting from community-based organizations
Financial management	• embezzlement • misapplication of funds	• audits unable to determine final use of funds • mixed financial accounts preclude accountability for use of funds
Regulations and inspections	• interference in setting standards or approval for drugs, equipment, and licensing • bribing inspectors or extorting funds from suppliers and providers to certify compliance	• alleged bribery of inspectors
Procurement	• kickbacks • manipulating specifications • collusion among bidders • special access to bidding documents	• performance audits show cases in which work was not done • audits reveal unverifiable expenditures • proper bidding procedures not always used in purchases of large commodities programs and in awards of construction contracts
Drug supply	• expired, substandard, or counterfeit medications • theft for use in private practice • theft for resale	• diversion to private practice and pharmacies • existence of a black market for drugs not available in the public sector
Health care delivery and patients	• side payments for favored placements • absenteeism • receiving or extorting illicit payments	• absenteeism to serve private patients • referral of patients to private practice for additional fees • priority services provided by patronage • pilfering of equipment and other services for use in private practice

Source: Authors.

Figure 2.3   Ethiopian Health System Actors and Vulnerabilities to Corruption

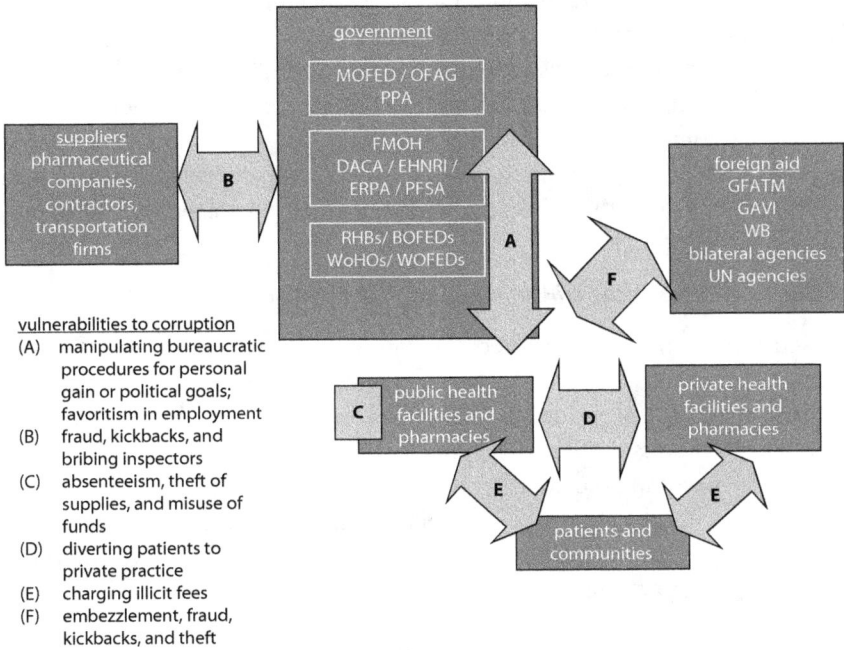

vulnerabilities to corruption
(A)   manipulating bureaucratic procedures for personal gain or political goals; favoritism in employment
(B)   fraud, kickbacks, and bribing inspectors
(C)   absenteeism, theft of supplies, and misuse of funds
(D)   diverting patients to private practice
(E)   charging illicit fees
(F)   embezzlement, fraud, kickbacks, and theft

Note: FMOH = Ministry of Health; MOFED = Federal Ministry of Finance and Economic Development; GFATM = Global Fund to Fight AIDS, Tuberculosis and Malaria; GAVI = Global Alliance for Vaccinations and Immunisations; RHBs = Regional Health Bureaus; WoHOs = Woreda Health Offices; PPA = Public Procurement Agency; UN = United Nations; ERPA = Ethiopian Radiation Protection Authority; PFSA = Pharmaceutical Fund and Supply Agency; OFAG = Office of the Federal Auditor General.

As table 2.1 showed, an estimated two-thirds of total health expenditure is financed through foreign aid. In most developing countries, this would mean that funding is governed by separate donor procurement and accounting systems. Yet a significant share of all foreign aid is channeled through the government of Ethiopia's national procurement and financial control mechanisms (table 2.1).

In 2006, Ethiopia directed about US$130 million of domestic revenues to health through the FMOH, Ministry of Education, and Ministry of Defense. Foreign agencies provided another US$475 million, of which US$264 million was channeled through MOFED or the FMOH. The funds channeled through the government were subject to normal federal procurement and financial management policies, which have been reformed with support from the World Bank and are considered acceptable by international standards (FDRE 2007a; World Bank 2007; Wolde 2009). Even in cases where foreign agencies use funds to procure pharmaceuticals and commodities, the government is trying to ensure coordination by having these products channeled through a newly created agency, the PFSA, responsible for managing the procurement and distribution of supplies to all public facilities.

This overview provides the context for the findings that follow, which assess the levels of corruption relative to other countries and sectors before analyzing vulnerabilities to corruption along the value chain—from budgeting and planning through health care delivery—and concluding with an assessment of corruption in relation to the rapid expansion of foreign aid.

Extent and Sources of Corruption: Findings

Based on our field research, corruption in Ethiopia's health sector does not seem to be as pervasive as in other countries or other sectors. Nevertheless, the sector is vulnerable to corruption, which could get substantially worse as the health sector expands. The main areas identified as particularly vulnerable to corrupt practices include the budgetary and financial oversight system; the procurement of drugs, equipment, and other health commodities; the pharmaceutical distribution system; regulation and inspections; the interaction between providers and patients; and the scale-up of new global health funding mechanisms.

Comparison with Other Countries and Sectors

Although this chapter focuses on opportunities for corruption in Ethiopia's own health sector, it is important to keep the issue in perspective. Ethiopia's health sector faces many problems related to limited resources, a high burden of disease, and weak institutions. Corruption is one part of the overall picture that should be addressed, but not without considering the effects on the larger system. Focusing exclusively on controlling corruption can end up creating further obstacles to extending health care provision and implementing system reform.

International comparison. This is particularly the case because corruption does not appear to be as pervasive in Ethiopia as in other countries. The interviewees who have international experience all told us that Ethiopia had fewer problems with health sector corruption than elsewhere. One staff person from an international NGO said, "We infrequently get shaken down or asked for bribes in Ethiopia. In other African countries that I've been in, it was a regular problem."

Another NGO staff member noted that the NGO is working with the government on health care delivery because it perceives that the public sector is serious about providing care—in contrast to experiences in other countries where NGOs have tried to distance themselves as much as possible from the government. Fewer Ethiopians report being charged illegal fees at public facilities than is common in other countries. For example, only 3.6 percent of Ethiopians in a 2008 survey reported illegal charges at public facilities compared with rates exceeding 20 percent in Ghana and more than 50 percent in Cambodia (Ethiopian data from FDRE 2008; others from Lewis 2006).

Sector comparison. In Ethiopia, health sector corruption also seems to be less problematic than in other sectors. In our interviews, people who were not employed in the health sector volunteered specific examples of corruption in land and resettlement programs, transporting food relief, construction, and industry. Though they also expressed concerns about public health care provision and criticized the government for not being more effective, they provided relatively few specific allegations of wrongdoing in the sector.

This finding is also reflected in a recent study of local accountability in eight woredas that identified 8 case studies of problems in public administration, 8 in education, 5 in water, 10 in agriculture, 6 in justice, and 3 related to gender and youth, but only 1 in health—involving a health post that was allegedly not built to standards (Pankhurst 2008). Similarly, a recent survey of local public services found that people were least satisfied with roads and city cleanliness and more satisfied with public health services, even though they expressed greater interest in improving health and water services (Urban Institute 2009). Thus, corruption is an issue for the health sector but apparently not as much as in other sectors.

Ethiopia also seems to be taking corruption in the health sector seriously. Most of the specific allegations in interviews had been formally reported and were under investigation, either internally by a government ministry, by the auditor general, or by the FEACC. The exceptions to this rule were a number of discrepancies and allegations of improper use of funds in audit reports for which we could not find follow-up actions. This issue was also noted in MOFED's Public Finance Management Assessments (FDRE 2007a; World Bank 2007).

Budget Allocations and Financial Oversight

Ethiopia has adopted internationally recognized procedures for classifying and reporting its budget as well as for documenting flows of funds and conducting audits. These procedures can limit corruption by linking funds to visible outputs and increasing the chances of detection and punishment.

Although Ethiopia's system of budgeting and financial oversight is structured appropriately, its implementation is weak except in the aggregate. A recent Public Finance Management Assessment gave Ethiopia high scores (A) on its federal budget execution, budget classification, and budget process but low scores (C+) on controls in procurement, effectiveness of internal audits, and quality and timeliness of annual financial statements (FDRE 2007a).

Regional public financial systems are modeled on the federal ones, and the recent Public Finance Management Assessment gave the regions a largely favorable report. Regions received high scores for budget classification comprehensiveness of information, payroll controls, and effectiveness of internal audits, but low scores on effectiveness of tax collection, value for money in procurement, and follow-up of external audits (World Bank 2007).

Health sector financial management. For the health sector, regional financial management systems are critical because the regions are responsible for most public health sector expenditures. A large part of the funds applied by the regions to health care services are received in block grants from the general public budget system. The formula for allocating block grants to the regions was recently changed to bring the amounts in line with population, and it takes revenue-generating capacity into consideration (FDRE 2007b). Most of our informants felt that the new formulas were more equitable and less subject to manipulation.

The regions themselves then allocate resources by applying a region-specific budget allocation formula to the various sectors, zones, and woredas. The regions have Bureaus of Finance and Economic Development (BOFEDs) that transfer funds directly to the RHBs for regional activities, including the funding of referral and regional hospitals. The BOFEDs also transfer finances to woreda-level Offices of Finance and Economic Development (WOFEDs) to finance the WoHOs, which generally do not have their own finance departments but instead rely upon the WOFEDs for financing processes.

Several reforms are in place to increase the woredas' capacity to manage their own finances, including training, investments in computerization, and simplification of accounting. A typical woreda manages between 7 and 10 bank accounts to be able to provide reports to different government and foreign agencies. For example, Asegede Tsimbele woreda manages seven accounts: for block grant funds; agriculture; health; HIV/AIDS (human immunodeficiency virus and acquired immune deficiency syndrome); the Productive Safety Net Programme; the UN Development Program; and the World Bank (Pankhurst 2008).

Donor funds. Donor resources are channeled into the country using several different mechanisms. Bilateral agencies channel resources directly into government budgets through the PBS program, the MDTF, and the MDG fund. Funds channeled through these mechanisms flow through the regular public financial management system and are therefore subject to the regular financial accounting and audit processes.

Public sector financial management procedures are appropriate, and our informants felt that the procedures, including keeping records of transactions, are generally followed. In fact, several interviewees were concerned that public officials may be too rigid in following financial accounting rules and argued that such inflexibility can obstruct efficient management of health services. They also conceded that it may be difficult for the system to generate timely reports and blamed these difficulties on lack of capacity and high turnover among the health sector and local government financial personnel. We were told that individuals who develop financial skills in the public sector frequently move to higher-paying jobs for international agencies or private sector firms.

Unfortunately, most of the audit reports that we reviewed detected serious record-keeping deficiencies that belied some of our informants' assurances. The audits that we reviewed regularly reported failures to produce records for financial transactions, particularly when these involved multiple governmental levels.

As one example, US$6 million was transferred from the FMOH to regional governments for a GFATM program, of which only US$2 million was accounted for in the statements of expenditures. The auditors could not verify whether the regional authorities still held the remaining US$4 million because funds had been deposited into general accounts (Audit Services Corporation 2008).

Many of the new multilateral global health initiatives—including the GFATM, the U.S. President's Emergency Plan for AIDS Relief (PEPFAR), and GAVI Alliance—rely upon other channels. Many of these programs provide project funding with separate accounts or operate through parallel financing control mechanisms. For example, PEPFAR reported that it issued grants to more than 100 international and local institutions in Ethiopia in 2007. Although the government is the main recipient of GFATM funds, it was not clear whether financial controls were primarily the responsibility of the government or of the GFATM's local financing agent.

Supervision of the Global Fund to Fight AIDS, Tuberculosis and Malaria (GFATM) funds appears to have changed significantly in the past five years, with an increasing number of regular supervisory visits to sub-recipients that started in 2006, and a change in the local financing agent from KPMG to UNOPS. Before these changes, audits for the GFATM found a large number of irregularities in the use of funds, and our own interviews uncovered allegations that funds were improperly diverted and used. We could not establish that large foreign aid programs were being held to adequate standards.

Mixed assessment. In sum, Ethiopia has appropriate financial systems in place and is making efforts to improve their implementation. However, compliance is still weak in critical areas such as record keeping and follow-up on external audits. Of particular concern were how few performance audits we could obtain and the high share of these that reported funds had not been spent as intended. It is unclear whether these irregularities are due to corruption, simple record-keeping errors, poor management and training, or even well-intentioned coping efforts by staff and officials to provide services under extremely difficult circumstances.

Procurement. It is often difficult to ensure the integrity of procurement in the health sector because it involves such a diverse range of specialized goods and services. Ethiopia's national drug formulary runs to 572 pages, listing hundreds of drugs, each with its own quality indicators and dosages. Supplies ranging from protective gloves to catheters, equipment ranging from diagnostic blood tests to x-ray imagery, and infrastructure ranging from health posts to hospitals are all objects of procurement that must be properly specified, put out for bids, verified upon delivery, and used properly.

Until 2003, salaries accounted for more than 60 percent of public health spending, but today pharmaceuticals and commodities are the largest and fastest-growing share of public and foreign expenditures in health. All of these factors make procurement a special area of concern.

Reformed standards and procedures. In Ethiopia's public health sector, procurement must follow rules of the PPA, an autonomous federal government agency created in 2005 to set standards, monitor compliance, and build procurement capacity. Although the regional governments are not obligated to follow the federal law, all nine regions have followed the federal government's lead and adopted similar standards, procedures, and organizational structures.

PPA standards include five procurement procedures: open bidding (international and national), two-stage bidding, restricted bidding (international and national), request for quotations, and direct procurement. In the past three years, PPA reports that it has received information from 75 percent of federal agencies and, among these, open bidding accounts for about 84 percent of all procurement; direct procurement for another 11 percent; and a combination of restricted bidding, two-stage bidding, and request for quotations for the remaining 5 percent (Wolde 2009).

Interviews with the PPA and procurement specialists from government and foreign agencies all reported that the capacity to properly conduct and control procurement has improved considerably in recent years. When asked about the negative conclusions of a 2002 audit, one foreign agency staff person said, "It could easily have happened because staff didn't know how to follow procedures, but if I were to see the same thing today, I wouldn't believe that it was lack of capacity." MOFED's Public Finance Management Assessments have also judged Ethiopia's procurement procedures to be satisfactory, even if they give lower marks for record keeping and follow-up on external audits (FDRE 2007a; World Bank 2007). To the extent that problems persist, they are blamed on lack of proper procurement planning, failure to use the standard bidding documents, and poorly trained staff.

Specialized health procurement reforms. More than in other sectors, health procurement involves technically specialized products that only one or a few manufacturers produce. Furthermore, the extensive network of public facilities requires timely distribution of these products, often under particular storage conditions.

Ensuring that procurement is fair and efficient under such conditions is difficult. For example, in one case, international competitive bidding for ELISA equipment (devices for testing antibodies, often used for HIV/AIDS diagnosis) elicited numerous bids from trading firms but none from the two international companies that produce the equipment. Therefore, the purchase cost was probably higher than it might have been directly from the manufacturers, requiring the Ethiopian government to contract separately with the manufacturers for technical support and maintenance. The efficient approach would have been to identify the two manufacturers and invite bids directly from them. However, the equipment is costly and surpasses the PPA threshold for requiring open bidding, so authorization to invite bids from the prequalified manufacturers would have required a special exception (Carl Bro Intelligent Solutions 2006).

In 2007, recognizing these particularities of health sector procurement, the government created a new agency, the PFSA, to procure, store, and distribute pharmaceuticals and commodities to all public facilities. It is hoped that by centralizing these functions in one agency, the system can be made more accountable and efficient. Furthermore, so that the PFSA can attend to the specialized nature of health sector procurement, the government gave it authority to promulgate its own procurement manual, so long as it remains compatible with the PPA.

As with financial controls, the recently reformed procurement system follows international standards in almost all respects. The government has committed significant effort to minimizing vulnerabilities to corruption in procurement by

- establishing the PFSA
- asking international agencies (such as UNICEF and UNFPA) to conduct procurement processes on major contracts
- committing resources to train and deploy capable staff.

Appropriate reporting systems are in place, but implementation is weak. It is unclear whether this weakness reflects the difficulty of getting information reported out of the control system or whether materials are actually being diverted at different stages. Evidence of stockouts at local health facilities could indicate inadequate supplies, inefficient management, diversion of materials to other legitimate public uses, or diversion of materials for personal gain.

The creation of the PFSA will change this situation considerably. Once it has completed its implementation, it will be responsible for forecasting, distributing, and controlling pharmaceuticals and supplies to all public facilities in the country. Its responsibilities will include training and monitoring staff responsible for receiving stock and managing stockrooms. By concentrating these functions in one institution, Ethiopia may, as planned, be creating an efficient and effectively controlled distribution agency that can minimize corruption. The risk of this strategy is that if PFSA is not well implemented and adequately supervised, it could itself become a locus for serious, large-scale abuse.

Infrastructure challenges. One procurement area that remains outside the PFSA's purview is construction. The FMOH is undertaking a large effort to expand the infrastructure necessary to reach the entire population, particularly in underserved rural areas. It has almost tripled the number of government health centers (from 243 in 1997 to 600 in 2005) and constructed 13,625 health posts (small structures in rural villages, staffed by health extension workers, that provide the most basic level of health care services) over the course of the past four years. This scale of construction, funded federally and regionally but executed locally, is vulnerable to corruption. Although proper bidding procedures are in place, informants told us of two ways in which the system has been corrupted: (a) manipulation of the process for selecting contractors, and (b) compromising the quality of construction by stealing materials.

In the Amhara region, we saw documentation of a few cases in which the selected contractors did not satisfy the contractually agreed specifications for a project. In another example, again from the Amhara region, construction materials were stolen. In both cases, those responsible had been prosecuted and sentenced to prison time and large fines. Also in the Amhara region, a contractor complained of favoritism in the awarding of construction contract by regional authorities. In another case, in the Afar region, community members alleged that a health post had not been built to standard; however, no investigation was ever conducted (Pankhurst 2008).

Strong, independent oversight essential. In sum, procurement is an aspect of the health sector that is highly vulnerable to corruption. The government is limiting opportunities for corruption by simplifying procedures, training staff, consolidating procurement into relatively few standardized systems, and investigating cases when they arise. However, it is too early to determine whether these reforms will resolve past difficulties with record keeping and compliance with procedures.

Regardless of progress in general procurement, two issues stand out for special attention in the future:

- The continuing need for procurement of high-value and specialized equipment and commodities will require the PFSA to ask the PPA for special exceptions. Managing this process with appropriate oversight and controls—but without hampering the efficiency of procurement and use of these supplies—will require substantial effort.

- Consolidating procurement in a specialized agency such as the PFSA has the potential to substantially improve the quality of procurement. However, the benefits of consolidation also come with the risk of concentrating opportunities for abuse. Therefore, the government would be well advised to establish strong independent oversight for the PFSA.

Pharmaceuticals

Within health systems, the production, sale, and distribution of pharmaceuticals are recognized as particularly vulnerable to corruption. Pharmaceuticals are highly regulated, markets are restricted, and manufacturers are often politically and economically powerful. It can be costly for regulators and purchasers to assess the quality and efficacy of pharmaceuticals. For all these reasons, as figures 2.2 and 2.3 previously enumerated, abuse and fraud are possible in almost every transaction involving pharmaceuticals—influencing policies, manipulating decisions about which drugs to include in national drug lists, corrupting prescription practices, overprescribing, encouraging kickbacks in procurement, and supplying substandard products. Corruption in drug system management can happen at any stage in the process, from basic research to prescription and use (WHO 2006). The following processes are especially vulnerable:

- *Drug selection for the national formulary.* As in most countries, Ethiopia has a list of registered medicines that can be legally imported, produced, and distributed. The process for including medicines in such a list can be corrupted by manufacturers who either want to sell products that do not meet accepted standards or want to exclude competitors. The most common way to insulate drug registration from abuse is to establish a procedure for disinterested individuals to serve on a public committee that applies explicit criteria according to established procedures.
- *Medicine promotion.* Pharmaceutical manufacturers and distributors can manipulate the public through advertising or improperly influence health professionals to increase profits at the expense of patients or patient health. Few developing countries have effective policies to regulate medicine promotion.
- *Pharmaceutical inspection.* Manufacturers, distributors, and retailers can evade regulations by corrupting inspectors, with detrimental impact on health and safety.
- *Drug distribution.* A variety of corrupt practices can also occur at all points where drugs are distributed, prescribed, purchased, or sold to patients.

WHO has assessed pharmaceutical governance in more than 20 developing countries and found that the greatest risks involved inspection, promotion, and selection, as figure 2.4 shows (WHO 2009).[4]

Regulation of pharmaceuticals. Ethiopia has enacted measures for regulating and controlling the pharmaceutical sector. Ethiopia's Drug Administration and Control Authority (DACA) began operation in 2001 as an agency within the FMOH aimed at ensuring the safety, efficacy, quality, and proper use of drugs. It is responsible for

- setting standards for drug quality, manufacturers, warehouses, and dispensaries
- licensing clinical trials
- controlling the quality of raw materials
- registering and licensing drugs for use
- promoting appropriate use
- inspecting manufacturers (including foreign manufacturers who seek to export to Ethiopia), health facilities, and pharmacies (whether publicly or privately owned).

We did not hear any allegations of corruption in policy and registration, and DACA appears able to exercise its authority: in several cases, it rejected drugs procured by the FMOH and the PFSA for noncompliance with safety, quality, or efficacy standards (Wolde 2009).

However, several interviewees reported that some pharmacies, drug shops, and rural drug vendors sell restricted or illegal items and avoid detection and penalties by learning about inspections in advance and preparing accordingly. One informant provided a particularly pessimistic view of the pharmaceutical sector, but we could not corroborate the individual's allegations that "at least 30 percent" of staff involved in regulating, distributing, and managing pharmaceuticals engaged in some form of abuse. The allegations do highlight the need for Ethiopia to pay attention to the opportunities for staff to accept bribes for issuing licenses to foreign or domestic manufacturers; awarding contracts; or certifying pharmacies, health facilities, and warehouses.

Public and private pharmacies. Interviewees were also concerned about the relationship between public and private pharmacies. Maintaining a public practice gives pharmacists access to certain resources, such as hospital clients, but they can generate more revenues in the private sector. We were told that public pharmacists commonly refer patients to

Figure 2.4 Corruption Vulnerability Scores in WHO Assessments, by Pharmaceutical Management Function, GGM Countries

number of countries

	Registration	Licencing	Inspection	Promotion	Clinical trials	Selection	Procurement	Distribution
Extremely vulnerable	0	0	0	5	0	1	0	0
Very vulnerable	2	0	3	5	2	3	1	0
Moderately vulnerable	10	3	10	9	1	9	4	1
Marginally vulnerable	11	3	6	1	3	10	17	7
Minimally vulnerable	1	0	1	0	0	1	2	4
Total no. of countries[a]	24	6	20	20	6	24	24	12

red circles and shaded column headings = most vulnerable to corruption

green circles = least vulnerable to corruption

Source: WHO 2009.

Note: WHO = World Health Organization. GGM = [WHO] Good Governance for Medicines Programme.

a. Total represents the number of countries that had undergone assessments since 2004. As of 2008, 24 countries had participated. However, the assessment of some functions was not carried out in all countries because new pharmaceutical functions were added to the assessment over the past four years.

their private practices when certain products are unavailable. Although this is not necessarily a form of corruption, it is difficult to monitor this process, and it is unclear whether patients are referred only when a product is truly unavailable.

In Ethiopia, certain medicines, such as antiretrovirals for HIV/AIDS, are available only in the public sector. Therefore patients who need medicines, even those who would not normally access health services in the public sector, must get them from public facilities. At least one pharmacist reported that because many patients with means want to avoid visiting a public facility, some pharmacists have offered to deliver medicines to the patients' homes in exchange for delivery fees.

Interviews have also suggested that pharmacists may use their access to public and private stores to improve their incomes. For example, a pharmacist with medicines that are close to expiration might transfer the product to a public pharmacy for faster sale. Although this represents an abuse of the individual's public office, the pharmacist justifies the action by arguing that it reduces waste of useful medicines.

By law, most pharmaceuticals can be dispensed from pharmacies only with a doctor's prescription, opening another avenue for abuse. We were told of one case in Addis Ababa in which an audit of a hospital pharmacy found many prescriptions written to a particular group of patients. Allegedly, the drugs were purchased at subsidized cost in the public pharmacy for later resale, at a higher price, in a private pharmacy.

A black market is growing for pharmaceutical products, many imported from Kenya, Somalia, and other countries (Jubat and Ongeri 2009). Many of the drugs available on the black market are either lower-cost versions of drugs available in public pharmacies or products that are not registered and available within Ethiopia. Some pharmacists reportedly sell such drugs by storing them in the trunk of a car parked outside the pharmacy and selling them in a way that is easily hidden and formally off-premise. Because these products are outside of the regular market, DACA and other authorities cannot monitor their quality.

Progress continues. In sum, DACA officials listed a number of measures they are taking to ensure the integrity of their regulatory functions. Some involve improving pay and educational opportunities for inspectors to improve morale and make them less vulnerable to corruption. They also have organized their teams of inspectors separately from those responsible for laboratory supervision and are trying to increase the number of inspections. The two areas that they are working on most are postmarket surveillance and laboratory quality control. [5]

Regulation, Licensing, and Inspection

The health sector involves goods and services whose quality is difficult for patients and their families to assess. Furthermore, patients do not want to bear the cost and discomfort of trying different providers and treatments to see which ones work. Consequently, countries use a variety of mechanisms to signal whether a medical provider or medication is genuine and to meet some basic standards of quality.

In many countries, health practitioners must be certified with specific training before they can legally practice or get employment. Professional associations sometimes establish codes of conduct and investigate complaints. Pharmaceutical companies are usually subjected to inspections, and medications must meet quality standards before they can be sold. Although such quality control mechanisms can be conducted by private companies and professional associations, most countries have chosen to establish governmental or quasi-governmental agencies to supervise medical licensing and drug registration. This interface between public regulators and those they supervise is an avenue that can be corrupted.

Quality control actors. In Ethiopia, several agencies are empowered to regulate, license, and inspect health care providers and associated businesses:

- *FMOH* has primary responsibility for regulating the health sector and is in charge of licensing physicians and monitoring the quality of health care provision in all public and private facilities; however other agencies and ministries also play a role.
- *DACA* is another significant actor, a decentralized agency that reports to the FMOH and is empowered to review all applications for importing, producing, and selling medications in Ethiopia.
- The *Ethiopian Radiation Protection Authority (ERPA)*, a dependency of the Ministry of Science and Technology, is responsible for licensing and inspecting all equipment with radiation, such as x-ray machines.

Risks in inspection, licensing processes. In interviews, people holding a range of different positions—both within and outside of health care provision—expressed concerns that inspections were prone to corruption. One person reported that four inspectors were under investigation by the Ministry of Science and Technology for allegedly pressuring people for bribes to certify that radiation equipment in their facilities complied with safety standards. Several individuals expressed concern over inspections of private and public pharmacies, stating that they knew of cases where noncompliant or expired medications remained on shelves for sale and use after inspectors agreed to overlook the violations.

The FEACC has also investigated allegations that licensing and inspections were not being conducted properly. It reported that some FMOH licenses had been issued to private health institutions even though these facilities were not in full compliance with regulations. It also reported inconsistencies in the licensing of health practitioners and private health institutions by the Addis Ababa Health Bureau (FEACC 2008).

Our informants argued that low pay and low per diems made it difficult for inspectors to make a living, and this is used as a justification for accepting or requesting bribes. They also noted that abuses were more common in rural areas, where visibility and the likelihood of detection were lower. Several individuals emphasized the nature of familial networks and social pressures that make it difficult for inspectors to sanction providers: if an inspector has family connections to the provider, this attachment can be used to pressure the inspector to overlook noncompliance because a negative report would either harm the provider's ability to conduct business or look bad on his or her employment report. Because of the low per diems, inspectors are also susceptible to being given meals or a place to stay. However, issuing a sanction to an individual who has just hosted an inspector breaks social norms.

Notably, most of those who mentioned corruption of the inspection process also cited examples where those who had allegedly broken the law were facing investigation. Ethiopia does have mechanisms in place for responding to complaints and investigating and punishing corruption in inspection processes.

Inspections, as an area of vulnerability to corruption, may not be of primary importance in terms of lost funds, but it is nevertheless important for its effects on the health of individuals who are treated and on the staff who are exposed unnecessarily to harmful working conditions. When the public is aware that government inspection is not effectively ensuring the quality of health facilities, it also erodes confidence in the public sector overall and casts a negative shadow over those facilities and inspectors who remain honest.[6]

Provider-patient interactions

Thus far, we have discussed aspects of health care that are largely invisible to most people. Now we turn to opportunities for corruption in direct patient-provider interactions. Corruption can affect patients at this level through the extraction of bribes or informal payments, favoritism in the allocation of services, staff absenteeism, or pilfering of supplies essential to the delivery of care. All of these corrupt practices can directly reduce the quality of care patients receive, increase the overall cost of care, lead patients to seek care from alternative providers who may be unskilled or more costly, or deter patients from seeking care altogether.

Overall, however, corruption does not appear to be a major issue in Ethiopia's front-line health service delivery. Recent surveys have not substantiated allegations of bribery and absenteeism. When asked about their satisfaction with public health care services, as figure 2.5 shows, a large share of people cite problems with the distances they have to travel

Figure 2.5   Reasons for Dissatisfaction with Public Health Services in Ethiopia
percentage

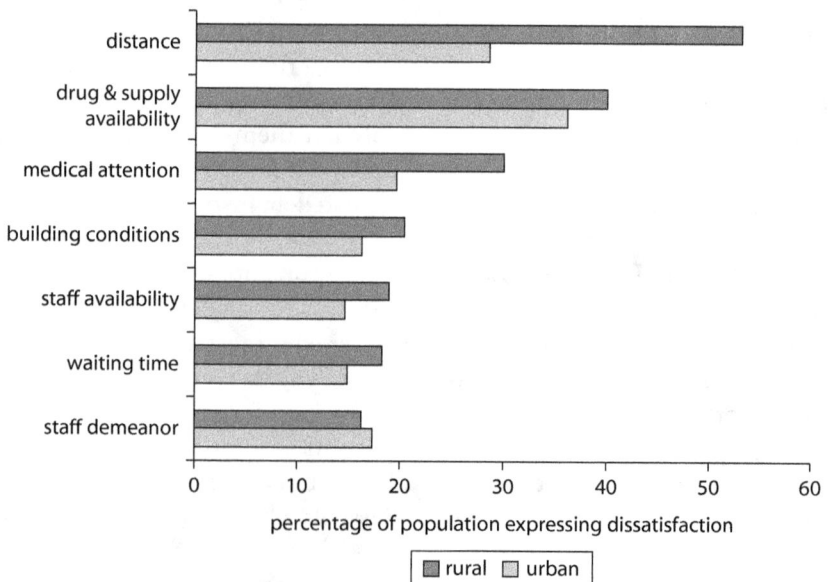

percentage of population expressing dissatisfaction

rural urban

Source: Urban Institute 2009, table 4.1, 37.

(44 percent) and with lack of drugs (40 percent) (Urban Institute 2009). However, relatively few (18 percent) cite problems with the availability of staff (absenteeism), long waits (17 percent), or disrespectful treatment by staff (16 percent). Except for drug availability, these results suggest that many of the resources expended on front-line delivery may actually be getting through to patients, although a more detailed public expenditure tracking study would be required to confirm such a judgment.

Bribery. Although illegal fees at public health facilities are a problem in many developing countries, they are not a significant issue in Ethiopia. A national survey of households found that the practice of extracting bribes from patients in Ethiopia exists but is relatively rare (FDRE 2008). Among households who had contact with a public health facility in the past year, only 3.6 percent reported paying more than the official fees to receive services. The most commonly cited reasons for paying any additional amounts were to gain admission to the facility or to obtain medicines, and most of those who reported making such payments said they had initiated the transaction rather than the provider.

Favoritism. In our interviews, respondents claimed that patients with personal connections to providers or of higher social status received preferential treatment in government health facilities. This finding was consistent with a 2005 study in which respondents frequently mentioned that health care providers provided priority access to services to friends or by patronage (Lindelow, Serneels, and Lemma 2005). Although this form of favoritism does not require patients to pay a bribe, it may account for some patients' willingness to voluntarily pay extra to visit a clinic and could limit equitable access to government facilities.

Dual public-private job positions. The most common problem cited by informants at public health facilities involved poor-quality care or lack of medicines, often leading patients with resources to seek private care. Although such a decision can be a legitimate choice between options, it appears that health care workers—including nurses, health officers, and doctors—sometimes intentionally divert patients to private practices where they can charge fees and earn more income. An earlier study of health care providers and patients identified the unregulated relationship between private and public practice as a large and growing threat to the integrity of health care provision (Lindelow, Serneels, and Lemma 2005).

The practice of holding dual jobs can compromise the care provided in public health facilities in several ways:

- Staff may work hard in their private practices, where they are paid in relation to the number of consultations or drugs dispensed, and exert less effort in their public sector jobs, where their salaries are fixed.
- Staff may use their public practices to identify patients who can pay more for private services and then refer those patients to their private practices, promising higher-quality services or access to more sophisticated equipment.
- Providers may transfer resources, such as lab equipment, from the public sector to their private practices.

Other studies have also cited such examples (Lindelow, Serneels, and Lemma 2005), and several cases have been referred to the FEACC.

Managing the public-private relationship. Private practice can contribute positively to the quality and quantity of health care services and increase access to care, but the rapid expansion of private provision in Ethiopia appears to be outpacing the government's capacity to regulate its relationship with the public sector.

Ethiopia's strategy for dealing with these tensions is to formalize and regulate public-private interactions. For example, the government is experimenting with the construction of private wings within public facilities, promoting the establishment of special for-profit pharmacies beside public facilities, and allowing dual practice among medical practitioners. Managing this relationship is not easy, and whether these arrangements will be functional in terms of performance and transparency remains to be seen.

Rapid Expansion of Foreign Aid

Foreign aid is just as vulnerable to corruption as domestic spending. In some respects, foreign aid is an even more attractive target because it is paid in highly valued foreign currency and involves large transactions. In other respects, foreign aid may be less of a target because external control mechanisms may be harder to evade. Regardless, the forms of corruption to which foreign aid is susceptible are as varied as the ones affecting domestic spending, ranging from theft of commodities and kickbacks to embezzlement and fraud.

Foreign aid to Ethiopia for the health sector deserves special attention because it is so large and increasing so fast. From 1998 to 2008, foreign aid to Ethiopia's health sector increased tenfold—from about US$50 million to more than US$500 million.[7] Two very different structural changes characterize this rapid expansion: One large part of this money is being organized by donors into pooled funds that are channeled through the government's normal financial management and procurement systems. Another major share is being channeled directly to NGOs, civil society organizations, and consulting firms with independent and parallel forms of financial supervision.

Ethiopia certainly needs these funds, but ensuring that they are used properly is a major challenge. The international community has increasingly recognized that new aid modalities create both challenges and opportunities for reducing corruption, and this is also true for the health sector (Kolstad, Fritz, and O'Neil 2008).

Corruption risks and mitigation. The efforts to pool funds and work within the government's financial management and procurement system includes funds going into the PBS program, the MDTF, and the MDG fund. In 2006, bilateral agencies and the World Bank provided about US$90 million through the PBS program, part of which financed local government block grants through MOFED, while the other part financed pharmaceuticals and supplies through the FMOH. The GFATM and GAVI Alliance are currently disbursing through government channels as well, leaving PEPFAR as the major source of foreign aid still disbursing outside of Ethiopia's public financial management and procurement systems.

Our research found concerns that abuses of foreign aid flows for the health care sector might be occurring in three ways:

- Diversion and theft of commodities
- Embezzlement and fraud of funds channeled through the public sector
- Misuse of funds channeled outside the public sector.

However, three factors mitigate the risks of corruption affecting foreign aid to Ethiopia:

- The funds that flow through the government's normal procedures should be verifiable and, if any abuses are detected, investigated and prosecuted.

- A large share of this funding goes to international procurement managed by foreign consulting firms (such as Management Sciences for Health, which procures for the PEPFAR program) or UN agencies (for example, UNICEF, which the FMOH has asked to purchase vaccines)—so the funds do not necessarily even enter the country.
- Even foreign aid disbursed directly to organizations in Ethiopia is subject to external, often foreign, audits. For example, the GFATM contracts with an international consulting firm to audit the programs managed by its country coordinating groups.

Diversion and theft of commodities. The Ethiopian government has anticipated the prospect of diversion and theft. One case, currently under investigation by the FEACC, came to light because the government was sweeping domestic markets for illegally obtained bednets. With financial support from the GFATM, Ethiopia undertook the largest program to date for delivery of insecticide-treated bednets in regions where malaria is endemic. With a goal of distributing 20 million bednets, the program is probably the largest of its kind anywhere in the world. At a cost of about US$5 per unit, this large volume of bednets is also a tempting target for theft and resale. At least one NGO purchased 5,000 bednets on the open market and discovered, upon delivery, that the bednets had been stolen from the FMOH; this is the case under FEACC investigation. Other allegations have been made about bednets purchased with foreign assistance being diverted for private resale within Ethiopia and abroad.

Other commodities that are potentially being diverted include high-value medicines such as antiretrovirals, antimalarials, and antibiotics. The Ethiopian government guarantees free access to particular medicines such as antiretrovirals for treating HIV/AIDS and insulin for treating diabetes. Because these medicines are available for free in public pharmacies, they are not supposed to be sold in private pharmacies. In fact, there shouldn't be a market for drugs that are provided free of charge in public facilities. Nevertheless, drugs are not always reliably available in public pharmacies—possibly because of manipulation by stock managers and pharmacists. Interviewees also told us that people will pay for these medications to avoid visiting public facilities. Some drugs are also allegedly being taken outside the country for resale.

Embezzlement and fraud through public channels. The second major risk of corruption involves foreign aid channeled through the government's financial management and procurement systems. Given the relatively high marks for foreign aid in public financial management assessments, we were surprised that foreign aid program audits we reviewed found that supporting records were frequently unavailable, compliance with procurement guidelines was weak, and accounting discrepancies were common.

For example, the GFATM awarded a grant to the government for preventing and controlling malaria. The audit, covering 2004 through 2007(Audit Services Corporation 2008), found

- duplicate entries (expenses entered once as an advance and again as a settlement);
- charges for medicines and supplies that were part of other programs (such as medicines for obstetric care that were charged to GFATM); and
- overstated charges (for example, US$3,000 of per diems paid out but recorded as US$2,000).

The audit also could not find cash receipts or goods receiving vouchers for transporting of bednets, purchasing of spare parts, medical supplies, and rental agreements, among other expenses. In one UNFPA program, the disbursements were validated, but the final balance of funds available was off by 30 percent or about US$1 million (Alia Abdulahi & Co. 2005).

Misuse of direct aid to NGOs and community organizations. Since 2000, the international sense of urgency to rapidly expand and scale up programs to fight major diseases has required the involvement of many new actors, in particular community-based NGOs that were not particularly active or well resourced in the past. Many of these organizations were created specifically to implement these programs. As a result, their capacity to monitor their own performance and to report back on their financial expenditure was initially weak.

Our informants reported that substantial resources are being channeled into regions and woredas for awareness creation, advocacy, and capacity building. However, the outcomes of such activities are difficult to monitor, making it easy to divert funds. The extent to which these resources are having any effect is unclear, and the limited amount of reporting and record keeping makes it difficult to know whether funds are being used as intended. Hence these funds are vulnerable to abuse of per diems and workshops through favoritism and embezzlement.

Finally, some informants mentioned that the influx of donor funding has contributed to the high turnover of public sector employees—in particular, the staff involved in the monitoring and reporting on financial flows—and the diversion of staff for travel and training purposes. Many interviewees cited the high turnover as the main reason for a lack of capacity in the financial management process.

In the Tigray region, regional health officials have limited the per diems that can be paid by government or outside agencies to keep some control over their employees. However, per diems from HIV/AIDS organizations have been exempted from this practice, and those we interviewed could not explain why. Donor organizations should be encouraged to abide by local standards where possible, avoid excessive recruitment of technically trained employees, and provide stronger justification for such workshops and training.

Next Steps

The weakness of Ethiopia's health care system appears to have more to do with limited resources and inefficiency than with corruption. Ethiopians do not generally have good or equitable access to health care, but this is largely due to constraints on financial and human resources. Fortunately, Ethiopia is receiving increasing resources to strengthen its health sector and expand service provision. The government is also undertaking many reforms and programs to improve the efficiency and integrity of public health care provision. Many of these reforms will simultaneously curtail corruption, though some also present risks.

Public sector modernization is advancing on a number of fronts that could substantially reduce opportunities for corruption. These advances include the following reforms:

- *Public procurement reforms.* Application of the PPA to all public procurement is improving procurement practices and transparency.
- *Pharmaceutical Fund and Supply Agency.* The PFSA is assuming responsibility for the procurement, management, distribution, and control of all pharmaceuticals and supplies used in the public sector.
- *Business process reengineering.* BPR is being implemented in federal and regional public administrations responsible for health care provision to improve personnel management, performance, and accountability.

- *Decentralization and improved planning.* The FMOH is implementing a new planning system that includes analysis of bottlenecks in service provision at the woreda level.
- *Protection of Basic Services.* The PBS program is simplifying and stream-lining the flow of block grant funds from and through the federal government to regional and woreda governments.
- *Investigation and prosecution.* The FEACC is actively investigating allegations of corruption, and its public reporting is increasingly trans-parent and open.

In fact, these reforms are so far-reaching, ambitious, and recent that many of the cases and allegations uncovered in this study may no longer be relevant for policy making. Still, this research has uncovered a number of issues that should be addressed if Ethiopia wishes to maintain and improve the integrity of its health care system. Ethiopia's health sector is less corrupt than in other countries and sectors. Nevertheless, irregulari-ties are still problematic, and factors such as rapidly rising expenditures, growing private provision, concentrated procurement, and financial inno-vations could increase the sector's vulnerability to corruption in the future. The recommendations below address the existing and future areas of vulnerability.

Recommendation 1: *Improve human resources involved in financial management and procurement.*
To the extent that improved human resource management and training are improving public officials' capacity to follow procurement guidelines, keep records, and undertake proper accounting, opportunities for corrup-tion may already have been significantly reduced. However, the diver-gence between the assurances we received from high-level officials regarding the effectiveness of the "paper trail" and the evidence provided in audit reports and other interviews suggests that more work must be done in this area.

Continued efforts to train, supervise, and motivate personnel are nec-essary until the government has regular evidence in its external audits that appropriate financial management and procurement procedures are being followed and that information can be reported out of the system readily. These efforts need to be redoubled, with special attention given to addressing the problem of high turnover among skilled financial and administrative staff.

Recommendation 2: *Ensure appropriate PFSA oversight and support.*

The PFSA will be responsible for a rapidly growing amount of procurement and is even supposed to manage distribution of donated commodities (bednets, antiretrovirals, and so forth). Ensuring transparency and appropriate oversight without hindering the PFSA's efficient operation is critical.

This agency could substantially reduce the scope of corruption in procurement and distribution of supplies and medicines in Ethiopia by better using the limited number of skilled personnel, standardizing procedures, improving forecasting and planning, and eliminating duplication. However, the PFSA's authority over an enormous portion of health sector spending also makes it an attractive target for corruption. It is extremely important to ensure appropriate oversight and support for this key agency.

Regarding the PFSA, two issues stand out: the difficulties of supervising specialized procurement and the potential tradeoff between performance improvements and abuses inherent in concentrating control in the PFSA. Addressing both of these issues requires increased public transparency and external oversight.

Supervising specialized procurement. The continuing need for procurement of high-value and specialized equipment and commodities will require the PFSA to ask the PPA for special exceptions. Managing this process with appropriate oversight and controls but without hampering the efficiency of procurement and use of these supplies will require substantial effort.

There is potentially a direct tradeoff here: any exceptions that are authorized to make procurement efficient—as in the example of ELISA equipment described earlier—can be exploited to restrict competition, raise prices, misuse funds, or generate kickbacks. Therefore, Ethiopia needs a clear and agile set of procedures under which the PFSA can ask the PPA for exceptions when market and technical criteria suggest this would be the most efficient route. Some form of external oversight, however, is necessary to ensure that these procedures are not abused.

Better procurement vs. Risk for abuse. Although consolidating procurement in a specialized agency like the PFSA has the potential to substantially improve the efficiency and quality of procurement, these benefits also come with the risk of concentrating opportunities for abuse. Existing oversight procedures seem adequate for an organization that already has a good track record, but to establish the PFSA's credibility, the government might find it advisable, initially, to establish stronger external supervision.

For example, it could create a group of rotating officials from other agencies to be included as observers on key PFSA committees who would report directly to the FMOH and the FEACC. Alternatively, an external commission—chaired by an FEACC representative—could be appointed to review quarterly reports on procurement during the PFSA's first few years of operation.

Whatever the specific mechanism chosen, some process for increasing the PFSA's transparency to the public or external authorities is necessary if this new agency is to develop the credibility and reputation for integrity that it needs as one of Ethiopia's largest and most prominent procurement entities.

Recommendation 3: *Improve inspections.*

Regulations, licensing, and inspections are not often viewed as high corruption risks because the amounts of money involved may be relatively small. However, in the health sector, these governance mechanisms are critical to ensuring the quality and integrity of health care provision, and progress on three fronts could significantly curb corruption among inspectors:

- *Reforming incentives* by addressing inspectors' pay, per diems, training, motivation, work programs, and supervision. Pay and per diems should be structured and monitored to meet inspectors' real needs while also creating significant chances of detection and punishment for failing to abide by the laws.
- *Improving information* by establishing random revisits by a core team of trusted inspectors.
- *Addressing social norms* by rotating inspectors to prevent development of personal relationships with the people at facilities they are inspecting. Training should emphasize the importance of the inspector's mission of protecting the public by upholding the law—one counterbalance to pressures to accept bribes or overlook noncompliance. Role-playing exercises could suggest tactful ways to resist unlawful approaches and subtle forms of influence. The government could implement these changes for inspectors at DACA and ERPA as well as for internal and external auditors in different ministries.[8]

Recommendation 4: *Address the public-private relationship.*

The most common concern raised by citizens and staff regarding irregularities in health care provision involves health workers, doctors, nurses, and pharmacists who divert patients to, or remove supplies and equipment for use in, private practices. Better regulation of the relationship between health care providers' public and private roles is needed, with particular attention to how the government's strategies affect the relationship between public and private health care provision.

One of the key complaints from citizens and health workers is that poor public sector working conditions and lucrative private sector opportunities are distorting health care provision. The government has a range of sensible programs to harness private sector activity in support of expanding health care access; however, it is not clear whether the government has a clear overarching strategy that addresses both the public-private institutional relationships and the impact on personnel management and health worker behaviors.

It is advisable for the government to reflect on how its different strategies are affecting the relationship between public and private health care provision. Improving human resource management in the public sector will address only one side of this equation, and it is necessary for the government to clearly delineate acceptable and unacceptable ways for public staff to combine public and private practices. Once these roles are delineated, systems must be implemented to enforce them.

Recommendation 5: *Improve surveillance of pharmaceutical sales.*

The relationship between public and private pharmacists, the existence of a private market for drugs that are formally available for free, and evidence of a black market in drugs from abroad all suggest that Ethiopia needs to strengthen its information gathering on pharmaceuticals. Ethiopia's drug agency, DACA, needs adequate resources to conduct postmarket surveillance and lab testing to conduct sweeps for counterfeit and stolen medications. Further recommendations are likely to come from an ongoing study that has been commissioned as part of WHO's assessment of pharmaceutical governance (WHO 2009).

Recommendation 6: *Monitor foreign aid inflows.*

Foreign aid to Ethiopia is increasing so rapidly that it has surpassed the government's own expenditures. These and other changes in international assistance are bringing both advances and risks: Coordination among major donor agencies is simplifying financial and administrative control functions and focusing technical support on improving one public system. However, some agencies continue to use their own financial control systems, which may be stronger or weaker than Ethiopia's own public system.

In general, donors should provide Ethiopia and the public with a full accounting of the amounts disbursed (whether financial or in-kind), the channels used, and subrecipients' use of these funds. More specifically, our research identified three major ways in which foreign aid affects Ethiopia's health sector and increases the risk of corruption—and we recommend the following steps to address each:

- *Increased funding through government channels* increases the stress on the country's financial management, procurement, and logistical distribution systems. More money and more supplies mean more attractive targets for abuse. The first recommendation, then, is to reemphasize the importance of strengthening the government's financial management systems, as discussed above.

- *Expansion of staff opportunities* for alternative private employment or for special travel and training increase the demands on public health care providers. The government must address these challenging public-private interactions in its human resource planning and management. Donors should collaborate closely with the government to ensure that their engagement with public health care providers truly supports, rather than undermines, the fulfillment of their public service commitments.

- *Funds distributed outside government channels* for major disease-targeted programs may be less susceptible to corruption if the donors or NGOs involved properly control them. However, in several instances, this does not appear to be the case. The scale of funding entering Ethiopia through the GFATM, GAVI Alliance, and PEPFAR is so large that it deserves special attention. Each organization should provide the government, and the public, with a clear annual report stating how much funding was actually disbursed in a given year, in what form (funds or commodities), and through which channels.[9] Funds flowing into HIV/AIDS support work, in particular, should be the subject of a special investigation to determine whether funds are being appropriately spent.

Recommendation 7: *Learn from other countries when introducing new financing schemes.*

The Ethiopian government is in the planning stages for new health financing schemes, including national health insurance and community health insurance. Before implementing newly proposed health financing schemes, however, Ethiopia should learn from other countries so it can have systems in place at the outset for addressing tax evasion, fraudulent claims, and embezzlement.

The goals of these programs are to provide households with protection against impoverishment due to health care expenses. Because these programs are still in the planning stages, there is no way to know how vulnerable they may be to abuse and fraud. However, Ethiopia should design policies that forestall common problems that afflict other countries with such systems, including payroll tax evasion, underreporting of income, sale or misuse of insurance cards, manipulation of claims, false claims, and embezzlement.

If the government creates such insurance schemes,[10] it should seek technical support from developing-country institutions with relevant experience. Some Caribbean countries recently adopted national health insurance schemes and might provide lessons in what did and did not work (in Jamaica, for example). Vietnam and Zimbabwe have also sought to address these problems in implementing national health insurance and could offer useful lessons (Ron 2001). Although their political and institutional contexts are very different from Ethiopia's, countries such as Chile and Estonia have some of the most advanced institutional frameworks and administrative systems for managing the vulnerabilities of national health insurance to corruption.

Recommendation 8: *Undertake systematic studies and audits.*

Instead of recommending new studies to assess health sector corruption, we recommend that ongoing sector work be strengthened to collect information useful for assessing and limiting corruption. To that end, we favor two kinds of follow-ups to this study: a strengthened system of random performance audits and facility surveys.

Performance audits. To establish which areas are most vulnerable to corruption and to provide a check on its own internal audit procedures, the FMOH could establish an internal investigative unit to conduct a systematic program of random performance audits. The government has a system for internal and external auditing, including provisions for performance audits. However, all the public finance management assessments note that Ethiopia is weak when it comes to reporting and following up on federal and regional external audits. The studies we reviewed included performance audits that could not show that funds were used as intended, and we could not identify follow-up actions in these cases.

The advantage of a systematic but random program of performance audits is that it provides intelligence on problematic aspects of spending— not just evidence on preselected areas based on guesses or ad hoc interviews.[11] Such a program would be even stronger if the investigative unit reported directly to the minister and were required to simultaneously disclose its reports to the Office of the Federal Auditor General (OFAG), the FEACC, or both. Given the amount of funding from GAVI Alliance and the GFATM through the FMOH, it would be appropriate for these organizations to provide some of the resources to support such a unit.

Facility-level surveys. We do not recommend that a full Public Expenditure Tracking Survey or new facility survey be conducted just to determine the amount of leakage or corruption in Ethiopia's public health care services. However, it would be useful to address the corruption issues raised in this report in any ongoing health sector work that involves facility-level surveys.

To improve human resource management, drug distribution, maintenance of supplies, and quality of care, the government needs regular and systematic information on the performance of health facilities. Any surveys used for this purpose should capture information about the amount of resources reaching facilities, the amount of time that staff members are absent, and diversion of resources to private practices.

Recommendation 9: *Support the FEACC, OFAG, and other auditors.*

Finally, the government has established a number of institutions—the FEACC, OFAG, regional auditors general, the PPA, the PFSA, and so on—to limit corruption in Ethiopia. These entities need continuing political and economic support to fulfill their responsibilities and to collaborate more closely with the health sector.

When anticorruption agencies and auditors begin to find and prosecute problems, they almost always find themselves accused of overzealousness and are frequently pressured by legislative representatives, executive branch officials, and sometimes even the courts, in ways that begin to undermine them. One of the simplest and most effective ways that Ethiopia can address corruption in its health sector is for the president, ministers, legislators, and media to courageously stand behind and support effective and responsible control agencies and investigators.

Notes

1. Data presented in the text refer to 2008 unless otherwise specified.
2. The Marginal Budgeting for Bottlenecks planning software is used for health policy planning, costing, and budgeting. It was developed by teams from the United Nations Children's Fund, the World Bank, and the ministries of health in several countries and can be found at http://www.devinfolive.info/mbb/mbbsupport.
3. These estimates are highly uncertain. Precisely because of the extent of coordination, it was difficult to know whether published reports adequately distinguished sources of funds. So, for example, portions of foreign aid that go through Channel 1 and Channel 2 may be double-counted. In addition, reports frequently fail to distinguish commitments from disbursements.
4. Ethiopia was engaged in such an assessment, but the results were not available for this study.
5. According to a response from the FMOH, many of the "risks entailed" in issuing licenses and regulating drug sales would be limited through ongoing interventions aimed at "institutionalizing and enforcing standards and codes of ethical conduct among all health sectors" (FMOH 2010).
6. According to a response from the FMOH, guidelines and procedures for addressing service users' complaints have been drafted as part of a larger regulatory framework on food products, drugs, health professionals, and health facilities (FMOH 2010).
7. WHO's National Health Accounts data show that Ethiopia received about US$50 million in foreign aid to health in 1998, rising to about US$100 million in 2001 (WHO 2004). The 2005 National Health Accounts study estimated foreign aid to the sector at US$193 million (HCFT 2006). Our calculations suggest that foreign aid to Ethiopia's health sector has more than doubled in the past few years, probably exceeding US$500 million in 2008.
8. According to a response from the FMOH, efforts were under way at the time of the assessment to address issues with the internal and external audit system, and this study could not assess progress that may have been made in this area (FMOH 2010).

9. Our research found clear records of disbursements from the GFATM but not from GAVI Alliance or PEPFAR, and clear statements of recipients from PEPFAR but not from GAVI Alliance or the GFATM.

10. Ethiopia may be able to achieve its goals without creating a new national health insurance scheme. For some ideas about the problems with social health insurance and alternatives, see Savedoff 2004 and Wagstaff 2007.

11. Although such systematic random audits are not a common practice in reviewing public sector procurement, they have become standard—and expected—practice in auditing tax revenue collection. Lessons from the tax revenue field show that the benefits of such an approach are quite significant (Campos and Pradhan 2007).

References

Alemu, Getnet. 2009. "A Case Study on Aid Effectiveness in Ethiopia: Analysis of the Health Sector Aid Architecture." Wolfensohn Center for Development Working Paper 9, Brookings Institution, Washington, DC.

Alia Abdulahi & Co. 2005. "Strengthening Integrated Reproductive Health Services and RH/IEC within the Framework of HSDP Project ETH/P05/01/02." Audit report and financial statements for the year ended December 31, 2004, for the United Nations Population Fund and the Government of Ethiopia, Addis Ababa.

Audit Services Corporation. 2008. "Malaria and Other Vector Borne Diseases Prevention and Control." Grant ETH-202-G02-M-00, management letter for the two years ended July 7, 2007, for the Global Fund to Fight AIDS, Tuberculosis and Malaria (GFATM) to the Ministry of Health, Government of Ethiopia, Addis Ababa.

Aweke Gebre Selassie and Company. 2008. "Project Title: Protection of Basic Services (PBS) – Component 2, Report and Accounts for the Period Ended 7th July, 2007." Addis Ababa. March 28.

Campos, J. Edgardo, and Sanjay Pradhan, eds. 2007. *The Many Faces of Corruption: Tracking Vulnerabilities at the Sector Level.* Washington, DC: World Bank.

Carl Bro Intelligent Solutions. 2006. "Independent Procurement Review of Selected Bank-Financed Projects." Report REP/IPR/FY05/TF03063 prepared for the World Bank, Washington, DC.

Central Statistical Agency [Ethiopia] and ORC Macro. 2001. "Ethiopia Demographic and Health Survey 2000." Central Statistical Agency and ORC Macro, Addis Ababa and Calverton, MD. http://www.measuredhs.com/Data/.

———. 2006. "Ethiopia Demographic and Health Survey 2005." Central Statistical Agency and ORC Macro, Addis Ababa and Calverton, MD. http://www.measuredhs.com/Data/.

FDRE (Federal Democratic Republic of Ethiopia). 2007a. "The Federal PFM [Public Finance Management] Performance Report." Final public expenditure and financial accountability (PEFA) evaluation report by DFC Group, Barcelona.

———. 2007b. "The New Federal Budget Grant Distribution Formula." House of Federation, Addis Ababa.

———. 2008. "Woreda and City Administrations Benchmarking Survey, Synthesis Report." Ministry of Capacity Building and Ministry of Works and Urban Development in Collaboration with PSCAP Donors, Selam Development Consultants, Addis Ababa.

———. 2009. "Joint Financing Arrangement between the Federal Democratic Republic of Ethiopia and Development Partners on Support to the MDG Fund." Addis Ababa.

———. 2010. "Ethiopia's Fourth National Health Accounts, 2007/08." Addis Ababa, April.

FEACC (Federal Ethics and Anti-Corruption Commission). 2008. "The FEACC Annual Performance Report, 2000 [Ethiopian Calendar] Budget Year." FEACC, Addis Ababa.

FMOH (Federal Ministry of Health). 2005. "HSDP III: Health Sector Strategic Plan 2005/6–2009/10." FMOH, Addis Ababa.

———. 2008. "Annual Performance Report of HSDP-III." FMOH, Addis Ababa.

———. 2010. "Response to the World Bank Anti-Corruption Assessment Report of the Health Sector." FMOH, Addis Ababa.

FMOH Irish Aid. 2006. "Support to Health Sector Development Program Auditor's Report and Statement of Income and Expenditure for the Year ended 31 December 2006."

GAVI Alliance (Global Alliance Vaccine Initiative). 2005. "Annual Progress Report Ethiopia." GAVI Alliance, Geneva and Washington, DC.

———. 2006. "Annual Progress Report Ethiopia." GAVI Alliance, Geneva and Washington, DC.

———. 2007. "Annual Progress Report Ethiopia." GAVI Alliance, Geneva and Washington, DC.

GFATM (Global Fund to Fight AIDS, Tuberculosis and Malaria). 2009. *The Five-Year Evaluation of the Global Fund to Fight AIDS, Tuberculosis, and Malaria: Synthesis of Study Areas 1, 2 and 3.* Geneva: GFATM.

HCFT (Health Care Financing Team,). 2006. "Ethiopia's Third National Health Accounts 2004/05." Report of the HCFT, Planning and Programming Department, Federal Ministry of Health, Government of Ethiopia, and produced by Partners for Health Reform (PHR) and Abt Associates Inc., Bethesda, MD.

Independent Review Team. 2008. "Ethiopia Health Sector Development Programme (HSDP III) Mid-Term Review." Volume I, Component Report, prepared by consultants for the Joint Core Coordinating Committee (comprising representatives of the FMOH, World Health Organization, UNICEF, the Netherlands, USAID, Irish Aid, Italian cooperation, UNFAP, ESHE/USAID, and the World Bank), Addis Ababa.

Jubat, Adow, and Boniface Ongeri. 2009. "Exposed: Sale of Government Drugs in Foreign Lands." *The Standard*, Nairobi. July 29.

Kolstad, I., V. Fritz, and T. O'Neil. 2008. "Corruption, Anti-corruption Efforts and Aid: Do Donors Have the Right Approach?" Working Paper 3, Overseas Development Institute, London.

Lewis, Maureen. 2006. "Governance and Corruption in Public Health Care Systems." Working Paper 78. Center for Global Development, Washington, DC.

Lindelow, Magnus, Pieter Serneels, and Teigist Lemma. 2005. "The Performance of Health Workers in Ethiopia: Results from Qualitative Research." Policy Research Working Paper 3558, World Bank, Washington, DC.

Pankhurst, Alula. 2008. "Enhancing Understanding of Local Accountability Mechanisms in Ethiopia: Protecting Basic Services Project." Protecting Basic Services (PBS) II preparation studies, final main report for the World Bank, Washington, DC.

Ron, Aviva. 2001. "New Strategies for the Formal Sector: Focus on Vietnam and Zimbabwe." In *Recent Health Policy Innovations in Social Security*, ed. A. Ron and X. Scheil-Adlung, 33–58. New Brunswick, NJ: Transaction Publishers.

Savedoff, W. 2004. "Is There a Case for Social Insurance?" *Health Policy and Planning* 19 (3): 183–84.

Urban Institute. 2009. "Ethiopia Financial Transparency and Accountability Perception Survey. (FTAPS) Final Report." The Urban Institute, Washington, DC, and Birhan Research and Development Consultancy, Addis Ababa. Accessed April 28, 2009.

Wagstaff, A. 2007. "Social Health Insurance Reexamined." Policy Research Working Paper 411, World Bank, Washington, DC.

Wolde, Damtew. 2009. "Assessment of Procurement in the Ethiopian Health Sector." Report prepared for Social Insight, Portland, ME.

World Bank. 2007. "Ethiopia: PEFA Regional Public Financial Management Performance Report." World Bank, Washington, DC. https://agidata.org/Site/DocumentSingle.aspx?d=104.

WHO (World Health Organization). 2004. *The World Health Report 2004: Changing History*. Geneva: WHO.

———. 2006. "Measuring Transparency to Improve Good Governance in the Public Pharmaceutical Sector: Draft Assessment Instrument." Working draft for field testing and revision, WHO, Geneva.

———. 2009. "Good Governance for Medicines Programme: Progress Report, February 2009." WHO, Geneva.

WHOSIS (World Health Organization Statistical Information System). WHO, Geneva. http://www.who.int/whosis/en/. Accessed October 14, 2009.

CHAPTER 3

Education Sector Corruption in Ethiopia

Michael Latham

Introduction

Recognizing the importance of education in the development of Ethiopia, the government of Ethiopia has over the past two decades focused efforts on a range of interventions to improve the delivery of educational services. Supported by donor partners and guided by the education Millennium Development Goals (MDGs), the government has embarked on a process of education sector reform and service improvement aimed at enhancing the levels of access for the poor and employing approaches that respond more closely to demands from end users.

In recent years education budgets in Ethiopia have been relatively high (6 percent in 2006) as a proportion of gross domestic product (CIA 2006) and significant (20–25 percent) as a proportion of government spending (Dom 2009), but they are still low in terms of absolute

---

Although this chapter results from studies completed by January 2010, the process of checking, reviewing, and securing agreement for publication was finally brought to conclusion only in late 2011. The chapter is therefore put forward with the caveat that while it reflects the situation at the time of the study, some details will have understandably changed.

per capita expenditure. The significant growth in spending since 2003, disbursed through block grant mechanisms, has resulted in greatly increased enrollment rates, but these have not been accompanied by clear improvements in the quality of services. As a share of overall government expenditure, education budgets have peaked and are now declining gradually.

In this context, attainment of the education MDGs is unlikely if the investment and capacity required to meet the significant and growing demand is inadequate or if resources allocated to the sector are lost through inefficiency or corruption.

Objective

This diagnostic study was conducted to map corruption risks in the education sector—an essential first step in a broader process of understanding possible constraints to service delivery. Such constraints may include both direct leakage of financial resources and other, less direct forms of loss resulting from distortions caused by corrupt practices.

In practice, it can be difficult to distinguish between corruption and a simple lack of capacity. This is particularly the case where, as with this study, many of the underlying data are based on reported perceptions rather than on more substantive evidence. The approach adopted therefore recognizes that, whatever the basis for the reported perceptions, any corrective action is likely to include capacity-building measures.

As in other sectors, corruption in education can be multifaceted, ranging from large distortions in resource allocation and significant procurement-related fraud to smaller amounts garnered through daily opportunities for petty corruption and nontransparent financial management. As a result of this complexity, the current understanding of the extent and nature of corruption in the education sector in Ethiopia is limited. Although it is possible to focus in detail on specific issues such as teacher absenteeism or ghost workers,[1] such studies provide a limited view.

The broader approach adopted here tries to achieve a better understanding of the overall pattern of corruption risks across the whole national education system. This overview extends across the levels of government and along the value chain of policy making to front-line service delivery. In doing so, it highlights areas that warrant special attention—be they policy reform; procedural change; or the need for further, more detailed analytical study.

Methodology

The scoping study findings are based on the following information sources:

- *Literature review*. In the absence of specific studies of corruption risks, the review focused on published reports relating more generally to education sector performance and plans.
- *Field surveys*. The perception-based survey methodology was developed in consultation with both local stakeholders and representatives of the donor education team.[2] Surveys were conducted in mid-2009 in 19 woredas in the regions of Oromia; Amhara; Benishangul-Gumuz; the Southern Nations, Nationalities and People's Region (SNNPR); and the city-state of Addis Ababa (map 3.1).[3]
- *Informal interviews*. Structured interviews with respondents from each stakeholder group provided further qualitative data, insights, and examples of perceived corruption in the sector.

Map 3.1   Ethiopian Regions Included in Education Sector Field Surveys

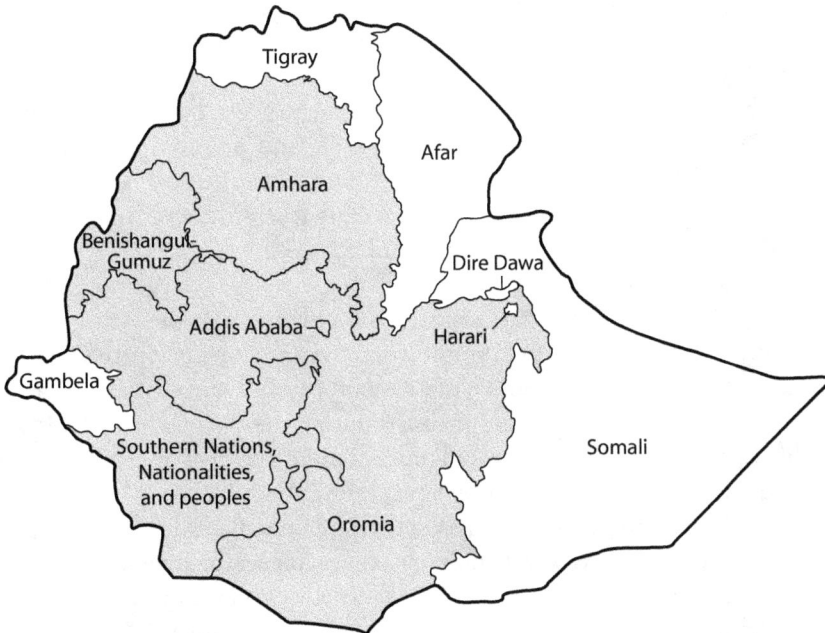

Source: http://mapsof.net.

- *Multistakeholder workshop.* A validation workshop at the end of the process involved diverse stakeholders who presented, discussed, and refined the emerging findings of the study.

Chapter Structure

The chapter is organized as follows:

- "Analytical Framework" presents an overarching framework for identifying and assessing corruption risks in education. The framework reflects a multifaceted view of corruption that seeks to understand each corruption risk within the context of a broader set of practices. This framework distinguishes between "upstream" risks (those related to policy development, planning and budgeting, and fiscal transfers) and "downstream" risks (those related to management; procurement, including teacher recruitment; and service delivery).

- "The Education Sector in Ethiopia: An Overview" establishes the general context with an overview of the sector. Ethiopia has made major strides in improving its human development indicators in the past 15 years, achieving significant increases in the coverage of basic education and health services. Improvements occurred during a period of marked decentralization of fiscal resources—to the regions in 1994 and to the woredas in 2002–03. As part of this process, decentralization in the education sector has given regional- and woreda-level officials extended powers and responsibilities, both administrative and fiscal, in delivering education services. However, it is still difficult to assess the quality of the accountability mechanisms.

- "Mapping Corruption in Education in Ethiopia"—the heart of the study—uses the analytical framework to map corruption risks in the education sector of Ethiopia, drawing on the full range of quantitative and qualitative information obtained during the study. This map establishes the basis for an integrated understanding of the governance issues and challenges in the sector by considering the full range of education-related corruption risks from a sectoral perspective. Although the perceived corruption risk in Ethiopia's education sector is generally lower than that typically encountered in many developing countries, or even in other sectors within Ethiopia, the country exhibits a relatively high risk of some specific forms of corruption, most notably those related to favoritism and falsification of documents.

- "Other Study Findings" presents findings of indirect relevance to the framework, including a brief review of accountability mechanisms. General perceptions of corruption are discussed in its various aspects, including levels of corruption; what constitutes corruption; where corruption occurs and who initiates it; and the role of discretionary powers. A range of accountability systems are in place in the sector, both on the supply side (government and its donor partners) and on the demand side (users and civil society). However, these systems are not always mutually supportive, and the various systems and their dynamics are also explained in this section.

- "Summary and Conclusions" and the final section, "Recommendations," wrap up the analysis. Several actions are recommended for consideration by the Ministry of Education (MOE).

Analytical Framework

Perceptions of corruption among the different stakeholders—be they government officials involved in education, staff employed within the sector, or parents and students receiving the service—tend to be specific, narrow, and often highly subjective. This subjectivity and diversity of perspective can make it difficult to develop a comprehensive understanding of corruption issues and related corrective action. To date, the international debate about corruption in the education sector has tended to focus on two specific teacher issues (absenteeism and ghost workers) and on financial issues such as fiscal transfers. As a result, many other forms of corruption risks have been overlooked, as has the need to address the potential links between them.

Establishing a robust and inclusive strategy for anticorruption action in the education sector requires consideration of the whole array of corrupt practices. A key feature of this broader approach is that it potentially identifies where corruption risks lie *and where they do not*. A number of frameworks have been developed for corruption, including corruption in the education sector (Patrinos and Kagia 2007), but none has considered corruption risks in different settings, taking due account of who is involved and at what stage of the service delivery chain. Ultimately, the goal of such an exercise is to provide a robust framework that is relevant and applicable to the sector, integrates project-level and cross-cutting governance diagnostics, and can be used as a tool for understanding and promoting change.[4]

The preliminary framework developed for this analysis is structured around a "value chain" of corrupt interactions in the education sector in key functional areas across two distinct (jurisdictional) sets of functions:[5]

- *"Upstream" functions* are primarily those in which corruption is most likely to occur between public officials and other public officials (although there may be some capture by private sector actors in education systems where there is a significant private interest). The three upstream functions are policy development, planning and budgeting, and fiscal transfers.

- *"Downstream" functions* involve management, procurement, and service delivery. They also involve three different types of potentially corrupt interactions: (a) between *public actors and other public actors* in teacher management and teacher recruitment; (b) between *public and private actors* in the provision and maintenance of equipment, supplies, and buildings; and (c) between *public actors and consumers* in relation to the delivery of teaching services. Consequently, these downstream functions are more complex because each can relate, in turn, to teachers, to supplies and equipment, and to buildings and related facilities.

The resulting framework is presented in tables 3.1 (for "upstream" functions) and 3.2 (for "downstream" functions).

This preliminary framework identifies 56 categories of potential corruption, 10 of which are upstream and 46 of which are downstream.

Table 3.1   "Upstream" Forms of Corruption in the Education Value Chain

Function	Form of Corruption
Policy development	Policy capture
	Regulatory capture
	Bribery or extortion over licensing
Planning and budgeting	Distortions in decision making by politicians
	Corruption in budget planning, from the center down to the regional and local levels
	Bribery to influence allocation of resources at central, regional, and local levels
	Corruption in budget planning, from the local levels up to the regional and central levels
	Corruption in sector budget management at the local level
Fiscal transfers	Bribery or extortion to ensure funding transfers

Source: Author.

Table 3.2   "Downstream" Forms of Corruption in the Education Value Chain

Function	Focus	Form of Corruption
Management	Teachers	Bribery, extortion, favoritism, or nepotism in selecting staff for promotion, access to scholarships, or access to opportunities for career enhancement
		Falsification of documents in support of applications for promotion and the like
		Collusion to ignore regulations regarding management of teaching and administrative staff
		Collusion with teachers over noncompliance with curriculum, academic calendar
		Extortion of facilitation payments from teachers for salaries and per diems
	Suppliers	Collusion with supplier when planning for supplies or equipment
	Builders	Collusion with contractor when planning the construction or maintenance of facilities
		Misappropriation of building funds by public officials or community leaders
Procurement	Teachers	Bribery, extortion, favoritism, or nepotism in the recruitment of teachers
		Fraud, falsification of qualifications (for example, teachers' certificates) to obtain teaching jobs
		Capture of recruitment by groups with vested interests
	Suppliers	Interdepartmental collusion to bypass procurement procedures
		Favoritism, nepotism, or bribery in the short-listing of suppliers or the provision of tender information
		Tendering companies owned by persons linked with the award of contracts
		Specifications that favor a specific supplier
		Fraud, falsification of tender documents, with or without associated bribery
		Collusion among suppliers
		Bribery to influence evaluation of tenders
		Supply of substandard, or low quantity of, supplies or equipment
		Overbilling by suppliers
		Extortion of facilitation payments to ensure settlement of invoices
	Builders	Favoritism, nepotism, or bribery in the short-listing of consultants or contractors or in the provision of tender information
		Tendering companies owned by persons linked with the award of contracts

(continued next page)

Table 3.2   *(continued)*

Function	Focus	Form of Corruption
Service delivery	Teachers	Bypassing of correct procurement procedures
		Specifications that favor a specific supplier
		Fraud, falsification of tender documents, with or without associated bribery
		Collusion among contractors or consultants in bidding
		Bribery to influence evaluation of tenders
		Bribery, extortion, favoritism, or nepotism in the selection of students
		Favoritism or nepotism in the assessment of students
		Fraud (and related bribery) in examinations
		Falsification of documents: for example, forged transcripts and certificates
		Teacher absenteeism
		Ghost teachers for payment of salaries or per diems
		Teachers using power to physically abuse students
		Teachers extorting fees for the provision of off-budget services (ID cards, sports, cleaning)
		Teachers shifting services to private tuition
		Private schools operating without requisite approval
	Suppliers	Extortion to provide access to supplies or equipment intended for all
		Leakage of supplies or equipment during distribution
		Theft and reselling of supplies or equipment
		Misappropriation of assets
	Builders	Bribery or extortion related to the granting of permits, licenses, and authorities
		Defective construction, supply of substandard materials, or overclaiming of quantities
		Bribery to cover up failure to meet specifications or other nonperformance
		Extortion of facilitation payments to ensure payment of certificates

Source: Author.

Depending on the circumstances, some of these forms of corruption can be further subdivided. Such refinements are highlighted in the narrative and in summary presentations, but in the interest of simplicity are not included within the framework itself.

By adopting this framework, every form of corruption risk identified has a place. This allows for the development of an overview that facilitates an improved understanding of interrelationships between different forms. It also makes it easier to make comparisons, both between different situations (including internationally) and in the same context at different times.

The Education Sector in Ethiopia: An Overview

In Ethiopia, "general education" comprises grades 1–12, encompassing both primary and secondary education. Primary education lasts eight years and is split into grades 1–4 (primary first cycle) and grades 5–8 (primary second cycle). Secondary education is also divided into two cycles, each with its own specific goals. Grades 9–10 (secondary first cycle) provide general secondary education and, upon completion, students are streamed either into grades 11–12 (secondary second cycle) to prepare for university or into technical and vocational education and training (TVET). Assignments to either secondary second cycle or TVET are based on performance in the secondary education completion certificate examination.

The provision of education is the concurrent responsibility of federal, regional, and local governments. The federal government plays the dominant role in the provision of postsecondary education while also setting standards and providing overall policy guidance and monitoring and evaluation for the entire sector. Regional governments are responsible for overseeing the training of primary school teachers, for providing primary textbooks, and for adapting the primary syllabus to local conditions. Woreda (district) governments are responsible for payment and recruitment of both primary and secondary teachers, as well as for their supervision and training.

Policies and Programs

The government prepared the national Education and Training Policy (ETP) in 1994 and, within the framework of the ETP, launched the first five-year Education Sector Development Program (ESDP I) in 1997 as part of a 20-year education sector plan. As a result of a series of important organizational, financial, and programmatic measures, the ESDP I target of raising primary enrollment from 3.7 million to 7 million was surpassed, with enrollment reaching 8.1 million in 2000/01 and 13.5 million in 2005/06, when ESDP III was launched. Over this period, the gross enrollment rate (GER) increased from 61.6 to 91.3 percent and net enrollment from 52.2 to 77.5 percent.

Grade repetition rates also dropped significantly—from 15.7 percent and 18.6 percent for boys and girls, respectively, in 1996/97, to 3.8 percent and 4 percent in 2003/04. First-cycle secondary enrollment trends show significant increases (the GER rising from 17.1 percent in 2001/02 to 33.2 percent in 2005/06), and although second-cycle secondary enrollment is low (3.9 percent in 2005/06), it is increasing. Figure 3.1 shows how primary completion rates have risen over 30 percent over the 2001–09 period. These advancements collectively are a remarkable achievement, occurring at the same time as a major expansion of both the TVET and higher-education subsectors.

This expansion has required a marked increase in the number of teachers. Until 2009, teacher trainee selection had continued to be centrally managed by the government, with selection generally limited to those failing to achieve the highest grades. This lack of individual choice, which extends to decisions over the allocation of teachers to schools, has been identified as a significant factor both in low teacher morale and the declining quality of several specific teaching outcomes.[6]

A further issue affecting quality is the fact that despite recent marked increases in sectorwide spending, per-student spending has, as a result of increased enrollment rates, remained low both in absolute terms and by comparison with international standards.

Nonstate provider education (NSP) in Ethiopia includes private schools and nongovernmental organization (NGO) or faith-based organization (FBO) schools. Despite recent growth, NSP remains well below the relative importance it attained in the mid-1970s. NSP exhibits marked regional variations, nationally providing about 5 percent of the total provision at the primary level and 12 percent at the secondary grade levels.

Figure 3.1   Grade 5 Primary Completion Rates in Ethiopia, 2001–08

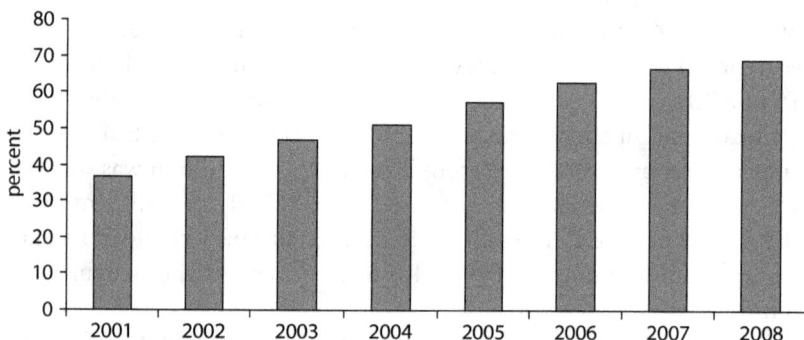

Addressing Quality, Capacity, and Resource Gaps

Despite rapid expansion, Ethiopia's education sector faces four key challenges:

- *Access.* Access to educational opportunities continues to be an obstacle, especially for females and other "most vulnerable children," poor students, and those in rural areas.
- *Quality.* Improved access has not been accompanied by adequate improvements in quality.
- *Financing.* The rapid expansion has left a considerable financing gap between available funds and the anticipated cost of investments needed to improve and maintain quality.
- *Capacity.* Some of the regional and woreda governments lack the capacity to adequately plan, manage, and monitor the sector. This includes the capacity to gather and report on key performance indicators on time to manage and monitor effectively the implementation of education reforms.

Ethiopia is currently implementing its second poverty reduction strategy, known as the Plan for Accelerated and Sustained Development to End Poverty (PASDEP). PASDEP shows a strong vertical coordination of sectoral strategies with the overall government strategy and is well integrated with the budget through the Macroeconomic and Fiscal Framework and the government-donor Joint Budget and Aid Review. PASDEP's strategic vision is one of rapid and sustained growth, being achieved primarily through scaled-up development assistance and large domestic investments targeted at eliminating the poverty traps that have hindered the development of the country.

The government's current vision for education development is described in PASDEP. Although education remains a high priority, it is evident from PASDEP that education has been receiving a smaller share of the overall budget, the decline starting in 2004/05 (MOFED 2006). The overarching framework for education provision is the ESDP. Currently in its third phase (ESDP III), this gives high priority to quality improvement at all levels and to an increasingly important role for the private sector in educational provision at all levels. Some observers have noted, however, that PASDEP does not include policy proposals which, by ensuring a level playing field, would permit the private sector to enter the market with confidence (Austrian Development Cooperation 2007).

Within the framework of the ESDP III, the Ministry of Education (MOE) developed a draft General Education Quality Improvement Program (GEQIP). A key recommendation of the education sector Annual Review Meeting in 2007 was that the MOE and development partners work together to implement the GEQIP through a pooled funding mechanism. The proposed program will support the implementation of the first four of the six GEQIP components:

- The Teacher Development Program, including the English Language Quality Improvement Program
- Curriculum, textbooks, and assessment
- The Management and Administration Program, with an education management information system subcomponent
- The School Improvement Program, with a school grants subcomponent.

The government has also prepared the preliminary cost estimates and financing plan of the proposed program, suggesting a financing gap of more than US$800 million over the next five years. The practice of planning on the basis of need and then demonstrating a financing gap—common in the Ethiopian context—contrasts with the more conventional approach of formulating detailed plans within the constraints of available resources and more clearly linking plans to budgets.

Within this context of ambitious but nevertheless constrained spending, low teacher morale, and related concerns about quality and capacity constraints, it is opportune to assess perceived and potential risks of corruption in the sector.

Mapping Corruption in Education in Ethiopia

Corruption is by its very nature hidden, so it is inherently difficult to study corruption with confidence. Even where, as in this study, attempts are made to triangulate the results of perception surveys and other more objective data, there remains a risk of misinterpretation, not least because of the difficulty in distinguishing corruption from other aspects of poor governance, including a simple lack of capacity.

Approach to Interpretation
In interpreting the results of this study, the approach adopted has therefore been to focus on identifying and understanding corruption *risks* that

need to be addressed, regardless of the extent to which those risks may currently be giving rise to actual corrupt practices.[7]

In view of the limited scope and scale of this study, the modest sample size, and potential distortion of some of the responses because of the sensitive subject matter, care has been taken not to read too much into the details of the responses within each stakeholder group. Instead, broad findings have been derived from an analysis of the overall response pattern within each group, with due account taken of triangulation of responses to different questions within each group. The resulting risk ratings are necessarily of a tentative nature, based as they are on an interpretation of a combination of stakeholder responses and the results of the literature review within the broader context of international experience in the sector.

Mapping of Upstream Corruption Risks

Public actors in Ethiopia's education sector include actors from the international community; national, regional, and woreda governmental departments; and agencies with both education and noneducation functions. Most upstream corruption risks within these government entities would typically entail interactions between public sector actors only. Such interactions could include either "vertical" interactions—down the education hierarchy from the center down to the region, woreda, institutions, and individuals—or "horizontal" interactions involving various line departments, agencies, and individuals at a similar level of government. In the case of policy development, there may also be collusion between public officials and private sector entities with a vested interest in promoting, or preventing, specific policies or regulations.

The risk of each of the specific forms of upstream corruption, referenced previously in table 3.1, will now be addressed in turn.

Policy development

Policy capture—risk: low. Policy capture occurs when a private company, or an elite group, improperly influences policy to further its vested interests. A hypothetical example for the former would be when one or more private companies make secret payments such that policies are adopted that allow for restricted competition, or effective monopolies, in the provision of goods or services to the education sector. An example of the latter could be the capture of policy by politicians with regional or ethnic biases, by particular social groups, or by any powerful individuals with a vested interest in promoting an agenda that benefits themselves or their allies. One indication of an education policy captured by an elite could be the neglect of basic education in favor of maintaining and developing private school interests and tertiary education for the few.

The federal government sets education policy in Ethiopia. Within the framework of the ETP, the overarching policy since 1994 has been to provide educational services for all. The details of this policy have been refined through successive ESDPs, which have markedly expanded the general provision of basic education.

The transparent and thorough nature of this policy development suggests greatly limited scope for policy capture. Although some risks of capture do exist—a concern raised by some stakeholders—they relate, in the main, to the formulae used to calculate block grants to regions rather than to the manner in which the formulae have been applied. Such concerns have focused on an apparent bias against larger, less-developed regions. Following a period of study and consultation, the House of Federation recently proposed a new formula, which takes account of disability factors and differences in tax base capacity. The new formula is expected to ensure a more equitable resource distribution among regional states (*Addis Fortune* 2009).

Ethiopia's national budget has been described by a major donor (the U.K. Department for International Development) as "the most pro-poor budget of Africa" (Dom 2009). This view is reflected through household-level survey responses suggesting a high degree of user satisfaction with the provision of basic education. Nevertheless, survey responses also indicate that central officials are significantly less likely than higher-education officials to consider that education services are accessible to the poor.

One general area of perceived policy capture lies in what for some stakeholders is an apparent general absence of a level playing field in terms of access to decision making and markets.[8] This upstream risk is difficult to disengage from political considerations that are beyond the scope of this study, but it does find practical expression in several of the downstream risks.

Regulatory capture—risk: low. Regulatory capture is similar to policy capture but refers to situations where regulatory or licensing agencies created to act in the public interest instead act in favor of commercial or special interests. In the education sector, such agencies would typically be responsible for developing and approving education programs, issuing school leaving certificates, determining scoring systems, and monitoring assessments. A theoretical example of regulatory capture, for instance, could occur if, under pressure from private universities, their examinations were to be exempted from the full scope of external moderation applicable within the rest of the sector.

Survey responses received during this study indicate that a strong majority of both central officials and public officials considered policies and regulations to be strictly defined, and a strong majority considered them to be both useful and easy to understand. A slimmer majority considered them to be stable, not too onerous, and well supervised.

According to ESDP projections, the private sector is expected to play an increasingly important role in the provision of educational services in Ethiopia. A reduction in private sector enrollments in grades 1–4 is expected to be accompanied by a doubling of enrollments in grades 5–8 and sevenfold or higher increases for grades 9–10 and 11–12, albeit from relatively low levels. These projections continue a trend that has in recent years seen a marked but geographically patchy increase in private education. In Addis Ababa, the rate of increase in private schools has exceeded that of government schools, though the overall percentage figures have not changed significantly, as government schools generally cater to larger numbers.

Although the current risks of regulatory capture appear to be low, broader general concerns among survey respondents and international observers about the absence of a level playing field within the sector suggest that, left unchecked, the risk could increase as the private sector plays a more prominent role in some regions where there is currently little or no nonstate provision.

Bribery or extortion over licensing or permits—risk: low. This form of bribery can occur in any situation where official licenses or permits are required to provide goods or services in the sector. Possible scenarios range from an FBO needing to obtain or renew a license to operate a private school, to a construction company needing a permit to draw water from a local supply when building a new university. In either case, the responsible official may abuse his or her discretionary power and threaten to block or delay approval unless a facilitation payment is made. Alternatively, the initiative may come from the applicant, seeking to bribe the official to speed up the process or to overlook certain areas of noncompliance.

Survey responses received during this study did not directly address this question but did indirectly suggest, on the one hand, that corruption risks exist at the level of procurement of goods and services and, on the other hand, that outright bribery is rare.

Table 3.3   Summary of Corruption Risks in Policy Development

	Perceived risk of corruption		
Form of corruption	Low	Medium	High
Policy capture	☐		
Regulatory capture	☐		
Bribery or extortion over licensing	☐		

Source: Author.

Summary of policy development risks. In light of the above, the perceived risk of corruption in each of the three aspects of policy development is, as tabulated below, considered to be low (table 3.3).

Planning and budgeting

Distortions in decision making by politicians—risk: medium. Planning and budgeting can also be subject to corruption as decision-making officials try to influence how established policies and procedures are implemented in practice. Typically, these attempts involve skewing the process of allocating scarce resources, either in return for favors from other political appointees or as a result of more overt bribery or collusion.

In Ethiopia, responsibility for the delivery of most basic services, including education, has been assigned to subnational government as part of the country's decentralization process. At these subnational levels, regions and especially woredas have primary responsibility in the allocation of treasury resources, decision making, management, and delivery of educational services. The fiscal decentralization strategy includes the procedures that govern intergovernmental fiscal transfers, through the regional block grant mechanism.

Survey responses received during this study generated a mixed message regarding this form of corruption. A strong majority of respondents considered the following:

- Budget administrative decisions are made transparently.
- Budgets are announced and made available to the public.
- Budgets are subject to regular audits (though these are often not independent).
- Internal control systems are in place to protect the resources against inappropriate use or loss.
- Budgets are based on specific criteria.
- Budgets are not influenced by illegal payments.

However, there are also some suggestions of malpractice. For example, although central officials indicated that the main factors affecting budget allocations are objective, and budget administration procedures well defined, they expressed concern that the practical implementation of those procedures is not well supervised and followed. More specifically, a minority considered planned allocations to be based in part on political ties or affiliations, regional preferences, and influential connections in the institution.

Examples were given of distortions of the process. In one reported case, funding allocated for the recruitment of new teachers was diverted to the payment of per diems for woreda staff. In two other cases, Woreda Education Offices (WEOs) considered their Woreda Offices of Finance and Economic Development (WOFEDs) to be involved in malpractice in budget administration.

Corruption in budget planning from the center to the regional and local levels—risk: low. The budget planning process, from the center down to the regional and local levels, can also be influenced by corrupt actions such as interministerial bribery for allocation of funds, bribery in the selection or project approval processes, or the misuse of funds. In Ethiopia, three main areas of risk were identified, albeit within the context of a general perception that budget planning is based on a well-defined system:

- *Distortions to the system of block grant allocations*, even when supposedly based on established formulae, as described above
- *Relatively lax monitoring and related controls* at the level of some regions, and many woredas, due in part to capacity constraints
- *Perceived shortcomings in the accountability mechanisms* associated with pooled support to the education sector, according to some observers.[9] (It was noted that although such mechanisms are robust at sector level in that continued disbursement depends on some broad assessments of sector performance, they can be less effective at the detailed level, where weaknesses have been reported in the timely flow of accurate data.) This risk has been recognized and is being addressed through capacity-building measures included under Protection of Basic Services (PBS) II and ESDP III.

These risks are compounded by an evident tendency to engage in needs-based (as opposed to resource-constrained) planning, which can itself undermine accountability mechanisms by weakening the links between plans and budgets.

Bribery to influence allocation of resources at central, regional, and local levels—risk: low. Survey responses received during this study showed that a strong majority of public officials perceived budget administration processes to be transparent and open to public scrutiny, and not to be influenced by illegal payments. A smaller majority considered the criteria used to allocate funds to be clearly defined. There were broadly spread views about the extent of external auditing and the degree to which allocations were subject to unforeseen reductions. A significant minority considered budget allocations to be influenced by regional ties, political affiliations, and influential connections. Overall, there was a strong perception that budget procedures are sounder in theory than in practice.

Documentary evidence indicates that budget allocations to the regions are based on the fiscal transfer formulae described above, which reflects current policies. The regional allocations, announced annually as a part of the budget cycle, are available on the Ministry of Finance and Economic Development (MOFED) website.[10] In such a system, it would in practice be difficult to bribe or extort bribes to increase allocations in what is a well-defined fiscal (national-to-regional) transfer system. It is at the regional level where discretion in the allocation of resources to woredas enters the system—and where transparency and accountability weaken.

At the woreda level, more than 50 percent of the total block grants received are typically allocated to education, but the allocation can change markedly from year to year within a given woreda, and the amount allocated per student might change depending on the woreda and region. The fact that there is no standard, or guide, per capita amount allocated to education across woredas and regions makes external monitoring difficult and greatly complicates any attempt to track funds down the vertical chain from the central ministries (MOFED and MOE) to specific schools. This difficulty in accessing relevant information does not itself suggest corruption but does give rise to risks at this level.

Woreda-level education budget allocations are reflected in "performance agreements" entered into between the WOFED and the regional Bureau of Finance and Economic Development (BOFED). Woreda representatives and council members do not have much discretion, given that their budgets are in practice generally based on the amounts disbursed in the previous year and there is little flexibility in the percentage of allocation that can be made across the different sectors. Woredas do audit expenditures at the kebele (neighborhood, or ward) level, and cases have been reported where this has led to money being returned by kebele-level officials if malpractice is identified.

Corruption in budget planning, from the local levels up to the regional and central levels—risk: low. Planning processes necessarily rely on the upward flow of reliable data. As such, they can be corruptly influenced by falsification or fraud in the provision of this data. In Ethiopia, such risks could potentially occur through the falsification of the numbers or factors used to calculate the formula for budget allocations. Though concerns have been expressed about such overreporting of demographic and poverty data (PBS JRIS 2008)—and indeed about the accuracy of the underlying census—more detailed consideration of this risk is beyond the scope of this study. However, reviews undertaken in support of the PBS II project preparation provide some assurances that the budget and fiscal transfer system to the regions appears to be relatively sound.

At the woreda level, there are a number of areas of risk in the planning and budgeting of the multifund system, and although procedures are clear, controls are not. Such areas of risk include (a) inflating of numbers to receive more funding, and (b) manipulation of off-budget funds by donors and NGOs.

Corruption in sector budget management at the local level—risk: medium. At the local level, there is a theoretical risk of corruption resulting in budget distortions, made possible by the relatively low capacity of formal monitoring systems (table 3.4). Survey responses received during

Table 3.4 Summary of Corruption Risks in Planning and Budgeting

Form of corruption	Perceived corruption risk		
	Low	Medium	High
Distortions in decision making by politicians		☐	
Corruption in budget planning, from the center down to the regional and local levels	☐		
Bribery to influence allocation of resources at each of the three levels	☐		
Corruption in budget planning, from the local levels up to the regional and central levels	☐		
Corruption in sector budget management at the local level		☐	

Source: Author.

this study suggested that any such risks are perceived by local stakeholders to be low, due in part to the monitoring role played by active parent-teacher associations (PTAs). This view is countered, however, by other reports of significant concern that funds allocated for capital works are not ending up in the bricks and mortar for which they have been contributed.

The lack of a capital budget at the woreda level influences the nature of such risks. At the village level, the lack of funding sharply limits planning and budgeting in schools. Only 14 percent of the total education budget is allocated to capital works, and 92 percent of the recurrent budget is spent on salaries.[11] This constraint places a large burden on schools to mobilize additional funding from the community—through either in-kind support or actual collection of funds. That these community funds are not subject to the same level of auditing and monitoring as the public funds raises concern because the WOFED does not audit school-generated revenues. This lack of oversight is potentially important, given that, according to responses from school-level staff, PTA fees represent a significant source of school development funds.

One other issue arising from the research is that if the WEO representative does not properly defend the education budget, the sector will get a smaller budget. New WEO officials are considered to be particularly vulnerable—suggesting that the allocation process is not entirely objective and may be unduly influenced by personality and political connections.

Summary of planning and budgeting risks. Although the scope of this study does not include a detailed analysis of the planning and budgeting process, a clear pattern differentiates it from education systems in other low-income countries:

- The national planning and budgeting processes are unlikely to be a point of leakage or diversion of funds. Government systems are sound, and the policy commitment to education protects the sector from a systemic loss of funds. The budgeting process at the national level is transparent.
- The resource allocation to the region is transparent and subject to predetermined criteria. The region-to-woreda allocation, however, is a higher area of risk.
- At the woreda level, the planning process is subject to more risk, though a transparent process ensures a fair degree of integrity and accountability.

Any capture would be opportunistic rather than systemic because woredas are controlled by party structures with an interest in service delivery.

- In a small proportion of woredas, the planning and budgeting process appears skewed, either geographically or ethnically. However, corruption is only one possible explanation for such distortions, and more detailed study would be required before firm conclusions could be drawn.
- One area of potential leakage at the woreda level concerns off-budget funds provided by donors and NGOs.

Fiscal transfers

Bribery or extortion to ensure funding transfers—risk: low. Fiscal transfers in the education sector can be affected by public officials corruptly exerting improper pressure to speed up or divert agreed funding transfers. The fiscal transfer process in Ethiopia is immediate and centrally controlled. The system is audited (through internal, external, and random audit checks) and has built-in checks and balances. It would appear that the money is getting through the system to its intended end accounting centers.

These findings are borne out by the results of a World Bank PBS Review conducted in the regions of Amhara, Oromia, and SNNPR using woreda-level budget and monthly block grant transfer data for 283 woredas (World Bank 2006). The review confirmed that the subnational budget envelopes and block grant disbursements from the federal to subnational levels were adhering to the established intergovernmental rules framework. Essentially, budget resources were being disbursed per the fiscal transfer formula, and there was no statistically significant deviation from the disbursed versus the entitled budgets across the woredas (World Bank 2006).

Summary of fiscal transfer risks. Although the scope of this aspect of the study is limited, initial indications both from stakeholder responses and from secondary sources are that disbursements from the federal to subnational levels broadly adhere to established rules (table 3.5).

Table 3.5   Summary of Corruption Risks in Fiscal Transfers

	Perceived corruption risk		
Form of corruption	Low	Medium	High
Bribery or extortion to ensure funding transfers	☐		

Source: Author.

Mapping of "downstream" corruption risks. Typical corruption risks related to teacher management, recruitment, and service delivery entail interaction between different groups, as follows:

- *Teacher management* typically involves practices between local officials, head teachers, community leaders, PTAs, and teachers.
- *Teacher recruitment* typically involves practices between public officials (in management) and teachers or other lower-level officials.
- *Service delivery* (that is, teaching) typically involves practice between teachers and students.

In Ethiopia, the overwhelming bulk of expenditure in the education sector is taken up by the recurrent salaries of teachers. As the sector has expanded rapidly, significant risks of corrupt practices have risen and are becoming established in relation to recruitment and management. The field survey provides a picture of how the sector is functioning and the risks related to typical corrupt practices.

Bribery, extortion, favoritism, or nepotism in selecting teachers for promotion, upgrading, or grants—risk: high. Although teachers in Ethiopia are poorly paid, they do have clearer promotion paths than other extension agents (Pankhurst 2008). There are, however, considerable perceived distortions to a related process of skills upgrading that forms part of a program of enhancing teacher qualifications through in-service training during holiday periods. Upgrading is perceived by some to be a relatively nontransparent management process that enables managers to use their positions to influence the selection of candidates. As one stakeholder stated, "Hidden relationships are used in teacher upgrading, with officials at the zonal or woreda level taking the first option on upgradation programs."

Survey responses received during this study suggested that favoritism[12] and nepotism are major, though not necessarily dominant, factors affecting upgrading. Out of 60 higher-education officials interviewed, 20 percent considered the upgrading process to be problematic. Out of 80 teachers, more than 50 percent noted that teacher upgrading is highly influenced by political connections, and 27 percent said it is influenced by relationships to committee members. Of school-level staff, 80 percent expressed general dissatisfaction with the procedures for upgrading. Bribery was also seen to influence upgrading opportunities, though to a lesser degree, being cited as a factor by just 9 percent of respondents.

Promotion procedures were also perceived to be problematic, with more than 50 percent of school-level staff expressing dissatisfaction with career promotion. This view is consistent with a parallel finding that most of the respondents at all levels believed there were no clear incentives for staff to perform well. Other surveys that have reached a similar conclusion, including a 2009 survey, found that "selection for promotion is not merit-based" (VSO 2009). Corrupt practices also were reported as influencing the award of grants, which were also affected by forged transcripts and certificates.

Falsification of documents in support of applications for promotion—risk: high. As a general pattern, the respondents viewed falsification of documents as being somehow less corrupt than more overt corruption such as bribery. In the case of applications for promotion, there is an apparently high risk that supporting documentation relating to qualifications and experience could readily be falsified by the applicant. For such falsification to go unnoticed, there is a related risk of the officials supporting or approving the application being implicated in the corrupt practice.

Collusion to ignore regulations regarding management of staff—risk: medium. This form of corruption could, for instance, occur if education officials chose to ignore regulations concerning the attribution of applicable salary scales to specific staff or any other management regulations. The assessment of this risk level as medium is based on two findings: First, there is a general sense that rules and regulations are less strictly applied in practice than in theory, suggesting a high degree of discretion on the part of some key decision makers. Second, there is a reported sense that favoritism by some officials is inevitable and cannot be challenged.

Collusion with teachers over noncompliance with curriculum, academic calendar, and similar practices—risk: medium. This form of corruption relates to semiofficial practices that benefit teachers but reduce the provision of educational services. As such, it requires collusion between teachers and their managers at the local level.

An indirect indicator of this risk occurs when teacher absenteeism is tolerated by head teachers, within the context of staff perceiving a need to supplement their income through private tutoring or other forms of income generation. Survey responses received during this study indicated that private tutoring is widespread, with 40 percent of school officials reporting it as a practice.

Extortion of facilitation payments from teachers—risk: low. This form of corruption relates to teachers being refused salary or other payments to which they are entitled unless they first pay a kickback to an official. In some countries, such a practice is commonly linked with initial recruitment—with jobs or promotion offered on the basis that the teacher involved will also make future kickbacks or contributions to a specific individual or political party.

Survey responses did not indicate this to be a problem in relation to salary payments—a finding consistent with a general distaste reported for such overt forms of corruption commonly encountered in other countries. Less conclusive was the situation in relation to the payment of per diems, with 48 percent of school-level staff reporting that per diems are not being paid according to regulations. This finding does not necessarily lead to a conclusion that facilitation payments are being extorted, but it does warrant further study as a possible form of corruption.

Bribery, extortion, favoritism, or nepotism in teacher recruitment—risk: high. Survey responses suggest nepotism and favoritism in recruitment were broad and frequent—namely that, in some woredas, the recruitment of teachers (and other community-based workers) is based on political affiliation, including paid-up membership of the Ethiopian People's Revolutionary Democratic Front (EPRDF). This process is perceived to start with the selection of candidates for technical training colleges (TTCs). Although the findings of this study are triangulated by other studies on accountability, it is difficult to judge the extent to which this reported favoritism and capture in the recruitment of teachers is actually occurring. Further, more specific, study would be required to determine this.[13]

This finding is related to a perceived lack of transparency in the recruitment process. Out of 60 higher-education officials interviewed, more than 20 percent considered this process to be nontransparent.

Nevertheless, only a small minority of respondents perceived a risk of bribery in teacher recruitment. This is in marked contrast with experience in some other countries in the region, where the payment of bribes for teaching jobs is considered to be a normal part of recruitment patterns. The context is unusual in Ethiopia, however, in that students do not generally choose to become teachers but are centrally selected from a pool of those who have failed to achieve high grades.

This system was set to change beginning in 2010, when those wishing to become teachers were to be able to elect to undertake an additional year of study. Once trained, the allocation of teachers to jobs is also centrally managed. Although most teachers express positive views about their profession, many resent being sent to work in remote rural communities, which can in some cases also constitute a risk to their personal security. Teachers from ethnic minorities can find themselves more likely to be posted to remote areas as a result of the policy of providing primary education in nationality languages.[14] In such circumstances, there is a clear potential risk of bribery to avoid unpopular postings, although that specific risk was not assessed in the survey.

Fraud to obtain teaching jobs—risk: high. Survey responses reveal a higher reported prevalence of fraud and falsification of teaching qualifications and other documents, reflecting weak controls, poor-quality documents (that are easily falsified), and the widespread belief that such a practice would not be detected.

Capture of recruitment by groups with vested interests—risk: high. Survey responses suggest widespread political capture of recruitment in the education sector. In addition to the previously reported perception of political influence over the recruitment and deployment of teachers, there are suggestions of broader influence being brought to bear. Among school staff respondents claiming to understand the appointments system, the appointment of local education officials was perceived, albeit by a small sample, to be more a matter of being "politically assigned" than competitive.

Bribery, favoritism, or nepotism in the selection of students—risk: medium. Survey responses suggest a risk of favoritism or nepotism in the selection of students, specifically as follows:

- Albeit from a small sample, a significant minority of the few public officials claiming an involvement in admissions considered political affiliation to be a factor, albeit less important than fulfillment of academic criteria. The student's home community was also considered to be an influencing factor.
- Although university and TTC students reported clear and publicly available criteria for admission, only 30 percent considered the admissions procedures to be completely fair.
- Twenty percent of school staff perceived favoritism in the selection of student teachers for TTCs.

- At the school household level, there were mixed views on the process of recruiting students to TTCs, with a slight majority considering it not to be fair to all students.
- Reported manipulation of the points system for selection of students to higher education entails allocating higher percentage points for results from transcripts and national exams than for entrance exams. Such manipulation is perceived to have enabled a large number of inadequately qualified students to join the affected institutes, sometimes with forged transcripts. This practice has affected the quality of students gaining entry to higher education and eroded the quality of the training program.

Favoritism or nepotism in the assessment of students—risk: medium. Survey responses paint a mixed picture of the risk of corruption in the assessment of students, specifically as follows:

- Higher-education and TTC staff members perceive assessment as depending entirely on academic achievement and attendance record.
- Of the university and TTC students, 92 percent believe academic factors influence the assessment of students. However, most consider students not to be judged fairly and report that teachers do not respect equality of students regarding religion, sex, or ethnic origin. Twenty-five percent consider a student's political affiliation to be a factor influencing the assessment of work; 20 percent consider the payment of gifts to be a factor in obtaining a degree; and 12 percent report political affiliation to be a factor. In addition, 42 percent report that staff members change marks; 33 percent report that staff favor their relatives; and 27 percent say the staff members selectively leak questions.
- School staffs report low levels of conflict between teachers and students over grades. When it occurs, the main complaints are that some students are favored more than others, including by receiving advance information about exams.

Fraud (and related bribery) in examinations—risk: high. Survey responses suggest a significant risk of corruption in examinations. Further discussions with key stakeholders identified generally high levels of perceived risk. The types of fraudulent practices in examinations include the following:

- *Forged admission cards* enable students to pay other students to sit exams for them. Such a practice is made possible by the poor quality of the admission cards. In one region, respondents estimated that more than 200 students took an exam for other students.

- *Collusion allowing both individual and group cheating in examinations.* Assistance from invigilators and school and local officials was noted in the survey to be common in all regions studied. Threatening or bribing strict supervisors and invigilators for their silence was reported to be a major problem in several centers.
- *Higher-level interference.* It was alleged that in 2008, in one region, action was taken to disqualify cheaters, but regional officials overturned that disqualification.
- *Fraudulent overscoring of examination papers* occurs when teachers are bribed by parents and students.

Fraud in certification (transcripts and certificates)—risk: high. Survey responses suggest there is a significant risk of corruption in certification, with 20 percent of TTC and university students perceiving that some students' certificates or transcripts are forged to help them graduate. Similar concerns are expressed by other stakeholder groups, including at the household level, where a minority of respondents consider that some students' certificates or transcripts are forged to help them pass to the next grade or level.

The corrupt practice identified as being most prevalent concerned the falsification of documents pertaining to student performance. Feedback in all regions suggested that there was an "industry" involved in falsification of documents and that it was most prevalent in the provision of certification for completing the primary or secondary school cycles.

Teacher absenteeism—risk: medium. In Ethiopian schools, teacher absenteeism is not common, nor is not common in the form and to the extent found in many other developing countries. In community interviews and surveys, 78 percent stated that the teacher was "always" at school for work, while 21 percent said "sometimes." If representative, this compares favorably with other estimates in the region: in Kenya, 26 percent absenteeism rates are reported, and in Uganda, 28 percent (Chaudhury et al. 2006). However, among Ethiopian TTC and university students, only 30 percent of respondents reported that instructors were "always" available.

Nevertheless, some practices seem to suggest an increased risk in this area. In a number of regions, the survey revealed the practice of certain teachers paying bribes or kickbacks to management, mostly school directors, to allocate shorter work hours in schools so that they can use the freed-up time to earn fees as teachers in private schools. This suggests that a form of teacher absenteeism or, more correctly, "informal part-timeism" is occurring, linked in some cases to bribery of other public officials who enable or provide their silence for this diversion of human resources to the private sector.

The lack of teacher absenteeism in the form found elsewhere is explained in part by an understanding of accountability systems in Ethiopia. In being recruited, teachers are required to meet certain expectations. Although there may be a need to also make additional money, there is a degree of community, party, and self-checking that makes teachers balance the need for more private income with the service they have been tasked with delivering.

Ghost payments—risk: low. Unlike many countries where this practice is rife, Ethiopia seems to have adequate controls to ensure that the number of "ghost teachers" is kept to a minimum. The supply-side systems that would enable false names to be registered for salary payments in Ethiopia have been overhauled and are reported to have improved as a result.

Nonetheless, survey reports suggest that a problem continues to exist in relation to the payment of per diems to "ghost participants," with some woreda officials or those controlling the payments allegedly embezzling funds through this practice. Further study would be needed to understand the precise nature of this problem.

Physical abuse by teachers—risk: medium. Survey responses suggest that physical abuse by teachers is generally rare. However, at the university level, respondents reported some isolated instances of university teachers demanding sexual favors from female students in exchange for fair marking. The seriousness of this risk is enhanced by related reports of a lack of confidence in the efficacy of mechanisms for reporting allegations of staff malpractice.

Extortion of additional fees by teachers—risk: low. This risk relates to other means by which teachers improperly extract fees from their students. The survey responses identified some instances of charging fees, but these were of an ambiguous nature, such as for the provision of ID cards, cleaning of classrooms, and sports activities. No instance was reported of students being required to pay for report cards.

Shifting services to private tuition—risk: medium. The survey found only a limited number of cases where teachers were found to be charging private teaching or tutoring fees. Although cases were reported, the practice was not considered to be systemic. Furthermore, communities appeared to be aware that it is not the norm. In one reported case, a teacher in a public school was teaching only part of the curriculum in the day public school classes, requiring students who wanted to complete the topic to attend night class and pay for private tutoring. In this instance, nonpaying students complained and the private tutoring ceased.

Despite this finding, an evident risk remains in relation to this form of corruption. With more than 40 percent of teachers reporting that teachers conduct private tutoring, and a strong majority of higher-education officials considering that moonlighting is necessary to some extent, there is a clear risk of improper pressure being brought to bear in this regard. This is borne out by the minority view that those who do not attend private tutoring are not favored by teachers.

In marked contrast to the responses from teaching staff and lecturers, only 4 percent of public official respondents reported other sources of income in addition to the official salary. This result may reflect the relatively low salaries of teachers. A major survey conducted in 2008 reported significant concern among teachers, both about the salary scales themselves and the extent to which these were not implemented correctly or efficiently (CfBT 2008, 42).

Private school operating without requisite approval—risk: low. Urban areas in particular have experienced marked growth in private education at all levels. The survey did not specifically seek to assess corruption risks associated with such private schools. However, the fact that such risks were not raised by respondents suggests that they are not perceived to be significant.

Summary of teacher management, recruitment, and service delivery risks. Based on the discussion above, the overall perceived risk of corruption in the three categories of teacher management, recruitment, and service delivery is considered to be medium to high, as shown in table 3.6.

Supplies and equipment. Procurement requires interaction between the public and private sectors because each of the three main levels of government in Ethiopia (central, regional, and woreda) and every type of government agency has to purchase goods and services, normally from the private sector. In the education sector, a number of public actors may be involved, depending on the size and type of the task. These include national and local government politicians and managers, operations staff,

Table 3.6   Summary of Corruption Risks in Teacher Management, Recruitment, and Service Delivery

Form of corruption	Perceived corruption risk		
	Low	Medium	High
Management			
Bribery, extortion, favoritism, or nepotism in selecting staff for promotion, access to scholarships, or access to opportunities for career enhancement			☐
Falsification of documents in support of applications for promotion or other considerations			☐
Collusion to ignore regulations regarding management of teaching and administrative staff		☐	
Collusion with teachers over noncompliance with curriculum, academic calendar		☐	
Extortion of facilitation payments from teachers for salaries and per diems	☐		
Procurement (recruitment)	*Low*	*Medium*	*High*
Bribery, extortion, favoritism, or nepotism in the recruitment of teachers			☐
Fraud, falsification of qualifications (such as teachers' certificates) to obtain teaching jobs			☐
Capture of recruitment by groups with vested interests			☐
Service delivery	*Low*	*Medium*	*High*
Bribery, extortion, favoritism, or nepotism in the selection of students		☐	
Favoritism or nepotism in the assessment of students		☐	
Fraud (and related bribery) in examinations			☐
Falsification of documents: forged transcripts and certificates			☐
Teacher absenteeism		☐	
Ghost teachers for payment of salaries or per diems	☐		
Teachers using power to physically abuse students		☐	
Teachers extorting fees for the provision of off-budget services (ID cards, sports, cleaning)	☐		
Teachers shifting services to private tuition		☐	
Private schools operating without requisite approval	☐		

Source: Author.

and procurement officers. From the private side, actors include suppliers of teaching and learning materials, utility operators, and suppliers of equipment ranging from chalkboards to vehicles.

During the course of the survey, respondents referred to several cases of apparent weakness in the processes used for the procurement of education-related supplies and equipment. Though it was not possible within the limited scope of this study to ascertain the degree to which these failings were the result of corruption per se, as opposed to simple mismanagement, corrective action is clearly required in the form of capacity building. As a general comment, the relatively low spending on procurement under education budgets means the scope for corruption is limited. On the other hand, low spending also means that the education officers responsible for procurement may, compared with their counterparts in higher-spending sectors such as public works, have less experience in developing and applying procurement-related controls.

Using the standard framework, each of the corruption risks related to supplies and equipment is now assessed in turn. Because of the relatively low spending on this part of the education budget, the field surveys addressed these aspects in less detail than those relating to teachers and teaching services. For this reason, the conclusions drawn are necessarily tentative in nature, though consistent with the totality of responses received.

Collusion with supplier when planning for supplies or equipment—risk: medium. Such collusion could, for instance, occur if those responsible for the procurement of furniture for a school or university were to draw up procurement plans with the secret support of a potential supplier. For such an approach to succeed, there must be either a lack of transparency or a lack of accountability in the procurement processes.

Survey responses from higher-education and TTC staff indicate that procurement processes are widely viewed as being transparent. However, 15 percent of respondents did not consider this to be the case, and 12 percent strongly disagreed with the statement that purchasing plans are publicly announced as required. Even if there is transparency, corruption could still occur if accountability mechanisms are weak, such as may occur if some people have sufficient influence to flout the rule of law, or bypass due procedure, with impunity. Given that independent external observers consider both law enforcement and public access to information in Ethiopia to be "very weak" (Global Integrity 2008), there is a potential risk in this area. However, survey respondents did not echo this view, suggesting less corruption than the high levels that would otherwise appear likely.

Interdepartmental collusion to bypass procurement procedures—risk: low. The survey responses provided no direct indication of interdepartmental collusion to bypass procurement procedures. Such collusion would require responsible parties in more than one department to work together to ignore or manipulate specified procedures to favor specific suppliers. Although the risk of such collusion appears low, there are indirect indications that it could occur through the practice, as reported by some respondents, of dismissing the need for open tendering on the grounds of remoteness or urgency. Although a strong majority say that purchasing plans are publicly announced as required, 12 percent "strongly disagree" that this is the case.

Favoritism, nepotism, or bribery in short-listing of suppliers or provision of tender information—risk: medium. Survey responses indicate that most higher-education staff do not believe procurement procedures to be at all influenced by political or influential connections or by illegal payments. However, about 20 percent of the respondents neither agreed nor disagreed that such influences occur, and about 15 percent perceived corrupt influences to occur, albeit in the form of influential connections and bribery rather than through political connections.

Tendering companies owned by persons linked with the award of contracts—risk: high. Interview responses suggest a widespread perception of family or other connections between tendering companies and officials responsible for procurement.

Specifications that favor a specific supplier—risk: low. This corrupt practice entails the writing of specifications in a manner that limits the number of suppliers capable of responding to the procurement request. Given the generally low-tech nature of most educational supplies and equipment, the risk of this form of corruption, though possible, is considered to be low. Any specific study of such a risk should ideally focus initially on the procurement of relatively high-tech specialist equipment, such as that required for the remote learning program.

Fraud, falsification of tender documents, with or without associated bribery—risk: medium. This corrupt practice could potentially entail a supplier falsifying documentation to qualify for or win the procurement contract. The falsified information may relate to the company status, its past experience or turnover, or the specifications of the supplies or equipment to be provided. In light of the pattern of risks indicated elsewhere through survey responses, there is considered to be a medium risk of this form of corruption.

Collusion among suppliers—risk: medium. This corruption risk could take many forms, including the formation of a cartel, obstruction of potential new entrants to the market, or other forms of uncompetitive practices that may or may not include a conspiratorial role on the part of those responsible for procurement. In view of suggestions of related practices, including perceived barriers to market entry, the risk of this corrupt practice is considered to be medium.

Bribery to influence evaluation of tenders—risk: medium. In general, survey responses suggest that outright bribery in the form of cash payments is relatively rare, and when it occurs, it is of a more minor nature than would typically be encountered in other countries in the region. Nevertheless, other less-direct forms of bribery were reported to have recently occurred, including an example of an overseas publisher offering international travel perks to Ethiopian officials responsible for the procurement of textbooks.

From an international perspective, the offering of such perks would normally be deemed to be a corrupt act in the country of origin of the company involved, as well as in Ethiopia. At the very least, any such perks would need to be openly declared and subject to public scrutiny, to ensure that it did not influence the tender evaluation. Survey responses suggest a low level of awareness of the corrupt nature of such inducements. For this reason the risk is assessed as being medium, despite an absence of any significant perception that it is a major corruption risk.

Supply of substandard, or inadequate quantity of, supplies or equipment—risk: medium. One of the clearest indicators of corruption in procurement is the purchase of substandard or defective supplies or equipment. For this to go unchallenged by those responsible for procurement strongly suggests either a lack of capacity, corrupt practices, or both.

Interview responses suggest that basic procurement controls are in place but that they do not always work as intended, resulting in some cases in the acceptance of goods that fail to meet the specifications set out in the procurement contract. For example, a large fleet of buses purchased by the MOE using Teacher Development Program funds and distributed to TTCs were found to be defective. The TTCs complained that the MOE had dumped the buses on them. The MOE subsequently sent auditors to determine whether the complaint was genuine.

Many schools continue to experience textbook shortages. It is beyond the scope of this study to analyze the causes of such shortages, which are understood to include capacity constraints, budget limits, the multiplicity of languages in which books must be printed,[15] and frequent changes to the curriculum.

Overbilling by suppliers—risk: low. Overbilling occurs when a supplier invoices for an amount that is higher than that stipulated in the contract or when the same amount is invoiced twice. Corruption occurs through the act of overbilling, whether or not the invoice is subsequently paid as requested. If such payment is made, it suggests either incompetence, or collusion, on the part of the officer responsible for procurement. Given the relatively sound nature of account controls in Ethiopia, the risk of this form of corrupt practice is considered to be low.

Extortion of facilitation payments to ensure settlement of invoices—risk: low. This form of corruption relates to suppliers being denied payments to which they are entitled unless they first pay a kickback to an official. It is a common practice in some other countries in the region. Survey responses did not indicate this to be a significant problem in the education sector in Ethiopia, though the hidden nature of such payments makes any such assessment uncertain. More broadly, however, there was a suggestion that a supplier may be inclined to express gratitude to a client through a small gift, but the amounts involved would be small and unlikely to be in the form of a crude cash payment.

Extortion of funds to provide access to supplies or equipment intended for all—risk: low. This corrupt practice, common in many developing countries, typically involves the charging for the use of textbooks that are supposed to be freely available. Survey responses suggested that this is not a significant problem in schools in Ethiopia. Respondents indicated that textbooks are normally free, or occasionally rented, while the high level of involvement of PTAs in schools has resulted in a widespread awareness of free services to which pupils are entitled.

Leakage of supplies or equipment during distribution—risk: low. Although this form of corruption is a theoretical possibility because of the low level of monitoring and controls in place in some woredas, the respondents did not highlight this risk. Secondary sources do, however, suggest a possible problem—one recent study concluding that even the modest (and at times inadequate) provision made for teaching and learning materials do not always reach the schools as intended.

Theft and resale of supplies or equipment—risk: medium. A theoretical possibility of this form of corruption also exists because of the low level of monitoring and controls in place in some woredas. Although controls are perceived to be stronger at the level of city education offices, there are indirect indications that this risk may in some cases occur. One such indication relates to the alleged illegal sale of education facilities, with related allegations of nepotism. A city education office is alleged to have sold valuable heritage buildings in a secondary school to a private developer and then to have requested land to rebuild the school facilities. Such allegations remain unproven and anecdotal, but the fact that stakeholders consider them to be plausible does suggest broader shortcomings in the systems of monitoring and control of supplies, equipment, and facilities.

Misappropriation of assets—risk: low. This form of corruption relates to the misuse of supplies or equipment intended for educational purposes. The general risk of this form of corruption is considered to be low, although isolated cases were reported of the misuse of telephones. (Technicians tapped office telephones to make international calls, and Internet service providers paid bribes for this access; the WOFED received a bill for Br 12,000 when the regular fee did not usually exceed Br 300.)

Summary of supplies and equipment risks—In light of the above, the overall perceived risk of corruption management, procurement, and service delivery concerning educational supplies and equipment is considered to be low to medium, as shown in table 3.7.

Buildings and facilities. Facilities development requires tendering and contracting processes similar to any public works procurement, construction, and ongoing operation and maintenance. It is therefore likely that corrupt practices in nonteaching functions will be influenced by experiences in other sectors.

Corrupt practices related to procurement of buildings and facilities can reasonably be expected to be similar in nature, but more pronounced, than those related to procurement of supplies and equipment. This is because of the nature of the construction sector, which can involve high expenditures and heavy reliance on the maintenance of high professional standards in all aspects of construction, including design and site supervision. An additional cause for concern is the absence of any independent

Table 3.7   Summary of Corruption Risks in Supplies and Equipment

Form of corruption	Perceived corruption risk		
	Low	Medium	High
Management			
Collusion with supplier when planning for supplies or equipment		☐	
Procurement	Low	Medium	High
Interdepartmental collusion to bypass procurement procedures	☐		
Favoritism, nepotism, or bribery in the short-listing of suppliers or provision of tender information		☐	
Tendering companies owned by persons linked with the award of contracts			☐
Specifications that favor a specific supplier	☐		
Fraud, falsification of tender documents, with or without associated bribery		☐	
Collusion among suppliers		☐	
Bribery to influence evaluation of tenders		☐	
Supply of substandard, or inadequate quantity of, supplies or equipment		☐	
Overbilling by suppliers	☐		
Extortion of facilitation payments to ensure settlement of invoices	☐		
Service delivery	Low	Medium	High
Extortion to provide access to supplies or equipment intended for all	☐		
Leakage of supplies or equipment during distribution	☐		
Theft and reselling of supplies or equipment		☐	
Misappropriation of assets	☐		

Source: Author.

professional bodies responsible in Ethiopia for the maintenance of standards among both companies and individuals.[16]

Such risks must, however, be considered within the context of spending patterns. With about 85 percent of education sector spending being taken up with direct costs of teaching, the budgets generally available for construction of new facilities are low. There are two important exceptions to this trend:

- At the woreda level, locally raised funds are often used for the construction or maintenance of school facilities.

- At the federal level, there has been a major capital program to construct 13 new universities. Commissioned and funded by the MOE, this ongoing program is jointly supervised by GTZ International Services, which is the project management and implementation agency with the primary task of capacity development. The objectives of the University Capacity Building Program (UCBP) extend beyond the construction of 13 universities, with a total capacity for more than 120,000 students. In addition, it is intended that the Ethiopian construction sector be modernized, and its competitiveness in the national and international markets improved. In 2009, following an independent review of corruption risks, the UCBP introduced a comprehensive Project Anti-Corruption System (PACS), an accountability mechanism described within the "Other Study Findings" section below.

Collusion with contractor when planning the construction or maintenance of facilities—risk: low. Survey responses from public officials suggest that corruption in contracting is considered to be rare but roughly twice as likely as corruption in service provision, with 12 percent of respondents considering corruption in contracting to be "widespread." Collusion between contractors and procuring officials is therefore considered to be a distinct possibility, albeit in relation to a relatively low level of expenditure.

Within the UCBP, such collusion is unlikely to succeed because it would also require collusion from the international managers involved. Given that part of the mandate of these managers is specifically to strengthen good governance, any such collusion would be unlikely.

Misappropriation of building funds by public officials and/or community leaders—risk: medium. At the local level, secondary sources report a significant loss of community contributions across the country, thus constituting a high area of corruption risk.

The context here is a strong reported willingness on the part of communities to mobilize for the construction of schools. This is associated with a positive attitude toward education and a local awareness of the costs and risks of sending children to schools farther away. Communities are therefore often more than willing to contribute labor and sometimes cash for the construction of schools. However the cash that communities contribute does not fall on-budget and is not monitored and audited to the same degree as public monies.

Such concerns are not, however, validated by the household-level survey responses, which indicate the following:

- A strong sense that the PTA provides a good point of liaison with the community
- High levels of awareness of PTA decisions
- High levels of involvement in the school, including a monitoring function
- A strong sense of knowing how school charges are spent
- An apparent awareness of formal reporting on the spending of school charges
- A strong view that collected fees are used exclusively for the good of the school
- A strong majority view that use of contributions is transparent.

In view of these responses, the assessment is downgraded to "medium risk" but not to "low risk" based on the relative lack of accountability in the case of locally generated funds, which constitutes an area of risk that needs to be addressed.

Favoritism, nepotism, or bribery in the short-listing of consultants or contractors or the provision of tender information—risk: medium. The short-listing component of this risk is related to concerns expressed in survey responses about the dominant market position of some favored contractors and consultants and reported cases of private contractors being awarded contracts for which they were not eligible to bid. However, such reports relate to the construction sector as a whole, which is beyond the scope of this study. The only specific report linking such risks to the education sector was an unsubstantiated report that the Finance and Administration Department—the agency within the MOE that is responsible for building maintenance—was under investigation for suspected unspecified malpractice.

Concerning the risk of unfair provision of tender information, interview responses included unsubstantiated suggestions of a corrupt relationship between some established universities and certain private contractors for the construction and maintenance of facilities.

Tendering companies owned by persons linked with the award of contracts—risk: medium. This risk is understood to exist within the construction sector as a whole but was not specifically identified as a risk in relation to the construction of educational facilities. In the case of the UCBP, no suggestion of any such risk was made.

Bypassing of correct procurement procedures—risk: medium. The only suggestions of such a risk in relation to construction contracts have been indirect, arising from

- A general perception among some respondents that sound procedures may exist in theory but can often be bypassed in practice.
- The reported practice of dismissing the necessity for open tendering on the grounds of remoteness and urgency.

In the case of the construction contracts under the UCBP, no suggestion of any such risk was made.

Specifications that favor a specific supplier—risk: low. This was not reported as a perceived risk. If it does exist, it is most likely to be in relation to specialist features or high-tech equipment rather than to standard aspects of facilities.

Fraud, falsification of tender documents, with or without associated bribery—risk: medium. This was not specifically reported as a perceived risk, but other reports indirectly suggest that unqualified contractors are short-listed for, and awarded, some construction contracts.

Collusion among contractors or consultants in bidding—risk: low. This was not reported as a perceived risk.

Bribery to influence evaluation of tenders—risk: low. Despite the suggestions of favoritism toward certain contractors, no indication was received that this extended to specific bribery to influence the evaluation of tenders. Reports of ambivalent attitudes by consultants and contractors toward the practice of expressing gratitude to clients do, however, suggest that such bribery may occur, albeit at a low to moderate level. The relatively tight controls put in place under the UCBP lead to this overall risk being assessed as low, even though the main construction contracts had been awarded by the time the full PACS was introduced into the program.

Bribery or extortion related to the granting of permits, licenses, and authorities —risk: medium. Survey responses included reference to contractors making facilitation payments to speed up the issue of licenses and permits needed to meet contract commitments to time schedules. Although not specifically related to this particular form of corruption, the dominant view among public officials is that such malpractice is initiated by the private entity. Sixty-five percent considered this to be the case, with about 15 percent considering that such corruption is initiated by the public official and 20 percent considering that both parties "know how the system works."

Defective construction, substandard materials, or overclaiming of quantities—risk: medium. Construction quality issues are considered a significant problem in the construction of educational facilities, particularly in the case of small, remote facilities where high standards of construction supervision can be difficult to achieve. For example, a toilet block in a school collapsed a month after completion. The contractor responsible for building the facility was not required to make the work good or repay the amount paid, nor was the contractor sanctioned. The matter was not investigated.

Such problems are a significant indicator of corrupt practices, particularly when the contractor is not ultimately held to account for its failures. Problems with quality can, however, also simply reflect low capacity on the part of the contractor (for failing to construct properly), the consultant or architect (for failing to supervise adequately), and the procurement agency (for failing to manage the process).

Bribery to cover up failure to meet specifications or other nonperformance—risk: low. This was not reported as a specific corruption risk, though the fact that poor-quality construction practices appears to be tolerated in some cases suggests either that there is either bribery to cover up failures, favoritism to prevent action against the contractor, or incompetence by those responsible for supervision. In the absence of any more specific information, this risk is tentatively assessed as being low.

Extortion of facilitation payments to ensure payment of certificates—risk: low. This was not reported as a specific corruption risk.

Summary of buildings and facilities risks. The overall perceived risk of corruption in each of the three aspects of buildings and facilities is, as shown in table 3.8, considered to be low to medium.

Table 3.8   Summary of Corruption Risks in Buildings and Facilities

Form of corruption	Perceived corruption risk		
	Low	Medium	High
Management			
Collusion with contractor when planning construction or maintenance of facilities	☐		
Misappropriation of building funds by public officials or community leaders		☐	
Procurement	Low	Medium	High
Favoritism, nepotism, or bribery in the short-listing of consultants or contractors		☐	
Tendering companies owned by persons linked with the award of contracts		☐	
Bypassing of correct procurement procedures		☐	
Specifications that favor a specific supplier	☐		
Fraud, falsification of tender documents, with or without associated bribery		☐	
Collusion among contractors or consultants in bidding	☐		
Bribery to influence evaluation of tenders	☐		
Service delivery	Low	Medium	High
Bribery or extortion related to the granting of permits, licenses, and authorities		☐	
Defective construction, substandard materials, or overclaiming of quantities		☐	
Bribery to cover up failure to meet specifications or other nonperformance	☐		
Extortion of facilitation payments to ensure payment of certificates	☐		

Source: Author.

Other Study Findings

The mapping exercise presented above represents only part of the overall picture of corruption risks affecting the education sector in Ethiopia. To be fully assessed, such risks must be considered in the institutional and political context in which they occur. People tend to engage in corruption when the risks are low, the penalties mild, and the rewards great (Klitgaard, MacLean-Abaroa, and Parris 2000). This dynamic suggests that corruption risks will be accentuated where there are wide-ranging discretionary powers or where accountability mechanisms are weak. Following a review of general perceptions of corruption arising from the study, each of these factors is briefly considered in turn.

General Perceptions of Corruption

Levels of corruption. Central officials and public officials were asked about their perception of general levels of corruption. Ninety-five percent of central officials and 60 percent of public officials indicated awareness of some instances of misappropriation of funds in the preceding two years. This suggests higher levels of awareness of corruption among the more senior, central officials.

The same groups of respondents provided their perceptions of changes in levels of corruption since 2004. Asked about perceived levels of corruption in 2004, 2007, and 2009:

- *Central officials* indicated that corruption levels among public officials in general had slightly decreased over this period and that corruption has never been widespread among public officials in the education sector.
- *Public officials* indicated that general levels of corruption had decreased markedly over this period. Corruption in the education sector was also perceived to have decreased, though from a much lower base than among public officials in general. Specifically, the proportion of responses considering general levels of corruption to be "widespread" among public sector officials fell from 22 percent in 2004 to 7 percent in 2009, while the equivalent figures for those involved in education were 7 percent and 2 percent, respectively.

Taken together, these responses reinforce the sense that levels of corruption in the education sector are perceived to be relatively low.

What constitutes corruption. In Ethiopia, the pattern of perception suggests that outright bribery is perceived to be more corrupt than, for example, favoritism or the falsification of documentation. There is also a sense that some practices, such as expressing gratitude to a client through the giving of a small gift, are normal business practice and not necessarily corrupt. Finally, there is an underlying acceptance among many that the state has the right to intervene in the market if that is considered to be in the national interest, and there is little sense that such interventions could be at variance with ongoing efforts to promote the level playing field needed for effective privatization of service provision, including in the education sector.

Where corruption occurs and who initiates it. The survey responses of public officials indicate that they hold the following perceptions:

- Corruption is perceived as the most likely in contracting, then in decision making, then in service delivery, in that order of significance. Responses to the same question were inconclusive when asked of higher-education officials.
- Bribes received are likely to be shared first with superiors, then with a political party, and then with colleagues, in that order.
- The value of bribes received is reported as increasing in relation to the annual income of the post holder. In other words, where public officials believe that more senior post holders are receiving bribes, they consider the value of such bribes to be higher than could realistically be demanded by themselves or by more junior officials.
- In most cases, the user (or private sector representative), rather than the public official, initiates corrupt deals. A similar pattern of responses was received from higher-education officials.

Discretionary powers. An Ethiopian proverb—"Sishom Yalbela Sishar Ykochewal"—roughly translates into English as follows: "One who does not exploit to the full his position when he is promoted will lament when he no longer has the opportunity."

One feature of Ethiopia's unique political heritage is the lack of discretionary powers available to middle-ranking and junior functionaries at each of the three administrative levels. Accounts abound of officials being unwilling to take responsibility for ad hoc decision making and instead referring matters up the hierarchy. In addition, cultural factors including tribal alignment can have a bearing on decision making. Combined with these factors is a strong sense that, although most people need to play by the rules, some do not and can act with impunity. This is expressed through a wide range of sentiments, ranging from politicized resentment to a grudging acceptance, bordering on admiration, for those able and willing to exercise power in this way.

In Ethiopia's decentralized yet authoritarian system, considerable powers exist among senior officials at the federal, regional, and woreda levels. Of particular relevance to this study is the discretion exercised by politically appointed officials at the woreda level, directly affecting the management of teachers. In cases where measures are taken against teachers and headmasters, including dismissals, they are generally initiated from the woreda level rather than by community action, with limited involvement of the semiformal institutions such as the boards and PTAs.

Accountability mechanisms. Accountability mechanisms in Ethiopia's education sector relate to all aspects of performance and include the monitoring of financial management, service provision to users, and the responsiveness or otherwise of management to the needs of employees. For the purposes of this subsection, and in view of the sectorwide approach to most aspects of the ESDP, a distinction is made between "supply-side" accountability to government and its donor partners, and "demand-side" accountability to users and the employees.

Supply-side accountability. Ethiopia's supply-side controls reflect a legacy of strictly defined procedures and hierarchical management. Within this context, the education sector is widely perceived to be better resourced, staffed, and managed than other sectors, with relatively clear structures, systems, and staffing. The guidelines and mechanisms are clearer, and the local institutions are more involved than in other sectors. As with other sectors, institutional capacity is considered to be stronger at the federal level than at the regional or woreda levels, though with a wide spectrum of capacity among both regions and woredas.

Within this context, national supply-side accountability mechanisms include audits (both internal and independent) and school inspections. Additional mechanisms undertaken by the donor community in collaboration with the government of Ethiopia include the following:

- *Fiduciary risk assessments* to assess whether funds were used for the purposes intended.
- *Public expenditure and financial accountability reports,* the most recent of which relating to Ethiopia were in 2007, looking specifically at the federal and regional levels.

In relation to the education sector, a specific mechanism undertaken jointly by the government of Ethiopia and the donor community is the annual ESDP Joint Review Mission (JRM). It is beyond the scope of this study to comment in detail on the efficacy of any one of these or other supply-side accountability mechanisms. General comments, however, include the following:

- Given the high levels of expenditure and apparent difficulty in obtaining timely and reliable data,[17] such mechanisms are only ever likely to provide a general view of corruption risks.

- The government's ambitious, needs-based approach to planning can result in weak links between plans and budgets, thus undermining accountability mechanisms. (Note the variability of aid flows to education, as figure 3.2 showed.) The more predictable aid flows provided by Direct Budget Support (DBS) were intended to reduce this risk. Following the suspension of DBS, it was recognized that the political vulnerability of aid flows risked undermining the long-term objective of sustainable provision of basic services. The decentralized PBS program made progress in this regard, but donors have not yet achieved a clear and transparent system of "graduated response." Such a system would ensure that aid structurally cofinancing basic services such as education would not be hostage to political difficulties.[18]

Taken together, the following observations suggest a degree of inconsistency between the supply-side accountability mechanisms of government and those of donors, with the result that reporting channels can

Figure 3.2   Overview of Corruption Risks in the Ethiopian Education Sector, by Function

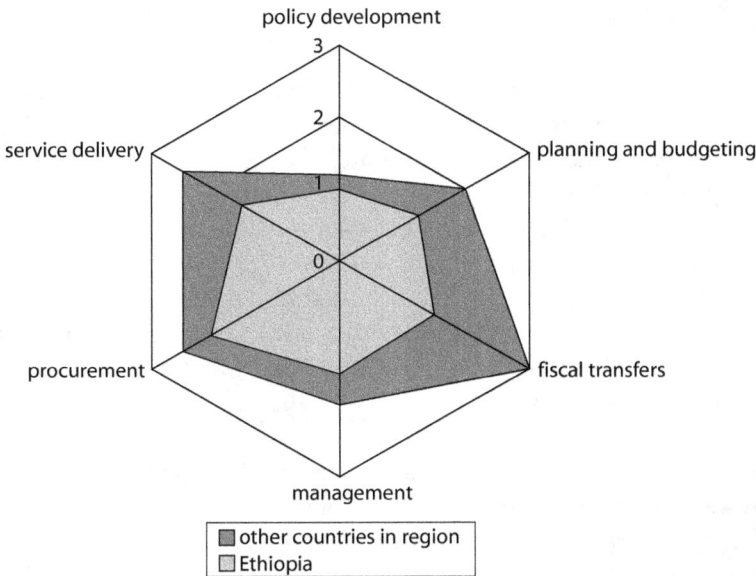

Source: World Bank 2009.
Note: Numerical values along the radii, depicted on the vertical axis, designate the degree of estimated average corruption risk within each education sector function, as follows: 0 = no corruption risk; 1 = low risk; 2 = medium risk; 3 = high risk.

become muddled. Although donors profess a desire, where possible, to rely on official accountability mechanisms, they also find themselves under demand-side pressure from their own taxpayers to undertake independent checks, not least because of the apparent unreliability of some official data flows.

- Independent Public Financial Management (PFM) studies conducted in Ethiopia in 2007[19] noted satisfactory progress in recent years but drew attention to scope for further improvement in public access to fiscal information and control of nonsalary expenditures.
- A 2008 World Bank risk assessment related to Ethiopia's education sector (World Bank 2008) noted "high" or "substantial" preproject risks related to financial management and a "high" risk related to procurement. The education management information system was considered to be weak, and PFM capacity at the woreda level was considered to be low.
- At the local level, the lack of influence that school directors have over school appointments (VSO 2009) can reduce both their authority and their accountability, as does the perception that some director appointments are political (CfBT 2008, 39).

Demand-side accountability. A prerequisite for demand-side accountability is transparency, meaning that information must be clearly available (to users, employees, and, where appropriate, to the public) as a basis for then assessing performance. Accountability systems then serve to reward or encourage good performance or behavior and to punish or discourage poor performance or behavior.

The field surveys included some questions related to demand-side accountability among employees. At the level of higher-education and TTC staff, a striking feature of the responses was that 80 percent of respondents disagreed with the statement that there were incentives to improve their performance. This suggests a system in which accountability mechanisms are extremely weak—meaning that good performance is not rewarded and poor performance is tolerated.

There is also a marked perception of intimidation toward those who complain. Survey responses indicate that 30 percent of central officials and 24 percent of public officials had considered reporting a case of malpractice in the past year but decided not to do so. The dominant underlying reason for this was a strong sense that there is no protection to guard against possible reprisals directed at those who report malpractice.

A minority perceived that complaining would result in a personal security risk. The same group of respondents expressed a wide range of views as to the sincerity of government efforts to fight corruption in education, with most considering the efforts to be sincere.

A law on charities and civil society organizations, passed by the parliament in early 2009, includes a number of restrictive provisions that some international actors view as limiting the role of civil society in demand-side accountability.[20]

Survey responses from users also generated some interesting data. Households revealed a strong perception that PTAs contribute to accountability at the local level. This view is echoed in responses from school-level staff, who expressed high confidence in school financial records (as far as they go) and who report a strict regime of school inspections.

Disciplinary procedures exist, and complaint mechanisms against unfair measures are available and sometimes used. However, these mechanisms seem to be used mainly by teachers seeking redress rather than by community members.

Secondary sources suggest flaws in broader accountability mechanisms within the teaching profession, including in the representation of teachers' interests. Teachers in Ethiopia have historically been represented by the Ethiopian Teachers' Association (ETA), founded in 1949. Following a long legal battle, a 2008 court ruling took away the right of the ETA to its name and all of its assets, creating a different organization with an identical name. Most teachers are now members of this replacement organization, for which dues are deducted from teachers' salaries. The original ETA, now reorganized as the National Teachers Association (NTA), considers the new ETA to be unduly influenced by the government and has complained of discrimination against its members. Such concerns have in turn been expressed internationally through a range of bodies including the International Labour Organization (ILO 2009).

Summary and Conclusions

This concluding section presents three levels of summary:

- *An overview* of the six functional areas identified, which lends itself to a comparison of the general corruption risks in Ethiopia's education sector with those perceived to exist in other countries

- *A subfunction view*, which identifies characteristics from the mapping of corruption risks along the education sector value chain
- *A focus on the areas of highest perceived risk of corruption*, which sums up the specific, locally identified risks in Ethiopia's education sector that urgently must be addressed, or at least studied in more detail.

Overview

The overview emerging from this study is that the full range of anticipated corruption risks exist within the Ethiopia's education sector but that the resulting risk map differs from that in other countries, or indeed within other sectors in Ethiopia. Specifically, the following tentative conclusions can be drawn and depicted:

- The "upstream" corruption risks related to policy development, planning and budgeting, and fiscal transfers are low compared with the "downstream" risks related to management, procurement (including recruitment), and service delivery.
- At this general level, corruption risks within each of the six functions are generally lower than would typically be encountered in other countries in the region. This is shown in figure 3.2, where the corruption risk, as expressed on the vertical radius, runs from zero at the center, through low (1), medium (2), and high (3) at the outer edges.
- Presented in this way, as an average of the estimated risks within each function, the "upstream" risks are low, and the "downstream" risks are in the low-to-medium range.

Subfunction View

A more detailed representation in figure 3.3 shows estimated risks of each of the downstream subfunctions, revealing some high risks and some low ones.

Here, the three highest areas of risk all relate to teachers, the area of highest spending in the education sector. Starting with teacher recruitment, extending to teacher management and, to some extent, teachers' delivery of services, there are strong perceived risks of corruption in the form of favoritism.

The relatively low perceived risks associated with functions related to supplies and equipment as well as buildings does not mean that corruption risks can be ignored. Although outright bribery is seen to be rare, corruption where it occurs is more likely to be in the form of either fraud or favoritism.

Figure 3.3   Corruption Risks in the Ethiopian Education Sector, by Subfunction

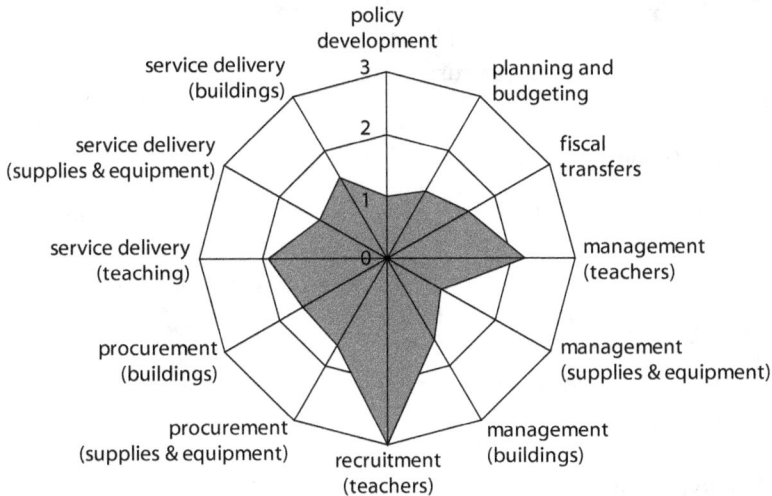

Source: World Bank 2009.
Note: Numerical values along the radii, depicted on the vertical axis, designate the degree of estimated average corruption risk within each education sector subfunction, as follows: 0 = no corruption risk; 1 = low risk; 2 = medium risk; 3 = high risk.

Areas of Highest Perceived Corruption

Drilling down further into the detail, the following corruption risks are perceived to the most pronounced in the education sector in Ethiopia:

- Bribery, extortion, favoritism, or nepotism in selecting staff for promotion, access to scholarships, or access to opportunities for career enhancement
- Falsification of documents in support of applications for promotion or other considerations
- Bribery, extortion, favoritism, or nepotism in teacher recruitment
- Fraud in the falsification of qualifications (for example, teachers' certificates) to obtain teaching jobs
- Tendering companies owned by persons linked with the award of contracts
- Fraud (and related bribery) in examinations
- Falsification of documents such as forged transcripts and certificates.

These risks can be grouped into four categories:

- Corruption affecting the selection of teachers for training, recruitment, skills upgrading, or promotion

- Falsification of documents to obtain qualifications, jobs, or promotions
- Fraud and related bribery in examinations
- Conflict of interest in procurement.

Recommendations

Even when correctly identified, there is no single, or simple, way of dealing with specific corruption risks. The recommendations that follow should therefore be considered within the context of an integrated approach characterized by the following:

- Sound understanding of the underlying drivers of behavior
- Laws and regulations that can realistically be applied and enforced fairly and impartially
- Adequate institutional capacity
- Transparency, meaning that the quality of service delivery can readily be assessed and shortcomings recognized
- Accountability, meaning that individuals and institutions are clearly identifiable as responsible for failures in service delivery or related breaches of procedure, while users and civil society organizations have the capacity and the mandate to demand such accountability.

Based on the findings of this scoping study, the recommendations below are proposed for consideration by the Ministry of Education.

Recommendation 1: *Establish a corruption risks working group to oversee a considered response to the tentative findings of this study.*

The group, whose composition should command the confidence of all stakeholder groups, would oversee a considered response to the tentative findings of this study. Such a response should include, but not be limited to, the following recommendations:

Recommendation 2: *Analyze the nature and extent of fraud in the examinations process and develop specific recommendations for remedial action.*

Recommendation 3: *Review the de jure and de facto procedures for recruiting, upgrading, and promoting teachers and develop specific recommendations for improving accountability.*

Recommendation 4: *Review asset management capacity, with a view to strengthening oversight mechanisms.*

Recommendation 5: *Develop disclosure requirements for the education sector and improve access to information.*

Recommendation 6: *Identify and develop the scope for more coherent accountability mechanisms, including the empowerment of PTAs and NGOs with further information related to service delivery.*

Recommendation 7: *Document and disseminate (both within MOE and in other sectors) the lessons learned from the pioneering experience of implementing PACS under the UCBP.*

Notes

1. A "ghost worker" is someone who does not exist, whose salary or per diem provision is drawn down corruptly by those in a position to manipulate the system.
2. Including, in particular, the U.K. Department for International Development education economist.
3. Data were collected using six different survey instruments from a total of 352 respondents at the central regional, woreda, and school levels as well as from households at the school or community level and students or trainees engaged in studies at the universities or technical training colleges (TTCs). The number of response fields generated by each survey interview ranged from 65 to 169 per respondent and included some identical questions for each stakeholder group to enable a comparative assessment of responses patterns between, as well as within, stakeholder groups. The groups surveyed, and numbers of respondents per group were as follows (references to these groups in this chapter correspond to the specific surveyed groups described above):

   - Central officials (47 respondents) from the Ministry of Education (MOE), Ministry of Finance and Economic Development (MOFED), and the regional Bureaus of Finance and Economic Development (BOFEDs)
   - Public officials (84 respondents) from Regional Education Bureaus, BOFEDs, Woreda Education Offices (WEOs) and Woreda Offices of Finance and Economic Development (WOFEDs)
   - Higher-education and TTC staff (33 respondents)
   - TTC and university students (33 respondents)
   - School-level staff (81 respondents)
   - Household-level individuals (74 respondents).

4. The requirement is for a framework that can also be used in each country context to locate concentrations of corruption, identify unknowns, plot shifts in corruption activity, and identify links within the corruption matrix.

5. This interactions-based approach is driven by (a) a need to build broad stakeholder commitment and a coalition for change and (b) a strong belief that the corruption problem in the sector should be articulated in terms of the actions of all public, private, and civil society actors and institutions. It is also pursued knowing that policy actions are more likely to influence the public sector than other actors and that more policy options are available to public actors. Understandably, given that education is usually a monopoly (the state provides, finances, owns, and regulates the sector), this approach places the public office at the core of the interaction framework and emphasizes that the public officer or agency interacts with three other sets of actors—the other public actors and agencies; the private actors and companies; and consumers, civil society, and its representative organizations—across the cycle, from central policy planning down to actual service delivery.

6. Trends for quality are mixed, with proxy indicators deteriorating, stagnating, or slowly improving. The last three years of National Learning Assessments results show that educational attainment at grades 4 and 8 has declined year on year, but grade 5 completion rates have improved.

7. The MOE notes that for many of the corruption risks highlighted below, regulations and guidelines are in place to mitigate them (MOE 2010).

8. Such concerns are not limited to the education sector and relate to both (a) the dominant role of the ruling party in decision making and (b) perceived obstacles to the role of the private sector. Although PASDEP places the private sector closer to the center of development policy than before, some observers say it does not yet include policy proposals that, by ensuring a level playing field, permit the private sector to play its true role. Neither of these areas of concern necessarily relates directly to corruption, but they do raise concern among some stakeholders about possible indirect corruption risks. The specific risk of political capture of budget support, as historically perceived by some donors in 2006, is described in the "Other Study Findings" section below.

9. In "World Bank vs. Ethiopia: Response to Dr. Ishac Diwan's letter," a 2006 exchange of open letters related concerns about an alleged lack of accountability in pooled donor support channeled through block grants under the Protection of Basic Services (PBS) program, which includes the education sector.

10. http://www.mofed.gov.et/English/Pages/Home.aspx.

11. From approximately 17 percent of the recurrent budget on general education in 2001/02, nonsalary spending fell to an average of 8 percent in 2007/08.

12. This favoritism is related in most cases to the influence of the ruling party. In this regard, as previously reported in this chapter, party control of woredas

can also have the effect of reducing other forms of corruption as a result of a party interest in service delivery.

13. Such study would entail comparing the recruitment rates of EPRDF vs. non-EPRDF candidates, which would itself be complicated both by the high proportion of the population claiming to be EPRDF supporters and by the related selection process for teacher training.

14. Section 3.5.1 of the Education and Training Policy (1994).

15. There are some 120 local languages. For ESDP I, 19 languages were identified.

16. Although the views of architects, consultants, and contractors are expressed to the government through their respective professional associations, decision making about the professional registration of both individuals and companies rests with the government alone.

17. The comment is made in several reviews, including the 2007 JRM reports, that it is difficult to obtain reliable data in a timely manner. Although this does not in itself constitute a reason to doubt the accuracy of available data, it does means that available statistics should be viewed with caution.

18. In 2009, Sweden suspended all its programs implemented by government agencies, including GEQIP, in protest against a new law restricting the activities of charities and civil society organizations. Some of the resulting shortfall was made up by other donors.

19. PEFA studies include one at the federal level and one covering seven regions.

20. The provisions include a strict limit on the extent of international involvement.

References

ADC (Austrian Development Cooperation). 2007. "Ethiopia Country Strategy 2008–2012." Program assessment, ADC, Vienna.

Addis Fortune. 2009. "Thumbs Up for New Grant Formula." February 9.

Chaudhury, N., J. Hammer, M. Kremer, K. Muralidharan, and F. H. Rogers. 2006. "Teacher and Health Care Provider Absenteeism: A Multi-Country Study." Working paper, World Bank, Washington, DC.

CfBT (Centre for British Teachers) Education Trust. 2008. *Study into Teacher Utilization in the Regions of Ethiopia (STURE) 2008.* Addis Ababa: United Nations Development Program.

CIA (Central Intelligence Agency). 2006. *The World Factbook.* Washington, DC: National Technical Information Service and U.S. Government Printing Office. https://www.cia.gov/library/publications/the-world-factbook/.

Dom, Catherine. 2009. "Country Desk Study: Ethiopia," discussion draft, "Mid-Term Evaluation of the EFA [Education for All] Fast Track Initiative." Program evaluation by Cambridge Education, Mokoro, and Oxford Policy Management for the World Bank, Washington, DC.

Global Integrity. 2008. "Ethiopia: Integrity Indicators Scorecard." Ethiopia scores for "The Global Integrity Report," Global Integrity, Washington, DC. http://report.globalintegrity.org/Ethiopia/2008/scorecard/.

ILO (International Labour Organization). 2009. "Report of the Committee on Legal Issues and International Labour Standards." Decision report, April 14, ILO, Geneva.

Klitgaard, Robert, Ronald MacLean-Abaroa, and H. Lindsey Parris. 2000. *Corrupt Cities: A Practical Guide to Cure and Prevention.* Oakland, CA: ICS (Institute for Contemporary Studies) Press; Washington, DC: World Bank Institute.

MOE (Ethiopian Ministry of Education). 2010. "Feedback." July 22.

MOFED (Ethiopian Ministry of Finance and Economic Development). 2006. "Ethiopia: Building on Progress: A Plan for Accelerated and Sustained Development to End Poverty (2005/06–2009/10)." MOFED, Addis Ababa.

Pankhurst, Alula. 2008. "Enhancing Understanding of Local Accountability Mechanisms in Ethiopia: Protecting Basic Services Project." Protecting Basic Services (PBS) II preparation studies, final main report for the World Bank, Washington, DC.

Patrinos, H., and R. Kagia. 2007. "Maximizing the Performance of Education Systems: The Case of Teacher Absenteeism." In *The Many Faces of Corruption: Tracking Vulnerabilities at the Sector Level,* eds. J. Edgardo Campos and Sanjay Pradhan, 63–87. Washington, DC: World Bank.

PBS (Protection of Basic Services) JRIS (Joint Review and Implementation Support). 2008. Report, Addis Ababa.

VSO. 2009. "How Much Is a Good Teacher Worth? A Report on the Motivation and Morale of Teachers in Ethiopia." VSO International, London.

World Bank. 2006. "Protection of Basic Services [PBS] Review." Project appraisal document, World Bank, Washington, DC.

———. 2008. "First Phase of GEQIP." Project appraisal document, World Bank, Washington, DC.

———. 2009. "Protection of Basic Services [PBS] Phase 2." Project appraisal document, World Bank, Washington, DC.

"World Bank vs. Ethiopia: Response to Dr. Ishac Diwan's letter." 2006. Ethiopian American Civic Advocacy. May 24.

CHAPTER 4

Rural Water Supply Corruption in Ethiopia

Roger Calow, Alan MacDonald, and Piers Cross

Introduction

In Ethiopia, investment in rural water supply underpins the government's poverty reduction efforts. The challenge is huge: roughly 50 percent of the (mainly rural) population still have no access to safe water, and the country has the highest number of people in Sub-Saharan Africa without access to improved water supply and sanitation. The consequences are dire: every year, roughly 250,000 children die from diseases related to poor water and sanitation, and many others face the daily grind of collecting water from distant sources.

To meet the challenge, the government has set ambitious targets under its Universal Access Program (UAP) to achieve full coverage by 2012, with major investment from government, donors, and (increasingly) communities. Considering the scale of the challenge, Ethiopia has made significant

The authors would like to acknowledge the contributions and field work by Derek Ball, Yemareshet Yemane, and Elizabeth Mekonnen.

Although this chapter results from studies completed by January 2010, the process of checking, reviewing, and securing agreement for publication was finally brought to conclusion only in late 2011. The chapter is therefore put forward with the caveat that while it reflects the situation at the time of the study, some details will have understandably changed.

progress in attracting finance to the sector. The government of Ethiopia estimates that to meet its UAP target for rural water supply, annual expenditure of more than Br 1.1 billion (US$99 million) is required, of which more than 90 percent is already committed. At the same time, dramatic reforms have resulted in the development of a programmatic approach to improve aid effectiveness in tandem with large-scale decentralization—both political and administrative.

The sheer scale of investment required to meet the UAP target raises inevitable questions about how well the money is spent: Is corruption a significant issue? Might it affect the delivery of basic services? If so, by how much? Internationally, water is viewed as a high-risk sector because of the financial flows involved, weak government oversight, and significant public-private interactions involved in infrastructure provision. However, there is little concrete evidence of specific risks or of the effectiveness of different interventions and reforms that might reduce them. In Ethiopia, no previous studies have attempted a systematic assessment of the nature and extent of corruption, either within the water sector in general or in the provision of rural drinking water supply in particular.

In view of the sums of money involved, ensuring that funding translates into improved services for poor people is a clear priority. Yet little is known about how robust or effective the current systems are to prevent corruption and enable the national program to meet its goals. Internationally, recent initiatives have identified corruption as a contributor to poor water governance and, more specifically, as a constraint on service delivery to those most in need. Is this the case in Ethiopia?

Objectives

Against this background, the study of corruption risk discussed in this chapter aims to shed light on the importance, scope, and nature of corruption in the provision of rural drinking water supplies.[1] The study has three broad objectives:

- Map the different forms, links, and scope of corruption in Ethiopia's rural water supply along the service delivery "value chain"—from policy development (at the top of the chain) to scheme implementation and management (at the bottom)
- Identify particular points along the value chain that are vulnerable to corruption, backed up with qualitative and quantitative data on perceptions and evidence
- Work with key sector stakeholders to validate findings and develop recommendations to address vulnerabilities.

Methodology

To meet these objectives, a team of international and local consultants developed a diagnostic approach for mapping corruption, interviewed sector stakeholders, and conducted a field survey of rural drinking water boreholes, specifically as follows:

- *At the policy making and federal level*, a stakeholder analysis of rural water supply policy making, planning, and budgeting included more than 50 interviews with sector stakeholders representing the government, donors, nongovernmental organizations (NGOs), and the private sector.
- *At the project and program level*, an evaluation of borehole procurement, construction, and management included contract specifications; actual construction standards and invoices; and a postconstruction survey of 26 shallow boreholes in the Southern Nations, Nationalities and People's Region (SNNPR) and Oromia—using down-the-borehole, closed-circuit television (CCTV) equipment—to determine whether completed infrastructure had been built to contract and invoiced correctly.
- *At the community level*, the team conducted a survey to ascertain village perceptions and governance associated with borehole development and management at the selected sites.

Key findings from the interviews and sample survey were then presented and discussed at a validation workshop in Addis Ababa, opened by the minister of water and hosted by the Federal Ethics and Anti-Corruption Commission. More than 40 sector stakeholders, drawn from the groups above, attended the workshop.

Why the focus on rural drinking water supply, particularly on groundwater-based rural water supply? Three reasons:

- The government's target to achieve full coverage depends crucially on developing groundwater; this provides (a) the only cost-effective way of meeting dispersed rural demand at relatively low cost and (b) a buffer against climate variability.
- The UAP emphasizes the importance of affordable technologies, including shallow boreholes.
- It has previously been difficult to assess the extent of corrupt practices in the provision of groundwater-based supply because groundwater is "out of sight and out of mind." By adopting a new technique for assessing subsurface construction standards and by comparing the findings with design specifications, invoices, and community perceptions of construction, the study has piloted an approach that could be applied

more widely in Ethiopia and other countries to monitor service provision and reduce corruption.

Summary of Findings

Broadly speaking, Ethiopia has made significant strides in policy development, financing, governance, and management, resulting in *generally low levels of corruption and perceptions of corruption along the value chain*. That said, the study highlights a number of vulnerable areas, particularly at the lower (procurement and construction) end of the value chain, and stakeholder perceptions of corruption vary significantly in some instances.

Chapter Structure

The chapter is organized as follows:

- "Corruption in the Water and Sanitation Sector" examines the causes, costs, and consequences of corruption in the water sector generally, drawing on recent international studies. The value chain approach to understanding corruption risk is presented in more detail.
- "Ethiopia's Water Sector" describes the characteristics of the water sector in Ethiopia before focusing on the rural drinking-water supply in particular. Recent sector reforms and financing are discussed, underlining the importance of providing secure water for highly vulnerable rural populations.
- "Rural Water Supply Corruption in Ethiopia" presents the study findings along the value chain of sector functions: (a) policy making and regulation; (b) planning, budgeting, and transfers; (c) design, tendering, and procurement; (d) borehole construction and payment; and (e) local management of completed infrastructure. The section includes an indepth discussion of the approach and findings of the field surveys.
- "Summary and Recommendations" recaps the key findings and presents 10 recommendations for reducing corruption risks and strengthening accountabilities at vulnerable points along the value chain.

Corruption in the Water and Sanitation Sector

Three recent documents provide comprehensive analyses and overviews on the extent of corruption in the water sector:

- Transparency International's *Global Corruption Report 2008: Corruption in the Water Sector* reviews the entire water sector through essays representing different perspectives (TI 2008).

- *The Many Faces of Corruption: Tracking Vulnerabilities at the Sector Level* includes an examination of the water supply and sanitation sector in Africa (Campos and Pradhan 2007).
- A comprehensive World Bank sourcebook on the urban water and sanitation sector was developed to help water and sanitation practitioners diagnose the extent and risks of corruption in urban areas (Halpern et al. 2008).

These sector reviews have two common themes: (a) the potential for, and risks of, corruption in the water sector; and (b) the paucity of empirical data, thus the need for further field research. Inclusion of the water sector in the Ethiopia country diagnostic studies is a timely addition to this growing body of knowledge.

Potential for Water Sector Corruption

The water sector is characterized by its diversity. Water, literally, is involved in most human activities, and predicting the actual scale of corruption in any specific water operation is hazardous without a specific local assessment.

There are many different types of water services and many actors involved at several levels—from politicians to pipe manufacturers, consultants to consumers, local government officials to lab technicians, public agencies to private enterprises, vendors to donors, and planners to philanthropists. Water corruption can be either *grand* (the misuse of vast amounts of public sector funds by a relatively small number of officials) or *petty* (a large number of officials abusing their public office by extracting small bribes and favors, generally directly affecting the poorest). Indeed, water corruption includes all of these forms:

- *Bribes*: the offering or payment of money, services, or valuables to public officials to persuade them to do something (quicker, better, or more in their interest)—for example, a bribe to get pipes repaired
- *Fraud*: an economic crime involving deceit or trickery for unlawful gains—for example, fraudulent CVs to get a job or license in water or the moonlighting of state-owned rigs
- *Nepotism*: the exploitation of an individual's own power and authority to procure favors for relatives or friends—for example, water sector jobs for relatives
- *Embezzlement*: the misappropriation of public resources (property or funds) legally entrusted to someone in his or her formal position as an agent or guardian—for example, the misuse of water funds.

Water supply and sanitation services in developing countries have a number of characteristics that make them appear highly prone to corruption, including the following:

- *Monopolistic public service providers* are associated with weak regulation; when public services fail, they are supplemented by informal, often illegal, private services, which distort sector pricing.
- *Large flows of public money* (high-cost assets) and uncoordinated donor contributions may be subject to few of the controls that would be expected in private financing. Furthermore, the sector rarely achieves full cost recovery, depends on government subsidies, and sector financing often fails to achieve its financial objectives.
- *Complexity of stakeholders' relationships* and no clear institutional leadership result in a lack of clarity of rules, regulations, roles, and responsibilities.
- *Asymmetry of information* on sector policies and procedures means there is little shared understanding of how systems work, who does what, and what the costs of water services are or should be.
- *Little accountability* in user-provider relationships means that, at best, most systems use "the long route to accountability," in which governments mediate between consumers and providers.

Many of the fundamental issues—such as low capacity, low wages, dysfunctional institutions, and large-scale procurement—are common to public service delivery. The water and sanitation sector is also part of the construction sector, globally thought to be the most corrupt of all sectors (TI 2005).

Water Sector Corruption Costs

What does water corruption cost? There is no clear answer. Hypotheses on the scope and incidence of corruption in the water and sanitation sector are largely untested, and the range appears large. An order of magnitude has been estimated at as much as 30–40 percent in "highly corrupt" countries; a path-breaking study in South Asia estimated 25–30 percent (Davis 2004). In the urban sector, if water utilities were operating in corruption-free environments, costs could be reduced by an estimated 64 percent (Estache and Kouassi 2002). If the 30 percent estimate is correct and water investment matches Millennium Development Goal (MDG) needs,[2] up to US$20 billion could be lost to corruption in the next decade.

Adding to the potential risks are the trends toward decentralization and the adoption of sectorwide approaches with weaker project controls. Many studies concentrate on bribery and direct consumer interactions and neglect to account for the types of corruption that occur higher up the value chain.

Causes of Water Sector Corruption

Klitgaard's (1998) diagnostic of corruption risk (namely, Corruption = Monopoly + Discretion − Accountability), provided in the context of municipal service delivery in Bolivia, is relevant to an understanding of the water and sanitation sector in developing countries because it highlights the aggregate effect of monopoly and discretionary power. A number of anticorruption advocates, including Klitgaard, identify four key factors that engender opportunities for corruption: monopoly power, wide discretion, weak accountability, and lack of transparency.

At the heart of the corruption problem in the water sector lies weak governance: ineffective public sector management, little political accountability, little private sector involvement, intentions to decentralize not borne out in practice, and limited engagement by civil society or the media.

Diagnosing Corruption in Water Supply and Sanitation Services

Plummer and Cross (2007) have posited a useful diagnostic model to establish a more comprehensive approach to understanding corruption in the water and sanitation sector, highlighting corrupt interactions within and between three broad stakeholders groups:

- *Public-to-public interactions*, ranging from public finance allocation distortions that favor projects that come with kickbacks, to corruption in public service management such as buying jobs or transfers
- *Public-to-private interactions*, including contract procurement and marked-up pricing or fraud in construction
- *Public-to-consumer interactions*, including "speed" money (bribes to give priority to repairs), illegal connections, or falsifying bills and meter readings.

These interactions occur along a value chain, encompassing a comprehensive framework of decisions and interactions—from high-level policy making to household payments—that differentiate between types of corrupt practice. The framework assists in identifying which corrupt practices exist in different settings, who is involved, and at what stage of water and sanitation service delivery they occur along the cycle of five sector functions:

- Policy making and regulation
- Planning, budgeting, and fiscal transfers
- Tendering and procurement
- Construction and operations
- Payment and access.

Figure 4.1 depicts a simplified version of the framework.

The current study provides an opportunity to apply the framework, and focus on interactions along the value chain, in a specific country case study and subsector. Tables 4.2, 4.3, and 4.4, later in this chapter, provide further detail on the corrupt practices typically found at each level of the value chain illustrated in figure 4.1 and identify the key issues investigated in Ethiopia. The tables formed the basis for stakeholder interviews and for discussions at the validation workshop.

Perceptions and Realities in Measuring Corruption

Corruption is difficult to measure with any reliability. Much of the literature relies on studies of *perceptions* of corruption. Although they provide an easily measurable indicator, even the best perception studies

Figure 4.1   Value Chain Framework of Corrupt Interactions in the Water and Sanitation Sector

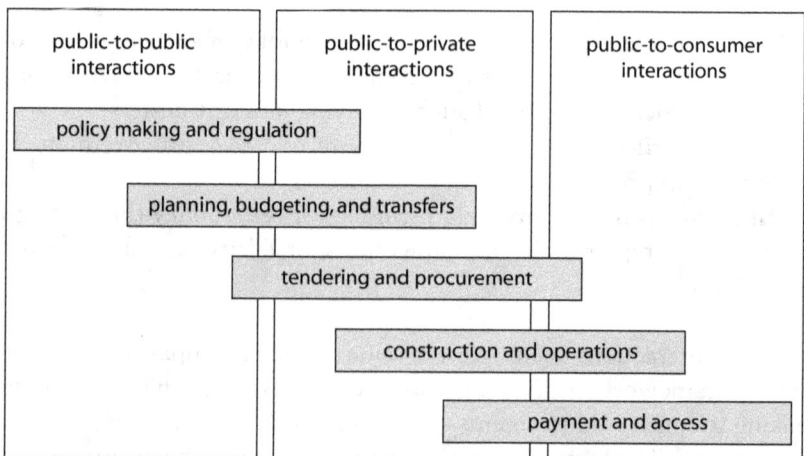

public-to-public interactions	public-to-private interactions	public-to-consumer interactions
policy making and regulation		
planning, budgeting, and transfers		
tendering and procurement		
construction and operations		
payment and access		

Source: Plummer 2008.

can be entirely misleading, especially in a sector as complex as the water sector, where there are so many different interactions and so many institutions with different perspectives and motivations. The written record is also an unreliable source on such a sensitive matter: facts and perceptions about corruption are not generally recorded, and even where they are, the facts are often in dispute, and researchers have little way of determining what is actually happening. Moreover, physical audits of exactly what was constructed are expensive and time consuming, hence rarely undertaken.

In short, to take our knowledge of the water sector forward, one priority is to document more cases of actual corrupt practice in the sector to set those cases alongside what potentially could happen. Research approaches must take into account the myriad types of interactions throughout the entire value chain of decisions made by actors at varying levels. A comprehensive approach would also study the written record; analyze the perceptions of the variety of stakeholders along the entire length of the value chain; and, where possible, investigate what was actually built as well as what monies were spent against what had been commissioned.

Ethiopia's Water Sector

Water plays a pivotal role in Ethiopian society and is an input to almost all production. Water is also a force for destruction: floods and droughts account for major swings in economic growth and significant losses of life and wealth. Unmitigated hydrological variability is estimated to cost the economy one-third of its growth potential (World Bank 2006b). Yet Ethiopia's investments to mitigate these impacts and use its considerable water assets for power, food production, livestock, manufacturing, and improvements in health and livelihoods have historically been limited.[3]

In recent years, the government of Ethiopia has recognized the scale and importance of the water challenge in Ethiopia and has embarked upon a wide range of water investment programs in the following areas:

- *Water supply and sanitation.* Priority has been given to water for human development and for livestock use, with a core focus on low-cost groundwater development for urban and rural supply. The Ministry of Water Resources (MOWR) has, over the past half-decade, led a process of studies, policy, and strategy development, resulting in much-improved sector coordination, institutional reforms, significant increases in water and sanitation coverage,[4] increased financial allocations, and the development of an ambitious plan not only to meet the water and sanitation

MDGs but also to achieve universal access to basic services in rural and urban areas. Current funding for rural water supply has, at least in nominal terms, reached the annual volumes required to meet either the MDG or UAP target, although aggregate expenditure in the subsector is only 60 percent of budget (World Bank 2009).

- *Agriculture and livestock.* Agriculture accounts for a dominant share of the Ethiopian economy (almost half of gross domestic product). Yet per capita food production has declined significantly, with roughly half the population classified as food insecure. The government's Participatory Small-Scale Irrigation Development Program plans to invest US$1.68 billion over 15 years (2002–16), substantially increasing the percentage allocated for irrigated areas. Twelve projects (adding about 259,000 hectares) are scheduled for completion by 2010, and Ethiopia's National Action Plan for Adaptation has a core focus on small-scale irrigation development to reduce dependence on rainfed agriculture. Ethiopia also has the largest livestock herd in Africa, and livestock is integral to livelihoods in highland and pastoral farming systems. Livestock use is a major driver of rural water development, especially in drought-prone regions.

- *Energy and hydropower.* Roughly 95 percent of Ethiopia's electricity generation is from hydropower. The country's economically feasible hydroelectric potential is estimated to be 100 times more than current production. With demand for energy growing rapidly, the MOWR has embarked upon an ambitious five-year development plan, with seven projects under implementation or in design, involving billions of dollars of investment.[5]

- *Emergency relief.* Water provision forms a part of the emergency response to national drought or relief programs, although drought planning continues to be dominated by food rather than broader public health or livelihood needs (Calow et al. 2010). The United Nations Children's Fund (UNICEF), supported by many NGOs, provides ongoing support to the recurring problem of drought—helping to repair critical rural supplies or trucking water to protect lives and livelihoods.

Rural Water Supply in Ethiopia

Although corruption amounts may be larger in other water domains that involve higher-value contracts, rural water supply directly affects the well-being of most of the population. In short, a corrupt transaction involving the rural water supply will have a direct or indirect impact on the poorest and largest sections of the population.

Facing extremely low access rates at the turn of the century, the MOWR embarked upon a substantial program of reforms and improvements in service development, undertaking sector studies from which they adopted a new policy frame and sector strategies. In 2001 the government adopted a water and sanitation strategy that called for the following:

- Promoting more decentralized decision making
- Promoting the involvement of all stakeholders, including the private sector
- Increasing cost recovery
- Integrating water supply, sanitation, and hygiene (WASH) promotion.

In 2005 the government announced highly ambitious targets to increase coverage in its Plan for Accelerated and Sustained Development and to End Poverty (PASDEP) for 2010. Soon afterward, it announced the UAP. The impact on the ground of these initiatives has been dramatic: in 1994 coverage was estimated at just under 15 percent, whereas the PASDEP progress report for fiscal year 2008 (based on sector administrative data) reports rural water supply coverage at 54 percent.[6]

A Framework for Progress
Within the current framework, the MOWR (and the Ministry of Health for sanitation) set national policies for rural water supply. The sector framework at the policy and strategy level seeks to incorporate several principles of good governance, including the following:

- Separating regulation from provision of services
- Decentralizing finance and management to the lowest appropriate level
- Seeking equitable access to water
- Seeking to strengthen consumer information and participation
- Making greater use of the private sector.

In October 2006 both ministries as well as the Ministry of Education signed a memorandum of understanding to define the roles and responsibilities of each.

The reforms have led to significant improvements in sector coordination and donor harmonization and alignment. The first Multi Stakeholder

Forum (MSF) in 2006 set a new standard for the sector in terms of consultation and transparency, followed by additional MSFs in December 2007 and October 2009.

Under the policy of decentralization, regional water bureaus and woreda water desks are in charge of investment planning, monitoring, and technical assistance to service providers. Although several mechanisms of financing rural water supply remain (as further discussed in the next section), the country's 700 woredas now receive block grants from the central government and can decide autonomously how to use these grants within broad criteria set by the Ministry of Finance and Economic Development (MOFED). In rural areas, community water and sanitation committees—or Water User Associations (WUAs)—operate water systems and promote sanitation, supported by woreda and regional water and sanitation government staff.

Challenges Ahead

Considering the ambition of the UAP, Ethiopia has done remarkably well in attracting finance to the sector. The combined budgeted volume of the financing modalities employed in Ethiopia (about Br 1.2 billion, or US$109 million) closely matches the government's estimated annual costs of meeting either the MDG for rural water supply (Br 900 million, US$81 million) or the UAP (Br 1.1 billion, US$99 million).[7] However, the World Bank's (2009) recent Public Finance Review added a number of caveats:

- High inflation and an increase in project costs have forced the government to revise the annual cost of implementing the UAP upward to Br 1.7 billion (US$154 million) for the 2009–12 period.
- Government and development partner support must be renewed to sustain this level of funding for rural water supply.
- Only 60 percent of budgeted finance is actually spent, with the result that funding is not being translated into an equivalent increase in service delivery.[8]

A joint technical review of rural water supply in January 2009 commended the progress made but identified the following main sector issue areas: underexpenditure, planning, capacity, procurement, and coordination at the regional and woreda levels.[9]

Table 4.1, drawn from the World Bank's (2009) recent Public Finance Review, summarizes costs and budgets for rural water supply and provides data on the types and numbers of water points that will need to be constructed or rehabilitated to meet targets.

In summary, the national rural water supply program in Ethiopia appears to be a remarkable success story. Dramatic reforms have resulted in the development of a programmatic approach, large-scale decentralization, engagement of many sector stakeholders, and significantly increased finance. Yet little is known about how robust or effective the systems are

Table 4.1   Rural Water Supply Costs, Budgets, and Investment Priorities in Ethiopia under MDG and UAP Targets

	MDG costing for RWS (2005–15)	UAP costing for RWS (2006–08 achievements in parentheses)	Adjusted UAP 2009–12 (revised 2009–12 targets)
Additional people to be served	31.8 million	50.9 million (13.5 million)	34.5 million
No. of new schemes constructed			
Hand-dug wells without hand pumps	0	70,000 (531)	32,742
Hand-dug wells with hand pumps	47,783	38,000 (8,762)	38,920
Spring protection works	16,635	14,000 (7,238)	20,845
Shallow boreholes with hand pumps	17,989	20,000 (3,339)	11,711
Deep boreholes or gravity systems with distribution	9,740	3,000 (1,750)	2,461
No. of existing schemes rehabilitated	30,701 existing schemes	maintenance of 47,397 schemes in 2 yrs.	
Program cost (birr)	Br 9.1 over 10 yrs.	Br 7.7 over 7 yrs.	Br 6.8 over 4 yrs.
Annual cost (birr)	Br 900 million	Br 1.1 B	Br 1.7 B
Annual beneficiaries	3.2 million	7.3 million (4.5 million)	8.6 million
Annual combined budget for RWS (birr)		Br 1.2[b]	
Annual combined actual spending on RWS (birr)[a]		Br 731 million[b]	

Source: World Bank 2009.
Note: MDG = Millennium Development Goal. UAP = Universal Access Program. RWS = rural water supply. The UAP aims to achieve 98 percent rural water supply coverage compared with the MDG target of 66 percent. However, investment requirements under the UAP are lower because of the focus on low-cost technologies and community financing.
a. Includes all domestic, official development, and NGO funding for rural water supply.
b. Includes an estimated Br 30 million from bilateral donors other than Finland.

in preventing corruption and enabling the national program to reach its goals. Indeed, risk factors for corruption include all of the following:

- The very speed of program development
- The extent of decentralization
- Questions about the lack of staff, experience, and skills at lower levels
- The substantially increased activity and money being invested in the sector.

Rural Water Supply Corruption in Ethiopia

Policy Making and Regulation

Corrupt practices may occur at the policy-making level within the public sector. Politicians and officials responsible for water sector policies might seek to influence the focus of policy (that determines investment priorities) to set up future opportunities for rent seeking. In turn, regulators can be bought by politicians and other stakeholders to determine standards and regulations (regulatory capture) or to allow projects to bypass established standards or procedures.

At higher levels of government, such corruption is typically opaque and complex, but distortions in the allocation of resources are achieved only by collaboration within water departments and between line departments such as financing and planning (Plummer and Cross 2007).

Risk: low to medium. The available evidence from Ethiopia, and the perceptions of water sector stakeholders, indicates that corruption risk at this level is generally low to medium. Table 4.2 summarizes the findings of the study team and the views of workshop participants on some of the key issues.

Few opportunities for rent seeking at the policy-making level appear to exist for politicians in the rural water sector in Ethiopia because funding mechanisms and prioritization are reasonably systemized, transparent, and rules-based (as discussed in further detail below). However, adherence to sector policies and strategies appears to vary by region, dependent partly on resource allocations and partly on the degree to which knowledge about sector policies and priorities filters down to lower levels of government.[10] At the regulatory level, there is good to excellent compliance.

Role of state-owned drilling companies. One potential area of concern is the position of the government-owned drilling companies favored for

Table 4.2 **Corruption Risk in Policy Making, Planning, and Budgeting in the Ethiopian Rural Water Supply Sector**

Value chain area	Typical corrupt practices in water delivery chain	Risk areas evaluated by study team in Ethiopia (RWS)	Risk ST	Risk WS
Policy making and regulation	• Policy capture (competition and monopolies) • Regulatory capture (e.g., waivers to regulations and licensing)	• Monopoly position of drilling companies (e.g., regional drilling enterprises in some areas or for some types of work) • Regulation of design and construction (standards for borehole design, evidence of overengineering, collusion between companies) • Licensing or registration practice and procedure for drilling companies (bias, selection)	Medium Low Medium	Medium Low High
Sector-level planning, budgeting, and transfers	• Distortions in decision making by politicians (affecting location and types of investments) • Corruption in national and sector planning and budget management (misuse of funds, interministerial bribery for fund allocation, collusion or bribery in selection and project approval) • Corruption in local budget management (fraud, falsification of accounts or documents) • Bribery to influence allocation of resources • Bribery in sector budgeting management (national and local) • Donor-government collusion in negotiations to meet spending or funding targets • Donor-government collusion or fraud with respect to progress and quality	• Distortions in on-budget and off-budget allocations to regions, zones, and woredas (preferential treatment, political bias) • Distortions in use of monitoring information (e.g., coverage) for political or funding ends • Link between planning and budgeting and the types of contracts used (do contracts determine the plans?) • Risk in shift to local-level procurement under decentralization (e.g., management and oversight of funds, local procurement) • Donor contribution to corrupt practices, e.g., through collusion in progress reporting or agreeing to fund moribund projects	Medium Low Medium High Low	High Low High Medium Low

Risk ☐ Low ▨ (medium) ■ High

Source: Author.

Note: RWS = rural water supply. ST = study team finding. WS = workshop finding.

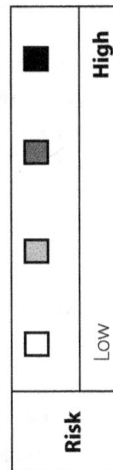

on-budget allocations. The state-owned drilling companies have their origins in an era when external aid gave drilling rigs to government, and the private sector generally was viewed with suspicion. State drilling capacity has been retained and increased, continuing to play an important role in drilling in remote locations and resettlement areas, emergency situations, and conditions deemed unsuitable for the private sector, as box 4.1 describes.

Box 4.1

An Uneasy Coexistence of State and Private Drilling?

Ethiopia's drilling industry is characterized by a mix of state, private, and NGO actors, significantly increasing financial commitments in the run-up to 2015 and rapid expansion in private sector activity, both home-grown and international (Carter et al. 2006).

- *State enterprises are often the first choice for regional bureaus contracting out borehole construction work.* They have their roots in the public authorities of the postimperial early Derg period. Six of Ethiopia's regions (Tigray, Amhara, Oromia, SNNPR, Somalia, and Afar) have enterprises engaged in borehole drilling, while some of the same regions and two others (Benishagul-Gumuz and Gambella) maintain drilling capacity within their water resource bureaus. In the past, state enterprises have received considerable support in the form of rigs and training from a number of donors, including the Japan International Cooperation Agency and UNICEF.
- *The emergence of private drilling companies is a relatively recent phenomenon.* The oldest private contractor, Hydro Construction and Engineering Co. Ltd., commenced business in Ethiopia in 1991. More recently, a number of international firms have entered the market, significantly undercutting the indigenous private sector and prompting claims from established companies that they must be taking shortcuts. There are currently around 25–30 private operators.
- *NGOs also maintain their own drilling capacity.* Others (for example, WaterAid [2008]) subcontract drilling to private or state enterprises but use their own in-house or consultant expertise for surveys, design, and supervision.

Where are the corruption risks? Although state enterprises are expected to operate in a financially viable manner without state subsidy—and to compete

(continued next page)

Box 4.1 *(continued)*

with the private sector—in reality they appear to capture work on unfair terms, often on a single-source basis. This situation may reflect the historical legacy of state control in the sector and a continuing suspicion of the private sector rather than corrupt practice *per se*. However, the opaque circumstances under which state enterprises compete or are single-sourced for bids, their higher costs, and reports that state drillers subcontract work to the private sector create conditions under which corrupt practices might emerge. That said, the private drilling companies interviewed did not identify unfair competition and corrupt practices as major issues. This response may indicate (for the moment, at least) that there is more than enough work to go around.

Sources: Authors' interviews (June 2009) and Carter 2006.

Drilling practices by these state-owned enterprises (SOEs) appears to be less efficient (incurring delays and higher economic costs) and less transparent (documentation is poorer and more difficult to access) than using private sector drillers. From a bureaucratic perspective, however, it is often easier for government officers to allocate required boreholes to government drillers because the processes are simpler and the responsibility gets transferred to another government department. Although this practice is arguably inefficient, there is little evidence to suggest there is more *corruption* in government-drilled boreholes, and oversight of all drilling operations remains at federal or regional levels.[11]

Licensing policy a barrier to entry. Licensing of drilling companies is another potential area for corruption. The current specifications require that licensees have the experienced personnel and equipment to undertake professional operations. However, some stakeholders argued that the requirements (for example, around rig ownership and not recognizing leasing) prohibit new market entrants and that the licensees are, in practice, a smallish, closed shop.

Addressing this issue would require a policy change to encourage the emergence of new drilling companies, especially indigenous companies that find it particularly hard to meet licensing criteria. Policy components might involve accepting leasing arrangements, facilitating credit, and supporting training for new Ethiopian drilling businesses.

Planning, Budgeting, and Transfers

Grand corruption—the misuse of vast amounts of public sector funds by a relatively small number of officials—is most likely to occur during the planning and budgeting processes associated with project and sector investments. Corrupt practices along this portion of the value chain may include the following (Plummer and Cross 2007):

- Favoring of large, capital-intensive works, where opportunities for bribery and rent seeking are greatest
- Manipulation of budgets, particularly where there is a disconnect between policy objectives and planning and implementation
- Corruption in local budget management (for example, fraud or falsification of accounts)
- Corruption in fund allocation and transfers (for example, through approval systems that operate between ministries and line departments).

Risk: low to medium. In poor countries, where the aid budget is a significant contributor of finance to the sector, the value chain is strongly influenced by the type of financing and conditions of use. A number of studies have highlighted the risk of corruption in donor-financed, poverty-focused projects—for example, where aid harmonization rather than spending efficiency becomes the key factor driving structural shifts in poverty reduction strategies. Indeed, the focus on budget support and alignment may provide a much greater degree of discretion, or fiduciary risk, in budget allocation and spending than traditional project-based investment.

In Ethiopia, sector-level planning, budgeting, and financial transfers have changed significantly over recent years—reflecting shifts in both government policy (particularly around decentralization and revisions to the UAP) and donor financing. Such major changes might be expected to increase the risk of corruption in sector budgeting and transfers as new systems "bed in," yet perceptions from Ethiopia indicate that corruption in these areas is viewed as generally low-risk, albeit with some variation among regions. Table 4.2 summarizes the findings of the study team and views of workshop participants about sector planning, budgeting, and fiscal transfer issues, highlighting moderate risk only in relation to local-level procurement and the use and abuse of monitoring information.

Sector planning issues. In terms of sector planning, there is a clear recognition that to meet UAP and MDG targets and to ensure sustainability, low-cost technologies that can be partially financed and maintained by local communities are preferable to high-tech options (as previously shown in table 4.1). Indeed, the revised UAP places a priority on low-cost household technologies, including self-supply, as a key means of extending water access in rural areas (MOWR 2008), although this approach is not without its critics.[12]

For rural water supply, then, low-cost, groundwater-based approaches (self-supply, shallow wells, boreholes) are recognized as the only realistic way of meeting dispersed demand across *most* areas of the country, with private sector involvement based on local artisans rather than large firms.

Budgeting and transfer-related risks. In terms of budgeting and transfers, the rural water supply sector is characterized by a range of discrete financing modalities, set against a background of political and administrative decentralization.[13] The study team therefore addressed these key questions: (a) whether the general shift toward budget support and alignment creates opportunities for the misappropriation of funds and distortion in on-budget and off-budget allocations; and (b) whether the decentralization of resources to lower levels of government, where administrative capacity is more limited, generates similar risk.

As noted above, corruption risk in both areas was assessed as generally low, albeit with some regional variation. In particular, there was broad consensus across stakeholder groups that budgeting and transfers are rules-based and reasonably transparent, with well-developed systems of monitoring and oversight, at least down to the regional level.

Specifically, on-treasury and on-budget funds managed through the government's core budget and expenditure system are allocated to regions through block grants according to a strict formula developed by MOFED and approved by the House of Federation, as further explained in box 4.2. Similarly, on-budget and on-treasury funds channeled through the new multidonor pooled fund—and ring-fenced, or earmarked, for WASH investments—are allocated to regions through a similar, formula-based approach, albeit through a parallel accounting system.[14] Remaining (bilateral) donor investment in the sector (from Finland, Italy, Japan, and the United States), and NGO investment in water projects, is generally provided directly to service providers and is therefore off-budget and

Box 4.2

The Intergovernmental Fiscal Transfer Formula: Dividing Money Fairly among Regions

A new formula for allocating the federal government's "general purpose" grants to individual regions was introduced in 2007. The new formula has three basic principles, or objectives:

- Ensure that all Ethiopians are entitled to a similar range and level of service delivery.
- Make the transfer independent of regions' tax efforts or expenditure levels (effort-neutral).
- Ensure that regions that are forced to spend more than the "standard expenditure"—for example, because of their dispersed populations or entrenched poverty—are entitled to budgetary support.

Variables included in the formula are population; differences in relative revenue-raising capacities; differences in relative expenditure needs (to meet basic needs, including water); and performance incentives. The approach strives for equal per capita distribution of grants while considering the regions' needs or capacities.

The formula has been the subject of intense negotiation. However, it has been agreed to and accepted by the regions and provides clear criteria for allocating funds.

Source: World Bank 2009.

off-treasury. Disbursement and reporting systems vary but are generally viewed as efficient and low-risk.

A subject of considerable debate is the allocation of regional block grants (through Channel 1) to lower levels of government, in particular allocations for rural water supply. Ethiopia's federal system gives regional states a high degree of autonomy over their public finances, and it is difficult to track levels of funding for different services—including rural water supply—at lower levels with precision (World Bank 2009). In practice, the discretion afforded to regions over the allocation of block grants is limited by existing commitments, capacity, and staffing levels. Public sector salaries set at the federal level absorb a major proportion of the grants: More established regions (Oromia, for example) tend to devolve more funds because they have greater local government capacity to prioritize and administer them. And some regions (the more established ones) have developed their own regional formulae for cascading funds down to zones and woredas.

A broad conclusion is that although corruption in the transfer and allocation of funds between different levels and sectors is probably minimal, there may be significant subregional variation in the transparency of budgeting, in the administration of budgets and procedures, and hence in corruption risk. In contrast, WASH funds allocated to regions and woredas through the donor trust fund (Channel 1b) are clearly ring-fenced through special accounts at each level, reducing the perceived risk of leakage to other sectors, corrupt or otherwise. The key issues here relate more to the *use* of funds (low utilization rates) than to *abuse* as well as to the potential trade-offs between procedural oversight, scheme quality, and the speed of implementation. Project-based investment, meanwhile, is also strictly controlled, albeit through a variety of different organizations and accounting arrangements.

Risks from decentralization. One policy shift highlighted as offering corruption opportunity is administrative decentralization. Although decentralization policies have devolved tasks and responsibilities down to lower levels of government, funding has not always followed. In particular, control of woreda budgets tends to remain at the regional and federal levels, with small shares transferred through block grant channels for capital expenditure. Hence, one reason why subregional corruption is viewed as low-risk is because of the small amounts of money filtering through, presenting few opportunities for the misappropriation of funds in spite of low pay and weak accounting systems.

Should there be more devolution to the woredas, or are the risks too great? Although it makes sense for woredas to plan and implement low-end technologies (for example, spring protection and self-supply) and to be funded accordingly, there are sound technical, economic, and anticorruption arguments for retaining borehole procurement at regional-zonal levels—where the core expertise exists, where economies of scale are present in the batching of contracts, and where procurement and oversight systems work reasonably well.

Needs for greater oversight and transparency. Monitoring and evaluation were also identified as weaknesses by both the study team and workshop participants, though the systems in place are arguably superior to those in many developing countries. Several priorities have a bearing on corruption risk:

- Regional inventories of infrastructure, though implemented, do not link schemes to financing modalities, making attribution impossible to verify except through field visits (World Bank 2009).
- Monitoring output data—what is being built where—is inadequate, making it difficult to know whether spending is cost-effective and whether (and where) money might be leaking. Better tracking of funds as they move along the transfer system toward water projects would reduce the risk of corruption and improve planning.
- Monitoring and information systems for assessing access to water supply and sanitation facilities were viewed as problematic, though improving.[15]

Many interviewees reported problems with "coverage inflation," or "information corruption," as one person put it. Coverage figures are routinely inflated as they pass upward from woredas to the regional and federal levels, with politicians eager to show progress against targets.[16] Whether this practice fosters real corruption is a moot point. Given that coverage inflation could lead to reduced funding under the block grant formula, the answer would appear to be "no," although the perception of corruption remains.

Design, Tendering, and Procurement

Procurement requires public-private interaction for the purchase of a wide range of goods and services, including borehole drilling and materials. For this reason, it is one of the most well-publicized and well-documented faces of corruption in the water sector (Plummer and Cross 2007). Depending on country context and project area, a number of public actors may be involved, from national to local. Private actors may include suppliers, contractors, operators, or local and national consultants. Corruption may influence the selection of contracts for services and supplies, payment schedules, profit margins, and the outcomes of the regulatory process (Plummer and Cross 2007).

In Ethiopia, the drilling sector is characterized by a mix of private operators, both national and international, and SOEs. Procurement can be carried out by government institutions (typically regional bureaus) or directly by donors and NGOs; the method depends on both financing modalities and whether the commissioning agent has in-house drilling capacity.

The tendering and procurement process for borehole drilling has undergone major changes in recent years. In particular, national procurement guidelines are now closely aligned with international or donor systems, such as those developed in the World Bank's WASH program. In addition, all public sector institutions in Ethiopia have recently been required to complete a business process reengineering plan, under which all organizations start with a clean slate in looking at ways to improve efficiency, effectiveness, and transparency.

The competitive tendering process. Well drilling financed by the Ethiopian government, UNICEF, and other United Nations agencies, including that financed through the government's Food Security and Productive Safety Nets programs, can either be competitively tendered or sole-sourced to SOEs.

Where drilling is competitively tendered, national procurement procedures are followed. Projects financed by the World Bank and the African Development Bank are always competitively tendered; those banks' procurement procedures are carried out in accordance with their respective procurement guidelines.[17]

National competitive tenders for drilling companies (consultants) follow these steps:

- The MOWR or regional water bureaus advertise bids in national newspapers. Interested bidders can either register for prequalification or, in the absence of a prequalification stage, purchase bid documents directly. A prequalification process is more common on larger bids.

- In the case of prequalification, a single expression of interest is submitted by each bidder and evaluated against preset criteria specific to the work involved. Criteria commonly include license status, prior experience of similar work, financial liquidity, and the capacity and number of drilling rigs and other equipment (vehicles, for example). Those bidders that meet prequalification criteria then receive the full tender document and are invited to submit a full bid.

- Separate technical and financial proposals (sealed) are submitted by each bidder and kept in a safe place before the advertised opening date and time. An evaluation committee then assesses the proposals in the bidders' presence, with all documents initialed by committee members. Technical proposals are evaluated first. Those bids considered substantially responsive, and that provide evidence of firm liquidity (including a financial guarantee or bid bond), are then considered for a separate financial evaluation. This two-stage "quality-quantity" evaluation is also weighted: typically the technical proposal is weighted more heavily (70–80 percent) than the financial proposal.

- Those firms that qualify for the final financial evaluation are invited to a separate meeting in which the total financial offer of each bid is read in public. The evaluation committee checks each offer—correcting for mathematical errors—to determine the lowest bid. The winning firm is then invited back, at a later stage, for final negotiation and contract signature.

Risk: low to medium. In contrast to other areas of the value chain, the stakeholders expressed no consensus on corruption risk in tendering and procurement: their views differed markedly. In particular, although serving government staff and drilling companies expressed confidence in the process—noting that the demand for drilling services is greater than available supply (reducing incentives for corruption)—other stakeholders were more critical.

Some of the most critical voices were those of ex-government staff with direct experience on evaluation committees, although their concerns may be outdated given recent changes to methods and systems. For these reasons, there was some disagreement over the risk scores assigned to different elements of the tendering and procurement process (shown in table 4.3), with the views of the study team (ST) (based on key informant interviews) contested by the validation workshop (WS) group.[18]

Box 4.3 summarizes some of the more critical observations on tendering and procurement relayed to the study team. These criticisms focus on how government officials and contractors, sometimes in tandem, can manipulate different steps in the process—from contract design to final award. That said, none of the stakeholders interviewed was able (or prepared) to cite *recent* cases of such corruption in rural water supply contract design, tendering, and procurement.

In addition, some interviewees expressed concerns about circumstances in which competitive bidding was not undertaken and about the SOEs' favored status in the process (as previously discussed in the "Policy Making and Regulation" subsection). For example, the precise circumstances under which SOEs acquire work in different regions and

Table 4.3 Corruption Risk in Contract Design, Tendering, and Procurement in the Ethiopian Rural Water Supply Sector

Value chain area	Typical corrupt practices in water delivery chain	Risk areas evaluated by study team in Ethiopia (RWS)	Risk ST	Risk WS
Contract design	• Influence on project-level decision making • Bribery for preferential treatment, elite capture • Distortionary decision making	• Program and contract design: favoring one particular contractor over another for corrupt reasons (e.g., by specifying one supplier's equipment or one contractor's rig)	□	□
		• Contract design: evidence of overengineering in design specification to generate more work for contractors or suppliers	□	▨
Tendering and procurement	• Administrative corruption (fraud, falsification of documents, silence payments) • Interdepartment or interagency collusion over procurement and construction • Bribery to influence contract or bid organization • Corruption in delegating management: fraud to over- or underestimate assets; selection, type, and award of concessions; decisions over duration, exclusivity, tariffs, subsidies • Corruption in procurement: inflated estimates for capital works, supply of chemicals, vehicles, equipment • Falsification of documents	• Tendering process: fully competitive tendering of contracts or unexplained or unwarranted exceptions	▨	□
		• Prequalification process: e.g., inconsistencies that favor a particular contractor or group of contractors	▨	□
		• Collusion in bids: e.g., decisions around which drilling companies compete for certain contracts, with payments offered or solicited	▨	□
		• Objectivity and transparency of the tender assessment process: e.g., can the process favor the wrong contractor for corrupt reasons?	▨	□
		• Contract award: potential for extortion by government officials from contractors (e.g., winning contractor asked to pay bribe to guarantee award)	▨	□

Risk

□	▨	▨	■
Low			High

Source: Author.

Note: RWS = rural water supply. ST = study team finding. WS = workshop finding.

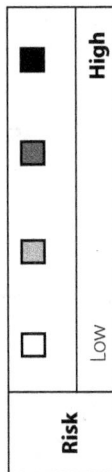

Box 4.3

Contract Design, Tendering, and Procurement: Corruption Risk Examples

Some interviewees cited examples of corrupt practices in contract design, tendering, and procurement, as summarized below.

- *Favoritism in design specs.* Preparation of design specifications may favor one company, or group of companies, over another. For example, if the tender includes the drilling of both shallow boreholes and deeper ones, only those companies with higher-capacity rigs would be able to compete. Similarly, tenders may require contractors to meet specific requirements in terms of equipment, personnel, and experience. Such preconditions may be entirely legitimate, but some interviewees noted that they can also be used to skew contracts unfairly to favored firms.
- *Spurious items or activities in the design specification.* For example, the tender may include activities that favored firms would know are unnecessary, such as a requirement to carry out five-day pumping tests on each borehole. Such activities might add considerably to costs, yet those close to the evaluation process would enter artificially low costs, or no costs at all, for this line item to undercut less-knowledgeable bidders.
- *Conflicts of interest in the selection of evaluation committee members.* For example, a regional bureau head may be serving on a committee evaluating a tender in which the regional (state) drilling company is competing (bureau heads usually chair or are board members of state-owned drilling companies).
- *Arbitrary exclusion of bids on spurious technical or licensing grounds.* Such exclusion of bids might cite criteria that are introduced only during the evaluation process.
- *Interference in the bidding process.* For example, a senior politician dictates the type of process to be followed (such as single-source or preselection) or directly determines the outcome.
- *Collusion among contractors to rig the bidding process.* For example, firms agree among themselves which tenders to bid for to reduce competition and inflate prices.
- *Use of "contract variations" to extend the work of a contracted company beyond the original contract.* For example, company X could be requested to complete a further 50 boreholes in area Y on the back of an existing contract, without the need for another tender.

through different financing modalities remains opaque; however, most of the private drilling companies questioned were sanguine on this matter, highlighting the sheer volume of work that all parties must carry out to meet the UAP target. Box 4.4 provides a more comprehensive summary of the drilling companies' views.

Box 4.4

The Drillers' Take on Corruption Risk

The views of 10 private drilling companies interviewed before the validation workshop are summarized in box figures 4.4.1 and 4.4.2, including views on the licensing process and on supervision and sign-off procedures for borehole construction and approval.

Box Figure 4.4.1   Corruption Risks Identified by Drilling Contractors in the Ethiopian Water Sector

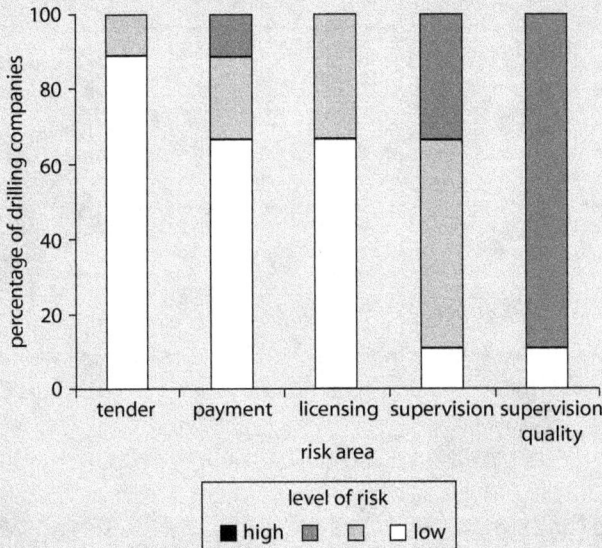

Source: Author.
Note: "Tender" refers to the tendering and procurement process. "Payment" refers to final payment for completed work. "Licensing" refers to the licensing procedure for drilling companies. "Supervision" relates to corrupt practices in on-site supervision and sign-off by government staff. "Supervision quality" refers to (noncorrupt) failures in on-site supervision (for example, officials' failure to arrive on site at agreed-upon time and poor technical knowledge of supervising officials).

(continued next page)

Box 4.4 (continued)

Box Figure 4.4.2   Corruption Risks Identified by Drilling Contractors in the Ethiopian Water Sector

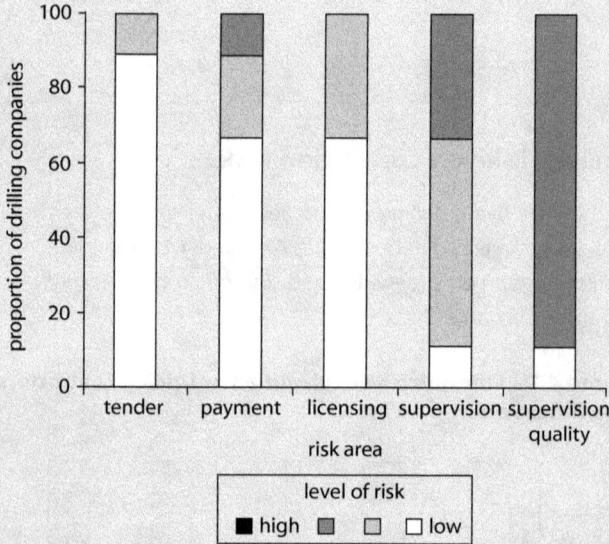

Source: Author.

Note: "Tender" refers to the tendering and procurement process. "Payment" refers to final payment for completed work. "Licensing" refers to the licensing procedure for drilling companies. "Supervision" relates to corrupt practices in on-site supervision and sign-off by government staff. "Supervision quality" refers to (noncorrupt) failures in on-site supervision (for example, officials' failure to arrive on site at agreed-upon time and poor technical knowledge of supervising officials).

Nine of the 10 contractors interviewed stated that corruption in tendering and procurement was not a problem, again citing the volume of work available and the low incentive for corrupt practice. However, the contractors were less enthusiastic about field supervision and sign-off by zonal and regional officials, highlighting delays in approval and noting that small bribes were occasionally offered or solicited. Several also remarked on delays in payment following contract completion and invoice approval as well as the need to "speed things along" occasionally with small payments or large lunches.

Construction and Payment: The Borehole Story

After the contracts are awarded, corruption can also be prevalent in the construction of infrastructure and in final invoicing for work completed—or not completed. In construction, bribery and fraud resembles that found in other parts of the construction industry: contractors may fail to build to specification, concealing substandard work and materials or paying officials to ignore it. Or oversight officials may demand payments to ignore instances where specifications are not adhered to. Fraudulent invoicing and documentation is another common problem.

Such practices help contractors to minimize costs and increase profit, but the outcome may be poor-quality work that affects the reliability and quality of services. Poor quality may be visible, as in the case of a dam or community tap, or it may be invisible absent a physical audit. Groundwater development is a case in point: A contractor that drills a shallow borehole and then claims payment for a deeper one, or who installs substandard materials inside the borehole and claims otherwise, can "hide" bad practice beneath the ground. Corruption then becomes difficult to detect.

In Ethiopia, groundwater development to meet dispersed rural demand underpins the UAP. Yet despite massive (and accelerating) investment in borehole drilling (as shown previously in table 4.1), little is known about corruption in drilling and water point construction. Could this be a serious problem, or is this part of the value chain reasonably clean?

The evaluation approach. To answer this question, the study team carried out a study of 26 boreholes in Oromia and SNNPR in tandem with water point interviews. The study had two main elements:

- *A postconstruction technical investigation,* using down-the-borehole CCTV equipment to assess what had actually been constructed. Findings were then compared with contract specifications, borehole completion reports, and final invoices to ascertain whether (a) what was actually built matched the design specification; and (b) what was claimed, or invoiced, matched what was actually built. In addition, data on borehole construction costs were analyzed to identify areas where major savings could potentially be made through corrupt practices.

- *A village survey,* including (a) the collection of basic information on village characteristics; (b) an assessment of the community development process in relation to water point planning and management; and (c) a simple assessment of borehole performance in terms of functionality, water availability, and water quality. In addition, a perception survey gauged community views about the location, design, and construction of the borehole to see whether community perceptions around construction standards and outcomes correlated with the technical results.

Ball (2009) provides further survey details. In summary, the postconstruction survey focused on shallow boreholes of up to 60m depth equipped with a hand pump. In Ethiopia, these are called shallow wells. Although the sample was small, site selection was designed to capture a range of different drilling contractors (private, state, and NGO); funding channels (Channels 1, 2, and 3); and funding sources (government, donor, and NGO). Selection was carried out by the study team alone, independent of the government.[19]

At each site, a CCTV camera was used to inspect the materials installed in the borehole and to measure its depth. Information on contract specifications, well completion reports, and invoices was collected from clients and drilling companies. Village and perception surveys were based on water-point interviews with community key informants and user groups.

Key findings.
Corruption risk: Analyzing the costs of borehole construction. To better understand the potential for corrupt practices in borehole construction, it is first necessary to understand the major costs involved and hence the opportunities for corrupt practice.

In Ethiopia, as elsewhere, costs are incurred in (a) mobilizing a drilling team and rig to site; (b) drilling the borehole itself; and (c) equipping the borehole with a pump and the materials needed to make it work effectively and prevent contamination. These materials include casing to prevent the sides of the borehole from collapsing, a slotted screen to allow water to enter the borehole, and grout to prevent contamination from the surface (see figure 4.2).

Drawing on cost data collected from drilling contracts and invoices in the current study, the average costs of drilling a shallow borehole of less than 60m depth were approximately US$3,700, excluding hand pump installation and taxes. This cost is similar to the average cost to construct shallow boreholes in Nigeria estimated recently by UNICEF (Adekile and Olabode 2009) and in other African countries (Foster, Tuinhof, and Garduno 2008), although international comparisons should be treated with caution.[20] For shallow boreholes, drilling is the most significant cost.

Figure 4.2   Typical Borehole Construction in Ethiopia

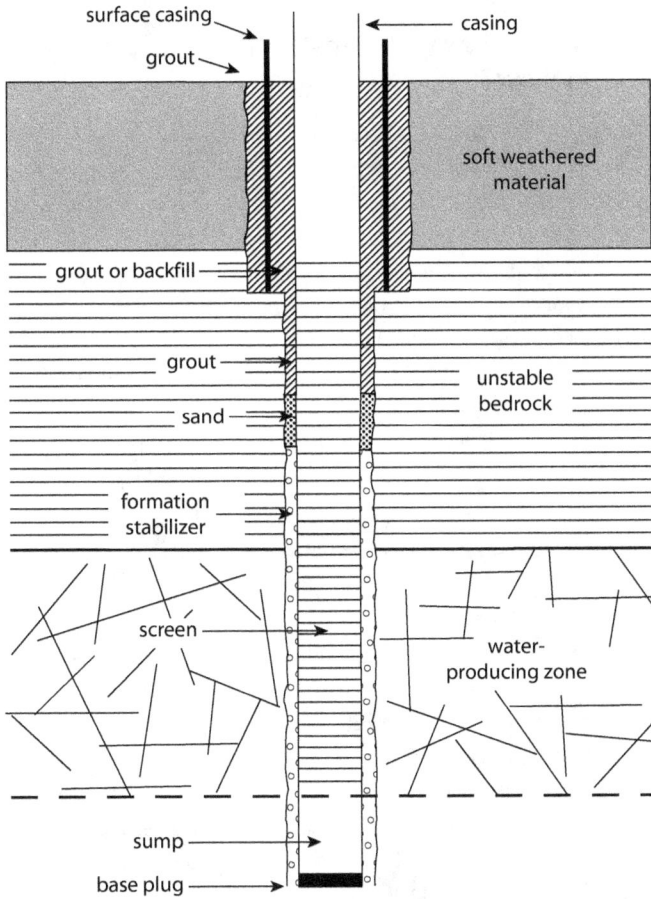

Source: Ball 2009.

For this reason, the most likely corrupt practice in the construction process is to drill short, as box 4.5 explains.

Risk: low to medium. The available evidence from Ethiopia, and the perceptions of water sector stakeholders, indicates that corruption risk at this level is generally low to medium. Table 4.4 summarizes the findings of the study team and the views of workshop participants on some of the key issues.

Survey results, summarized in the annex, were also discussed with workshop participants in Addis Ababa (as specified in table 4.4). In

Box 4.5

The Costs of Shallow Well Construction: Where Are the Corruption Risks?

An analysis of invoiced costs for the boreholes in this study indicates that drilling costs make up roughly half the total cost of a shallow borehole, with total costs varying between US$2,700 to US$4,800 per borehole (excluding hand pump installation and taxes, both minor costs). These numbers are similar to those found in other African countries. For example, a recent study of borehole costs across Nigeria found median costs per shallow borehole (< 50 meters [m]) of approximately US$5,000 (Adekile and Olabode 2009), although costs of around US$120 per meter are not unusual for shallow boreholes in Africa (Ball 2004; Foster, Tuinhof, and Garduno 2008).

Deeper boreholes, drilled at a larger diameter and equipped with motorized pumps, cost considerably more. The two deeper boreholes included in the current survey cost US$12,000 and US$20,000 for depths of 99 m and 174 m, respectively, before pump installation and taxes. This falls within the cost range reported by the Carter et al. (2006) for deep boreholes in Ethiopia. This type of borehole is rarely used for rural water supply in other areas of Africa, so cost comparisons are difficult. However, Adekile and Olabode (2009) quote similar numbers for deep boreholes in Nigeria, with costs of US$18,000–$26,000 for boreholes of 100–150 m depth.

The particular hydrogeology of Ethiopia makes deeper boreholes successful: similar boreholes would fail over much of the continent. In addition, a culture of deep borehole drilling in Ethiopia, even in circumstances where shallow boreholes would be successful, means that deep boreholes are often preferred. Box figure 4.5.1 provides a detailed breakdown of costs based on survey data collected for the present study.

Drawing on the data for shallow boreholes, it is clear that the easiest way of saving money is to drill short. However, given that in Ethiopia a supervising hydrogeologist must, in theory, sign off on every borehole, such a scheme would require collusion between supervisor and driller. A further option would be to drill a borehole of narrower diameter than specified, although this would save less money. However, if the supervisor at does not identify the too-narrow drilling at the time, it would be difficult to identify later if the correct-diameter screens and casings were then installed.

In terms of materials, shallow wells are generally equipped with unplasticized polyvinyl chloride (uPVC) screens and casing (as seen in the cost breakdown in

(continued next page)

Box 4.5 *(continued)*

Box Figure 4.5.1   Cost Breakdown for Shallow and Deep Boreholes in Ethiopia

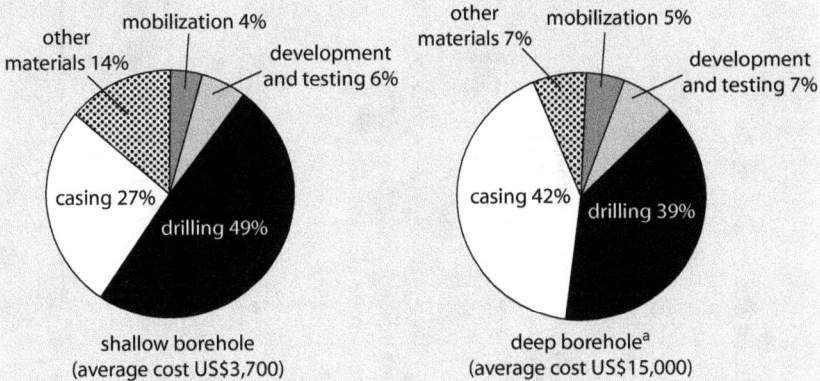

shallow borehole
(average cost US$3,700)

other materials 14%
mobilization 4%
development and testing 6%
casing 27%
drilling 49%

deep borehole[a]
(average cost US$15,000)

other materials 7%
mobilization 5%
development and testing 7%
casing 42%
drilling 39%

a. Only two deep boreholes in sample

box figure 4.5.1). This material is already some of the cheapest available (at US$15 per meter), so substitution to save money is unlikely. Other materials used in the construction of the borehole, such as washed river gravel and grout, are insignificant costwise but essential for the reliability of the borehole and to ensure a safe seal from contamination. If these materials are omitted, it is unlikely to happen on cost (and hence corruption) grounds. A likelier explanation would involve poor management in getting the materials to the site on time for construction.

What conclusions can be drawn? For shallow wells, the most likely corrupt practice during construction is to drill short. This would allow significant savings in both drilling costs and casing material. For example, drilling to 50 m instead of 60 m would save roughly 13 percent of contracted cost, amounting to $15,000 on a contract for 30 boreholes using the cost data above. For deeper boreholes (over 60 m), although drilling short would still be the most effective way of saving money, the cost of materials is more significant.

contrast to discussions about tendering and procurement, there was broad consensus in the workshop around corruption risks in borehole construction, which validated the findings of the construction and perception surveys. In particular, areas of elevated (albeit low-to-medium) risk focused on substandard construction and, related to this, weaknesses

Table 4.4 Corruption Risk in Borehole Construction and Payment in the Ethiopian Rural Water Supply Sector

Value chain area	Typical corrupt practices in water delivery chain	Risk areas evaluated by study team in Ethiopia (RWS)	Risk ST	Risk WS
Construction and payment	• Corruption in construction: bribery and fraud, including (a) not building to specification; (b) concealing substandard work or materials; and (c) failure to complete works or underpayment of workers • Fraudulent invoicing: marked-up pricing, overbilling by suppliers • Corruption in community-based construction (with practices similar to public-private interactions)	• Contractor failure to build the specified number of boreholes	□	□
		• Failure to build boreholes to specification: substandard construction (e.g., not drilling to required depth, not constructing to required width, not using required quantities of equipment or materials, using substandard equipment or materials, and so on)	■ (dark)	■ (High)
		• Fraudulent claims for variations to the contract (e.g., claimed payment for adverse site conditions when the conditions were OK)	▨	□
		• Collusion between contractor and site engineer to issue an extension of time or variation, with the result that the contractor gets additional payment and shares it with the site engineer	▨	□
		• Bribery by contractor of site engineer to overlook construction or performance defects		■ (dark)
		• Extortion of payments by government officials from contractors (e.g., for approving completion reports and invoices)	■ (dark)	■ (dark)
		• Preferential treatment or bribery in borehole siting decisions	□	□

Risk: □ Low ▨ ■ ■ High

Source: Author.

Note: RWS = rural water supply. ST = study team finding. WS = workshop finding.

in oversight and sign-off procedures. Nonetheless, participants high-lighted the need for a larger survey to strengthen the evidence base and the need for accurate (GPS) recording of borehole locations to ensure that inspection evidence can be linked with complete confidence to contract and invoicing documentation.

Corruption evidence: Comparing contracts, construction, and invoices. Contracts for borehole drilling in Ethiopia typically specify the depth to which boreholes should be drilled, their diameter, the likely drilling con-ditions, and the casing material to be used.[21] Often the type of drilling rig is also specified (as previously discussed in the "Design, Tendering, and Procurement" subsection). Typically, the responsibility for siting bore-holes, supervising drilling operations, and authorizing payment for com-pleted works rests with the regional water bureau.

The subsections below look briefly at how contract specifications com-pare with what was actually built (based on evidence provided by CCTV footage) and what was finally invoiced by the driller and paid for by the commissioning agency. Box 4.6 summarizes overall variance (measured versus invoiced) in the sample, focusing on three cost-weighted indica-tors: borehole depth, diameter, and materials. In addition, we look at the relationship between construction variance (as above), community par-ticipation in water-point implementation, and community perceptions of construction quality.

Variation between contracted specification and drilled depth. A borehole had been constructed at each of the locations the study team identi-fied for inspection. For the 16 boreholes where an estimated depth had been specified in a contract, few (25 percent) were within 10 percent of the target: most were both measured *and* invoiced for less depth.

Given that measured depths, completion reports, and invoices for this group were consistent, the most likely reason for the discrepancy was that sufficient water was found at shallower depths and the supervisor sug-gested that drilling should cease before the target depth had been reached, saving time and money. This conclusion is supported by Carter et al. (2006), which found that reported completion depths in a survey of rural water supply boreholes across 14 zones in Ethiopia were often 10–20 percent lower than in the design specification, largely because tenders erred on the side of caution.

Box 4.6

Calculating Total Variance in Borehole Construction

To estimate total measured versus invoiced variance in borehole construction, three key indicators of construction standard (depth, diameter, and materials) were weighted and then combined to give an overall measure of variance. The weights assigned to each indicator were based on their relative costs, drawing on the cost data for shallow boreholes previously discussed in box 4.5.

Three scenarios were used to construct weights: (a) drilling short by 50 percent; (b) using cheap casing of 50 percent of the invoiced value; and (c) drilling a narrow diameter borehole wide enough to install casing but too narrow to accommodate gravel pack. These scenarios and cost figures give the following weights: drilling short has the highest weight (60 percent), diameter (15 percent), and materials (25 percent).

What results does this calculation produce for the current sample? The cost-weighted approach to measuring the construction-invoicing difference indicates that *10 percent of the boreholes have high variance that is likely to be caused by corrupt practices.* A further *20 percent have moderate variance* that may be the result of corruption and deliberate short-drilling but could also be caused by poor construction.

Extrapolating beyond the current survey to look at the overall investment in shallow boreholes needed to meet UAP targets (as previously shown in table 4.1), these results would imply that 2,000–6,000 shallow boreholes (10–30 percent of the 20,000 required) could be compromised over the next three years of the plan period. Using the cost breakdown previously presented in box 4.5, and assuming that each compromised borehole is drilled to 50m instead of 60 m, corruption costs attributable to short-drilling could run between US$1 million and US$3 million. However, given the small sample size of the study and difficulties confirming with absolute certainty the identities of all boreholes, such projections are tentative.

Variation between drilled and invoiced depth. However, the results presented in the annex, table 4A.1, also indicate that for a significant minority of boreholes (some 35 percent), the actual measured depth was 10 percent less than that reported in the completion document and claimed in the invoice.

Figure 4.3 indicates that, for two boreholes, the difference was particularly large but that there was also a cluster of boreholes where the variance was 10–25 percent. For the entire sample, the total variance of

Figure 4.3   Measured versus Invoiced Depths in Sample Boreholes in Ethiopia

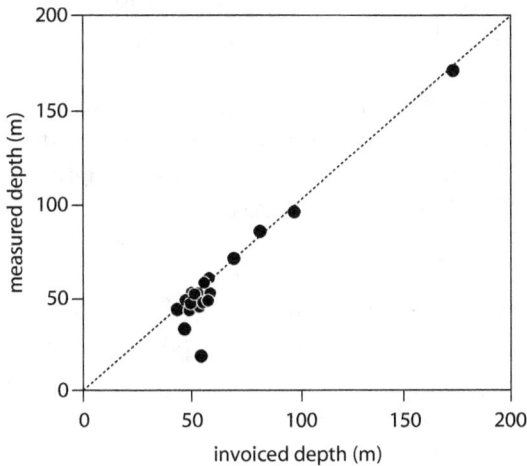

measured depth versus invoiced depth was 18 percent. Much of the variance is accounted for by one agency: an indigenous NGO using its own drilling rig, contracted by the regional water bureau.

It is conceivable that such "overshallow" boreholes have, in fact, silted up because of poor construction or difficult geological conditions. However, other observations point toward deliberate short-drilling, at least for two boreholes where both screen and pump were installed at a much shallower depth than reported in the completion certificate. For the remaining boreholes where measured depth was within 15 percent of the invoiced amount, it is more difficult to attribute variance to deliberate short-drilling and corruption.

Variation in borehole diameter and materials. CCTV was also used to check whether the borehole casing had been installed. However, the process of removing the pump and rising main created significant turbidity in the borehole water, making it difficult to evaluate construction standards in detail. Instead, an attempt was made to merely observe whether casing was present above the water table. In addition, it was not always possible to measure the total length of screen in the borehole. However, because uPVC screen and casing are similar in price in Ethiopia, drillers are unlikely to economize on (normally more expensive) screen by substituting casing.

It was only possible to measure the diameter of the installed screen and casing, not the drilled diameter. In all cases, the diameter of the screen and casing was as recorded on the invoice.

Borehole outcomes: construction variance and borehole performance. Might corrupt practices in borehole construction affect the quantity, quality, and reliability of water supply? To shed light on this question, community interviewees were asked a series of questions around (a) borehole functionality, (b) seasonal variation in water availability, and (c) the perceived quality of water, including turbidity and perceived "healthiness." Responses were summarized, ranked, and equally weighted to generate the scores (shown in annex table 4A.1) and then compared with the scores for overall construction variance (measured versus invoiced), as discussed in box 4.6. Figure 4.4 shows the results.

Six of the boreholes were reported as performing poorly. Interestingly, there is an observable relationship between borehole performance and variance in borehole construction, suggesting that substandard construction has a negative impact on borehole performance, even though all of the boreholes surveyed were less than three years old.

Figure 4.4   Relationship between Construction Variance and Borehole Performance in Ethiopia

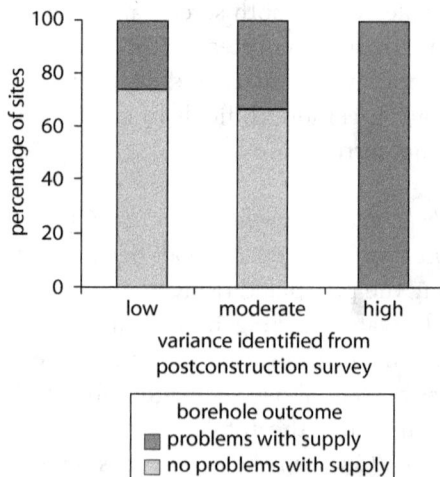

Note: "Construction variance" refers to differences between actual and invoiced construction measures. The "borehole outcome" ranking combines indicators of borehole functionality, water availability, and water quality.

Community perceptions of borehole design and construction. Villagers were also asked questions about the borehole construction process to highlight any corrupt practices around (a) site selection, (b) borehole drilling and construction, and (c) borehole payment. Several conclusions can be drawn:

- *The site selection process was regarded as fair*, with no reports of siting "bias" that might favor, for example, more influential or wealthier households. In all cases, respondents stated that siting had been carried out by "an outside expert" (a technician from the water bureau) and that drillers simply drilled at the specified location, with no input from community members.

- *Villagers had no involvement in the construction process itself*, except in one instance where villagers contributed labor to help move materials.[22] As one villager put it, "We know nothing about drilling boreholes. The drillers came, did their work, and then left." As a result, villagers had no firm views on the quality of the drilling process specifically and hence on whether the boreholes had been correctly drilled and equipped. However, some villagers did have strong views on the design and construction quality of visible headworks. Perhaps surprisingly, most criticism came from villages where community participation in project design and implementation was rated highly by the survey team (roughly half of the villages), suggesting that where communities are treated as active development partners, people are more likely to raise concerns about the quality and design of their water points, although not about the *drilling* process. Box 4.7 provides further details about the community discussions.

- *Village interviewees were adamant that no payments in cash, labor, or materials occurred between drillers and communities* except in the one instance noted above. Interviewees were unanimously clear that the drilling teams were accountable to external agencies (government or NGO) rather than to the village or the village water committee and were therefore paid by others. In most villages, community members had offered drilling teams food, drink, and in some instances shelter. In all instances, this hospitality was offered rather than solicited.

Local Management and Payment Systems

Corruption that directly involves communities and households includes situations where a householder or community leader acts as a bribe

Box 4.7

Borehole Design and Construction: What Role for Community Oversight?

Discussions with community members indicate that they have little knowledge of, let alone input into, the borehole drilling process. In most villages, the arrival of a drilling team on site is the first indication that a new water point has been planned. Drilling teams then work independently, with community support restricted to offering hospitality.

Communities did, however, express views on the quality of the headworks constructed by the drilling teams, at least in those villages where community members had been actively involved in water point planning and management (where the "development process" was rated highly). Box figure 4.7.1 shows how overall perceptions of construction quality, determined largely by views on headworks, relate to the quality of the development process followed in each village.

Box figure 4.7.2 shows a positive correlation between the construction quality of headworks rated by the survey team and community perceptions of (overall) construction quality.

Box Figure 4.7.1   Perceptions of Ethiopian Water Point Construction Quality and Community Involvement in Project Design and Management

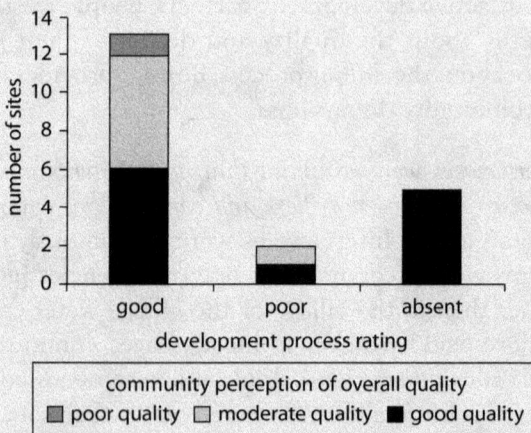

(continued next page)

Box 4.7 *(continued)*

Box Figure 4.7.2   Community Perceptions of Headworks Construction and Actual Construction Variance

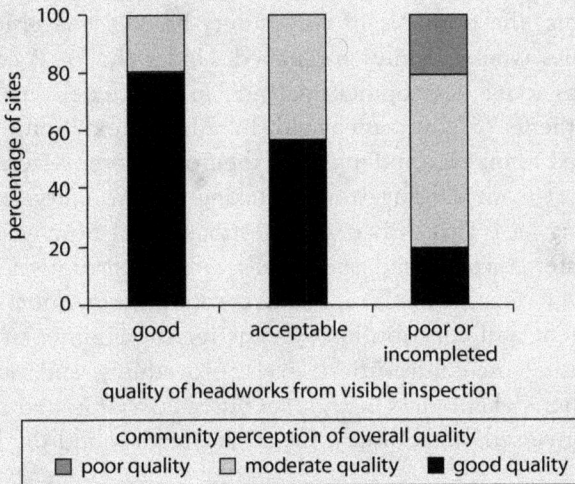

Note: "Construction variance" refers to differences between actual and invoiced construction measures.

A general conclusion is that although communities may have strong and well-informed views on the "nondrilling," lower-cost elements of borehole construction—particularly where they have been actively involved in a project—these views do not provide a robust indicator of corrupt practice in higher-cost drilling.

giver—bribing officials to gain access to water, or water infrastructure, that might otherwise go to another village or household. Such community or household corruption might also include the embezzlement of funds by committee members in charge of collecting money for an operation and maintenance (O&M) fund or nepotism in the selection of committee members to secure kickbacks and bribes.

Evidence from rural development projects and governance assessments, within and outside the water sector, suggests that this type of petty corruption can be significant because many small transactions gradually mount up for a household or village (Plummer 2007). Moreover, broader policy shifts toward cost recovery and user financing raise the stakes: under cost-sharing arrangements, the poor are paying for leakages caused by corruption throughout the system in the form of higher (absolute) contribution levels and higher bribes to secure (more costly) access to water (Plummer 2007).

In Ethiopia, the principle of community-based management of rural water supplies is now firmly entrenched. Under the UAP, communities are viewed as active development partners in service delivery rather than passive recipients of government aid. In this context, communities are now expected to manage and maintain their own water systems following initial support from the government, taking responsibility for collecting and managing fees. This shift raises questions about how well local contribution systems work—and, specifically, around corruption risk.

The survey team therefore asked community members questions about payment and contribution systems for the maintenance of water points, focusing on contribution levels, procedures, and outcomes. In addition, other stakeholders in regional bureaus, NGOs, and donor agencies were canvassed. In summary, the survey team found the following:

- In all of the villages surveyed, water and sanitation committees had been established. However, the quality of the mobilization and management process differed markedly. Only in those projects funded by the World Bank WASH program or implemented by NGOs were expressions of demand for improved supplies actively sought by project-implementing agencies in the form of up-front contributions to capital costs, the opening of a bank account, and the formation of committees prior to borehole construction.

- In those villages where the development process was rated highly (WASH program and NGO), contribution systems appeared to be much more robust and rules-based. That said, none of the users interviewed during the course of the survey voiced concerns about the embezzlement of fees (typically amounting to Br 1 to Br 2 per month per household) by those responsible for collection, banking, and spending. In each village, contributions were collected and periodically banked.

- In contrast, interviews conducted with those outside the community identified embezzlement of funds and "interference" in user group formation as serious issues. Examples of corrupt practices cited included

(a) interference in the selection of committee members by powerful village members; (b) nomination of noncommittee members for training; (c) failure to bank all of the money collected from users; and (d) unauthorized withdrawal and theft of funds by committee members. Interference in committee selection and hence training has a financial implication because those attending courses receive an allowance.

A general conclusion is that although our survey did not highlight evidence of corrupt practice in local payment systems,[23] there are clear risks—particularly in larger schemes, where banks are distant, where money is left in the care of individuals for long periods of time, and where woreda officials find it difficult to keep tabs on community-held funds. Partly as a response to these risks, civil society organizations have lobbied government to grant WUAs legal status through a Proclamation on the Establishment of Rural Water Users' Associations (see box 4.8), under a task force coordinated by the MOWR. One of the key aims is to reduce the risk of local, village-level corruption.

Box 4.8

Proclamation on the Establishment of Rural Water Users' Associations

Although household contributions to local O&M funds are small (Br 1 to Br 2 per month), combined funds can quickly add up. A village of 500 households, for example, would contribute Br 6,000 to Br 12,000 over the course of a year. Funds should be deposited regularly in a bank account, but where banks are difficult to reach, cash is often kept in the house of a committee member. Moreover, although woreda officials are supposed to authorize the opening of a WUA bank account and are responsible for investigating any reports of misuse, the job is a difficult one, especially when there are repeated changes in committee membership. Over time, woreda oversight becomes weaker.

NGOs that work with communities on a long-term basis are more aware than most of the opportunities that local oversight creates for the misappropriation of funds. One NGO staff member interviewed reported how a committee member had disappeared with more than Br 15,000 from a large village project—a major

(continued next page)

Box 4.8 *(continued)*

setback for both the NGO and the community. In 2005, three NGOs actively involved in the promotion of community management of water supplies commissioned a report on the legal aspects of WUA formation and management, arguing that legal status would help prevent the mismanagement of funds because money collected from community members would no longer be in the care of individuals but held in the name of a legal entity.

In 2006, a consultative and validation workshop was held by the NGOs, the MOWR, regional water bureaus, and other stakeholders to discuss the issue. A national task force was set up under the authority of the minister, and a consultant was hired to prepare a generic proclamation and implementation guideline. The proclamation is currently being adapted and adopted in a number of different regions.

Sources: Study team interviews and RiPPLE 2008.

Summary and Recommendations

In view of the scale of investment required in rural water supply in Ethiopia and its importance in reducing poverty, ensuring that service delivery is efficient, corruption-free, and reaches the poor is a clear priority. The risks are potentially high: internationally, the water sector is viewed as "high-risk" for corruption because of the financial flows involved, weak government oversight, and significant public-private interactions. In Ethiopia (as elsewhere), however, there is little concrete evidence of specific risks or about the effectiveness of different interventions that might reduce those risks.

To address this gap, the current study has reviewed both evidence and perceptions of corruption in the provision of rural water supply in Ethiopia through a mix of field surveys and interviews with sector stakeholders. The study has drawn on a framework that helps focus on corruption, in various forms, through a value chain, with the aim of identifying risk points and mitigation measures.

One of the study's major conclusions, broadly speaking, is that Ethiopia has made significant strides in policy development, financing, governance, and management, resulting in *generally low levels of corruption and perceptions of corruption along the value chain*. That said, the study has also highlighted a number of vulnerable areas, particularly at the lower (procurement and construction) end of the value chain, and stakeholder perceptions vary in some instances. Moreover, given Ethiopia's experience with decentralization, there may be significant *regional* variation in corruption risk.

The 10 recommendations below—focused on how to reduce risks and strengthen accountabilities—are aimed primarily at federal and regional governments.

Policy Making and Regulation

Available evidence—and the perceptions of government, donor, civil society, and private sector stakeholders—indicates that corruption risk in the policy and regulation area of the value chain is low. For example, few opportunities for rent seeking at the policy-making level appear to exist for politicians because funding mechanisms and prioritization are systematized, reasonably transparent, and rules-based. Nonetheless, it is clear that knowledge of and adherence to sector policies vary by region: established regions such as Oromia enjoy a better reputation for good governance and low corruption (at this and other levels of the value chain) than others.

Sector stakeholders identified three particular areas of concern:

- The privileged position of state-owned drilling enterprises in borehole construction
- Licensing procedures for private drilling companies
- The cost-effectiveness of drilling operations generally.

In each case, however, concerns relate more to governance and efficiency than to corruption per se. State drilling capacity has been retained and strengthened, providing government with capacity to operate in remote areas or emergencies when risks may be too high for private contractors. Nonetheless, SOEs are also engaged in routine drilling works, and in some instances reportedly subcontract surplus work to the private sector. The circumstances under which SOEs bid for work or are sole-sourced (and subcontract to others) remain somewhat opaque, creating the perception (at least for some stakeholders) of malpractice.

Recommendation 1: *Clarify the position of SOEs and restrict their operations to high-risk situations.*

The position of regional drilling enterprises in the drilling market requires clarification. In particular—to reduce perceptions of malpractice or unfair competition and to increase confidence in tendering and procurement more generally—the federal government should clarify the circumstances and procedures for contracting SOEs. In a competitive market with many different drilling companies, the role of an SOE should be as a "driller of last resort."

Concerns about licensing focus on generating healthy competition and competitive pricing in the drilling sector. An argument by some stakeholders was that the current (onerous) licensing requirements are prohibitive for new entrants to the market, in effect creating a smallish, closed shop in which SOEs inflate the costs.

Recommendation 2: *Lower the entry barriers for private contractors.*

A relaxation in current licensing requirements would encourage new entrants into the market (particularly from within Ethiopia) and encourage greater competition. Measures could include accepting leasing arrangements (rather than outright ownership) for rigs and trucks and facilitating credit for start-up enterprises.

Recommendation 3: *Commission an independent study of the efficiency and effectiveness of state-owned drilling companies.*

The study should include a detailed breakdown and analysis of drilling costs for both shallow and deep boreholes under different contracts and in different areas.

Planning, Budgeting, and Transfers

There have been major changes in sector planning, budgeting, and transfers in Ethiopia over recent years, but both evidence and perceptions suggest that the corruption risk in these areas is generally low. With respect to planning, for example, low-cost technologies that can be part-financed and maintained by local communities are favored under the UAP, recognizing the need to adapt service delivery choices to the circumstances of the poor instead of to, say, the "big-project, high-tech" wishes of contractors.

In terms of sector budgeting and fiscal transfers, the shift toward general budget support and decentralization does not appear to have created new or significant forms of corruption. For example, the allocation of block grants is transparent and formula-based; the growing multidonor pooled fund is similarly disbursed (and in this case ring-fenced) according to strict criteria; and the remaining off-budget, project-based investment appears to be tightly controlled, albeit through a variety of different organizations and accounting procedures.

What of political and administrative decentralization? Does this carry the risk of devolving money and power to tiers of government where oversight and accountability remain weak? A conclusion from our study is that although it makes sense for woredas to support self-supply and other low-end technologies (spring protection, for example), there are sound reasons for retaining borehole planning and procurement at regional or zonal levels, in part to reduce corruption risk.

Recommendation 4: *Retain borehole planning and procurement responsibilities at regional or zonal levels.*

Decentralization policy raises the question of which tasks and responsibilities should be retained and which should be devolved. There are sound technical, economic, and anticorruption-related arguments for retaining borehole planning and procurement at regional or zonal levels. This is where core expertise exists, where economies of scale can be found in the "batching" of contracts, and where government oversight and supervision probably work best, albeit with some reservations, as specified below.

Recommendation 5: *Improve the quality and accessibility of monitoring data about rural water supply investment, infrastructure, and functionality.*

One area that sector stakeholders singled out for attention was weak monitoring and evaluation, which includes several elements:

- Infrastructure inventories do not link schemes to financing modalities, making attribution difficult.
- Infrastructure inventories themselves are inadequate or fragmented among different stakeholders at different levels, making it difficult to know what has been built where. (One of the major obstacles faced in the postconstruction survey was compiling information on boreholes—from initial contract documents to site locations and final completion reports).
- Information systems for monitoring access to water—beyond theoretical coverage—remain inadequate despite being vital to support planning and to guide the allocation of funds. Significant distortions in the reporting of access to water occur at different levels of government, leading to perceptions of corruption as figures are inflated for political ends.

Taken together, these weaknesses are perceived as contributors to corruption risk by making it difficult (for government and for donors) to link investment with infrastructure and outcomes. Efforts under way to roll out a national WASH inventory should go some way toward addressing these problems.

In contrast to many developing countries, monitoring and information systems for tracking spending and progress in rural water supply at least exist in Ethiopia. However, their quality and accessibility could be significantly improved. In particular, there is an urgent need to compile accurate inventories of rural water supply (and sanitation) infrastructure funded through different channels and to increase confidence (and reduce *perceptions* of corruption) in coverage data.

Tendering and Procurement

In contrast to other areas of the value chain, there was no general consensus among stakeholders about corruption risk in tendering and procurement. In particular, although serving government staff and drilling companies expressed confidence in the process—noting that the sheer demand for drilling services makes corruption rather pointless—other stakeholders were more critical. That said, none of the stakeholders interviewed was able or prepared to cite recent cases of corruption in the rural water supply sector—although examples of how the process *could* be manipulated were readily provided. A tentative conclusion is that recent changes in process and procedure have reduced opportunities for corrupt practice and that the current demand for drilling services, coupled with a reasonably competitive drilling market, also mitigates risk, though perceptions vary.

Where are the remaining vulnerabilities, and how could they be addressed? A key finding from the study is that tendering and procurement records are not easy to find and check. In theory, information should be available from the regional bureaus that commission, oversee, and approve work. Regional and zonal bureaus should also compile and use well completion reports, not only as a check on what has been built and where but also to inform future contract design. In practice, records are sometimes incomplete or lodged with different levels of government, and archived data are lost or inaccessible.

Recommendation 6: *Strengthen record-keeping procedures in regional and zonal bureaus, providing clear guidelines for the compilation and use of well completion reports and contract information.*

Regional and zonal water bureaus responsible for commissioning, overseeing, and approving borehole construction should compile and maintain complete file copies of contracts, design specifications, completion reports, and invoices. Drilling contractors should submit well completion reports (including the GPS coordinates of completed boreholes) to bureaus as a matter of routine and as a prerequisite for payment.

Recommendation 7: *Increase the transparency of the tendering and procurement process through a public disclosure program.*

A broader point concerns transparency and access to the information compiled on tendering and procurement. To date, efforts to curb corruption in this area have been largely prescriptive—establishing better rules and procedures for tendering and bid evaluation, for example. However, steps can also be taken to increase the transparency of tendering and procurement, creating opportunities for public scrutiny of tender documentation, evaluation reports, overall costs, and unit rates. Experience from other countries indicates that greater transparency and access to information can change the behavior of public officials and private contractors, increase the probability of detection, and generate *demand* for accountability.

Information relating to the tendering process and outcomes should be made available for public scrutiny. There are various ways of doing this, and lessons can be learned from the experience in other countries. One approach would be to present records online through a contracts portal on the ministry website.

Construction, Operation, and Payment

The postconstruction technical and perception surveys conducted for this study have proved useful in identifying corrupt practices in borehole construction. The cost-weighted comparison of design specifications, measured construction parameters, and invoices indicates *probable* corrupt practice in 10 percent of the sample through short-drilling. A further 20 percent showed moderate variance that *could* be caused by deliberate short-drilling but could also result from other factors. Most boreholes— the remaining 70 percent of the sample—had been properly constructed and were functioning well. Although international comparisons should be treated with caution and data are limited, the costs of borehole construction (albeit from a small sample) *appear* comparable with those found in other African countries.

Extrapolating beyond the current survey to look at the total number of shallow drinking-water boreholes needed to meet UAP targets, this finding would imply that 2,000–6,000 shallow boreholes could be compromised over the next three years. Using sample cost data, and assuming each compromised borehole is drilled to 50 m instead of 60 m, corruption costs attributable to short-drilling of could total between US$1 million and US$3 million. There may be other costs, too: survey results suggest that corrupt practices in construction affect borehole performance and hence people's access to improved water supplies. Projections should be treated with caution, however, because the sample size was small and the identity of some village boreholes (and hence links to contracts, borehole logs, and invoices) could not be confirmed with complete confidence in the absence of GPS coordinates.

Beneath the headline numbers, what key conclusions and recommendations emerge from the borehole story? To begin with, the study highlights the importance of understanding borehole construction costs as a means of identifying likely corrupt practice. Our analysis of borehole costs indicates that the most likely corrupt practice during the construction of *shallow* boreholes is to drill short, generating significant savings in both drilling and materials. Depth can be measured with the CCTV equipment used for the current study, but it could also be measured using a simple measuring line by government staff or by communities themselves. For *deeper* boreholes (those > 60 m) the cost of materials is more significant, and use of CCTV would be the only way of assessing both depth and the correct use of casing and screen.

Recommendation 8: *Adopt the survey approach piloted in this study to monitor, and improve, construction standards in borehole drilling and to deter future corruption.*

For shallow boreholes, the critical indicator of corrupt practice is drilled depth; this can be measured in a number of ways. For deeper boreholes, it is more important to use CCTV equipment to assess both depth and the use and quality of materials. In both cases, spot checks on construction, as well as the announcement that checks might be made, could provide a powerful means of reducing corruption risk.

Recommendation 9: *Strengthen on-site supervision of drilling contractors by government personnel.*

We note that procedures are already in place for monitoring construction standards through on-site supervision of contractors by regional or zonal hydrogeologists. However, staff members are few in number and often hard pressed to monitor the numbers of boreholes being constructed in rural areas.

Appropriate monitoring can be achieved by increasing of the number of regional and zonal staff assigned to monitoring duties and by ensuring they receive the training necessary to spot deliberate malpractice with respect to short-drilling and use of substandard materials.

Recommendation 10: *Strengthen community oversight and monitoring of headwork construction in parallel with government supervision of drilling.*

Finally, study findings suggest that community perceptions of construction are determined largely by the quality of borehole headworks, at least in those villages where communities have been actively involved in project planning and management. However, perceptions alone do not provide a robust indicator of corrupt practice in drilling—the part of construction that is most vulnerable to corruption but that community members know least about.

For this reason, we conclude that the potential for community oversight of construction as a means of reducing corruption risk is limited but that opportunities do exist for improving accountability in the design and quality of headworks. The most effective way of achieving this is to ensure that communities can make informed choices about the pump they want and about any additional water uses (such as for livestock) that need to be factored into final design.

It is good practice to ensure that communities have a say in the design of surface headworks and, where feasible, in the siting of a borehole. However, although community monitoring may improve project outcomes, it is unlikely to affect corrupt *drilling* practices. Community oversight of drilling is unrealistic; this should remain a government responsibility.

Annex 4.1 Ethiopian RWS Borehole Study and Perception Survey Results

Table 4A.1 Summary of Ethiopian RWS Borehole Construction Variance Study and Perception Survey Results

	Site information		Depth information			Variance				Final scores			
Site	Woreda	Driller	Suggested depth in specification (meters)	Actual depth from survey (meters)	Depth invoiced (meters)	Depth invoiced compared to actual depth (percentage)	Actual depth compared to specified depth (percentage)	Material type invoiced compared to actual	Diameter invoiced compared to actual (percentage)	Post-construction survey variance[a]	Borehole outcomes[b]	community perception of construction standards[c]	community perception of community development process[d]
0	Omo Nada	Private driller	70	70.0	70	0	0	L	0	low			
1	Omo Nada	Private driller	60								excellent	good	poor
2	Sokoro	Private driller	60	52.5	60	15	-13	L	0	low	excellent	good	poor
3	Kersa	Regional enterprise		146.0		3			0	low		moderate	good
4	Amaya	NGO	60	18.5	55	197	-69	M	0	high	problems	good	good
5	Amaya	Private driller	50	52.0	60	15	4	L	0	low	problems	good	good
6	Amaya	NGO	60	44.8	54	21	-25	L	0	moderate	excellent	good	poor
7	Amaya	Private driller		47.4	57	20		L	0	moderate	problems	good	good
8	Nanno										failing	moderate	good
9	Goru	Private driller	60	58.0	57	-2	-3	L	0	low	excellent	poor	good
10	Amaya	NGO	60	32.4	47	45	-46	L	0	high	problems	good	poor
11	Amaya	NGO	60	42.9	50	17	-29	L	0	moderate	excellent	good	good
12	Amaya	Private driller	50	52.3	54	3	5	L	0	low	problems	moderate	good

No.	Location	Provider											
13	Goru	Private Driller	60	46.5	50	8	−23	L	0	low	excellent	moderate	good
14	Goru	Private Driller	60	51.5	53	3	−14	L	0	low	excellent	moderate	good
15	Goru	Private Driller	60	47.6	60	26	−21	L	0	moderate	excellent	moderate	good
16	Shebedino	Regional Enterprise		53.0	52	−2		L	0	low	problems	good	
17	Shebedino	Private Driller		121.5						low			
18	Shebedino	Regional Enterprise		42.7	44	3		L	0	low	excellent	good	moderate
19	Dale	Private Driller	150	95.0	99	4	−37	L	0	low		good	
20	Dale			50.4						low	problems	good	
21	Dale	Private Driller	150	145+	174	5	10	L	0	low		good	
22	Gedebe	Regional Enterprise		48.4	49	1		L	0	low	excellent	good	good
23	Abeshgehu	Private Driller	70	60.6	60	−1	−13	L	0	low	excellent	moderate	moderate
24	Abeshgehu	Private Driller	70	84.1	83	−2	20	L	0	low	excellent	moderate	
25	Abeshgehu	Private Driller									excellent	moderate	poor

Source: xxxxx

Note: RWS = rural water supply. NGO = nongovernmental organization.

a. Score based on a weight of depth, diameter, and materials variance of 60%, 15%, and 25% respectively, according to cost.

b. Score based on even weight of answers to survey questions on functionality, seasonal quantity, and quality (turbidity) of water.

c. Score based on even weight of answers to questions on borehole location, construction, and payment.

d. Score based on even weight of answers to questions on community participation, management arrangements, and contributions.

Notes

1. The provision of basic drinking water is of direct relevance to the rural poor. However, an assessment of corruption risk in hydropower, irrigation, and urban water supply—where contract values are higher—was beyond the purview of the current study.

2. The Millennium Development Goal for water is to halve those without access by 2015.

3. Grey and Sadoff (2007), citing a World Bank study (2006b), highlight two key challenges: First, Ethiopia lacks the water resources infrastructure and institutions to mitigate hydrological variability directly. For example, Ethiopia has less than 1 percent of the reservoir storage capacity per capita of North America to buffer its hydrological variability. Second, it lacks the market infrastructure that might help mitigate the economic impacts of variability by facilitating agricultural trade between affected and unaffected areas.

4. Between 2002 and 2005, total access to potable water increased from 30 percent to 42 percent.

5. The Gilgel Gibe III hydroelectric dam, Ethiopia's largest infrastructure project to date, will more than double the country's electricity generation capacity, provide much-needed water storage, and reduce flooding in downstream areas. However, the US$2 billion dam has attracted significant controversy over its environmental and social impacts as well as the procedures followed by the African Development Bank in assessing them.

6. Estimates from other sources also show considerable gains, though the level of increase is more modest: the WHO-UNICEF Joint Monitoring Program (JMP) (2008) reports that 31 percent of the rural population use water from improved sources (protected wells and springs or piped systems) as their main source of drinking water. (Government figures are based on theoretical access, regardless of functionality; WHO-JMP figures measure actual use of improved sources.)

7. The effective exchange rate is that used in the World Bank Public Finance Review (2009): US$1 = Br 11.06.

8. The Public Finance Review (World Bank 2009) singles out for blame the parallel accounting systems imposed by financial partners, noting that modalities with low annual utilization rates (as low as 27 percent for African Development Bank projects) had set up parallel procedures that centralized control of decentralized service delivery, particularly for accounting and procurement.

9. See JTR 2008.

10. Lack of knowledge about federal policies at lower levels of government is a widely acknowledged problem.

11. Although decentralization is giving lower tiers of government new rights and responsibilities, government policy also takes into account the economies of scale present in tendering higher levels of technology to higher levels of government. Hence for borehole drilling, where it makes sense to batch or package contracts rather than tender one at a time, regional and zonal staff will retain contracting and oversight responsibilities (World Bank 2009).

12. The criticisms relate to both the technology itself and the government's motives in promoting it. Concerns around the former relate to water quality and reliability from sources regarded as "unprotected" (WHO-UNICEF 2008) and more sensitive to variations in rainfall. Hence some have argued that that the government's primary motive in promoting self-supply relates to cost and speed rather than provision of *secure* water.

13. Government and donor funding for rural water supply flows through three channels: *Channel 1* is "on-budget" and "on-treasury," with funds allocated through the government's core budget and expenditure system (through MOFED and the regional [Bureaus of Financial and Economic Development] and woreda [Woreda Offices of Finance and Economic Development] offices of finance and economic development) and allocated to regions through block grants. *Channel 2* funds are made available direct to the MOWR and transferred down through line departments. As such, they are on-budget but off-treasury. *Channel 3* resources are allocated directly to implementers and service providers, with funding from some bilateral donors and NGOs. These funds are therefore off-budget and off-treasury. A new channel (*Channel 1b*) has recently been created to pool donor and government funds for sectorwide WASH. This money is managed by the finance ministry and bureaus (and is therefore on-budget and on-treasury) through a cascade of special accounts at federal, regional, and woreda levels.

14. Supplementary to sector-specific funding, the Ministry of Agriculture and Rural Development manages two related special-purpose grants through its Food Security Commission: the Food Security Program and the Productive Safety Nets Program. These are managed outside the core government budget and expenditure management system through Channel 2. Because these programs are intended to smooth household income fluctuations through "food for work" and other activities, they do not focus on borehole drilling and were not examined in detail by the study team.

15. Draft guidelines for national WASH monitoring and evaluation were published and discussed at the October 2009 multistakeholder forum.

16. In SNNPR, for example, data on access to WASH services has been highly contested because of differences between aggregated results at the regional level and variations in underlying woreda and zonal data. Disputes have arisen between some woredas and zones about the level of water supply coverage, creating difficulties in budget allocation. The regional water bureau in SNNPR has now established a task force to generate a consistent dataset.

17. "Guidelines on Procurement under IBRD Loans and IDA Credits" (May 2004, revised 2006) and "Guidelines for Selection and Employment of Consultants by World Bank Borrowers" (2004, updated 2006).

18. The workshop group that was asked to validate the study team's findings was dominated by serving government staff.

19. Sample size was restricted to 26 boreholes, although CCTV measurement was limited to 23 boreholes, and invoices *and* CCTV measurements could be obtained for only 20 boreholes. The sample was limited because (a) gathering the background information needed (namely, contract documents, well completion reports, and invoices) to identify sites and evaluate performance proved difficult, with the data fragmented among drilling companies, regional and zonal bureaus, and NGOs; (b) finding sites in the field was not always easy without global positioning system (GPS) coordinates; and (c) preparing each borehole for CCTV filming was time-consuming. In particular, the hand pump and rising main had to be removed before the camera could be lowered down the borehole. The process could take up to one day depending on distance traveled and technical difficulty. The survey focused on shallow boreholes equipped with hand pumps rather than deeper boreholes. This focus reflects the importance of shallow wells to the UAP target (see table 4.1) and the need to pilot the CCTV survey method at shallower depths.

20. Drilling costs in India, for example, are typically less than one-tenth of those in Sub-Saharan Africa, but there may be good reasons for such differences (distances involved, the state of road networks, drilling conditions, and so on). Hence Carter (2006) cautions against simplistic international comparisons.

21. Contracts are not employed for drilling programs when drilling is commissioned and conducted by one of the state-owned drilling enterprises or when an NGO drills boreholes with its own rig. In the current survey, four boreholes commissioned and drilled by regional enterprises were not formally contracted.

22. In this village, the drilling team reportedly asked village elders to organize help with the transport of materials and equipment to the borehole site on the understanding that labor would be paid. However, the drilling team left without making any payments. None of the contracts or invoices viewed by the survey team included provision for local (contractor to village) payments.

23. In each of the surveyed villages, discussions on contribution systems for water-point operation and maintenance were held with committee members and ordinary water users. Although malpractice was not reported, comprehensive checks on local accounts were not possible in the time available.

References

Adekile, D., and O. Olabode. 2009. "Study of Public and Private Borehole Drilling in Nigeria." Final report for the WASH (Water, Sanitation, and Hygiene) Section, United Nations Children's Fund (UNICEF) Nigeria, Abuja.

Ball, D. 2009. "Ethiopia: CCTV Well Field Review 2009." Report CR/09/080 for the British Geological Survey, Keyworth, Nottingham, U.K.

Ball, P. 2004. "Solutions for Reducing Borehole Costs in Rural Africa." Water and Sanitation Program, Rural Water Supply Network (RWSN) and SKAT Foundation Field Note, RWSN, St. Gallen, Switzerland.

Calow, R. C., A. M. MacDonald, A. L. Nicol, and N. S. Robins. 2010. "Ground Water Security and Drought in Africa: Linking Availability, Access, and Demand." *Ground Water* 48 (2): 246–56.

Campos, J. Edgardo, and Sanjay Pradhan, eds. 2007. *The Many Faces of Corruption: Tracking Vulnerabilities at the Sector Level.* Washington, DC: World Bank.

Carter, R. 2006. "Ten-Step Guide Toward Cost-Effective Boreholes: Case Study of Drilling Costs in Ethiopia." Rural Water Supply Series Field Note, Water and Sanitation Program, Rural Water Supply Network, St. Gallen, Switzerland.

Carter, R. C. H., Desta, B Etsegenet, B. Eyob, D. Eyob, N Yetnayet, M. Belete, and K. Danert. 2006. "Drilling for Water in Ethiopia: A Country Case Study by the Cost-Effective Boreholes Flagship of the Rural Water Supply Network." Final Report, Volume 1—Main Report of the Water and Sanitation Program, World Bank, Washington, DC; Rural Water Supply Network, St. Gallen, Switzerland; and Ethiopian Ministry of Water Resources, Addis Ababa.

Davis, J. 2004. "Corruption in Public Service Delivery: Experience from South Asia's Water and Sanitation Sector." *World Development* 32 (1): 53–71.

Estache, A., and E. Kouassi. 2002. "Sector Organisation, Governance, and the Inefficiency of African Water Utilities." Policy Research Working Paper 2890, World Bank, Washington, DC.

Foster, S. S. D., A. Tuinhof, and H. Garduno. 2008. "Groundwater in Sub-Saharan Africa: A Strategic Overview of Development Issues." In *Applied Groundwater Studies in Africa: IAH Special Publications in Hydrogeology, volume 13*, ed. S. Adelana and A. M. MacDonald, 9–21. Leiden, Netherlands: CRC Press.

Grey, D., and C. W. Sadoff. 2007. "Sink or Swim? Water Security for Growth and Development." *Water Policy* 9 (6): 547–71.

Halpern, J., C. Kenny, E. Dickson, D. Ehrhardt, and C. Oliver. 2008. "Deterring Corruption and Improving Governance in the Urban Water Supply & Sanitation Sector: A Sourcebook." Water Working Note 18, World Bank, Washington, DC.

JTR (Joint Technical Review). 2008. "Joint Technical Review Report and Agreed Actions." Submission discussed and agreed at June 27, World Bank, Washington, DC.

Klitgaard, R. 1998. *Controlling Corruption*. Berkeley: University of California Press.

Kolstad, I. 2005. "Direct Budget Support and Corruption." U4 Issue 1, U4 Anti-Corruption Resource Centre, Chr. Michelsen Institute, Bergen, Norway.

MacDonald, A. J. Davies, R. Calow, and J. Chilton, J. 2005. *Developing Groundwater: A Guide for Rural Water Supply*. Rugby, U.K.: Practical Action Publishing.

MOWR (Ministry of Water Resources). 2008. "Reformulation of Strategies and Plans for an Accelerated Implementation of the UAP for Rural Water Supply." Draft of Main Report, Volume 1, by the Task Force for UAP Review, Government of Ethiopia, Ministry of Water Resources, Addis Ababa.

Plummer, J. 2007. "Making Anti-Corruption Approaches Work for the Poor: Issues for Consideration in the Development of Pro-Poor Anti-Corruption Strategies in Water Services and Irrigation." Report 22, Swedish Water House, SIWI (Stockholm International Water Institute), and WIN (Water Integrity Network), Stockholm.

Plummer, J., and P. Cross. 2007. "Tackling Corruption in the Water and Sanitation Sector in Africa: Starting the Dialogue." In *The Many Faces of Corruption: Tracking Vulnerabilities at the Sector Level Campos*, ed. J. E. Campos and S. Pradhan, 221–63. Washington, DC: World Bank.

RiPPLE (Research-inspired Policy and Practice Learning in Ethiopia and the Nile Region). 2008. "Policy Engagement Strategy for the RiPPLE Research Program Consortium." Draft report, Addis Ababa.

Rose-Ackerman, S. 1999. "Corruption and Government: Causes., Consequences, and Reform." New York: Cambridge University Press.

TI (Transparency International). 2005. *Global Corruption Report 2005: Corruption in Construction and Post-Conflict Reconstruction*. Cambridge: Cambridge University Press.

———. 2008. *Global Corruption Report 2008: Corruption in the Water Sector*. Cambridge: Cambridge University Press.

WHO and UNICEF (World Health Organization and the United Nations Children's Fund). 2008. "Progress on Drinking Water and Sanitation 2008: Special Focus on Sanitation." Update report of the Joint Monitoring Program for Water Supply and Sanitation, UNICEF, New York, and WHO, Geneva.

Woodhouse, A. 2002. "Combating Corruption in Indonesia: Enhancing Accountability for Development." East Asia Poverty Reduction and Economic Management Unit, World Bank, Washington, DC.

World Bank. 2006. "Ethiopia: Managing Water Resources to Maximise Sustainable Growth." A Country Water Resources Assistance Strategy report, World Bank, Washington DC.

———. 2009. "Ethiopia Public Finance Review." Report 50278-ET, Poverty Reduction and Economic Management Unit, Africa Region, World Bank, Washington, DC.

CHAPTER 5

Justice Sector Corruption in Ethiopia

Linn A. Hammergren

Introduction

This study explores the incidence of corruption in Ethiopia's justice sector (including not only the courts but also several other organizations). Within the institutions covered here—or, indeed, within the sector more broadly defined—corruption usually has a far lower monetary value than it does in other sectors. Moreover, except in extreme cases, corrupt practice directly threatens public well-being less often. Nonetheless, corruption in the justice sector is important because it undermines the peaceful resolution of conflicts, the control of corruption in other sectors, the strengthening of the normative framework underlying private and public actions (the rule of law), and the creation of a predictable environment for public and private transactions.

The World Bank and the government of Ethiopia agreed to include justice in the overall exercise presented in this book to better understand

---

Although this chapter results from studies completed by January 2010, the process of checking, reviewing, and securing agreement for publication was finally brought to conclusion only in late 2011. The chapter is therefore put forward with the caveat that while it reflects the situation at the time of the study, some details will have understandably changed.

the nature and extent of corruption and political interference in sector operations. Although no country completely avoids these two ills (both treated here as "corruption" writ large), the available information on expert evaluations and public perceptions shows that countries do differ markedly concerning the *extent* of justice sector corruption and the form it takes.

In developed countries, corruption is less widespread than in many developing nations and usually takes the form of individual rather than organized malfeasance. In developing regions, corruption is often systemic, orchestrated, and frequently linked to political interference whereby political elites assert control over the sector agencies to influence decisions and actions; guarantee immunity for themselves and their allies; and, if less typically, partake of the monetary rewards. The lack, or weakness, of internal control systems in many of these countries also encourages higher levels of individual corruption.

This report begins from an agnostic standpoint—attempting only to document reality in Ethiopia's justice sector and to compare it, where possible, with the situation elsewhere in African and other countries where sector corruption is believed to be rampant.

Methodology

As in the sector studies elsewhere in this volume, research for the justice sector study examined corruption risks along a value chain, depicting the usual forms of justice system corruption with information on the Ethiopian situation derived from informant interviews (including a short structured questionnaire; focus groups; data analysis; and a review of relevant documents including studies, some surveys, official publications, and laws).

The research methodology relied heavily on informant interviews, covering some 60 individuals in Addis Ababa and Bahir Dar (capital of the Amhara region) and thus focusing on the federal system and one of the country's nine regions. Respondents were drawn nearly equally from among judges, prosecutors, police, private attorneys, nongovernmental organizations (NGOs), donors, and an "other" category comprising specialized staff and members of other organizations.

The interviewees did not include ordinary citizens with no special exposure to the sector. However, efforts (not always successful) to get information about complaints filed with relevant offices were intended to tap, at least partially, citizen reactions to the justice system. Aside from those offices' inability to provide detailed information, reviewers suggested that certain cultural constraints ("Ethiopians do not complain") might have interfered with this approach.

The interviews were supplemented with two formal and two informal focus groups. The latter used "windows of opportunity"—when other workers spontaneously joined interviews conducted with one of their colleagues. A structured questionnaire (of eight questions) was also used in the informant interviews and focus groups, but because respondents were not picked randomly, the questionnaire has no statistical significance and was used simply to track the dominant trends in the informants' answers for entry into the value chain.

A further impediment was that many respondents felt they could not answer questions that required experience they lacked (for example, how bribe amounts were determined or what happened in other organizations). Nonetheless, this "impediment," like the lack of information on citizen perceptions, may also have been an advantage because it eliminated answers based only on impressions and conventional wisdom.

Overview of Findings

The results—indicating where corruption was most or least common (or nonexistent)—can hardly be considered definitive given (a) the dependence on "knowledgeable actors'" perceptions and willingness to recount them; (b) the considerable disagreement among the roughly 60 persons interviewed individually and in focus groups; and (c) the fieldwork's limitation to the federal system and that of one more-developed region (Amhara).

Nonetheless, the following generalizations can be forwarded:

- Sector corruption appears less extensive in Ethiopia than in many African or Latin American countries. Although personnel management has some problematic aspects, one major conclusion is that justice sector positions are not purchased, thus eliminating an incentive often found elsewhere.
- Corruption, where it occurs, takes one of two forms: (a) political interference with the independent actions of courts or other sector agencies, or (b) payment or solicitation of bribes or other considerations to alter a decision or action.
- An ongoing modernization program, which is most advanced in the courts, has eliminated or sharply reduced some forms of corruption common elsewhere (such as petty bribes to perform normal duties).

- Other types of bribes are uncommon (though some would disagree) and relatively small, and political intervention appears to be decreasing (though some informants contend that political loyalty has reemerged as an important consideration in personnel actions).
- The most common form of corruption involves bribes solicited by or offered to police to ignore a criminal offense, not make an arrest, or not bring witnesses or suspects to court (which can cause a provisional adjournment of the case). Traffic police are the worst offenders.
- A second reputedly common form of corruption—payment of court staff to misplace case files or evidence—has nearly disappeared because of new judicial policies on archive management introduced under a Canadian International Development Agency program (FJA 2005).
- Although no one denied their existence, study participants disagreed about the frequency of (a) sales of judgments or other judicial actions in civil disputes; (b) lawyers' solicitation of "bribes" that never reached the bench; (c) prosecutors' misuse of their own powers, in response to bribes or political directives, to advance or paralyze a case; and (d) the corrupt actions of various officials entrusted with enforcement of judgments, especially in civil cases.
- The lack of consensus and the likely gap between perceptions and reality are partly a function of the persistent lack of transparency in personnel policies and the focus of sector modernization programs on other objectives (such as efficiency and increasing access). Internal mechanisms (complaints and disciplinary offices) also suffer weaknesses, and sensitivity about corruption (in this and other sectors) may be discouraging agencies from attacking it more directly and openly.

Overview of Recommendations

Both to decrease the perception-reality gap and to attack the problems that really exist, the following actions are recommended (in addition to more study on procurement and budgeting issues and institutions [traditional mechanisms, social and sharia courts] not covered here):

- *Greater accessibility and transparency.* The agencies' complaint-handling and disciplinary offices as well as the anticorruption commissions should become more accessible (through decentralization and more-predictable hours). They also need better databases on their own actions and should consider publicizing their reasons for not pursuing vaguely presented complaints.

- *More proactive approaches*. These same offices might fight corruption more proactively instead of waiting for complaints to be filed. Automated databases and further analysis could identify emerging problems, problematic actors, and areas requiring more citizen education. Agencies, including the ethics and anticorruption commissions, should develop more explicit strategies to address issues. Having proved they can investigate and prosecute corruption once it is reported, they must now create stronger disincentives by organizing their own inspections.
- *Greater clarity on personnel policies*. Especially in the courts, which receive the most criticism here, personnel policy reform is long overdue. As the courts are already considering, recruitment should be advertised, candidates should be ranked on explicit criteria, and lists of final nominees should be published before their appointments. The same is true of transfers and promotions.
- *Better self-policing by the bar*. Independent bar associations should be encouraged to police their own members instead of relying only on the ministry and bureaus of justice for this role. In the best of worlds, the bar associations would also be invited to evaluate judges and prosecutors.
- *Improvement of internal performance monitoring systems*. To combat corruption and improve performance, the police and prosecutors need to improve their internal monitoring systems along the lines of the judiciary's case management system (CMS).
- *Greater admission of the problem overall*. All agencies should admit that corruption remains a problem, if not a major one, and give it the same emphasis as other goals. Understandably, the courts do not want to admit any degree of corruption, thus possibly subjecting themselves to outside interference. However, admitting a problem while outlining a program to resolve it indicates that an agency is on top of the matter.

Chapter Structure

The next sections provide the broad context for the sector study: background about the Ethiopian justice sector and a discussion of the importance and usual types of corruption that affect the justice value chain. Further analysis follows in three parts:

- "Corruption and Intervention in Ethiopia's Justice Sector," which relates the study's findings in the context of the value chain
- "Conclusions on Justice Sector Corruption in Ethiopia," a comparative analysis in light of other country studies and the perspectives of participants interviewed for this study

- "Recommendations," which details the research-based approaches for improving the situation.

In addition, some initial caveats are in order: First, the next section—an introductory discussion of the justice system and forms of corruption therein—is necessarily long because many readers may not be familiar with the sector and thus need explanatory guidance.

Second, because field research was limited to courts on the federal level and in only one of Ethiopia's nine regions, conclusions about the incidence (and thus impact) of corruption in the sector are necessarily partial. As knowledgeable reviewers have suggested, the situation may be quite different and far more negative in Ethiopia's less-developed regions. However, because documentation on notoriously corrupt countries is also often limited to their more-developed regions, a comparative evaluation is not unreasonable. Still, for a more thorough picture, future studies might focus on Ethiopia's other regions as well as on some specific topics and institutions beyond the scope of the present study.

The Justice Sector and Corruption Defined

Although the justice sector can be defined broadly—as those formal and informal institutions involved in the rule-based resolution of disputes and the authoritative application of sanctions to rule violators—the focus here is only on the courts, prosecutors, police, and private attorneys, thus omitting some admittedly widely used mechanisms such as traditional dispute resolution, sharia, and social courts.

What constitutes a justice sector remains a matter of debate. It clearly is more than the courts and, broadly construed, it would include

- a host of core governmental agencies and actors (courts, police, prosecutors, administrative agencies with quasi-judicial powers, and public and private attorneys[1]);
- certain formal institutions that support their work (credit bureaus, registries, notaries, bar associations, prisons, and those in the executive and legislative branches responsible for enacting the laws and regulations governing their operations); and
- informal or customary bodies that carry out similar rule-based dispute resolution and sanctioning of rule violators (the term "rule" being used as opposed to "law" to include norms other than state-sanctioned laws used by alternative bodies[2]).

This study uses a more limited definition, focusing only on the courts, prosecutors, police, and private attorneys.[3] (Public defenders were not surveyed because there are few of them in Ethiopia.) At present, it is estimated that only some 15 percent[4] of the Ethiopian population has access to the services of these entities; for the rest, most conflict resolution and rule enforcement is conducted through traditional bodies or the system of social courts introduced in 1987.[5]

Apart from the time constraints, there is a strong justification for this narrower focus given that (a) the most widespread complaints about and dissatisfaction with sector performance are addressed at these agencies; (b) the government is actively trying to improve access to the state organizations; and (c) the government has also been engaged in a series of reform programs to improve formal sector performance.

As one sign of this interest, Ethiopia, with 3.4 judges per 100,000 inhabitants (although below the ratio for more-developed regions), does remarkably better than other Sub-Saharan African nations such as Ghana, Kenya, Malawi, Tanzania, and Uganda, where the ratio is closer to 1 per 100,000 (Van de Vijver 2006; author's data on Ghana and Kenya).

As part of ongoing reform, the government also has installed a fairly sophisticated system for tracking court performance at both the federal and regional levels. Unfortunately, the police and prosecutors lag behind in this area, and the ratio of police to population is extremely low.[6]

Importance of Justice Sector Corruption

Corruption within the institutions covered here—or, indeed, within the sector more broadly defined—generally has a far lower monetary value than corruption in other sectors, and, except for extreme cases,[7] offers fewer direct threats to public well-being. However, justice sector corruption is important for a number of reasons (even apart from the sector's central role in establishing a rule of law):

- Justice sector organizations are vital to the identification and sanctioning of corruption in other sectors. Where they are themselves corrupt, their activities in this area are severely compromised, both literally (they cannot perform their functions) and symbolically (their rulings will bear no legitimacy).
- Where justice sector agencies are perceived as corrupt or otherwise compromised, they will not be used to resolve conflicts except by those wishing to use the corruption to their own ends or with no choice in the matter (for example, defendants in criminal cases). Instead, citizens

will use other, possibly less effective, mechanisms or simply let conflicts fester until they explode.

- Conflict resolution is a private good provided by the sector, but its actions in this area create an important public good: the strengthening of the normative framework guiding public and private actions (Shavell 1997). Where the organizations are regarded as corrupt, this rule-strengthening function will not occur (thus compromising the rule of law).

- Finally, the rule-strengthening function contributes to another public good: creation of a predictable environment for public and private transactions (North 1990). Corruption undermines this predictability or, at best, makes it a function of who can pay most or who has the strongest political "godfathers."

The jury is still out as to the importance of justice-sector quality to attracting domestic and foreign investment (Hewko 2002; Jensen 2003; La Porta and López-de-Silanes 1998; Sherwood, Shepherd, and Souza 1994; Stone, Levy, and Paredes 1996). Still, even if there are other inducements (for example, market size or resource base) for investing in a country with notoriously corrupt courts and police, investors take steps to reduce their risks that also cut into overall productivity and thus into competitiveness.[8] The same can be said for other systemic vices, most notably egregious inefficiency, against which Ethiopia has made significant strides, especially in civil justice.

Still more important, justice sector corruption reduces the quality of life for a country's citizens, leaving them defenseless in the face of abuses committed by the sector's members or by other private and public actors. Hence, even if corruption is less directly economically harmful in the justice sector than in others, it represents a significant threat to the citizenry's well-being, to the pace of economic and social development, and to the returns on investment by public and private agencies (La Porta and López-de-Silanes 1998; World Bank 2005, 2009).

Challenges to Identifying and Combating Corruption

Corruption in the justice sector is a universal phenomenon that no country has completely eliminated. The underlying problem is the nature of the services delivered and their dependence on myriad decisions at the discretion of individual officials. Robert Klitgaard's (1988) formula—C = M + D – A (Corruption equals Monopoly plus Discretion minus Accountability)—meets its match in this sector, which (a) by definition holds a monopoly or quasi-monopoly on its basic functions; (b) requires a large measure of discretionary decision making; and (c) faces practical and ideological constraints on the use of accountability mechanisms.

These same factors also make it difficult to identify corruption conclusively, and they posed certain obstacles to this research—which, in the end, had to rely on the observations and perceptions of "knowledgeable" individuals and their willingness to divulge their own experience or what they believed was going on around them. To illustrate this comment, we can place Klitgaard's three factors in the context of any justice sector's operations.

Monopoly. Although alternative forums have been proliferating for civil disputes (hence the popularity of alternative dispute resolution [Williams 2002]), they cannot help to strengthen the legal framework because their decisions are individualized and private. The advantage of the official forums (be they state or traditional) is that they leave a public (if unwritten) record whereby individuals can calculate their risks should they or others decide to ignore the rules. In criminal cases, a monopolistic system is more important because the state (or the local community) will have more interest in ensuring that the rule-based and public decisions constitute a disincentive to rule violation.

Discretion. Despite occasional efforts to reduce the discretionary powers of sector actors by establishing bright-line rules to guide their actions, there are practical limits to the feasibility of this approach. When pushed to extremes, it quickly leads to gridlock and its own injustices. Judicial reactions to sentencing rules in the United States are one example. Both judges and the public want greater flexibility and individualization of sentencing rather than conformity to an ironclad set of regulations.

However, even when rules are introduced, they are difficult to enforce because so many of the sector actors operate in relative isolation:

- *The police officer* confronted with a possible crime and suspect must and will make a context-based decision as to whether to ignore the possible offense or arrest the likely perpetrator. Corruption can enter here, of course, but there are other reasons for "letting the offender off": a first-time minor offense, more important matters to pursue, and so on.
- *Prosecutors* must decide how much evidence is required to go forward with a case, whether they have a chance of collecting that evidence,

what charges to file (evaluated against the chances of getting a conviction), and whether, given their other pending cases, it is better to drop one of lesser importance. Often termed the "principle of opportunity," the legal recognition of prosecutorial discretion is an important component of modern criminal justice systems because it allows prosecutors to emphasize cases with more impact.

- *Judges* in the end must weigh the evidence and the facts presented to them according to their own appreciation of the legal truth of the matter, and in this there is ample room for disagreement among equally competent and honest experts.

Corruption can influence all these decisions, but there is also a large element of subjective appreciation that another observer might calculate differently. Short of a video recording of a police officer, prosecutor, or judge receiving money to sway his or her decision, it becomes nearly impossible to determine conclusively whether an "odd" ruling or other decision was the result of corruption, ineptitude, or just a different assessment of the situation.

Accountability. Given the considerations cited above, augmenting accountability might appear to be the solution, but again the sector faces some peculiar constraints:

- Judicial independence protects judges (if not their appealable decisions) from having to provide additional explanations of their actions. The concept of absolute independence is gradually being eroded and generally no longer applies to nonjurisdictional activities (for example, how courts manage their budgets, their personnel policies, or even productivity figures). However, in most countries, judges still enjoy greater immunity than other public servants from personal responsibility for their decisions and related actions (see NJI 2008, however, for a recommendation to loosen traditional immunity in Ethiopia).
- Transparency, one aspect of accountability, is also constrained throughout the sector because of privacy rights and the need to protect the parties or ongoing investigations.
- Because the sector's services depend on a multitude of individual decisions, there are practical limits on reviewing every one or even requiring written explanations. Where such explanations have been required (for example, that a prosecutor or other government attorney

justify a decision not to appeal an adverse decision), they often have perverse consequences (in this case, a plethora of needless appeals).

International Experience with Justice Sector Corruption

Countries differ markedly in the levels of justice sector corruption estimated by experts and perceived by the public—and those experts' estimates and public perceptions need not coincide. Recent surveys in European countries, for example, show markedly low (50 percent or less) public faith in the judiciaries of Belgium, France, Germany, Spain, and the United Kingdom (Toharia 2003, 29), although most experts would contend that those countries are relatively corruption free. Likewise, in the United States, public surveys indicate that a large portion of citizens do not believe they will "get a fair trial," although it is not clear whether they attribute these anticipated outcomes to bias and the power of the wealthy to hire a better lawyer or to out-and-out corruption. One suspects the answer is more toward the former end.

Developed countries. Of course, the United States and most European countries have had their share of judicial corruption cases. One of the most famous was the Operation Greylord investigations of corruption networks in the Cook County (Chicago) courts, which produced the indictment and conviction of some 70 officers of the court (judges, lawyers, and clerks responsible for assigning cases [Special Commission 1998]). A more recent (April 2009) example involved two juvenile court judges in Pennsylvania who were tried and convicted for accepting money from private detention centers to send young offenders to serve time there—also known as the "kids for cash" case. Corruption in various U.S. police departments has also been well documented over the years.

These examples aside, justice sector corruption in developed countries is considerably less extensive than in many developing nations and usually takes the form of individual rather than organized malfeasance. The Chicago investigation and convictions represented an exceptional case, but even there, the networks were internal to the judiciary, not directed by higher-level political and government elites.

Developing and undeveloped countries. In other regions, corruption is often linked to political interference whereby political elites assert control over the sector agencies as a means of influencing decisions and actions; guaranteeing immunity for themselves and their allies; and, if less frequently, participating in the monetary rewards. In many of these countries, the lack or weakness of internal control systems also tends to encourage higher levels of individual corruption.

In a few countries—such as the Democratic Republic of Congo (then Zaire) under Mobutu (Meredith 2005); Cambodia in the 1990s (Hammergren et al. 2008); and Haiti over the past several decades—low, infrequently paid salaries seem an official policy to undercut judicial integrity. Where judges, police, and others do not make enough to live on, they are virtually forced into corruption, and this becomes still more urgent, when, as reported in Cambodia, judges pay bribes to be placed on the bench (Hammergren et al. 2008). The admonition to "live from the people" attributed to Ethiopian Emperor Haile Selassie (quoted in several interviews) was thus not unique.

Latin America: A case for comparison. In Latin America (chosen for comparison because of relatively ample documentation of the problems), the level of sector corruption is notoriously high. Throughout Central America, with the exception of Costa Rica, ordinary citizens and experts coincide in identifying police, judicial, and prosecutorial corruption as well as corruption of private attorneys as systemic problems (DPLF 2007). Police not only take bribes but also participate actively in criminal activities (kidnappings, collusion with drug traffickers, murders, and other violent crimes).

Many South American countries show similar patterns: underpaid and undertrained police moonlight as thugs-for-hire, and informed observers claim to know the price to buy each level of judge. Under the Fujimori administration in Peru (1990–2001), an initially promising judicial reform quickly deteriorated into both organized and freelance corruption when the president's chief adviser, Vladimiro Montesinos, set up his own corruption rings within the courts, using them to harass government opposition and to turn a tidy profit for himself (Hammergren et al. 2008; McMillan and Zoido 2004).

Mexico's current situation—drug traffickers' penetration of the federal and many state justice organs—is well documented (Bailey and Godson 1999), as is the Carlos Menem administration's control of the Argentine federal courts through an "automatic majority" in the Supreme Court of Justice and manipulation of other appointments (Abiad and Thieberger 2005; Helmke 2005). Several African countries experience similar levels of state-sponsored corruption among judges, police, and prosecutors (USAID 2009; TI 2007), and as in Latin America, once the state captures these organizations, this encourages additional freelance corruption on the part of other members who know that all that matters is loyalty on those cases that count politically.

In both Latin America and much of Africa, corruption is also found in organizational management—misuse of budgets, manipulation of procurements, and mishandling or theft of agency physical resources. However, the most critical aspect is human resource policy and its use to provide jobs for followers, create docile internal networks, or threaten personnel who refuse to participate in corruption or countenance its practice by others. Purchase of positions or their award against promises of future favors is also not uncommon.

Unfortunately, reforming this area has proved difficult because doing so would pose a threat to political business as usual. Throughout Latin America, the introduction of judicial councils to recruit and discipline judges and sometimes prosecutors has, as often as not, reproduced the old party controls (Hammergren 2002). Laws have been manipulated to ensure that the political elites keep their voice, or they have been circumvented to ensure that the supposedly neutral members of selection committees are chosen for party affiliations. And even when the judiciary, through either the councils or the Supreme Court, increases or maintains control of appointments when corruption has already infiltrated the bench, these agencies may be no better than the politicians in discouraging its proliferation. In many cases, the only significant change is that the selection process is negotiated among various parties rather than being controlled by one.

Universal concerns: Other system actors. Finally, the role of private attorneys can hardly be overlooked. In many countries, they have stronger political connections than the judges, so their efforts to influence judges may be backed by implicit or explicit threats. Lawyers can also feed public perceptions of corruption by telling clients they lost the case because the judge was on the take or by collecting "bribes" that never reach the bench. Because lawyers are usually licensed by government (or by the courts), they are included in this analysis as "entrusted" officials.

Many justice systems have other actors in this category: nonpublic officials who are licensed to perform certain public functions. In addition to private attorneys, they include notaries; Brazil's *cartórios* (who carry out functions elsewhere performed by courtroom staff); the French *hussier* (private bailiff); and court-appointed experts and officials responsible for evaluating assets, administering receivership of companies undergoing restructurings, and conducting judicial auctions. Because of their arms-length relationship with the core justice agencies (which may not even pay them) and the imperfect coincidence of their interests with those of their clients, their roles in sector corruption differ from those of purely public or private actors.

Justice Sector Value Chains

Table 5.1, prepared for this research, outlines the usual sites where corruption may appear in any justice system. Its three sections focus on organizational aspects and criminal and civil proceedings, further divided into subareas or stages. Although the value chain approach always features a "production line" logic, there is still considerable variation as to how authors present their contents (Campos and Pradhan 2007).

In contrast to other versions of the value chain in this volume, table 5.1 does not feature a further division—linking types of corruption to types of actors (public, private, entrusted, and citizen) because, with few exceptions, the actions listed may be perpetrated by any of them. However, the means of their exercise usually differs: use of political pressure by political authorities and bribes or other considerations by private citizens or entrusted actors.

The table is based on the author's prior research in some 25 countries and a review of studies from other countries (for example, see TI 2007; USAID 2002, 2009). Because of time limits, the present research did not cover all areas; both the criminal and civil justice chains were incorporated in full, but in the organizational section, only human resource management was considered. Future work in Ethiopia might profitably explore the excluded areas (for example, budgeting and procurement) as well as institutions specifically excluded: public defense, prisons, social courts, sharia courts, and traditional dispute resolution.

Ethiopia's Justice Sector: An Overview

Historical Development

An understanding of a country's governance institutions cannot ignore their broader political context. This chapter does not review the latter, but as a preface to the institutional overview of the present-day justice sector, a few points merit emphasis:

- *Ethiopia has a long tradition of autocratic governments, and its post-1991 democratic transition is not complete,* either regarding government

Table 5.1   Three Value Chains for Justice Sector Corruption Risk

a. System Organization
Potential forms of corruption

Passage of laws shaping sector operations	• *Political actors* collude to ensure that rules increase their control over personnel decisions and influence other internal operations. • *Political actors* collude to increase their immunity from legal actions. • *"Entrusted" actors* bribe or offer other considerations to lawmakers to enhance their own positions and powers. • *Private actors or citizens* offer bribes or other considerations to executive and legislative officials to secure the most favorable legal framework for their own operations.
Development, passage of sector budgets	• *Political and governmental actors* include earmarks for unnecessary services and facilities for their own benefit or that of protégés. • *Potential providers of goods and services* offer bribes or other considerations to executive and legislative officials to insert earmarks. • *Political or governmental actors* engage in trade-offs or favoritism to locate service units to favor certain groups. • *Political authorities* set salaries for classes of actors (or even individuals) based on favoritism, political trade-offs.
Human resource management	• *"Entrusted" actors* reduce the merit component in selection of judges, prosecutors, defenders, police, and their own staffs through politically directed selection based on nepotism, political contacts, or the selection group's desire to create their own internal networks (e.g., Venezuela, RB's *tribus legales*). • Potential candidates for positions as judges, prosecutors, defenders, police, their staffs, and private entrusted actors use bribes, exchanges of favors, or networks of influence to shape the selection system. • *Political and governmental actors* assign personnel to positions and direct promotions based on favoritism and political contacts or, influenced by employees, based on bribes or promises of future favors. • *External (nongovernmental) patrons* buy or otherwise influence decisions regarding assignment of personnel. • *Political actors* use the disciplinary system to punish those (including *private entrusted actors*) who resist pressures and bribes and to reward those who acquiesce. • *External (nongovernmental) patrons* buy or otherwise influence disciplinary decisions. • *Public actors* who oversee private bar performance and licensing of these and other officers of the court accept or solicit bribes or succumb to favoritism in making their decisions.

(continued next page)

Table 5.1   *(continued)*

a. System Organization	
	• *Government-accredited bar associations* sell licenses or award them on a nonmerit basis or manage discipline of own members to either favor colleagues or ignore their misbehavior.
Execution of budget	• *Public sector actors* create slush funds or divert funds to nonofficial uses.
	• *Private and public actors* collude through bribes, kickbacks, and sweetheart contracts.
	• *Public actors* manipulate salaries or other benefits to reward or punish other public (and *entrusted*) actors.
	• *Private citizens* make "contributions" to augment public actors' salaries or improve benefits and so ensure favorable treatment.
Management of nonfinancial resources	• *Public employees* steal equipment and materials.
	• *Public and private actors* collude through bribes or kickbacks on maintenance contracts.
	• *Public actors* distribute equipment and other resources based on political clout or favoritism.
Management of funds collected by courts	• *Public actors* who collect funds do not turn them over in full, but pocket some or all.
	• *Public and private actors* collude to falsely record what is paid and split the difference.
	• *"Entrusted officials"* charged with collecting fees (e.g., Brazil's *cartórios*) do not turn them over to the court.

b. Criminal Justice	
Potential forms of corruption	
Detection of alleged crime	• *Political authorities or higher-level officials* direct police to ignore a complaint, undertake an investigation, or arrest a "suspect" without probable cause.
	• *Police* take regular payments from those running criminal activities or ordinary businesses in exchange for ignoring infractions.
	• *Police* solicit or accept bribes or other considerations to process or ignore complaints.
	• *Police* solicit or accept bribes or other considerations to arrest or release suspects.
	• *Lawyers* collude with private clients to threaten criminal complaints to extort money or force other actions of "probable suspect."
Investigation of crime and pretrial procedures	• *Political authorities or higher-level officers* direct police to falsify or ignore evidence.
	• *Police* steal valuable evidence.
	• *Political authorities or higher-level officers* direct prosecutors to file or not file charges.
	• *Political authorities* manipulate assignment of the "right" judge (prosecutor or investigator) to handle the case.

(continued next page)

Table 5.1   *(continued)*

b. Criminal Justice

	• *Political authorities* pressure prosecutors or judges to request or require pretrial detention, refuse bail, or set bail higher or lower than necessary.
	• *Political authorities* pressure judges or prison staff to restrict pretrial detainees' legal rights.
	• *Public authorities* solicit bribes from detainees for access to counsel or other legal rights.
	• *Political authorities* instruct judges, prosecutors, or public defenders to speed up or slow down proceedings.
	• *Political or higher-level officers* pressure judges or others (including private attorneys) regarding decisions on evidence or other matters.
	• *Police or prosecutors* solicit or accept bribes or other consideration from parties to falsify or hide evidence.
	• *Lawyers or other court experts* falsify or retain evidence to aid principal clients or as means of extorting money from other parties.
	• *Prosecutors* solicit or accept bribes or other consideration from parties to drop or reduce charges.
	• *Prosecutors* file charges to "punish" the suspect (abuse of authority).
	• *Political or governmental actors* pressure potential witnesses to not come forward.
	• *Lawyers or clients* purchase false testimony from civilian or expert witnesses.
	• *Public or private actors* solicit or offer bribes to influence case assignments.
	• *Lawyers or clients* offer (or accede to) bribes or other considerations to affect decisions on pretrial detention and bail.
	• *Lawyers* ask clients for money to "pay off" the judge or prosecutor but instead pocket the funds.
	• *Public or "pro bono" defenders* solicit fees from defendants or clients.
	• *Lawyers or clients* offer (or accede to) bribes or other considerations to influence scheduling of events.
	• *Lawyers or clients* offer (or accede to) bribes or other considerations to affect responses to motions to eliminate evidence, exclude witnesses, or dismiss parts of complaints.
Trial and appeal	• *Political or higher judicial authorities* direct judges as to how to rule.
	• *Political authorities* direct public defense lawyers or private attorneys to mishandle cases.
	• *Political authorities or higher-level officials* direct judges to accept or not accept appeals.
	• *Parties or political authorities* engage in jury tampering (if juries are used).

(continued next page)

Table 5.1   *(continued)*

b. Criminal Justice	
	• *Judges* "sell" judgments or other preferential treatment to parties.
	• *Public officials or political authorities* pressure or bribe witnesses.
	• *Police or bailiffs* take bribes to not bring witnesses (or defendants) to trial.
	• *Lawyers or clients* offer or agree to pay court staff to "lose" files.
	• *Lawyers or clients* offer (or agree) to pay to delay or accelerate issuance of written opinions (this may be delayed for a long time).
	• *Private defense attorneys* accept bribes from interested nongovernmental parties to mishandle cases.
	• *Court staff members* accept or request bribes to show judgments to parties (or to offer to sell an outcome already determined by the judge).
	• *Lawyers* solicit money from clients to bribe any of the actors but keep the funds.
	• *Lawyers or parties* offer or agree to pay to affect decisions on licenses to appeal and appellate judgments.
Enforcement of judgment	• *Political authorities or higher judicial leaders* direct whether and how enforcement will be effected.
	• *Parties* offer or agree to pay to arrange early release, nonincarceration, or reduction or nonpayment of damages.

c. Civil Justice	
	Potential forms of corruption
Filing of claim and pretrial stages	• *Public officials* (in judiciary or outside) direct staff to admit or not admit cases.
	• *Public authorities* coerce or bribe private attorneys to file or not file cases.
	• *Court staff* offer bribes or other considerations to accept and process claims.
	• *Lawyers* accept bribes from other parties to mishandle cases or accept fees from parties on both sides.
	• *Lawyers* solicit money from clients to bribe judges or staff but instead pocket the money.
	• *Lawyers* encourage clients to take cases to court that they are bound to lose.
	• *Process servers* accept or solicit bribes for nonservice, faster service, false service, and so on.
	• *Public officials* (in judiciary or outside) direct staff to speed or delay initial processing of cases.
	• *Lawyers or parties* offer or agree to pay court staff for faster or slower scheduling of events or for misplacement of case files.

(continued next page)

Table 5.1   *(continued)*

	c. Civil Justice
	• *Public officials* (in judiciary or outside) direct judges' decisions on pretrial motions.
	• *Judges* solicit or accept bribes for handling of pretrial motions.
	• *Lawyers* add unnecessary motions or appeals to be able to charge clients more.
	• *Public officials* (in judiciary or outside) direct court staff to misplace files.
	• *Public officials* (in judiciary or outside) direct staff to give them premature access to judicial decisions.
	• *Court staff* accept or solicit bribes for access to judicial decisions before they are announced.
Trial and appeal stage	• *Higher authorities or political elites* direct judgments or licenses to appeal.
	• *Private attorneys* collude with judges for mutual benefit.
	• *Judges (or higher-level judges on appeal)* accept or solicit bribes for favorable judgments.
	• *Public or private actors* engage in jury tampering (if juries are used).
	• *Court staff* use knowledge of judgments to "sell" them to winning parties.
	• *Lawyers* accept bribes from other parties to mishandle cases.
Enforcement	• *Governmental actors* ignore judicial orders to pay judgments or take other actions.
	• *Lawyers or parties* negotiate with judges, bailiffs, or other parties so that enforcement does not occur.
	• *Court-appointed experts* issue under- or overvaluations of assets.
	• *Court-appointed agents* (in the case of public auction) collude to manipulate price, take over assets at reduced price, or arrange with private parties to sell for low bid.

Source: Author.

practices (for example, lack of transparency and restrictions on opposition movements) or, perhaps more important, citizen expectations. As interviewees and reviewers repeatedly stressed, Ethiopians are cautious about the views they express publicly and careful about openly registering complaints. However, they compensate for what they believe government is *not* telling them with a rich rumor mill, part of which may also feed into government's preoccupation with alleged conspiratorial movements.

- *The post-1991 administration has reinforced the rule of law, but its interest in it conflicts with its desire to maintain control* (and thus with the law's application to its own activities and various requirements of accountability). This poses some constraints, real or imagined, to optimizing the independent operations of the judiciary and other sector organizations, further complicating their situation as institutions unused to independence.
- *Ethiopia has a large, ethnically divided population, and the adoption of a governance system based on ethnic federalism is still seen as a risky means of holding the nation together* (Turton 2006). There is a widespread perception that some nationalities are favored under current arrangements. Moreover, although the constitution does allow for regional secession—and acceptance of that principle is one of the tests of constitutional loyalty applied to judges—the ruling party's own actions demonstrate a more ambiguous stance.
- *In line with a distinction made by corruption experts, the government's approach to controlling corruption is closer to the top-down (Singapore) model than a bottom-up reliance on civil society monitoring* (Zook 2009). This does not mean the Ethiopian government depends on corruption to hold power (as appears to be the case in some African nations), but the top-down approach can easily encourage this development.[9] As a fully democratic polity, Ethiopia is still a work in progress—as are the justice sector institutions that are central to its completion.

The organization and operations of Ethiopia's justice sector have changed considerably since the 1960s, when the emperor controlled all agencies and judicial independence was virtually nonexistent (although it did figure in the 1931 and 1955 constitutions). Until 1987, the country had a unitary court system, police, and prosecution, and it returned to a unitary system in the early post-Derg years.

Judiciary and prosecution pre-1974. Even before the Derg's arrival, the judicial structure was relatively complex, with (post-1942) a supreme imperial court; the high courts (numbering 118 judges in 1967 [Tesfaye 2004, 108]); provincial (*teklay gizat*) courts; district (*woreda*) courts; subdistrict (*meketel woreda*) courts; and local arbiters (*atbia dagnas*). The courts were placed under the Ministry of Justice, but the minister had no legal authority to interfere in court proceedings. Post-1942, the minister's powers were further reduced, but he retained the responsibility for disciplining judges (Tesfaye 2004, 99). Up to the early 1970s, the emperor appointed judges (with advice from the minister of justice).

Until a law school was established in Addis Ababa (in the mid-1960s), most judges were not lawyers but rather "members of the clergy or persons well versed in the canon law of the Ethiopian Orthodox Church" (Tesfaye 2004, 105). In 1973, on the eve of the Derg revolution, a Judicial Commission was created to screen candidates for the emperor's approval.

Until the 1942 creation of the Office of Public Prosecution, most prosecution was private (by the victim or his or her relatives). The new office was located in the Ministry of Justice, and the minister appointed all prosecutors except the advocate general and his deputy; the emperor appointed both. The first advocates general were foreigners; an Ethiopian did not hold this position until 1961. Until the late 1960s, most prosecutors were police officers because of the shortage of trained lawyers.

Police. Ethiopia's police force evolved gradually, with considerable foreign influence from the late 19th and early 20th centuries. Following the expulsion of the Italians, a national force began to take shape and by 1971 had reached 28,467—which, for a population of about 27.4 million (Tesfaye 2004, 23)—is a higher police-population ratio than the country has today.

Under the Derg (1974–1991), the organization of the police force was not much affected. However, because of the Derg's reliance on the army, the number of police actually on duty (as opposed to in official positions) dropped considerably (to 8,039 by 1981–82) and rose again only toward the end of the decade (to 17,773) but still without reaching the levels of the pre-Derg period.

The Derg and Transitional Governments. The Office of the Procurator (prosecutor) General, while remaining in the Ministry of Justice, assumed more powers under the Derg, including extensive supervisory control over other agencies involved in law enforcement (prisons, the police investigators, and "the legality of the administration of justice" [Tesfaye 2004, 70–71]). The courts became less important (because of the creation of special tribunals [Jembere 2002, 514]), and their organization was simplified. Proclamation 53 of 1975 reinstituted the Judicial Commission for the appointment of judges, prosecutors, and registrars, except for the presidents of the Supreme Court, the High Courts, and the attorney general (all appointed by the head of state pursuant to consultations with the minister of justice). Further changes made in 1987, with the establishment of the People's Democratic Republic of

Ethiopia, included the creation of regional courts, the separation of the special courts from the regular judiciary, and the notably greater degree of government interference even in the latter's decisions.

After its victory over the Derg, the Ethiopian People's Revolutionary Democratic Front (EPRDF) effectively annulled the court system and all other agencies dealing with criminal justice for roughly 18 months. In August 1993, the Transitional Government, through Proclamation 40, created the three-instance Central Courts.

Not until 1995 did the current system of regional and federal courts, prosecution, and police emerge; and for all the usual reasons (dearth of financing and recruits), setting it up has taken time. The obstacles were compounded by the prior exodus of many professionals, not only from the institutions but also from the country, and the inevitable dismissal of many Derg appointees. For the courts, this may not have been a great loss: a ca. 1990 study indicated that only 7 percent of the bench had law degrees while only another 8 percent had two-year diplomas (author's interviews in Federal Supreme Court).

Contemporary Situation and Sector Reform

The current system comprises the federal courts, nine regional court systems, and two independent municipal systems—one for Addis Ababa and one for Dire Dawa. (Within regions, some municipalities also enjoy a quasi-independent status and are able to set up local police forces and special tribunals, often for land cases).

The federal and regional courts have three levels: Supreme, High (zonal in the regions), and First Instance (woredas in the regions), with High Court judges often "riding" circuit. The division of labor among them is determined by seriousness of offense or size of claim, but it is generally agreed that the ceiling for woreda courts should be raised because, despite being more numerous, they currently receive far fewer cases. The division of responsibilities between the federal and regional benches appears to pose few conflicts, especially because the federal system has only High and First Instance Courts in Addis Ababa and Dire Dawa—meaning that many federal cases are delegated to the regions. Much the same is true of police and prosecution.

Reform programs. Although, like the rest of the region, Ethiopia faces enormous challenges in improving sector performance and thus the rule of law, it has made some notable advances meriting recognition.

Compared with other African countries, the numbers of judges (reportedly 2,739 in 2007 [NJI 2008]) and prosecutors (an estimated 200 at the federal level, according to the director of criminal activities, surpassing the 118 federal judges; figures were not available for the regions) are relatively high. In fact, according to one estimate, there are considerably more judges than private lawyers (a less common but not unique situation in Africa) (Bourassa 2009).

Police numbers per population remain low, as they do in the rest of Africa. Although all agencies have expansion plans, they face financial limitations and a lack of suitable recruits. In terms of work levels, expansion may not be necessary. Workloads for police may be heavy, but those for judges and prosecutors are moderately high but manageable. However, the government's main interest appears to be increasing access and making all sector actors available to a greater range of the population.

Productivity gains from modernization. This gradual expansion of the size and reach of the sector institutions is part of a modernization program that began in the middle of the last decade. Although the program theoretically incorporates all institutions, the judiciary has advanced more rapidly than the prosecution and the police, and in fact has introduced innovations seen in few developing countries. This is especially evident in its adoption of an automated CMS (fully installed at the federal level and partially installed in the regions) and its use to monitor productivity. As a result, the judiciaries have reduced delays substantially and increased output. A similar system was developed for the Ministry of Justice, but it has never been expanded beyond one pilot office in Addis Ababa, and even there it is said not to work.

With data, systematic tracking. The courts (both federal and regional) track productivity, clearance, and congestion rates; appeals rates; execution of judgments; numbers of adjournment; and percentages of cases resolved within 0–30 days, 1–3 months, and so on up to more than six years. Since the installation of the system (in 2001), the numbers have all improved, although as shown below, congestion rates remain moderate. This is hardly surprising given the recent increases in filings.

With the exception of South Africa, no African country has these kinds of statistical data, nor do they attempt to track efficiency so systematically. Moreover, although case management systems have been spreading since the early 1990s in other regions, a comparable emphasis on productivity is rare (World Bank 2004b). In some Latin American countries, a few provincial or state judiciaries do keep track, but the clearance and congestion rates are not as good.

Appellate and adjournment benchmarks. Ethiopia's federal courts also track appeals rates, which are relatively low, and the percentage of rulings overturned on appeal, estimated at 10 percent and 5 percent, respectively. Hence, for the federal courts, the frequent contention that "everything is appealed" would appear to be erroneous.

Adjournments are also controlled, and the federal courts have set a benchmark of no more than four adjournments per case. To the extent they can meet that goal, this is a vast improvement over the experience in other African countries (such as Ghana, Tanzania, and Uganda) where frequent and lengthy adjournments create enormous delays (Amegatcher 2007; IMMMA Advocates 2008) and doubtless encourage corruption.

Table 5.2, prepared by the statistical office of the Federal Supreme Court, shows some illustrative figures for the 2006–09 period. Figures for the First Instance Courts include only the Lideta Bench, which is one of the two busiest court complexes in Addis Ababa and accounts for 25–30 percent of annual First Instance filings. It also provides better time series data because it has been relatively unaffected by recent temporary closings and transfers of judges in the other 11 complexes.

Challenges, boons for prosecutors. One reason for the courts' high clearance rates is a policy of provisionally closing cases that have been adjourned repeatedly because of the absence of witnesses (or even of the defendant, in criminal cases). Half the criminal cases in the federal First Instance courts reach closure for this reason, according to interviews and court data. Unfortunately for the prosecutors, these closures also reduce their conviction rates to between 30 percent and 38 percent.

In line with the business process reengineering (BPR) exercise introduced by the government for the entire public sector, the prosecutors are attempting to rationalize internal procedures and so raise their conviction rates to 50 percent, still short of what might be considered acceptable—at least 75 percent.[10] Clearly their biggest challenge here is the lack of a case tracking system (like the judiciary's CMS) that would enable them to identify bottlenecks and individual poor performers.

Fast-track courts. However, prosecutors' efforts will be aided by another judicial innovation: the introduction of fast-track courts to

Table 5.2 Disposition of Civil and Criminal Cases in Ethiopian Federal Courts, by Instance, Clearance Rate,[a] and Congestion Rate,[b] 2006–07 to 2008–09[c]

Court	Cases filed			Cases disposed			Clearance (C) and congestion (CG) rates		
	2006–07	2007–08	2008–09	2006–07	2007–08	2008–09	2006–07	2007–08	2008–09
SC	5,746	7,446	6,766	5,836	7,665	6,436	1.02 (C) 1.38 (CG)	1.03 (C) 1.27 (CG)	0.95 (C) 1.38 (CG)
HC	9,108	11,684	10,996	12,291	14,346	11,913	1.35 (C) 1.15 (CG)	1.23 (C) 1.44 (CG)	1.08 (C) 1.53 (CG)
First Instance Lideta Bench only	19,039	29,565	23,581	22,786	28,489	30,301	1.18 (C) 1.34 (CG)	0.96 (C) 1.43 (CG)	1.28 (C) 1.29 (CG)

Source: Statistical Office of Federal Supreme Court.

Note: SC = Supreme Court. HC = High Court. C = clearance rate. CG = congestion rate.

a. Clearance rates are calculated as cases disposed in one year / new entries. A figure at one or above indicates that pending cases are being reduced.

b. Congestion rates are calculated as (pending cases + new cases + reopened cases) / cases disposed in one year. The higher the number, the greater the congestion.

c. Statistics are calculated from May 31 to June 1. The 2008–09 figures are from only the first nine months of that period.

handle "minor"[11] crimes where a suspect has been immediately apprehended. Because 80 percent of defendants in these "real-time courts" (the name and the model are adopted from the French system) plead guilty, conviction rates are high from the start. The other 20 percent are given time to organize their own defense. Because they usually have to do this while in detention and without legal assistance, it is no surprise that the overall conviction rate is 95 percent or more. The real-time courts process high numbers of cases; in 2007/08, the two judges operating in Addis Ababa resolved 2,500 cases each. As their numbers increase (three more were added in Addis, and several regions have also introduced them), conviction and final disposal rates should also rise.

As the judiciary is aware, these courts do raise problems concerning due process—the internationally recognized right to defense, and if one cannot pay for a lawyer, the state's provision of one. Obviously, such a system has proven impossible to organize in Ethiopia, and the only indigent defendants given state subsidized services are those facing very serious charges (and capital offenses). A few more receive assistance from specialized NGOs. Although the statement of some of those interviewed—that these defendants are "all guilty anyway"—may be true, fast-tracking does pose serious risks to the innocent suspect caught in the system. Although defendants receive more leeway than prosecutors regarding adjournments for witnesses' failure to appear, this innovation does have its downside in the potential for abuse. However, as the judges also argue, the lack of subsidized defense is not limited to fast-track courts, and being judged and sentenced rapidly rather than waiting in jail for months may have its advantages.[12]

Staffing issues and initiatives. The prosecutors place much of the blame for low conviction rates on poor police investigation. Inadequate numbers of police (relative to judges and prosecutors) may be another problem, but here, as with the other agencies, faster staffing increases are seen as risking the addition of too many poorly trained officials.

All three agencies have training programs, although again the courts are the most advanced. The centralized judicial training institute now shares the terrain with a series of regional institutes. Amhara's judicial institute currently provides additional training to 700 law diploma holders (a diploma is earned in two years of post-high school study) who will subsequently be deployed as assistant judges or prosecutors and may eventually be promoted to full professional status. Assuming the extra training and on-the-job experience can fill in the gaps, participants may be better prepared than law school graduates (who, as is nearly universally true, are trained to practice law as private attorneys, not as judges or prosecutors).

The appointment systems for all these officials have also been further developed, with some agencies instituting written examinations to screen candidates. However, as further discussed below, there are many complaints that the recruitment, promotions, and discipline processes lack transparency, especially for the judiciary. Some regional courts have begun to recruit more openly, but the federal system remains pretty much a black box in this regard. Federal and regional judges are evaluated on productivity, but other elements that may affect promotions, transfers, and discipline remain known only to the judicial administrative councils that manage them.

Shortage of "entrusted" attorneys. Finally, regarding "entrusted" officials, the panorama is not complex, and the principal actors (and the only ones covered here) are private attorneys. As noted, a first problem is their scarcity, a situation only gradually being resolved with the creation of more law schools and even then subject to the added concern of reduced educational standards.[13] Attorneys must be licensed to practice by the Ministry (or the regional Bureaus) of Justice. At the federal level, an examination or five years of practice are required, but once a lawyer is accepted, the subsequent requirements are only payment of fees.

The ministry also receives complaints about malpractice, but it appears, at least at the federal level, that the major cause of suspension is a failure to reregister. Of the 81 lawyers subject to investigation in 2007/08, nearly all were suspected of working without a license or not keeping up with their fees. Only a handful were under investigation for other reasons, and in any event only 15 cases were fully processed, with the remainder being carried over to this year, according to ministry documents.

With the courts taking the lead, it is evident that the government as a whole, as well as the individual agencies, has made efforts to improve its performance, especially to upgrade the quality and quantity of staff and to improve efficiency. The period since 1991 has seen its ups and downs, but generally the trends have been positive. However, with most emphasis on productivity and efficiency, issues like corruption have arguably received insufficient attention.

Corruption and Political Intervention in Ethiopia's Justice Sector

Overview of Research Results

Three general points can be made at the outset:

First, none of the 60 individuals interviewed for this study denied the presence of corruption in the Ethiopian justice system. The one who came closest eventually admitted that "there was some, but it was very rare."[14] Other responses ranged from "a moderate amount" (limited to the bad apples) to the extreme of holding that "every civil judgment is sold." Participants in the two formal focus groups (the first composed of six federal prosecutors and the second of eight federal First Instance judges, all picked by their agencies) were less forthcoming than those interviewed individually, but they were willing to acknowledge the potential for corruption, both in their own agencies and in others. The two "spontaneous" focus groups with police and the Federal Ethics and Anti-Corruption Commission (FEACC), organized on the spot in Bahir Dar and Addis Ababa, brought what appeared to be franker reactions: a discussion of the problems of petty corruption and the difficulty of investigating more serious offenses based on the frequently vague complaints.

Second, on the topic of political intervention in agency operations and especially in personnel management, opinions were much more dichotomized. Even a judge who had been exposed to political interference (and later resigned, apparently for that reason) claimed this was rare—as did most, but not the entire, seated bench. Those who felt otherwise are largely but not exclusively now outside the system. One-on-one interviews with active members of all three agencies did elicit some negative comments. However, even the outsiders could point to few real examples (except for the recent case of a federal High Court judge, criticized for voicing complaints in a meeting with donors). Instead they referred (both in the judiciary and the prosecutorial offices) to a sense that (a) party membership and an ability to please politicians, one's superiors, and (in the case of the judges) political members of the Judicial Administration Councils was what counted, and (b) the lack of transparent criteria left ample room for purely arbitrary decisions. Similar reactions were reported in earlier studies (World Bank 2004a; NJI 2008) and in interviews with donors and NGOs. However, in both formal focus groups, the prosecutors and judges defended the personnel system as merit-based and therefore just.

Finally, efforts to contrast the interview data on corruption (if not political interference) with evidence from investigative bodies were frustrated because none of the three agencies, at either the federal or the regional level, appears to have a program for actively seeking out and investigating corruption among its members. One high-level judge did note that, faced with suspected corruption, the usual response was to encourage the person to resign, given the difficulty of proving anything decisively. All agencies have complaints offices and disciplinary bodies (often combined), but these appear (as some interviewees admitted) to be relatively underused by the public (Gidey 2007). The complaints office for the federal police is used largely by employees to register labor grievances. For the most part, citizens concerned about corruption turn to the regional and federal anticorruption commissions. Both the FEACC and the Amhara commission reported receiving most complaints about police; the FEACC said it had received 41 in the last two years. The Amhara commission estimated perhaps 50 complaints about judges annually; the FEACC could not provide an estimate.[15] Representatives of both commissions agreed that complaints about judges often give them little to work with and that they turn most complaints about police back to the police themselves because the amounts in question are so small.[16] According to interviews with FEACC staff, in the past two years, one federal judge has been convicted and two are still under investigation; five prosecutors have been investigated and prosecuted. A former FEACC prosecutor was also convicted, but for corruption incurred after he transferred to the customs agency. An earlier report noted that four judges had been removed for ethical violations, and three had been admonished in prior years (World Bank 2004a).

Now the discussion focuses on the three value chains and the areas where corruption and political interference were either present or absent.

The System Organization Chain: Personnel Management

As previously noted, personnel management is the only area of system organization covered in this study because it is frequently (in other systems) a focus of corruption in its own right and a contributor to corruption in other areas. The system by which personnel are chosen, evaluated, promoted, transferred, and disciplined has an enormous impact on their own incentives; can be a means of controlling their actions; and can also create internal networks for influence trafficking, political intervention, or simple rent extraction. For the most part, corruption in other areas of system organization may impede operations (especially when it

Table 5.3   Corruption Risks in Human Resource Management in Ethiopia's Justice Sector

Human resource management	• **Selection of judges, prosecutors, defenders, police, their staffs (*and entrusted officials*): merit component reduced by politically directed selection based on nepotism, political contacts,** or the selection group's choice to create their own internal networks
	• Selection of judges, prosecutors, defenders, police, their staffs, and private entrusted actors: **merit component ignored, and replaced by** bribes, exchanges of favors, or networks of influence mobilized by candidates
	• **Assignment of personnel to positions and promotions directed by political authorities: based on favoritism and political contacts** or influenced by employees, based on bribes or promises of future favors
	• Assignment of personnel: based on bribes or other influence by external (nongovernmental) patrons
	• **Disciplinary system: used by political actors to punish those (including private entrusted actors) who resist pressures and bribes and to reward those who acquiesce**
	• Disciplinary decisions: based on bribes or other influence by external (nongovernmental) patrons
	• Public sector oversight of private bar performance and licensing of these and other officers of the court: decisions based on bribes or favoritism
	• Licenses and discipline from government-accredited bar associations: sold or awarded on nonmerit basis or discipline of own members managed to either favor colleagues or ignore their misbehavior

Source: Author.

reduces or misallocates budgets and equipment) but is less likely to provide an incentive to corruption in other parts of the agency.[17]

As shown in the table 5.3 (an extract from table 5.1), the possibilities are various—ranging from systems where jobs are bought (with the expectations that the incumbent will then recoup his or her losses accordingly) to those where the process is tightly controlled from the top or outside to create a chain or network of faithful followers. Many of these problems were not reported in Ethiopia; only those in bold were reported to be in effect, although as further discussed, there was disagreement even here. The same system and caveats apply to the following sections as well.

As indicated by the bolded comments, Ethiopia's personnel management within the sector has some flaws, but they hardly extend to the full range of interference found in many other countries. Most important, there was universal agreement on one point: people aspiring to work in the justice sector or to be licensed for court-related duties do not buy their positions in Ethiopia, nor are such positions bought for them by external patrons. This finding is consistent with general findings on public sector positions as a whole (World Bank 2008) and is an important point because it eliminates one potential cause of further corruption frequently reported in other countries: the need to recoup one's "down payment" on a job.

Likewise, there was no suggestion that appointment mechanisms were used to form internal networks of corruption, as has been reported in some other countries.[18] And judging from the patterns of disciplinary actions against private attorneys, it does not appear that the Ministry of Justice uses such actions to punish political opponents or those openly critical of practices in the sector. Private practitioners did express fear of reprisals for speaking out (including in the interviews), but they seemed to believe reprisals would come in the form of negative decisions in their court cases or perhaps legal action against them—not from the ministry itself.

Police personnel management. Regarding personnel management in general, the police (at least at the federal level and in Amhara) came under the least criticism for the prevalence of political or other kinds of favoritism in appointments and downstream personnel policies. This relatively clean status may be because police work, at least at the lower levels, is not regarded as an attractive job and furthermore is less politically critical (and less likely to attract political activists of any stripe). Although the federal police do remove an estimated 200–300 members from their ranks annually, none of the informants suggested this was for any but legitimate reasons. Corrupt police were not believed to have patrons to protect them, and there were only minor complaints about a lack of transparency in promotions and training opportunities.

There was some criticism of a tendency to put "civilians" in high-level positions, but this practice is hardly unique to Ethiopia and has its adherents, especially in countries attempting major reforms.[19] Without knowing more about why the individuals were chosen or how well they have performed in this capacity, it is impossible to say whether political connections played an excessive role in Ethiopia.

Prosecutors' and judges' personnel management. Prosecutors and judges were more controversial among the study informants, and there are more indications of a political element in selection, promotions, transfers, and discipline. The courts, and especially the federal judiciary, are remarkably nontransparent in their personnel management—not even (in contrast to the prosecutors) advertising openings.[20]

However, for both agencies, there is a perception among current and former professional staff as well as among outsiders that since about 2004, there has been an effort to recruit judges and prosecutors who, as one informant noted, are active rather than passive members of the ruling party (or its regional affiliates). This may mean—as several commented of the federal courts in particular—that better-qualified candidates are passed over in favor of those with political ties. A few interviewees mentioned this as a particular problem in regard to assistant judges hired several years earlier but not promoted, for reasons that remained obscure.

Informants also mentioned an increasing tendency to favor federal candidates with degrees from the Civil Service College. Such candidates are regarded, at least by the Addis Ababa graduates (and two professors interviewed), as inferior students who need party ties to get into the program. The federal judiciary's efforts to "nationalize" the bench by drawing in judges from other regions also came under attack for (a) the nontransparency of the process, and (b) the suspicion that political connections counted here as well. However, the major problem may be a reliance on personal recommendations, for want of a better screening process. For example, the recent recruitment of several judges from the Amhara region (already overrepresented on the federal bench) was attributed to the prior transfer of the former regional court president who naturally recommended colleagues he thought worthy of consideration.[21]

The less-than-spontaneous participation in the two focus groups, combined with comments from most of the one-on-one interviews, do suggest that, whatever the truth of the matter, members of the public and the judges and prosecutors themselves perceive that loyalty—not just "to the constitution" but also to the administration—counts, and that an ill-considered comment or decision could have serious career impacts.

Post-1991 (after the EPRDF came to power), the only large-scale purge of the bench (and prosecution) occurred in 1996, when the government not only dismissed 336 judges from Addis Ababa and Amhara National States and 270 from Oromia (Kitaw 2004)—removing many incapable and probably corrupt officials—but also, it is believed, some judges who simply incurred the displeasure of those responsible for these decisions. However, interviewees also referenced subsequent unexplained transfers, dismissals, and some resignations by "victims of harassment." Few specific examples were cited, and it is impossible to verify the claims in any case. Still, given the ongoing evolution of the system and the novelty of performance-based evaluations, it is not surprising that judges, despite their constitutionally guaranteed independence and tenure, are cautious about how their behavior is perceived by their immediate superiors and by the members of the judicial administrative commissions.

To their credit, the federal courts and some regional ones are attempting to alter their own procedures to combat the impression that personnel policy is systematically politicized, whatever real practices may underlie it. The Federal Supreme Court is considering the introduction of an examination for all candidates as well as the announcement of openings and the publication of the list of nominees before their appointment. Both would be positive steps.

The court is also working toward standardizing salaries and thus reversing a federal rule (apparently not applicable to regional courts) that sets salaries for entering judges based on what they earned in their prior positions. Currently, the situation leads to injustices, as in the case of a First Instance judge hired from a state bank whose entering salary of Br 3,000 exceeded the Br 2,100 normally paid to entrants and the Br 2,600 earned by a colleague who had six years on the bench.

A more transparent policy and more open competition for the transfer of judges from regional courts would also help. Even the two former regional judges who had "received invitations" to the federal bench could not explain why they were chosen. Similar comments apply to the federal prosecutors (no regional prosecutors were interviewed). Although the federal ministry does advertise openings, the criteria used for selecting among the applicants (or for transferring individuals from regional positions) are anything but transparent.

Lack of transparency does not translate into a conspiracy, but it certainly leaves room to imagine one. It does not help that party recruiters in the law schools are reputed to tell students that party membership is a ticket to a government job. The claims are doubtless exaggerated, but absent a better understanding of what does count, they may convince a lot of people and affect their decisions about whether to join the sector and remain within it. Informants also mentioned that the prevailing uncertainty could encourage corruption: where individuals are unclear about how long they will keep their jobs, they may be more easily convinced to take advantage of them while they can.

The Criminal Justice Chain

In table 5.4 (extracted from table 5.1), the areas of most concern are bolded. Lack of bolding indicates that a problem was not mentioned and thus is either nonexistent or not significant. It should be stressed that even the bolded items were not deemed as highly common but simply as areas where corruption sometimes occurs.

Again, the bolded items suggest that what corruption occurs in the criminal justice system is relatively limited regarding where and how it operates. Current wisdom holds that the sense of insecurity among sector personnel gives rise to two forms of corruption in criminal cases:

- Willingness to make decisions in politically sensitive cases in accord with the perceived wishes or actual instructions of political actors
- Greater vulnerability to bribes because one never knows how long one will hold his or her current position.

Police. Except for the traffic police, whose tendency to shake down drivers for imagined faults or offer to ignore real ones is pervasive (if still not at the levels seen in much of the region), neither type of action is seen as frequent, but they do occur. The ethics and anticorruption commissions receive numerous complaints about police in this regard and, as opposed to complaints against judges and prosecutors, seem to have some success in investigating them, either directly or by delegation to the respective police forces. Among the most common complaints involving police are these:

- Bribe taking by traffic police
- Abuse of power or excessive use of force—not always corruption, although in some cases it may involve threats of false arrest or falsification of evidence
- Taking of bribes to alter evidence
- Taking of bribes to harass witnesses, or in the case of legal actions against police, doing it to help out a colleague
- Theft of evidence when it has some value
- Taking of bribes to not make or to delay an arrest—it was mentioned that some suspects ask to delay the arrest until a Monday, thus avoiding a weekend in jail and avoiding jail entirely by paying bail
- Taking of bribes to (a) not find the defendant so that he or she does not appear for the charging hearing, or (b) not bring witnesses for the prosecution.

Table 5.4 Corruption Risks in Criminal Justice in Ethiopia's Justice Sector

	Potential forms of corruption
Detection of alleged crime	• *Political authorities or higher-level officers* **direct police to ignore complaints, undertake investigations, or arrest "suspects" without probable cause.** • *Police* take regular payments from those running criminal activities or ordinary businesses to ignore infractions. • *Police* **solicit or accept bribes or other considerations to process or ignore complaints.** • *Police* **solicit or accept bribes or other considerations to arrest or release suspects.** • *Lawyers*, in collusion with private clients, threaten criminal complaints to extort money or force other actions of "probable suspects."
Investigation of crime and pretrial procedures	• *Political authorities or higher-level officers* direct police to falsify or ignore evidence. • *Police* steal valuable evidence. • *Political authorities or higher-level officials* **direct prosecutors to file or not file charges.** • *Political authorities* **manipulate assignment of the "right" judges (prosecutor or investigator) to handle cases.** • *Political authorities* **pressure prosecutors or judges to request or require pretrial detention, refuse bail, or set bail higher or lower than necessary.** • *Political authorities* **pressure judges or prison staff to restrict pretrial detainees' legal rights.** • *Public authorities* solicit bribes from detainees for access to counsel or other legal rights. • *Political authorities* instruct judges, prosecutors, or public defenders to speed up or slow down proceedings. • *Political or higher-level officials* pressure judges or others (including private attorneys) about decisions on evidence or other matters. • *Police or prosecutors* **solicit or accept bribes or other consideration from parties to falsify or hide evidence.** • *Lawyers or other court experts* falsify or retain evidence to aid principal clients or as a means of extorting money from other parties. • *Prosecutors* solicit or accept bribes or other consideration from parties to drop or reduce charges. • *Prosecutors* **file charges to "punish" suspects (abuse of authority).** • *Political or agency actors* pressure potential witnesses to not come forward.

(continued next page)

Table 5.4   *(continued)*

Potential forms of corruption

	• *Lawyers or clients* purchase false testimony from civilian or expert witnesses.
	• *Parties* offer or accede to bribes to influence how cases are assigned.
	• *Lawyers or clients* offer or accede to bribes or other considerations to affect decisions on pretrial detention and bail.
	• **Lawyers asks clients for money to "pay off" the judge or prosecutor but instead pocket the funds.**
	• *Public defenders* solicit fees from defendants; *"pro bono" defenders* solicit fees from clients.
	• *Lawyers or clients* offer or accede to bribes or other considerations about scheduling of events to either rush or slow down cases.
	• *Lawyers or clients* offer or accede to bribes or other considerations to affect responses to motions to eliminate evidence, exclude witnesses, or dismiss parts of complaints.
Trial and appeal	• ***Political or higher judicial authorities* direct judges as to how to rule.**
	• *Political authorities* instruct public defense lawyers (or private attorneys) to mishandle cases.
	• *Political authorities or higher-level officials* direct judges to accept or not accept appeals or direct rulings.
	• *Political authorities or parties* engage in jury tampering (if juries are used).
	• ***Judges* "sell" judgments or other preferential treatment to parties.**
	• ***Public officials or political authorities* pressure or bribe witnesses.**
	• ***Police or bailiffs* take bribes to not bring witnesses (or defendants) to trial.**
	• *Lawyers or clients* offer or agree to pay court staff to "lose" files.
	• *Lawyers or clients* offer (or agree) to pay to delay or accelerate issuance of written opinions (which may be delayed for a long time).
	• *Private defense attorneys* accept bribes from interested nongovernmental parties to mishandle cases.
	• ***Court staff* accept or request bribes to show judgments to parties (or offer to sell an outcome already determined by judge).**

(continued next page)

Table 5.4   *(continued)*

	Potential forms of corruption
	• ***Lawyers* solict money from clients to bribe any of actors, but they pocket the funds.**
	• *Lawyers or parties* offer or agree to pay to affect decisions on licenses to appeal and appellate judgments.
Enforcement of judgment	• ***Political authorities or higher judicial leaders* direct whether and how enforcement will be effected**.
	• *Parties* offer or agree to pay to arrange early release or nonincarceration. Same with any payment of damages.

Source: Author.

All of these examples were mentioned in interviews with police, the ethics and anticorruption commissions, and outside observers. Unfortunately, it was impossible to get data from any agency to determine how frequently these complaints were made, let alone how often they were true. Many of the resulting problems (failure of witnesses or defendant to appear, problems with evidence) could also be attributed to overwork, incompetence, or inadequate logistical support (for example, vehicles, address directories, and so on). Aside from simple monetary corruption (bribes), it was mentioned that relationships or political pressures (often from a local authority) could also be at fault. This is corruption but of a different kind.

Interestingly, no one expressed a belief that higher-level political corruption was a frequent explanation—and all seemed to believe that, in most cases, the monetary values involved were relatively small. This is one reason the FEACC prefers to send these cases back to the police for investigation and possibly for disciplinary action short of dismissal. The FEACC does its own investigation only when high police officials are involved or when the police take too long to do it themselves. Police records, to the extent they exist, did not allow for a winnowing out of corruption cases as opposed to other types of complaints (for example, abusive treatment, insubordination, excessive force, or shirking of duty).

Prosecutors. A national commission established to review problems of criminal justice has developed a long list of shortcomings related to prosecutorial performance. As with the police, some of these could involve corruption, but others may be overwork, incompetence, or inefficient work procedures. The anticorruption commissions had received relatively few complaints against prosecutors, and NGO interviewees tended to cite incompetence as more of a problem. In Amhara, two of the handful of cases mentioned involved "abuse of office," that is, a personal vendetta in which the prosecutor harassed someone with whom he already had a quarrel.

The criminal justice commission's list is too long to cite here. For example, just in the charging process, the following shortcomings were mentioned:

- Failing to file charge within 15 days
- Failing to file in accord with formats provided by the law
- Filing charges under inappropriate provisions
- Filing charges jointly when they should be separated or vice versa
- Failing to attach individual responsibility to the person charged, failing to assign level of responsibility to the actors, charging all together
- Failing to indicate the appropriateness of evidence
- Making the charges too long
- To avoid giving reasons why there is no case, simply filing the charge
- When there are strong grounds for the charge, to avoid responsibility filing charge without strong grounds (killing the charge slowly)
- Poor drafting of the charges, misidentification of the elements of the offense and of proof of those elements
- Thinking the number of files charged determines efficiency and effectiveness
- Bringing charges in the wrong case
- Filing charges where there is no evidence
- Failing to differentiate the grounds under article 40 (identifying legal grounds for charge)
- When in doubt, laying a charge instead of asking for direction.

To a suspicious mind, any of these actions (as well as the problems itemized in the four additional pages) could be motivated. Some of those interviewed suggested that prosecutors might be bribed or might act on friendship or political instructions to delay a case, mischarge the suspect, or otherwise plan for failure. However, no one seemed to believe this practice was frequent (in part because the same results might be purchased at a lower cost from the police). Moreover—because at the moment the federal ministry's greatest concern seems to be improving its conviction rate—such practices are likely to become more difficult and could cause the prosecutor to lose his or her job. One person suggested that the effort to reinforce the working relationship between prosecutors and police could lead to more corruption among the former, but again the emphasis on efficiency may drive out any such tendency, and otherwise the proposal seems a practical one.

As with the courts, greater monitoring of productivity and an emphasis on reducing delays and raising efficiency may drive out any petty corruption. Political intervention, including directions to press forward with cases against opposition members or anyone who had fallen out of favor with the government, is another matter, but although few discounted its presence, it was seen as restricted to a limited number of cases. In an ongoing, politically charged case, it is also reported that prison authorities illegally restricted detainees' access to counsel. Whether this was corruption or simple abuse would depend on why the authorities acted this way (that is, to extort bribes, on instructions, or just because they could do it).

Judges. For judges, corruption in criminal cases was mentioned less often. Here the major charge was that, in cases important to the government, judges were more likely to sway their decisions (a) in line with explicit instructions, or (b) still more likely, with what they believed the government wanted. A few ex-judges and outside observers mentioned the phenomenon of "looking over one's shoulder": the sense that judges feared making a decision that would negatively affect their careers or even lead to dismissal. A few examples were given: a judge who lost his driver and his per diems after a decision the government clearly disliked, and another who was denied certain benefits (leave for training, for example) because, he believed, he was too independent and too critical.

Out-and-out dismissal is apparently no longer common, but critics claimed that a series of subtle pressures could force a judge to resign. To avoid these circumstances, it was said that judges sometimes asked to be removed from cases or simply granted more and longer adjournments to avoid the hard decisions.

There are other kinds of pressures—from family, acquaintances, and even colleagues. One judge mentioned being contacted by the parties and even the prosecutor regarding certain cases; the guess was that there might have been corruption behind some of these requests, but no money was offered to the judge.

One innovation at the federal level that may curb some of these pressures is the introduction of a bail bench. Bail amounts tend to be relatively low, and although there are some nonbailable offenses, it is conceivable that an individual judge might be convinced to ignore that prohibition or to set bail even lower, thus giving the defendant a chance to flee. In a few cases, albeit not recently, the government has rearrested defendants released on bail and recharged them as they left the courtroom. Although not constituting corruption, this practice is a clear abuse of respect for judicial decisions, part of the rule of law.

Court staff and private attorneys. Finally, in criminal cases, the roles of courtroom staff and the independent bar should be considered. The bar was not seen as active in any likely corruption in criminal justice, probably because few defendants have a lawyer. Although courtroom staff once may have had a critical role (by "losing" files), it is said that the color-coded file system (an innovation of the modernization program) has made this less possible. In table 5.4 above, that item is thus not bolded, but it might be if other regions were included. One observer did note the possibility of misplacing cases in the transition from the prosecutor's office to the judiciary. The bench representatives admitted this was possible, but no one else saw it as a major problem. A high-level judge also noted a problem (in both civil and criminal cases) with court staff "selling" a decision to the winning party—based on the staff's foreknowledge of the outcome. This practice is bolded in table 5.4, but at least at the federal levels, it appears to be under control.

Thus, in criminal justice, most observers concluded that real or perceived political intervention was the major source of corruption for the judiciary. Other types of corruption centered on the police, with its ability to either advance cases or stop them in their tracks.

Regarding the judiciary, political influence (real or imagined) was assumed to affect the judgment and any appeals. Many of the judicial details potentially subject to political intervention (for example, admission of evidence or decisions on interlocutory motions) were not mentioned; whether this is because they do not occur or simply because they are subsumed under the general rubric of presumed political pressure (or a desire to please political leaders) is unclear.

The police's role in causing provisional closures for failure to bring witnesses or defendants to hearings was also cited. Data do indicate such closures are common, but there is no means of determining how much of this is a result of corruption as opposed to poor working procedures or logistical problems.

The Civil Justice Chain

Again, we begin with the relevant section of table 5.1, shown below as table 5.5, with bolding to indicate where corruption is most likely. As

Table 5.5   Corruption Risks in Civil Justice in Ethiopia's Justice Sector

	Potential forms of corruption
Filing of claim and pretrial stages	• *Public officials* (in judiciary or outside) direct staff to admit or not admit cases.
	• *Public authorities* coerce or bribe private attorneys to file or not file cases.
	• **Court staff solicit or accept bribes or other consideration to accept and process claims.**
	• *Lawyers* accept bribes from other parties to mishandle cases, or lawyers accept fees from both parties.
	• **Lawyers solicit money from clients to bribe judges or staff, but instead pocket the money.**
	• *Lawyers* encourage clients to take cases to court that they are bound to lose.
	• **Process servers solicit or accept bribes for nonservice, faster service, false service, and the like.**
	• *Public officials (in judiciary or outside)* direct staff to speed or delay initial processing of cases.
	• *Lawyers or parties* offer or agree to pay court staff for faster or slower scheduling of events or for misplacement of case files.
	• *Public officials (in judiciary or outside)* direct judges' decisions of pretrial motions.
	• *Judges* solicit or accept bribes for handling of pretrial motions.
	• *Lawyers* file unnecessary motions or appeals to be able to charge clients more.
	• *Public officials (in judiciary or outside)* direct court staff to misplace files.
	• *Public officials (in judiciary or outside)* direct staff to give them premature access to judicial decisions.
	• **Court staff solicit or accept bribes for access to judicial decisions before they are announced.**
Trial and appeal stages	• *Higher authorities or political elites* direct judgments or licenses to appeal.
	• **Private attorneys collude with judges for mutual benefit.**
	• **Judges solicit or accept bribes for favorable judgments (or to higher-level judges on appeal).**
	• *Lawyers or parties* engage in jury tampering (if juries are used).
	• **Court staff use knowledge of judgments to "sell" them to winning parties.**
	• *Lawyers* accept bribes from other parties to mishandle cases.
Enforcement	• *Government agency officials* ignore judicial orders to pay or take other action where judgments are against the agency.
	• *Lawyers or parties* negotiate with judges, bailiffs, or other parties so that enforcement does not occur.
	• **Court-appointed experts issue under- or overvaluations of assets.**
	• Court-appointed agents, in public auctions, collude to manipulate prices, take over assets at reduced prices, or arrange with private parties to sell for low bid.

Source: Author.

above in the criminal justice chain, many of the multiple actions that might influence a judgment (such as admission of evidence or other interlocutory motions) were not mentioned, but this may be because they are subsumed under the general rubric of "purchased" or "directed" judgments. Still, the failure to report them could be significant because in very corrupt countries, interviewees usually provide a wealth of such details.

The informants and reviewers, even government representatives, generally agreed that civil cases offered the greatest potential for judicial corruption—logically, because here only judges and entrusted officials (attorneys, expert witnesses, and those charged with enforcement) have a role.[22] Civil justice is also an area where political authorities are less likely to have an interest except in cases involving state-owned enterprises (SOEs) or where they or their allies happen to have economic dealings.

Although the federal courts have used their database to demonstrate that private citizens do win cases against the government, it would probably be worthwhile to do further analysis to determine whether there are types of cases where this is less true. Critics suggested, for example, that cases involving SOEs were less likely to be won, or more likely to have excessive delays and adjournments, because the judge was reluctant to come to a final decision. If such patterns can be identified, a case could be made for the exercise of political influence here. Determining political influence in cases of interest to, but not directly involving, political actors or agencies would be far more difficult, but this was another hypothesis offered by critics.

Nonetheless, the strongest claims about corruption in civil cases involve those between nongovernmental actors and generally took two forms: (a) the spontaneous (and often small) bribe offered to a judge to alter his or her decision, and (b) the parties' reliance on attorneys with a special relationship with certain judges.

Although no further information was given on the case of the Federal High Court judge recently convicted for accepting a bribe (based on 17 recorded entreaties to the party) if it was a civil case, it was clearly one of the former because the bribe requested was said to be between Br 7,000 and Br 10,000 (less than US$1,000). Apocryphal examples provided by other interviewees suggest that this is not an unusual amount for those judges who do initiate the process. One informant gave an example of a judge presenting a party with two judgments—one against the client and the other worth Br 50,000 in his favor. That these cases exist is undeniable, but their frequency is much in debate. The judiciary claims they are rare; other observers hold that they are not that unusual. Whatever the answer, proving judicial complicity is a difficult charge, especially given the simultaneous emphasis on augmenting judicial independence.

The role of private attorneys in this process is highly relevant, and for this reason that role has been treated separately in the value chain. Many attorneys served on the bench (if only to fulfill the requirements for licensing) and then left, either attracted by high salaries and greater independence in private practice or because they had problems with the evolving evaluation system. However, they retain contacts with their former colleagues, and this, many believed, is a foundation for corrupt practices. Certainly, in common parlance, the first question asked by a client is said to be "Do you know the judge?" It is presumed that if the answer is "yes," the lawyer will be able to negotiate a favorable decision. Moreover—and contrary to the example cited above—when larger amounts are involved, "experts" assert that lawyers or other go-betweens are used and that the party and the judge never discuss the matter.

A third scenario—not stressed by informants but certainly visible in some discussions—concerned large lawsuits involving foreign clients, some of whom were said to instruct their lawyers to "just make the judge happy." Given relatively low judicial salaries (from Br 2,100 plus housing and transportation allowances for a federal First Instance judge to roughly Br 6,000 plus free housing and a car for Supreme Court justices), a sizable payment could be tempting, but such cases were only discussed hypothetically; no one offered examples.

A final piece of information, which could not be verified, involved the rumored investigation of 12 judges in the Addis Ababa municipal land courts. Informants did not specify whether they were "real" judges (part of the Addis municipal courts) or members of a special executive tribunal. In any event, the FEACC refused to comment on the rumor although its own publications do confirm its ongoing investigation of the land agency. Both FEACC members and other informants did agree that taxes, land, and customs attract corruption, although they were probably referring to what occurs within the executive branch. Administrative manipulation of land issues does generate cases between private parties; in the other areas, any litigation is likely to be administrative or criminal (corruption).

Labor cases were also mentioned because of a presumed pro-labor bias on the part of some judges. The one example given was of a woreda judge (thus a member of a regional judiciary, although not in Amhara) who wrote the pleadings for a labor case on which he later presided. Like most of the other examples, this could not be checked, but it does fit with another common belief that woreda judges, because they are less experienced, younger, and more susceptible to executive interference, are among the most problematic. Earlier studies did report that local (woreda) administrators seemed to regard judges as virtual executive staff (World Bank 2004a; NJI 2008).

If civil cases are the most susceptible to corruption, the forms taken do not appear to be terribly complicated. Many of the possible corruption sites listed in table 5.4 seem unnecessary in the Ethiopian context where, if corruption occurs, it is most likely to be the purchase of a judgment or some finagling of the execution process (where the federal courts admit there are still problems but largely with nonjudicial experts and enforcement agents, including those running auctions). Two former sites—staff's misplacement of files and excessive and lengthy adjournments—have become less feasible because of new judicial policies, but it still may be possible for staff to collect fees for performing other regular duties.[23]

Compared with other countries within and outside the region, where informants could state the price for a judgment at different levels, it appears that, whatever its incidence, corruption in the civil justice process is less common in Ethiopia. In some sense, this is also the bad news because sporadic corruption is more difficult to combat than the more systemic and systematic type. The courts, having introduced practices to combat the more institutionalized vices, are now faced with combating corruption as they would ordinary, unorganized criminal actions—and doing so without reversing their simultaneous efforts to make judges more independent and less fearful of political interventions.

Conclusions on Justice Sector Corruption in Ethiopia

Compared with other regional and nonregional examples (the Latin American countries cited previously for comparison), Ethiopia's justice sector, if not corruption-free, is hardly a worst-case scenario. In terms of frequency, police may be the worst offenders, but we are largely talking about relatively petty corruption perpetrated by individuals in response to monetary offers, ties of friendship or kinship, or occasionally political influence (in cases where an ally or enemy of political authorities is involved).[24] Some of the most egregious practices identified in the most corrupt countries (for example, police involvement in criminal activities, their availability as thugs-for-hire, or their regular receipt of protection money from criminal operations or legal businesses) were not mentioned at all and probably do not exist in Ethiopia.

Prosecutorial and judicial corruption appears less frequently, which again seems to be largely a function of individual susceptibility either to monetary inducements or ties of kinship and friendship. (However, some observers noted that kinship, friendship, and ethnic ties might have a stronger impact in regions not visited for this research). There were no indications of internal corruption networks (except in the unverifiable example of the Addis land "judges"), and at most some informants suggested that certain lawyers may have special relationships with a few judges. Nor was there any suggestion that monetarily induced corruption was a top-down controlled phenomenon.

The practice in some other countries of sector (or "entrusted") officials buying their jobs and then engaging in corruption to recoup their "investments" was reported as entirely absent in Ethiopia. Judges and prosecutors do seem attuned to government requirements, real or imagined, in the occasional high-profile case, but such cases have become less frequent over time. Such sensitivity is linked to a perceived emphasis in personnel policies on party loyalty—an emphasis that agency officials insist is largely imaginary. To the extent they are correct, one contributing factor is the current larger number of qualified applicants and the persistent lack of transparent selection criteria. Whereas once, anyone with a law degree (and such degrees were nearly exclusively from the University of Addis Ababa) could get a job, there is now more competition and there are more law faculties in operation. Under these circumstances, for their own good and for the reassurance of the candidates, it clearly behooves those responsible for the selection process to become more explicit about the criteria they will apply. Now that they have the luxury of rejecting some candidates, they must offer the explanations that were unnecessary before.

Two additional areas of corruption—that of courtroom (or prosecutorial) staff and lawyers and other officers of the court—have developed differently. The courts' CMS has made staff malfeasance more difficult to proceed undetected. Because the prosecutors still lack a CMS, they also lack control over this situation although no one suggested that their staffs had much opportunity to affect the progress of cases.

For lawyers, it appears that little has changed. At the federal level, the Ministry of Justice seems most concerned with ensuring they are up to date on their fees, and in any case, receives complaints about little else. Passing some responsibility on to the bar association to police its own members might be a good idea, but the government's relationship with the major organization, the Ethiopian Bar Association, has been fraught with problems.

A relatively gray area involves other officers of the court (enforcement officials, expert witnesses, and those involved in evaluating and auctioning assets), and it probably requires more investigation. None of those interviewed mentioned this spontaneously, but when judges were asked, they admitted it could be a problem. As revealed in studies elsewhere, the lack of attention is universal despite the vast opportunities for abuses, even in the more-developed regions (for example, see Henderson et al. 2004).

Unfortunately, this generally positive situation relative to the rest of Africa is not fully appreciated by citizens. Although recent surveys suggest that citizens do not see the courts as the worst offenders (Transparency International 2007; APAP 2001), the public also seems unaware of agencies' efforts to do better.

Recommendations

One universal problem with citizen perceptions of corruption or, for that matter, of other sector vices is that they lack a basis for comparison. At best, citizens can compare current conditions with the situation ex ante in their own country, but rarely can they contrast it with even neighboring nations.[25]

It is the conclusion of this report that justice sector corruption, while not nonexistent in Ethiopia, is at relatively lower levels than in many comparator countries. However, because most citizens do not have contact with the sector (or if they do, have at most one experience, and moreover may be more influenced by a few recent scandals), their basis even for assessing recent developments is limited. Furthermore, citizen mistrust and the government's own lack of transparency may encourage the belief that corruption is happening behind the scenes.

More important, Ethiopia's sector reform programs have not focused on corruption, preferring to emphasize increased access, improvements to the quality of personnel, and efficiency. The lack of emphasis on corruption is understandable because (a) it arguably is not the principal problem, and (b) it is a negative goal (and does require admitting a problem that agencies may prefer not to recognize for a variety of reasons). However, without discounting the other objectives, it may be time for the sector to take a more decisive stance against this vice and so address citizens' possibly exaggerated perceptions of its frequency. The following are some suggested steps in that direction.

Recommendation 1: *Improve the mechanisms for receiving complaints.*

The complaints-handling and disciplinary offices common to all agencies are underused and for good reason. They are usually centralized and inconveniently located (for the federal police, on the seventh floor of the relatively impenetrable main office; in the courts and Ministry of Justice, no easier to find). These offices also appear to have few staff—possibly logically so, given their inactivity, but also creating problems for those wishing to register complaints.

Thus, a first step—already under consideration by the ethics and anti-corruption commissions—would be to ease access by decentralizing the reporting centers and making sure their hours of operation (if staffing does not permit these to be full-time) are well publicized and respected.

None of the offices appears to have good databases, for which reason none could provide information on complaints regarding corruption as opposed to all the other complaints they receive. Apparently the cases are kept in individual files, and the offices rely on the memories of those in charge to locate them. This weakness could be easily eliminated with, as discussed below, several advantages. Because, in the case of alleged judicial corruption, the standard answer of both the agency offices and the ethics and anticorruption commissions is to recommend an appeal, it is not clear how much value-added these offices and commissions supply for complainants. Admittedly, most complainants come with vague charges, but perhaps a public education campaign would help, focusing less on why corruption is bad than on *what it is* and *what it takes* to prove its existence. Some of the officials interviewed did report efforts to explain why certain complaints could not be pursued. This is good practice, and if any are not following it, they ought to do so.

Recommendation 2: *Take a more proactive stance in rooting out corruption.*

It would also help—even at the risk of redundancy with the anticorruption commissions—if the sector agencies took a more proactive stance in combating corruption instead of waiting for complaints to be filed. The courts certainly could use their CMS databases to identify irregularities, even if such irregularities do not prove corruption. Tracking win rates of lawyers with certain judges, or even tracking the rates of judge-lawyer assignments, might be a start.

If the respective complaints offices, including those in the courts, also created databases for their own cases, they could do further analysis to help identify emerging problems, problematic actors, and areas requiring more citizen education. In the end, this may mean reconceptualizing the role of the complaints offices: converting them from their current status as a sort of human suggestion box to a more technical, analytic focus on quality control and the development of strategies to enhance it.

Development of more explicit strategies might also be recommended to the FEACC and regional ethics and anticorruption commissions. They report having the means to prioritize their attention, but it might be useful to publicize their policies and to specify the objectives behind them. As a criminal investigator once explained to the author, the point is not just to catch criminals but also to focus on the best means to reduce crime. The ethics commissions have proved they can do the former, and it is now time to move on to the latter.

Recommendation 3: *Increase the transparency of personnel policies.*

Greater clarity on personnel policies is long overdue, especially in the courts, which come under the most criticism in this area. The steps under consideration by the federal courts should be adopted rapidly and imitated by those regional judiciaries that have not already started them.

The courts have finally entered a period where they no longer have to accept all comers, but that means the intrinsic guidelines they may have formerly followed should now be made explicit. Many more countries guarantee judicial independence and lifetime tenure than actually practice either. Ethiopia needs to place itself clearly among the practitioners and thereby end the impression among judges, lawyers, and the general public that party loyalty is what counts. This impression is probably in error, but without explicit guidelines there is too much room for systemic bias and arbitrary individual assessments.

Recruitment should be advertised, candidates should be ranked on explicit criteria, and lists of final nominees should be published before their appointments. The same is true of transfers and promotions. The courts could also use and enhance their databases to demonstrate that these guidelines are being used. The author's attempt to do so as part of this research proved impossible because the data on "judicial experience" turned out to include not credentials or evaluations of performance but rather former positions on the bench.

Recommendation 4: *Encourage bar associations to police their own members.*

Admittedly, professional associations often afford excessive professional courtesy to errant members, but given the government's inattention to attorney malfeasance, a little redundancy might be a good thing. Independent bar associations should be encouraged to receive complaints (which they do not do now) and police their own members instead of relying only on the ministry and bureaus of justice for this role.

In the best of worlds, the bar associations would also be invited to evaluate judges and prosecutors, adding their own assessments to those provided by the principal agencies. Some regional judiciaries (for example, Amhara) do include bar members in their judicial administrative councils, but they are conspicuously absent from the federal body. An external reviewer's suggestion that citizens be allowed to sue their attorneys for injurious representation might be considered, but giving the government an additional role in the process (beyond that already included in the licensing process) might invite political harassment.

Recommendation 5: *Improve the internal monitoring of the police and prosecution (and, once developed, public defense).*

Whether the government continues with the Singapore (top-down) model or eventually invites citizens to take a more active role in monitoring corruption, this step will be critical, not only to control corruption but also to improve performance overall. The BPR exercise may force this step, as both agencies will have to fix and track indicators of performance, but whether or not this happens, the agencies will not improve if they cannot monitor outputs and link them to individual employees and work units.

Recommendation 6: *Admit that corruption is a problem and may become more so as agencies grow.*

It would behoove all agencies to admit that corruption remains a problem, if not a major one, and to stress that they are giving the fight against corruption the same emphasis as their other goals. One important step here might be to conduct an annual survey on user experience with all agencies, especially regarding corruption. A similar survey was initially considered for this research, but because of the time limits, could not be done. A well-crafted survey might focus on general perceptions, negative experiences with any of the agencies, whether respondents made complaints, and if so, how they assessed the results. Over time such surveys could help agencies monitor their own progress as well as identify areas needing more attention.

Ideally, future surveys would also examine some of the areas not addressed here: traditional dispute resolution, sharia, social courts, and the remaining organizational themes. This recommendation does not stem from strong suspicions that all those areas feature corruption but simply from concern about the thoroughness of analysis.

It is understandable, especially for the courts, why they do not discuss corruption: to admit its existence is to lay oneself open for outside interference. One suspects a similar logic lies behind the various offices' "inability" to come up with precise figures on complaints received. However, admitting a problem and at the same time outlining a program for its resolution may be less dangerous because that would indicate the agency is on top of the matter. Aside from improving current perceptions, such a stance could also help fend off any emerging problems.

A few of those interviewed believed that the corruption situation in Ethiopia's justice sector was getting worse, and although this was a minority view, it is not entirely without foundation. As the agencies increase their size and recruit more widely, they will face problems of monitoring performance or running adequate background checks on new members. Thus, minor problems would escalate into major ones if strategies to prevent this are not put in place.

Notes

1. Private attorneys, although not government actors, are included because they are considered "entrusted officials" and commonly must be licensed or recognized by the state. In this status, they serve as a gateway to purely public services and thus are critical in defining both the supply of and demand for the latter (managing what is called a credence good).

2. This is clearly important in Ethiopia because of the major role of traditional dispute resolution (see Pankhurst and Assefa 2008 for examples, and Turton 2006 is also relevant).

3. The sharia courts now recognized as part of the Ethiopian judiciary—and thus falling under the supervision of the federal judicial administrative council—have also been excluded. No data were made available on the number of cases they handle.

4. Where this number comes from is anyone's guess, but it is frequently cited in the literature.

5. Some sources (Mariam 2002) trace the origins of the social courts to far earlier practices. Currently, these government-appointed bodies operate at the level of the *kebele* (the lowest administrative unit). They are composed of lay members who are supposed to operate based on a combination of local values and formal law, although for the most part they have little training in the latter (Mariam 2002; NJI 2008). Despite many criticisms of their operations (including corruption linked to favoritism and political influences), it seems unlikely that they can be eliminated quickly (NJI 2008, 183–84) and thus the current strategy seems to be to restrict their jurisdiction (removing some highly controversial areas including land) and train their members.

6. Accurate figures were elusive, but the authorities interviewed guessed that police staffing is currently under 60,000 (with 70,000 as a new goal)—providing a police-population ratio of about 75 to 100,000. Such a ratio is possibly usual for Africa (figures are unattainable elsewhere as well) but far below the standard recommendation of 300 police per 100,000 of population. However, the 60,000 total figure seems low, especially because the Federal Police (which provided it) claims to have a 30,000 staffing level and because other sources note that the Amhara region has another 15,000 (Bourassa 2009).

7. The extreme cases are nations where corrupt institutions have become predatory in their relations with citizens or have been fully captured by elites for the principal purpose of eliminating opposition.

8. Frequent risk reduction tactics including hiring private security, inflating costs (to compensate for the difficulty of collecting payments), and relying exclusively on known suppliers and contractors (see World Bank 2009 for comments on the latter practice in Ethiopia). The authors do not cite corruption but rather delays and inefficiency as the motivating factors.

9. As Zook (2009) and others have noted, Singapore's reputed success depends on factors not common to less-developed countries: sufficient resources to establish a complex internal mentoring system (and to pay extremely high salaries) and the country's small size. If this is, as some writers hold, "the Asian model," its application in countries such as China has proved a far less successful check on corruption, especially at the local level.

10. The prosecutors have also tried to argue that provisionally closed cases should not be counted, but unfortunately this is the international practice. If not counted, their conviction rates would be in the 80 percent range, according to Ministry of Justice interviews.

11. "Minor" is a relative term, and as Bourassa (2009) notes, in some regions, cases with up to 15 years' imprisonment as a penalty are handled in these courts.

12. The percentage of detainees who are still awaiting trial is unsatisfactorily high, as it is in most of Africa and other developing regions (EHRC 2008). It is worth noting that the federal judiciary contested the commission's numbers.

13. Apparently some donors have encouraged Ethiopia to develop paralegal services to make up for the shortage of lawyers, but progress has been slow.

14. This same individual also tried to argue that "corruption" was a Western concept and had a different meaning in Ethiopia but eventually desisted there as well.

15. These figures are approximations. As discussed later, apparently none of these offices has databases to track their work, or if they do, they are not organized to allow an identification of different types of cases.

16. The FEACC noted only one exception, a case that involved a "substantial amount" of money.

17. Corruption in other system administration areas also was not mentioned by interviewees even when presented with the full table. A recent audit did suggest errors in the federal judiciary's management of funds but without implying corruption (Tadesse 2009). In other countries, mismanagement of budgets and procurement (especially for police forces) is a common complaint, and any corruption may involve not only administrators but also higher-level officials. In Brazil, where judicial corruption is only moderate, one famous case from the late 1990s involved a federal judge who took kickbacks on a court construction project.

18. This practice has been reported in various Latin American nations, beginning with the *tribus legales* ("legal tribes") formed around Venezuelan political parties represented in that country's judicial council, from its creation in 1969 to its elimination in 2000 (Hammergren 2002). The practice has also been reported, albeit not as well documented, in several African countries.

19. Two examples are (a) a former federal minister of justice in Argentina who twice took control of the Buenos Aires police (a notoriously corrupt body), and (b) a former university administrator in Mexico who directed the Mexico City police during the early 2000s. Both attempted major reforms and encountered considerable hostility from career officers and their political patrons. Although not serving as police commissioner, Mayor Rudy Giuliani's championing of the New York City reforms of the 1990s is another example—and his conflicts with a series of commissioners are also well known.

20. This lack of transparency also contrasts with reportedly more transparent practices in the rest of the public sector.

21. The recruitment of judges from an overrepresented region not only conflicts with the underlying policy (to increase ethnic diversity) but also feeds the general impression that certain nationalities are inevitably favored.

22. It should be noted that one external reviewer stressed that corruption was less likely in civil than in criminal cases (except for civil cases involving administrative matters) because both parties would be equally motivated to pay bribes. In theory this may be true, but experience in many countries suggests a high level of corruption in civil, nonadministrative cases, if only because one party can outbid the other, has better political contacts, or is savvier about the rules of the game.

23. The color coding system previously mentioned would not prevent payments to court staff. However, references to such practices fall far short of those in other countries in the region. For example, a high-level administrator and a lawyer in another African country told the author that courtroom staff would have to be paid a "tip" to retrieve files. Whether or not this still happens in Ethiopia, one can hardly imagine such a practice being treated as standard procedure by high-level staff.

24. Such authorities need not be at the highest levels: it was mentioned that both mayors and woreda officials sometimes leaned on police.

25. Were citizens able to do so with a few of the increasingly available international databases (see, for example, CEPEJ 2006 and later biennial editions), they might better appreciate the judiciary's efforts to increase efficiency. Comparative data on corruption are also available but unfortunately not reliable, and as even their authors sometimes caution, they are most appropriate for tracking change in a single country, not for cross-national comparisons.

References

Abiad, Pablo, and Mariano Thieberger. 2005. "Justicia Era Kirchner: La construcción de un poder a medida." Buenos Aires: Marea.

Amegatcher, Nene Abayaateye Ofoe. 2007. "The Challenges to Commercial Dispute Resolution in the Ghanaian Courts: Is Order 58 of the High Court (Civil Procedure) Rules, 2004 (C.L47) the Panacea?" LLM dissertation, Nottingham Trent University, U.K.

APAP (Action Professionals' Association for the People). 2001. "Baseline Survey Report on APAP's Intervention in Areas of Human Rights." Research report, APAP, Addis Ababa.

Bailey, John, and Roy Godson, eds. 1999. *Organized Crime and Democratic Accountability: Mexico and the U.S.-Mexican Borderlands.* Pittsburgh: University of Pittsburgh Press.

Bourassa, Laura. 2009. "Briefing to USAID/Ethiopia on Justice Sector Reform." From notes transcribed by Jennifer Whelan, April 7, on file with author.

Campos, J. Edgardo, and Sanjay Pradhan, eds. 2007. *The Many Faces of Corruption: Tracking Vulnerabilities at the Sector Level.* Washington, DC: World Bank.

CEPEJ (European Commission for the Efficiency of Justice). 2006. *European Judicial Systems Edition 2006 (2004 data)*. Strasbourg: Council of Europe.

DPLF (Due Process of Law Foundation). 2007. "Evaluation of Judicial Corruption in Central America and Panama and the Mechanisms to Combat It." Regional comparative study report, DPLF, Washington, DC.

EHRC (Ethiopian Human Rights Commission). 2008. "Report on Visits to 35 Federal and Regional Prisons." Translated document, EHRC, Addis Ababa.

FJA (Office of the Commissioner for Federal Judicial Affairs Canada). 2005. "Court Administration Reform Project in Ethiopia." Final report of the Court Administration Reform Project II, FJA, Ottawa.

Gidey, Abadi. 2007. "The Relevance of Complaints Hearing System in the Ethiopian Federal Police to Protect and Promote Constitutional Rights." Senior thesis, Institute of Legal Studies, Ethiopian Civil Service College, Addis Ababa.

Hammergren, Linn. 2002. "Do Judicial Councils Further Judicial Reform? Lessons from Latin America." Working Paper 26, Rule of Law Series, Carnegie Endowment for International Peace, Washington, DC.

Hammergren, Linn, Naomi Bang, Jan Perlin, and Ugu Agomoh. 2008. "Balanced Justice and Donor Programs: Lessons from Three Regions of the World." Report for the Open Society Justice Initiative, New York. http://www.Justiceinitiative.org/db/resources.

Helmke, Gretchen. 2005. *Courts under Constraints: Judges, Generals, and Presidents in Argentina*. Cambridge: Cambridge University Press.

Henderson, Keith, Angana Shah, Sandra Elena, and Violaine Autheman. 2004. "Regional Best Practices: Enforcement of Judgments—Lessons from Latin America." Rule of Law White Paper Series, IFES (International Foundation for Electoral Systems), Washington, DC.

Hewko, John. 2002. "Foreign Direct Investment: Does Rule of Law Matter?" Working Paper 26, Rule of Law Series, Carnegie Endowment for International Peace, Washington, DC.

IAES (Institute of African Economic Studies). 2008. "Transparency Ethiopia Corruption Diagnostic Baseline Survey." Final report, Transparency Ethiopia, Addis Ababa.

IMMMA Advocates. 2008. "The Study on Court Cases Involving Banks in Mainland Tanzania." Unpublished manuscript, IMMMA Advocates, Dar es Salaam.

Jembere, Aberra. 2002. "Ethiopia." In *Legal Systems of the World: A Political, Social, and Cultural Encyclopedia*, Vol. II, ed. Herbert M. Kritzer, 510–15. Santa Barbara, CA: ABC-CLIO.

Jensen, Erik. 2003. "The Rule of Law and Judicial Reform: The Political Economy of Diverse Institutional Patterns and Reformers' Responses." In *Beyond*

Common Knowledge: Empirical Approaches to the Rule of Law, ed. Erik Jensen and Thomas Heller, 336–81. Stanford, CA: Stanford University Press.

Kitaw, Getachew. 2004. "Judicial Reform for Harnessing Economic Growth and Development." Unpublished presentation, Ethiopian Bar Association, Addis Ababa.

Klitgaard, Robert. 1988. *Controlling Corruption.* Berkeley and Los Angeles: University of California Press.

La Porta, Rafael, and Florencio López-de-Silanes. 1998. "Capital Markets and Legal Institutions." In *Beyond the Washington Consensus: Institutions Matter,* ed. Shahid Javed Burki and Guillermo Perry, 67–86. Washington, DC: World Bank.

McMillan, John, and Pablo Zoido. 2004. "How to Subvert Democracy: Montesinos in Peru." *Journal of Economic Perspectives* 18 (4): 69–92.

Meredith, Martin. 2005. *The Fate of Africa: A History of Fifty Years of Independence.* New York: Public Affairs.

Mariam, Abera H. 2002. "APAP's Experience on Social Court Judges Training." Discussion paper, APAP (Action Professionals' Association for the People), Addis Ababa.

NJI (National Judicial Institute of Canada). 2008. "Judicial Independence, Transparency, and Accountability: Assessment Report." Final report for CIDA (Canadian International Development Agency) and the Federal Supreme Court of Ethiopia, NJI, Ottawa.

North, Douglass. 1990. *Institutions, Institutional Change and Economic Performance.* Cambridge: Cambridge University Press.

Pankhurst, Alula, and Getachew Assefa, eds. 2008. "Ethiopia at a Justice Crossroads: The Challenge of Customary Dispute Resolution." Unpublished manuscript, Centre Français des Etudes Ethiopiennes, Addis Ababa.

Shavell, Steven. 1997. "The Fundamental Divergence between the Private and the Social Motive to Use the Legal System." *Journal of Legal Studies* 26 (2): 575–61.

Sherwood, Robert M., Geoffrey Shepherd, and Celso Marcos de Souza. 1994. "Judicial Systems and Economic Performance." *The Quarterly Review of Economics and Finance* 34 (Supplement 1): 101–16.

Special Commission on the Administration of Justice in Cook County. 1998. Final report on reforming the Cook County Circuit Court, Chicago.

Stone, Andrew, Brian Levy, and Ricardo Paredes. 1996. "Public Institutions and Private Transactions: A Comparative Analysis of the Legal and Regulatory Environment for Business Transactions in Brazil and Chile." In *Empirical Studies in Institutional Change,* ed. Lee J. Alston, Thrainn Eggertsson, and Douglass North, 95–128. Cambridge, U.K.: Cambridge University Press.

Tadesse, Kirubel. 2009. "Federal Auditor Reports Huge Accounting Errors." *Capital*, Addis Ababa, May 24.

Tesfaye, Andargatchew. 2004. *The Crime Problem and Its Correction*, Vol. II. Addis Ababa: Addis Ababa University Press.

TI (Transparency International). 2007. *Global Corruption Report 2007: Corruption in Judicial Systems.* Cambridge: Cambridge University Press.

Toharia, Jose Juan. 2003. "Assessing a Judiciary's Performance through Public Opinion." In *Beyond Common Knowledge: Empirical Approaches to the Rule of Law*, ed. Erik Jensen and Thomas Heller, 21–62. Stanford, CA: Stanford University Press.

Turton, David, ed. 2006. *Ethnic Federalism: The Ethiopian Experience in Comparative Perspective*. Addis Ababa: Addis Ababa University Press.

USAID (United States Agency for International Development). 2002. "Guidance for Promoting Judicial Independence and Impartiality." Technical Publication PN-ACM-003, USAID, Washington, DC.

———. 2009. *Africa Regional Rule of Law Status Review: Right to Justice.* Washington, DC: USAID.

Van de Vijver, Linda, ed. 2006. *The Judicial Institution in Southern Africa: A Comparative Study of Common Law Jurisdictions.* Cape Town: Silver Ink.

Williams, Jackson. 2002. "What the Growing Use of Pre-Dispute Binding Arbitration Means for the Judiciary." *Judicature* 85 (6): 2667.

World Bank. 2004a. "Ethiopia: Legal and Judicial Sector Assessment." Report of the Legal and Judicial Reform Practice Group, Legal Vice Presidency, World Bank, Washington DC.

———. 2004b. "Making Justice Count: Measuring and Improving Judicial Performance in Brazil." Report 32789-BR, World Bank, Washington, DC.

———. 2005. *Doing Business in 2005: Removing Obstacles to Growth*. Washington DC: World Bank, the International Finance Corporation, and Oxford University Press.

———. 2008. "Diagnosing Corruption in Human Resource Management in the Civil Service." Unpublished manuscript, World Bank, Washington, DC.

———. 2009. "Toward the Competitive Frontier: Strategies for Improving Ethiopia's Investment Climate." Report 48472-ET, World Bank, Washington, DC.

Wrong, Michela. 2000. *In the Footsteps of Mr. Kurtz: Living on the Brink of Disaster in Mobutu's Congo*. New York: HarperCollins.

Zook, Darren. 2009. "The Curious Case of Finland's Clean Politics." *Journal of Democracy* 20 (1): 157–68.

CHAPTER 6

Construction Sector Corruption in Ethiopia

Hamish Goldie-Scot

Introduction

Corruption in the construction and public works sector—consistently ranked worldwide as one of the most corrupt—can be attributed to a combination of high spending and the ease with which many corrupt practices can be hidden. Any capacity constraints, lack of transparency, or lack of accountability systems tend to accentuate the risk, both by

This report was commissioned by the World Bank as a part of an ongoing study of corruption in several sectors in Ethiopia. Thanks are due to all those contributors and participants from government, the private sector, civil society, and the donor community who made the work possible. The anonymity of these respondents has served to encourage the frank sharing of information and ideas that underpins the ongoing process of assessment and reform. Vision, dedication, and practical support were needed to ensure that the construction sector study could be conducted in an effective and independent manner. Special thanks are due to Janelle Plummer, who initiated and supported the work, and to H.E. Ato Ali Sulaiman, Commissioner of the Federal Ethics and Anti-Corruption Commission, who helped ensure access to government respondents.

Although this chapter results from studies completed by January 2010, the process of checking, reviewing, and securing agreement for publication was finally brought to conclusion only in late 2011. The chapter is therefore put forward with the caveat that while it reflects the situation at the time of the study, some details will have understandably changed.

increasing the opportunities for corrupt practices and by strengthening the drivers of corrupt behavior.

Through the use of structured expert interviews, confidential questionnaires, behind-closed-doors workshops, document analysis, and site visits, this preliminary study has started a process of mapping corruption and perceptions of corruption at each stage of the value chain in parts of Ethiopia's construction sector.[1] The approach adopted has recognized the close relationship that exists between corruption and poor governance. This, and the resulting focus on *perceptions* and *examples* of corruption in the sector—rather than on hard evidence of specific cases—led to high levels of interest and participation among most of the stakeholder groups consulted.

The resulting picture that emerged is complex but plausible. Ethiopia exhibits most of the classic warning signs of corruption risk, including instances of poor-quality construction, inflated unit output costs, and delays in implementation. In turn, these factors appear in some cases to be driven by unequal or unclear contractual relationships, poor enforcement of professional standards, high multipliers between public sector and private sector salaries, wide-ranging discretionary powers exercised by government, a lack of transparency, and a widespread perception of hidden barriers to market entry.

Despite such risks, corrupt practices at the operational level appear to be largely opportunistic and relatively minor, capable of being kept under control through professionally managed systems and procedures. However a widespread perception remains of higher-level corruption within the sector.

Mixed Perceptions

An inconsistent picture emerges from existing information on perceived levels of corruption in Ethiopia's construction sector and government attempts to address the issue. Feedback from international consultants suggests that, compared with many other developing countries, construction-related corruption within Ethiopia is relatively low and tends to be the exception rather than the rule. Such a perspective also tends to highlight the significant recent advances made by Ethiopia in infrastructure provision, compared with less-marked progress by other countries where construction-related corruption is known to be rife. These same international stakeholders are also inclined to point to the work of the Federal Ethics and Anti-Corruption Commission (FEACC), which has been bearing down on corrupt land deals related to construction projects, as evidence of government commitment to curbing corruption.

By contrast, some international media and web-based sources paint a much less positive picture, identifying the construction sector as being particularly corrupt and portraying the FEACC to be at best ineffective and at worst unduly influenced by government. As one extreme of a broad spectrum of views that may be unduly motivated by political considerations, such a perspective needs to be viewed with some caution. However, other more mainstream web-based sources present a view that, although less extreme, nevertheless includes strong statements about alleged high levels of corruption. Such a view derives in part from international contractors who previously worked in Ethiopia but no longer do so, considering access to the market to be affected by corrupt practices despite relatively low levels of petty corruption. Taken at face value, these perspectives would be sufficient to deter some responsible potential new entrants from trying to compete in the construction market in Ethiopia.[2]

The view is widely held that market entry is difficult for newcomers and that some individuals, companies, or groups of companies enjoy favored status. Fueling this perception of favoritism is the perceived hidden influence of the ruling party on the sector, a tendency toward top-down development planning, and the government's dominant role as client, regulator, and upholder of professional standards. Though this study encountered no evidence of such powers being abused, it was found that limited competition may be playing a role in driving up unit output costs.

The polarization of views may be self-reinforcing. Prospective new entrants to the market may either decide that the risks are too high and look elsewhere, or alternatively conclude that they have no choice but to bribe their way into contracts. Both such categories of businesses may report high levels of corruption, whereas some more-established businesses may not. By exploring and looking beyond these initial perceptions, this study represents a modest attempt—in itself only a small step—to clarify and help address both the perception and the reality of corruption within the construction sector.

Methodology

The lack of any existing sectoral analysis of corruption in Ethiopia led the World Bank, with the agreement and cooperation of the FEACC, to commission this study. It has been conducted in two phases, each of which comprised about three weeks of in-country consultation.[3] These two phases are considered as a single study. A simple stakeholder survey initiated in the first phase was extended in the second phase using an identical questionnaire.[4]

In addition, to better understand the rises in costs, a small study was undertaken of unit costs of federal roads managed by the Ethiopian Roads Authority (ERA), where Chinese contractors dominate the market, and rural roads (managed by regional road authorities [RRAs]) where the emerging institutional arrangements and related procedures remain relatively weak. In both cases, a lack of effective competition appears to be a significant factor contributing to increasing costs.

A participative approach allowed stakeholders to express their views freely while contributing to the development of practical solutions. This was achieved through a combination of confidential surveys, face-to-face structured interviews, group meetings, and workshops, complemented where necessary by a Web-based review of secondary sources.

To encourage open participation and stimulate constructive dialogue, it was made clear to all those consulted that the study had no investigative purpose and was not looking for attributable *evidence* of corruption. Rather, the focus was on identifying and understanding generic *examples* and *perceptions* of corruption that could be used eventually to help formulate appropriate policy responses. A key component of the strategy adopted for the study was to harness the evident desire on the part of most stakeholders to reduce both the practice and the risk of corruption within the sector.

An opportunistic approach was taken to the identification of and approach to stakeholders. Initial consultations with consultants (both international and domestic), donors (both bilateral and multilateral), and government officials (at the federal level) provided an opportunity to test a draft questionnaire and identify additional stakeholders. These included government officials and representatives of civil society organizations, domestic contractors, consulting engineers, and architects. Although detailed feedback was received from 50 stakeholders, the sample was skewed toward those working in the road sector: many of these had experience of the relatively high-spending ERA, though some also had experience or knowledge of other parts of the construction sector, including buildings.

A specific feature of the approach adopted in this study was to ensure that the issue of corruption was genuinely looked at from the perspective of all the main stakeholder groups. Each of these groups has different priorities and different underlying motives determining behavior. The lack of success of many past anticorruption initiatives championed by specific stakeholders—whether donors, governments, civil society, or construction sector professionals—has demonstrated that corruption cannot be "solved" by looking at the problem from a single perspective.

Corruption in Construction

International Perspective

As previously noted, the public works and construction sector is consistently considered to be one of the three most corrupt of all sectors, alongside defense and the extractive industries. Globally, it has been estimated that corruption accounts for at least 10 percent of turnover in the construction sector, or well over US$1 billion per day (ASCE 2005).

Both the problem and its effects are most acute in developing countries, where construction sector corruption can account for leakages of 20 percent or more (Campos and Pradhan 2007, 159). In many countries, construction-related corruption underpins what is often an opaque approach to funding the political process and is related to other forms of crime. As a result of corruption, project planning is distorted, construction quality undermined, maintenance neglected, and professional standards compromised.

In the roads sector, the classic pattern of corruption in many countries is that the consultant pays a percentage of consultancy costs in bribes, while the contractor pays a higher percentage of the (much higher) construction costs, generally in return for preferential treatment during the procurement process. Through various forms of fraud, including attempts by the contractor to recover his outlay, vested interests then divert a further proportion of construction costs. The result can be that, *even when proper procurement procedures have apparently been followed and when all financial audits appear to be in order*, it is quite possible for as much as 25 percent of the project resources to have been lost in corruption. A postconstruction technical audit may be able to identify some of the fraudulent activities such as the use of substandard materials, but otherwise most of the corruption cannot necessarily readily be detected.

In the past, some donors and many governments have turned a blind eye to, or even encouraged, such corruption. Since the late 1990s, however, a consensus has emerged that corruption not only harms the poor but is also bad for business, for national development, and for international security. The growing influence of international instruments such as the United Nations Convention against Corruption reflects this consensus. Some responsible international companies have now reformed their practices. Where previously they may have turned a blind eye to their staffs' engagement in corrupt practices, they have now established robust internal procedures in support of strict anticorruption policies. Yet corruption persists in the sector, spurred on by the ease with which it can be hidden and by the competitive pressures of globalization. There is no single, or simple, solution to this problem, but much can be achieved by creating more incentives for good practice and by better using existing tools to improve transparency and accountability.

Warning Signs of Corruption in Construction

The link between weak governance and corruption. In any country, many of the typical manifestations of corruption may also be the result of innocent, though equally damaging, weaknesses in governance at any level. It is therefore important not to jump to hasty conclusions. One of the most effective ways to reduce corruption is to improve, clarify, and communicate basic management processes and procedures so that when corruption does arise, it can be readily identified as such and dealt with accordingly.

Such processes include the establishment of an objective, quantifiable basis for measuring whether, and to what extent, anticorruption measures are proving effective. This study considers typical high-level indicators and warning signs (both direct and indirect) of the risk of corruption without addressing the more complex issue of ongoing monitoring of progress against an established baseline.

The increased attention to corruption as a result of anticorruption initiatives can have the effect of generating a temporary rise in perceptions of corruption before the benefits of reform become fully apparent. It is therefore quite possible that one of the short-term effects of the Ethiopian government's recent decision to assess and address the risk of construction-related corruption may, ironically, be to increase the perception of corruption in the sector.

Direct indicators. Direct indicators of corruption include the numbers of prosecutions, and convictions, occurring as a result of corruption in the construction sector. Even in developed countries, however, such data should be viewed with caution because they are highly dependent on the authorities' willingness and capacity to detect and prosecute corruption.

The hidden nature and ease of concealment of corruption in construction means that it can go undetected. Anticorruption agencies do not necessarily possess the skills, nor the full authority, needed to understand construction-related corruption. In some cases they are prone to political interference. It is not unusual for allegations of corruption to be leveled against the very people who are seeking to improve transparency in the sector.

Direct warning signs. Direct warning signs do not necessarily mean that corruption is occurring but would tend to arise if corruption was affecting the sector. These signs include the following:

- *Poor-quality construction.* If a bribe has been paid to win a construction contract, the bribe payer will seek to recoup that cost. This may be achieved by intimidating or simply bribing the supervising engineer to turn a blind eye to fraudulent activity. A typical scenario would be to claim full payment for substandard or incomplete work while also having that work certified as meeting the specification. The consequences may not come to light for many years and may be difficult to attribute to corrupt practices. Where such corruption results eventually in structural failure, the impact on users of that infrastructure can in extreme cases be fatal.

- *Inflated costs.* When corruption results in an uncorrected loss of quality, the result can be an apparent reduction in costs, reflecting the reduced value of the asset. But corruption can also result in cost inflation in many ways:
  - If the original bid has been rigged (readily achievable unless specific safeguards are in place to ensure genuine competition), the unit rates used by all the bidders may be inflated to include a provision for payment of kickbacks. Such a scheme commonly includes a combination of collusion between bidders, intimidation of other possible bidders to deter them from competing, and manipulation of the procurement process.
  - Alternatively, the original bid may be competitive, but the contract value is repeatedly increased through a succession of claims and variations, some or all of which may be spurious, and achieved through collusion with the supervisor or client.
  - There may also be collusion between the contractor and the supervisor in increasing the final measurement of some high-rate items.
  - Inflated costs can arise as a result of any barrier to market entry, whether intended or not. Such barriers include poor client reputation; unfair contract conditions; and discretionary access to professional

registration, professional certification, finance, equipment, or materials.

- *Delayed implementation.* Delays can arise as a result of a lack of capacity or accountability of the contractor, who fails to mobilize when awarded the contract or lacks the resources needed to respect the specified program. This in turn raises questions about the integrity of the processes of registering, shortlisting, awarding contracts to, and monitoring the performance of, contractors. Another effect can be that the contractor experiences cash flow problems because payments were withheld in the expectation of facilitation payments. More generally, any trust deficits in project relationships are likely to result in delays.

- *Neglected maintenance.* The connection here is less direct but nonetheless common. Corrupt arrangements tend to favor high-value, new construction contracts where major companies are involved and deals can be arranged, sometimes offshore. Therefore, the limited available funds tend to be spent on new construction instead of on maintenance— which normally involves a large number of smaller contracts on which corrupt deals can sometimes be more difficult to hide. In the absence of appropriate safeguards, even such smaller contracts remain prone to corruption risks.

Indirect warning signs. Indirect warning signs do not necessarily mean that corruption is occurring but would tend to allow corruption to flourish. Such signs include the following:

- *Unequal relationships between parties to the contract.* If one party to a construction-related contract is in a position to exert undue influence over the other party, there is a strong risk of corrupt practices. Such a situation could arise when, for instance, the government is a contractor's only client. It can also arise when contractual provisions are insufficiently defined and rely too heavily on the engineer's interpretation.

- *Poor enforcement of professional standards.* For an engineer to engage in corrupt practices is not only illegal and unethical but also unprofessional. The prospect of being debarred from practice as an engineer is a powerful deterrent for those tempted by corruption. For such a deterrent to work, however, there must be a strong sense of what is meant by professional standards and a powerful professional body with the independence and integrity to enforce them fairly. Any indication of weak enforcement of professional standards makes it more likely that corrupt practices may occur.

- *High multiplier between public sector and private sector salaries.* If a government official is poorly paid relative to the private sector yet is responsible for administering major construction contracts, he or she will have powerful incentives to engage in rent seeking. These incentives may, to some extent, be offset by other benefits attached to public office, including job security, prestige, and valuable work experience. However, a high multiplier between private sector and public sector salaries can be an indirect warning sign and can lead to moonlighting at best and rent seeking at worst. This issue is typically addressed by managing major contracts through quasi-governmental authorities or agencies, in which the normal limitations of civil service pay do not apply.

- *Discretionary powers and barriers to entry to market.* If government officials have discretionary powers that permit them in an unaccountable manner to overrule or unduly influence normal contractual processes—or if other factors unduly favor one player in the market over another—considerable scope will exist for corrupt, or seemingly corrupt, practices. These can either be personally motivated, politically motivated, or a combination of the two.

Framework for Mapping Perceptions
The value chain. In mapping the perceptions of corruption, reference is made to the entire construction sector value chain:

1. Policy making and regulation
2. Planning and budgeting
3. Management and performance monitoring
4. Tendering and procurement
5. Construction and operations
6. Payment and settlement of certificates.

Corrupt practices are commonly encountered in each stage of this chain. A standard list of such corrupt practices, as developed by the Global Infrastructure Anti-Corruption Centre,[5] was used in the initial stakeholder workshop as part of the general mapping exercise.

The risk versus reward model. To help understand what drives an individual to engage in corrupt practices in the construction sector—or deters that individual from doing so—the study adopted an approach of balancing risks and rewards. In such a model, the risk is typically built up from a combination of elements: (a) the risk of detection, (b) the risk of prosecution and loss of face if detected, and (c) the consequences of prosecution.

Countering these elements is the corrupt act's reward, which may be either personal or indirect—that is, a perceived benefit to one's company, political party, or other organization.

In the absence of any ethical considerations, a decision about whether to engage in corrupt practices would be based simply on this risk versus reward balance, with the result that anyone who thought they could get away with it (that is, have no risks) would act corruptly where there was a perceived benefit. This dynamic potentially gives rise to a particular problem in the construction sector, where opportunities abound for corrupt acts to remain undetected along with many situations in which those responsible for high-value contracts earn low salaries.

In practice, however, ethical considerations do play a role in that most people, given the choice, would prefer not to engage in corrupt practices. Within the engineering profession, such an ethical stance can be reinforced by professional standards and related training that encourages fair-minded professional behavior even when opportunities exist for shortcuts. Realistically, though, such ethical and professional considerations are not always strong enough to overcome a strong sense that the only choice is to engage in corrupt activities.

Corruption Risks in Ethiopia's Construction Sector

This study provides a preliminary overview of the nature and scope of corruption in Ethiopia's construction sector in order to identify areas of concern and those requiring more detailed study. The findings are therefore necessarily tentative, given the size and diversity of the sector and the limited scope of the study. However, they do reflect an internally consistent view of those parts of Ethiopia's construction and public works sector that have so far been studied. As such, this mapping exercise may help guide both further study and initial policy development, but it should in the process be treated with due caution.

Sector Overview

In broad terms, Ethiopia's construction sector falls into four categories: roads, water supply and irrigation, power, and other public works, each of which is summarized below.

Roads. Annual spending on roads in Ethiopia is estimated at approximately US$1.2 billion, including spending on community roads. The following entities and other factors affect road spending:

- ERA, in managing the road sector program, is by far the biggest spender, accounting for about 20 percent of the national budget. It has a reputation for being relatively professional and well managed but is increasingly at risk of capacity constraints and is heavily reliant on the work of a small number of experienced staff.

- "Direct labor" operations persist, under which government departments own equipment and employ staff and labor directly engaged in the construction and maintenance of some rural roads. In this regard, Ethiopia is unusual compared with most other African countries, which have already fully privatized the design and construction of public works.

- In recent years, the RRAs have reduced their spending, mostly on maintenance, as available funds are focused on the federal or woreda levels. Regional capacity is reported to be variable but generally weaker than federal capacity. The four largest RRAs operate autonomously, with the remaining regions receiving ad hoc support from ERA. The scope of this study does not extend beyond the four large RRAs.

- Community roads are set to see a rapid expansion, with more than 100 woreda development plans nearing the approval and implementation stage. Meanwhile, a reported 40,000 kilometers (km) of community roads are already being built each year under Ethiopia's food security program but with limited technical oversight. ERA's inclusion of about 27,000 km of community roads in Road Sector Development Program (RSDP) 3 represents an attempt to bring a degree of improved coordination and oversight to this major area of investment.

Water supply and irrigation. For more information about this category, see chapter 4 of this volume.

Power. This category of the construction sector was outside the scope of this study.

Other public works. Public works include universities, schools, hospitals, and markets. Though some study respondents referred to features of the major construction program for university buildings and associated infrastructure, the scope of this sectoral study has not included any consultation with the Ministry of Capacity Building.

Differing Perspectives among Stakeholders

The adoption of a multistakeholder approach revealed a common resolve to address the problem of corruption but also marked differences of perspective as to how, or even why, to do so. As a general pattern, donors appeared to be motivated by concerns about demonstrating that due process was being followed and was effective. Government officials tended to point to the need for enforcement of existing regulations, or the introduction of new ones, while those working for private companies in the sector were most interested in broader improvements in sector governance and project design that would result in a level playing field where they could compete fairly on equal terms.

Tabulated Overview of Findings

Tables 6.1–6.6 present, for each stage of the value chain, a summary overview of

- Typical risks experienced internationally at each stage
- Indicators of such risks as perceived in Ethiopia, drawn primarily from the stakeholder surveys and supplemented by the broader stakeholder consultations (some risks being stage-specific and others more general but indirectly related to a stage)
- Specific examples of corruption reported by stakeholders as having recently occurred in Ethiopia, stripped of any identifying features[6]
- Underlying factors affecting each cited risk in Ethiopia
- Corrective measures as recommended by stakeholders in Ethiopia, drawn primarily from survey responses.

Following the tables, the next section discusses the implications of these findings.

Table 6.1 Corruption Risks in Policy Making and Regulation of the Construction Sector in Ethiopia

	Corruption risks at each stage of the construction value chain	Perceived corruption risk at this stage of the value chain	
Value chain stages	1. Policy making and regulation 2. Planning and budgeting 3. Management and performance monitoring 4. Tendering and procurement 5. Construction and operations 6. Payment and settlement of certificates	Now (international comparison) High ☐ High Med Low	Likely trend (without corrective measures) High ☐ High Med Low
		Perceived possibility of abuse of dominant role of government in controlling the construction sector	

Typical risks as experienced internationally

The regulatory and policy environment in which the construction sector operates has a major effect on sector governance and on the associated risk of corruption further down the value chain. Policies and regulations that encourage, or help hide, corrupt practices in the sector are not necessarily themselves indicators of deliberate state capture or the result of more specific, ad hoc corrupt intentions. But a failure to amend such policies when their damaging effect has become evident may be the result of pressure from groups or individuals who stand to benefit from such corruption. Typical examples where regulations or policies, or the lack of them, can feed corruption or the perception of corruption include

- nonexistent, unclear, or inconsistently applied procurement regulations;
- lack of transparency in the application of procurement regulations;
- nonexistent, unclear, or inconsistently applied performance audit functions;
- unclear or overlapping responsibilities for application or enforcement of procurement regulations;
- large discretionary funding for development or maintenance of infrastructure;
- political capture of leadership of infrastructure or anticorruption agencies;
- lack of an independent judiciary; and
- lack of protection of civil society's role in holding government and industry to account.

Indicators of such risks as perceived in Ethiopia

Specific	General
• Government control of price of construction materials, access to finance, and access to equipment • Government control of professional and company registrations in the sector • High-level, bilateral infrastructure deals planned with China • Lack of independent performance audits	• Concerns over quality • Increasing unit costs • Weak enforcement of professional standards • Lack of transparency

Examples reported by stakeholders as having recently occurred in Ethiopia[a]

- Construction sector professional considers himself (and his company) to be a victim of improper practices but dares not complain for fear of being victimized, believing there is no truly independent body to which he can appeal.

(continued next page)

Table 6.1   *(continued)*

Underlying factors affecting this risk in Ethiopia

The government's dominant role in Ethiopia's construction sector is a natural result of its political history. Many functions in controlling the sector are conducted in a committed manner that is focused on serving the national interest. But such powers are open to abuse, particularly in a market where the government is a major client and where there is a reluctance to express dissent. Many stakeholders are concerned about the possibility of a connection between the dominant role of Chinese contractors in the road sector and high-level links between the Ethiopian and Chinese governments.

Corrective measures recommended by stakeholders in Ethiopia

- Government should communicate and consistently enforce existing regulations while raising awareness of the damaging effects on society of construction-related corruption.
- Government should strengthen procurement policy and related regulations to improve transparency, reduce its own discretionary powers, allow more investigative reporting and challenges by civil society and the media, favor domestic firms, take more account of past performance, allow a sample of bid evaluations to be subjected to independent external scrutiny, and give specific powers to independent bodies to define and maintain professional standards.
- There should be more open debate about the role of Chinese contractors in the road sector.
- Consultants and contractors' associations should actively combat corruption among members.

Source: Author's compilation.

a. Though accepted by other stakeholders as being plausible, these examples are neither backed by hard evidence nor necessarily widespread in the sector.

Table 6.2   Corruption Risks in Planning and Budgeting in the Construction Sector in Ethiopia

	Corruption risks at each stage of the construction value chain	**Perceived corruption risk at this stage of the value chain**	
		Now (international comparison)	Likely trend (without corrective measures)
Value chain stages	1. Policy making and regulation		
	2. Planning and budgeting	High ☐ High Med Low	High ☐ High Med Low
	3. Management and performance monitoring		
	4. Tendering and procurement	Tendency toward top-down planning combined with a perceived conflict of interest for some officials	
	5. Construction and operations		
	6. Payment and settlement of certificates		

Typical risks as experienced internationally

The risk of downstream corruption through collusive alliances is introduced whenever planning, budgeting, and project preparation procedures deviate from the use of a rational, objective basis for prioritizing the allocation of limited resources on the basis of need, anticipated rates of return, or other objective criteria. Such risks are typically greatest when there is evidence of

- lack of separation between policy making, budget allocation, and implementation functions;
- top-down planning by decree;

(continued next page)

Table 6.2   *(continued)*

- projects that are not responding to a prioritized need and (when combined with weak procurement regulations) can sometimes be negotiated directly between a corrupt official and a specific construction company;
- adoption of inappropriately high construction standards to enhance contract values;
- focus on constructing new infrastructure while neglecting to maintain existing facilities;
- conflicts of interest for officials with a stake in the construction sector;
- construction companies with party political allegiances; and
- increasing unit costs when estimates are based on past output unit costs (which may have been influenced by corruption) rather than on future margins.

Indicators of such risks as perceived in Ethiopia

Specific	General
• Tendency toward top-down planning	• Delays in project execution
• Adoption of inappropriately high construction standards	• Lack of transparency
• Perceived conflict of interest for some officials	
• Party-related companies operating in the construction sector	
• Increasing unit costs	

Examples reported by stakeholders as having recently occurred in Ethiopia[a]
- Packaging of contracts in a manner intended unfairly to favor some contractors over others
- Lack of transparency in planning some design-build contracts and off-budget engineering, procurement, and construction contracts

Underlying factors affecting this risk in Ethiopia
Ethiopia has taken some decisive actions to address these risks, including (a) separating policy making and implementation functions in some parts of the sector; (b) defining appropriate technical standards; and (c) developing and publishing strict rules governing the roles of party-owned companies and party and government officials in the sector. But across the sector the overall picture remains patchy, with many perceived risks remaining. Such perceptions tend to be aggravated by an underlying tendency toward top-down planning and leadership styles. Specific concerns expressed relate to the risk of reduced competition arising from the dominance of Chinese firms on International Competitive Bidding (ICB) contracts, the proposed renewed use of tied Chinese aid in the transport sector, and an apparent distortion in some cases of the appraisal and prioritization procedures for proposed road investments overseen by some of the weaker RRAs.

Corrective measures recommended by stakeholders in Ethiopia
- Review of construction standards to identify areas at risk of overspecification or design
- Requirement for all government and party officials to declare any commercial interests
- Extension and more transparent application of proper project appraisal and ranking procedures for all construction sector investments
- Encouragement of increased and fairer competition in the sector through strict enforcement of both the spirit and the letter of all relevant provisions of the Public Procurement Agency (PPA) regulations

Source: Author's compilation.
a. Though accepted by other stakeholders as being plausible, these examples are neither backed by hard evidence nor necessarily widespread in the sector.

Table 6.3   Corruption Risks in Management and Performance Monitoring in the Construction Sector in Ethiopia

	Corruption risks at each stage of the construction value chain	Perceived corruption risk at this stage of the value chain	
Value chain stages	1. Policy making and regulation 2. Planning and budgeting	Now (international comparison)	Trend (without corrective measures)
	3. Management and performance monitoring	**High** □ Medium Med Low	**High** □ Medium Med Low
	4. Tendering and procurement 5. Construction and operations 6. Payment and settlement of certificates	Inconsistent quality of governance and performance management leading to unjustified shortlistings	

Typical risks as experienced internationally

Management weaknesses can lead to corruption in three main ways: (a) Without basic good management controls, individuals (whether working for the client, the consultant, or the contractor) can find themselves free to take shortcuts that may cross the line into corruption. (b) Without good data management and reporting systems, the management information needed to identify and address corruption does not exist. (c) If the management is so incompetent that it gives rise to administrative or technical obstacles that are otherwise impossible to address, corrupt activities may be seen as the only realistic way for otherwise professionally minded individuals to deliver results. Such risks are typically greatest when there is evidence of
- low remuneration of managers and procurement staff;
- poor record keeping, data management, and reporting;
- lack of independent oversight of professional standards;
- contract awards to companies with a reputation for poor performance; and
- lack of clearly specified debarment procedures, including a related transparent procedure for reinstatement following a period of debarment.

Indicators of such risks as perceived in Ethiopia

Specific	General
• Low remuneration of some managers and procurement staff • Companies performing poorly yet shortlisted for new work • Companies shortlisted despite lack of relevant capability • Difficulty of obtaining public information about contracts • Corruption seen as being easy to hide • Lack of independent professional bodies	• Concerns over quality • Increasing unit costs • Delays in project execution • Weak enforcement of professional standards • Lack of transparency

Examples reported by stakeholders as having recently occurred in Ethiopia[a]
- Lack of transparency and clarity in systems used by some (weaker) procuring entities for performance monitoring and debarment

(continued next page)

Table 6.3   *(continued)*

- Client rejection, without explanation, of candidacy of suitably qualified professionals
- Reluctance by construction sector professionals to voice concern about apparently corrupt practices, for fear of being victimized

Underlying factors affecting this risk in Ethiopia
This stage of the value chain is particularly prone to the effects of capacity constraints. ERA is relatively strong in this regard, with some highly experienced senior staff and well-considered procedures enjoying strong support and some oversight from donors. ERA's management system serves as a model to which the RRAs and some other parts of the construction sector aspire. But as a result of high staff turnover, ERA itself remains fragile, and cases are believed to occur where due procedures are either bypassed or manipulated. Without corrective action, the corruption risks within ERA are likely to increase, but within the sector as a whole, such deterioration may be offset by improvements elsewhere.

Corrective measures recommended by stakeholders in Ethiopia
- Focus anticorruption efforts on improvement of management capacity in the sector
- When management information exists, make it available to the public where this does not undermine commercial confidentiality
- Share management information more freely between construction-related ministries, the PPA, and the FEACC to build capacity in understanding and addressing corruption risks
- Create an independent body for contractor registration (possibly including transparent computerized screening of qualifications)
- Create independent bodies for setting and maintaining professional standards

Source: Author's compilation.
a. Though accepted by other stakeholders as being plausible, these examples are neither backed by hard evidence nor necessarily widespread in the sector.

Table 6.4   Corruption Risks in Tendering and Procurement in the Construction Sector in Ethiopia

	Corruption risks at each stage of the construction value chain	Perceived corruption risk at this stage of the value chain	
Value chain stages	1. Policy making and regulation 2. Planning and budgeting 3. Management and performance monitoring 4. Tendering and procurement 5. Construction and operations 6. Payment and settlement of certificates	Now (international comparison)	Trend (without corrective measures)
		High □ Medium Med Low	High □ Medium Med Low
		Suggestions of possible collusion between contactors, including for federal road contracts	

Typical risks as experienced internationally
Although contributory factors are likely to exist in upstream stages of the value chain, corrupt arrangements tend to be agreed-on in principle during the tendering and procurement stage. Commonly encountered risks, which can be interrelated, include

(continued next page)

Table 6.4   *(continued)*

- unofficial sale by client officials to prospective bidders of additional information or services (ranging from marking schemes to help in preparing bids) to enhance the prospects for submitting a successful bid (which may or may not follow a prior bribe to ensure prequalification and is normally associated with a prior agreement to pay a requested percentage of fee if successful);
- collusion between contractors in the form of price fixing (sometimes including provision for a loser's fee) and intimidation of aspiring new entrants;
- unofficial quota system for the award of contracts on the basis of political affiliation of the companies involved;
- bribery (in the form of a percentage of fee, often paid through a third party) to obtain the main contract; and
- manipulation of design to favor a particular consultant or contractor.

Indicators of such risks as perceived in Ethiopia

Specific	General
• General lack of transparency in procurement processes	• Concerns over quality
• Shortlisting of companies known to be poor performers or lacking requisite experience or capability	• Increasing unit costs
	• Projects delivered late
• Shortlisting procedures not fair and transparent	• Weak enforcement of professional standards
• Some capable companies effectively being excluded	• Difficult for public to obtain information
• Collusion between contractors bidding for some contracts	
• Difficulties facing newcomers to the construction market	
• Procurement procedures not always consistently applied	

Examples reported by stakeholders as having recently occurred in Ethiopia[a]
- Unfair selective restriction of access to advance information about bidding opportunities
- Manipulation, by persuasion, of which contractors will bid for a job and which will not
- Sale of tender documents deliberately delayed or advertisement limited to benefit favored bidders given advance notice
- Price fixing, including collusion between contractors
- Manipulation of the tender evaluation process unfairly to favor a specific contractor
- Deliberately misleading unsuspecting bidders by including irrelevant items in the bill of quantities
- Client pressure to modify the engineering estimate to benefit favored bidders
- Approach to bidders by intermediaries claiming (falsely) to be client's staff seeking incentives in return for manipulation of bid evaluation

(continued next page)

Table 6.4   *(continued)*

Underlying factors affecting this risk in Ethiopia

Since 2002, Chinese contractors have become major players in the construction of federal roads in Ethiopia. Initial low prices led many other contractors to leave the market. Prices have now increased, and there have been several instances of concerns about possible collusive practices. Some projects have been retendered, but no hard evidence has been found of such collusive practices occurring in Ethiopia.

Corrective measures recommended by stakeholders in Ethiopia

• Engineer's estimate should be built up from input costs and made available to all bidders.
• Bid evaluations should be conducted by experienced staff and undertaken in a replicable, objective manner that cannot be unduly influenced by subjective considerations or bias.
• A sample of bid evaluations should be subject to independent external scrutiny.

Source: Author's compilation.
a. Though accepted by other stakeholders as being plausible, these examples are neither backed by hard evidence nor necessarily widespread in the sector.

Table 6.5   Corruption Risks in Construction and Operations in the Construction Sector in Ethiopia

	Corruption risks at each stage of the construction value chain	**Perceived corruption risk at this stage of the value chain**	
Value chain stages	1. Policy making and regulation 2. Planning and budgeting 3. Management and performance monitoring 4. Tendering and procurement	Now (international comparison)	Trend (without corrective measures)
		High □ Low Med Low	High □ Medium Med Low
	5. Construction and operations 6. Payment and settlement of certificates	Reported examples of operational-level corruption in Ethiopia tend to be opportunistic and fairly minor	

Typical risks as experienced internationally

Where there is a lack of transparency, low ethical and professional standards, and weak internal controls, this implementation stage of the value chain offers a wide range of opportunities for corrupt practices. In particular, where a contractor has agreed (at an earlier stage) to pay a bribe to help secure the contract, he is likely to try to recoup his outlay during the construction phase. This is most commonly achieved through various forms of fraud, including supply of inferior materials, falsification of quantities, inflated claims, and concealment of defects. In many cases, either the client's staff or the supervising consultant's staff will be implicated in such fraud, typically through agreement to unnecessary variations or approval of incorrect certificates.

(continued next page)

Table 6.5 *(continued)*

By contrast, there are cases in which the construction operations are characterized by a high degree of transparency, high professional standards, and effective controls where corrupt practices may occur but are the exception rather than the norm. The relative absence of corruption in such cases does not necessarily mean that the overall project is unaffected, as corrupt deals may have been completed at an earlier stage and effectively built into the unit rates.

Indicators of such risks as perceived in Ethiopia

Specific	General
• Contracts rarely completed on budget • Many contracts typically delayed significantly • Some contractors submit exaggerated claims • Often a problem with poor-quality construction • Some contractors knowingly underbid then recoup costs through variations	• Weak enforcement of professional standards • Difficult for public to obtain information

Examples reported by stakeholders as having recently occurred in Ethiopia[a]
- Consultant overdesigns, contractor builds to standard, and savings are shared out.
- Contractor fails to notify client of the identity and involvement of a subcontractor.
- Client instructs contractor to include additional works without first consulting the consultant.
- Member of consultant's staff is engaged by the contractor as subcontractor.
- Contractor fails to notify client of the involvement of a subcontractor, thus avoiding checks.
- Member of consultant's soils laboratory staff is paid by contractor to falsify test results.
- Contractor's and consultant's staffs exaggerate quantities to take advantage of high unit rates entered for ghost items at the tendering stage.
- Contractor submits exaggerated claim for variations.
- Contractor conceals construction defects or improperly influences client or consultant to accept substandard materials
- Consultant or contractor submits falsified documentation.
- Plant hire company receives exaggerated payments as result of falsified utilization records.

Underlying factors affecting this risk in Ethiopia

Despite the wide range of specific examples provided by stakeholders, such instances were in most cases reported as being the exception rather than the norm and considered to be rare in those high-spending agencies (such as ERA) where relatively strong controls are in place. This is in keeping with the perception that, at earlier stages, it is rare for contractors or consultants to agree to a specific percentage payment to a client official. In stakeholder consultations, the relatively blatant forms of corruption described here were generally considered to be more corrupt than those at earlier stages, thus tended to be frowned upon and resisted.

Corrective measures recommended by stakeholders in Ethiopia
- Build capacity to manage and supervise construction using all available tools.
- Increase transparency so that projects are more accountable to the public.

Source: Author's compilation.
a. Though accepted by other stakeholders as being plausible, these examples are neither backed by hard evidence nor necessarily widespread in the sector.

Table 6.6   Corruption Risks in Payment and Settlement of Certificates in the Construction Sector in Ethiopia

	Corruption risks at each stage of the construction value chain	Perceived corruption risk at this stage of the value chain	
Value chain stages	1. Policy making and regulation 2. Planning and budgeting 3. Management and performance monitoring 4. Tendering and procurement 5. Construction and operations 6. Payment and settlement of certificates	Now (international comparison) High □ Low Med Low	Trend (without corrective measures) High □ Medium Med Low
		Facilitation payments are common but not necessary, and they are generally small when they do occur	

Typical risks as experienced internationally

Three main categories of risk are typically related to the settlement of payment certificates: (a) Because of the ease with which a client can fabricate a justification for refusing payment, the withholding of payment can be used as a means of punishing companies that have refused to honor understandings (whether formally agreed to or not) entered into at earlier stages in the value chain. Such agreements typically entail the corrupt reallocation of an agreed-on percentage of each payment received. (b) Individuals may seek to extract small facilitation payments from those wishing to avoid undue administrative delays in payment. (c) Often in parallel with one or both of the first two categories, the party to whom the payment is due may be guilty of fraud for having submitted falsified documentation in support of reported progress or associated claims. These risks can be particularly acute when there is no realistic means of complaining, as typically occurs when one client dominates the market or when there is no outside body to which a complainant can refer the matter and expect a fair hearing.

The above three categories relate to clients, consultants, and contractors. Connected to these are further forms of corruption related to legal advisers, including in dispute resolution. Such advisers may be implicated in the submission of incorrect claims, concealment of documents, the supply of false witness statements, bribery or blackmail of witnesses, or excess billing, all of which contribute to overall levels of corruption in the project.

Indicators of such risks as perceived in Ethiopia

Specific	General
• It is commonly (though not universally) reported that facilitation payments may be required to speed up settlement of certificates. • Contractors sometimes curtail progress because cash flow problems arise as a result of late payments.	• Difficult for public to obtain information

Examples reported by stakeholders as having recently occurred in Ethiopia[a]
• Consultant or contractor perceives that payments are being withheld unfairly but has no realistic means of complaining or appealing to an independent body.

(continued next page)

Table 6.6   *(continued)*

Underlying factors affecting this risk in Ethiopia

Stakeholders report that it is relatively rare in Ethiopia for corrupt deals to be arranged based on bribes amounting to a significant percentage of fees, paid on settlement of invoices. In cases where a successful consultant or contractor does pass on a proportion of the income from a project, it is more likely to be in the form of a small "thank you" paid either to an individual with whom there is a special connection or to an agreed-on third party.

By contrast, the need for small facilitation payments to avoid deliberate delays in the administrative process (as opposed to more substantial bribes paid to secure preferential treatment) is fairly common—as is (albeit still reportedly on a smaller scale than elsewhere) the falsification of supporting documents on which a certificate is based.

Corrective measures recommended by stakeholders in Ethiopia

• Increase civil service pay.
• Increase transparency so that projects are more accountable to the public.

Source: Author's compilation.
a. Though accepted by other stakeholders as being plausible, these examples are neither backed by hard evidence nor necessarily widespread in the sector.

Assessment of Corruption Risk in Ethiopia's Construction Sector

Direct Warning Signs

Based on the responses received, the construction sector in Ethiopia appears to show most of the classic warning signs of the risk of corruption, as generally described in the previous subsection, "Warning Signs of Corruption in Construction." These signs include the following:

- *Poor-quality construction.* There was strong stakeholder *agreement* with the questionnaire statement, "There is a problem with poor-quality construction." This is not to suggest that infrastructure is necessarily of poor quality at handover (though that was reported as sometimes occurring), but it does clarify that tight supervision and control is required to ensure that quality is maintained. Such tight controls are not always in place.
- *Inflated costs.* There was strong stakeholder *disagreement* with the statement, "Contracts are normally completed on budget," pointing to a high cost from claims and variations. In addition, unit output costs used for budgeting purposes were rising at a rate that could not readily be explained by rises in the cost of construction materials. This issue was identified as warranting additional, more detailed study.
- *Delays in implementation.* There was strong stakeholder *disagreement* with the statement, "It is rare for construction contracts to experience

significant delays after approval for mobilization." This response suggests weaknesses in the underlying procedures for shortlisting, awarding contracts to, monitoring the performance of, and paying contractors.

- *Neglected maintenance.* This was referred to as a general issue in the sector, but this study does not specifically explore the reasons for and nature of such neglect. The road sector benefits from about US$100 million per year of funding for maintenance through a dedicated road fund established under the RSDP.

Indirect Warning Signs

- *Unequal relationships between parties to the contract.* For many private sector companies in Ethiopia's construction sector, the government is their primary or only client. In the less-well-managed parts of the sector such as with RRAs, there are reports of this unequal relationship being abused through the imposition of unreasonable contractual provisions. In extreme cases, it has been made clear to contractors that, no matter what the contract says, they will not be allowed to submit claims regardless of the merits of any case that may arise.

- *Poor enforcement of professional standards.* The bulk of stakeholders *disagreed* with the statement, "High professional standards are maintained in the sector." Though various industry associations define the professional standards to which they expect member companies to adhere, there are no professional institutions in Ethiopia to provide guidance and oversight to individuals. Unusually, the government retains control of the process of individual registration. Whether or not this process is ever abused, the arrangement itself serves to further reinforce the unequal relationship mentioned above.

- *High multiplier between public sector and private sector salaries.* This issue falls outside the immediate scope of this study but remains of fundamental importance. In broad terms, private sector salaries in Ethiopia's construction sector are about eight times higher than the equivalent salaries in the public sector. Sometimes other benefits associated with public service can offset this disparity, but the fundamental challenge remains one of retaining competent and committed staff within the various government client entities. Some officials report that they have joined public service to gain the experience needed to move into the private sector. Others carry out their public duties in a committed manner while supplementing their income with private engineering services unrelated to their work. But so long as such a marked discrepancy in incomes persists, the widespread perception will remain that some public officials believe they have little choice but to engage in corrupt activities.

- *Discretionary powers and barriers to market entry.* A company wishing to operate in Ethiopia's construction sector must overcome many barriers. To have the confidence to enter a new market, any business must be able to anticipate its likely future costs, its access to market opportunities, its access to capital and equipment, the margins to be made in those markets, and the related cash flows. In Ethiopia none of these can readily be predicted, and all are affected by discretionary powers assigned to government officials. Even if none of these powers are abused, many companies, when faced with so many risks over which they cannot with integrity exercise control, are likely either to increase their prices, withdraw from the market, or try to control those risks by engaging in corrupt activities.

Perceptions of What Constitutes Corruption

The following findings emerged from one of the workshop exercises conducted in the course of the study:

- No respondent considered it to be "very corrupt" for a procuring entity deliberately to benefit favored bidders by providing advance notice of opportunities.
- No respondent considered it to be "very corrupt" for a contractor intending to bid to be contacted by another bidder and dissuaded from doing so.
- Views were polarized about collusion between staff from the consultant, the client, and the contractor to overdesign, build to standard, then share the savings. Some respondents considered this to be only "slightly" corrupt, while an equal number considered it to be "very" corrupt.
- There was a similar polarization of views over cases where a member of the client's staff instructs the contractor to include additional works without prior consultation with consultant.
- All respondents considered it to be only "somewhat" corrupt for a contractor to engage a member of the consultant's staff as a subcontractor or provider of equipment.

- All respondents considered it to be only "slightly" corrupt for a contractor to fail to notify the client about the involvement of a subcontractor, thus circumventing checks on capacity and competence.
- All respondents considered it to be either "somewhat" or "very" corrupt for a contractor to arrange for the falsification of soil test results.

Though the numbers involved in this workshop were too small to allow any firm conclusions to be drawn, they are consistent with a general view expressed by domestic stakeholders that blatant corruption is unacceptable, while less blatant forms may be regrettable but cannot realistically be prevented. This in turn is consistent with the perception that most serious corruption occurs at the shortlisting and bid evaluation stages, and even then tends not to be at all blatant.

Within the context of minor operational-level corruption affecting day-to-day operations, international participants with experience of working in other developing countries generally expressed less concern about levels of corruption than domestic respondents. This contrast suggests that what a domestic respondent considers to be "high" levels of such corruption may well be relatively low by international standards.[7]

No evidence was encountered of public officials declaring small gifts understood to be given by grateful consultants and contractors. Clear guidelines governing the disclosure of such gifts would serve to clarify when the line is crossed between a gift and a bribe.

Cultural Paradoxes
In the course of the study, several cultural paradoxes became apparent that help explain some of the perceptions of corruption in the sector:

- *Lack of trust.* This widely reported feature of attitudes within Ethiopia could generate a false perception of corruption and could in theory reduce the risk of conspiracy between corrupt parties. However, it could equally generate a sense of being wronged or of being left out, which can itself be used as a justification for corrupt behavior.
- *Rigid hierarchical approach.* This can ensure that due procedure is followed, but equally can lead to flawed decisions when strict adherence to the rules does not permit officials to use their judgment or initiative. This can create both a motive for, and a perception of, corruption.

- *Ambivalent attitudes toward corruption.* Partly because of an ethical bias in society, and partly because of the fear of being caught, there is a strong sense in Ethiopia of not wanting to appear corrupt. Yet there also appears to be an underlying resignation to, bordering on admiration for, the possibility of the abuse of power. This is expressed in the Amharic saying "Sishom Yalbela Sishar Ykochewal" (literally "in power, not eat; out of power, regret"), which suggests that someone who does not engage in corrupt practices when in a position of power will regret it when he or she no longer has that power.

Overview of Current Perceived Corruption in the Value Chain

Table 6.7 below summarizes the perceived levels of corruption within the value chain. Given the high risk factors, it is surprising that perceived corruption levels are not reported as being higher. The low reported levels may be the result of methodological bias in that Ethiopians are reluctant to make foreigners aware of their country's shortcomings. However, any such reluctance did not keep stakeholders from volunteering many specific examples of corruption or from indicating their perception that the dominant role of the government and ruling party may lie behind the apparent lack of genuine competition in some parts of the sector.

The most notable feature of this analysis is the perceived lack of competition in the sector. This issue is considered in more detail in the "Perceived Lack of Effective Competition" section below.

Balance of Risk

In terms of the balance of risk, the overview presented above suggests that most Ethiopians working in the construction sector have a strong aversion—based both on ethical considerations and on the high risks associated with being caught—to engaging in overtly corrupt practices. This aversion is less pronounced when it comes to less overt bending or manipulation of the rules. Yet there is also a widespread assumption—verging on acceptance—that for some favored people or companies working in the sector, the potential rewards are so high, and the likely risks so low, that they can engage with impunity in thinly disguised corrupt practices.

Interventionist Policies

Compared with many other developing countries, Ethiopia is unusual in the interventionist policies that are currently adopted in the construction

Table 6.7   Overview of Perceived Corruption along the Construction Sector Value Chain

Stage of value chain	Risk level			Comments
	Low	Medium	High	
1. Policy making and regulation			☐	Perceived possibility exists of abuse of the dominant role the government plays in controlling the construction sector.
2. Planning and budgeting		☐		Perceived risk is present in parts of the sector that collusive practices drive up prices through reduced competition, higher-than-necessary technical standards, and weak associated planning.
3. Management and performance monitoring		☐		Strong perception exists that inconsistencies in the quality of governance in the sector, combined with external pressures, can give rise to unjustified shortlistings.
4. Tendering and procurement		☐		Persistent unsubstantiated perceptions of improper collusion are present in the sector, including between Chinese contractors.
5. Construction and operations	☐			Reported examples of operational-level corruption tend to be opportunistic and fairly minor, though some corrupt practices do not appear to be considered particularly corrupt.
6. Payment and settlement of certificates	☐			Provision of small facilitation payments are a common, though not necessary, part of ensuring prompt settlement of certificates.

Source: Author's analysis of stakeholder responses.

sector. Central planning, control, and influence are evident in many aspects of the sector:

- Access to some construction materials at preferential prices
- Allocation of some specially imported equipment
- Access to finance and to land
- Registration and professional certification.

Such controls can readily be understood in the context both of Ethiopia's political history and of the scale of the development challenges it faces. But however well intentioned, the controls also bring with them the possibility of abuse. Whether or not such abuse occurs, government control and influence can generate a perception of unfairness or corruption. Such perceptions are reinforced by a lack of appreciation in some quarters that any market gives rise to losers as well as winners. Whether justified or not, this attitude can result in strong perceptions of corruption, which in turn may deter some potential bidders from competing. Such restrictions can have the effect of driving up prices.

The detailed workings of such a process vary within the road sector. With federal roads, the government is known to have made considerable efforts to persuade non-Chinese contractors to reenter the market now that prices have reached attractive levels. The reluctance of some such contractors to do so may reflect a lingering perception that there is not a level playing field.

With regional rural roads, a significant factor appears to be the unfair allocation of contractual risk, which has contributed to high unit costs. Several cases were reported of contractors being required to sign contracts that did, at face value, share risk fairly while being warned that in practice all risk lay with them. Other factors include weak institutional capacity, limited experience of competitive bidding, and untested procedures. All of these concerns are currently being addressed with the assistance of a European Union–funded capacity-building program.

Government Efforts to Address Corruption Risks

Ethiopian roads authority. As a leading, high-spending agency in the construction sector, ERA has a reputation for relatively strong professionalism in its approach to project planning, procurement, and management. In response to the perceived risk of possible collusion between contractors in the sector, ERA has, on a pilot basis, experimented with the use of a postqualification (rather than prequalification) procedure for major roads contracts.

ERA's role extends beyond federal roads and includes some capacity building and other activities in support of District Maintenance Organizations, RRAs, and woreda-level infrastructure planning. In recognition of the risk that ERA's own capacity is limited and is undermined by high turnover of junior staff, the RSDP 3 includes specific capacity-building interventions within ERA designed to consolidate and build on existing initiatives related to the issuance of a new Procurement Manual in 2008.

Federal ethics and anti-corruption commission. The FEACC has a twin role in combating corruption, in its mandate both to educate and to investigate. Related sections headed by ethics officers are established in most government offices. Some government agencies managing large budgets are considered strategic and vulnerable to the risk of corruption and therefore are subject to continuous monitoring. These include ERA and the Land Administration Division of the Addis Ababa City Administration.

The government has encouraged respective regional governments to establish their own ethics and anticorruption commissions. With a few exceptions, the FEACC's primary role on construction-related issues has been to investigate allegations of improper land access as well as collusion in the setting of compensation for resettlement of properties within the reserve of proposed new road developments.

A recent FEACC annual report refers to several construction-related matters, including a review of the working practices and procedures of the Addis Ababa City Roads Authority (AACRA). Cases studied included (a) procedures relating to valuation of compensation payments at ERA and AACRA for properties expropriated as a result of road construction, and (b) cancellation of a tender floated by the Road Fund Office for the technical monitoring of rural and urban roads. The FEACC has taken a keen interest in Ethiopia's participation in the pilot phase of the international Construction Sector Transparency initiative described below.

Public procurement agency. The Federal Public Procurement Directive of 2005 constitutes the legal framework regulating public procurement in Ethiopia. A related proclamation determines the procedures of public procurement in Ethiopia and established its supervisory agency, the PPA.

The agency has extensive powers to investigate suspected breaches of public procurement procedures but due to capacity constraints tends to be reactive rather than proactive in relation to suspected malpractice in the construction sector. Most allegations investigated by the PPA involve alleged failure to follow due process in the award of contracts. Some cases are upheld, but most prove to have arisen as a result of a complainant's misunderstanding about the nature of competitive bidding.

The procurement directive sets out the details of good practice for procurement based on competitive bidding, including the adoption of internationally accepted tender procedures for externally funded contracts. It also grants considerable powers to the minister in matters of procurement and limits the direct award of some contracts. The 2005 directive is currently under review in response to both the experience gained during implementation and the feedback received during a stakeholders workshop organized by the Ministry of Finance and Economic Development.

Construction Sector Transparency (CoST) Initiative. Ethiopia is one of seven pilot countries for the Construction Sector Transparency (CoST) initiative.[8] Launched in 2008, CoST commits participating countries to a series of measures to improve transparency within the construction sector through the disclosure of material project information about participating projects. Such information would be designed to facilitate greater accountability by disclosing, for instance, details of the applicable bid evaluation procedures, contract value, works program, and cost overruns. In each country, the initiative is overseen by a national multistakeholder group (NMSG) comprising representatives from government, civil society, professional bodies, and the construction sector. This NMSG in turn appoints an independent "assurance team" of respected professionals whose job is to interpret material project information and ensure that it is not presented in a misleading manner.

One of the early results of the CoST pilot will be the establishment of a baseline against which future changes in transparency within the sector can be measured. In the medium to long term, it is also intended to assess changes in accountability and performance within the sector, though these will only be indirectly attributable to the initiative.

Ethiopia's participation in the CoST pilot and the establishment of an NMSG represents a potentially significant, though of itself insufficient, contribution to the broader challenge of tackling both the perception and the reality of corruption within Ethiopia's construction sector.

Perceived Lack of Effective Competition in Parts of Ethiopia's Road Sector

In view of the reported perceptions of hidden barriers to entry to some markets within Ethiopia's construction sector, this section attempts to assess in more detail whether the market is functioning in a manner consistent with true competition. Because of its high spending, available data, and concerns about rising costs, this analysis will focus on the road sector, specifically on ERA (responsible for federal roads) and RRAs (responsible for rural roads).

Indicators of Competition

If engineers' estimates are accurate, and market forces working well, then competitive tenders should result in lower prices. The level of competition is normally measured based on (a) the number of bidders and (b) the spread and pattern of bids received.

Such an analysis is beyond the scope of this study and is of little value if conducted superficially because both the number of bidders and the pattern of bids can readily be manipulated through collusive practices. However, based on monitoring of such indicators, ERA, some RRAs, and the World Bank have each in recent years expressed concern about a possible lack of effective competition in the sector.

An alternative approach to studying the issue is to focus on

- the process of preparing engineers' estimates; and
- the degree to which any changes in unit costs can be attributed to the cost of inputs, capacity constraints at times of increased spending, or increased margins due to restricted competition in the sector.

It is recommended that such a study be undertaken in the context of the Ethiopian road sector. Meanwhile, using data readily available from secondary sources, a preliminary analysis of such issues follows.

Growth in Road Sector Spending

The rapid growth in spending in Ethiopia's road sector has been particularly marked since 2004.[9] The bulk of this spending is on federal roads, managed by ERA. In a constrained market, such a pattern of high and growing spending increases the risk that a few favored contractors will dominate the market. Experience in other countries suggests that when this happens, it can lead to the construction of unnecessary roads and to increases in unit costs.

In Ethiopia's case, there is evidence that the rate of increase in the use of the federal road network exceeds the rate of increase in network length, suggesting that Ethiopia's growing classified road network is broadly consistent with demand. But the rate of increase in spending exceeds the rate of increase in network length, reflecting a significant rise in unit costs.

Federal Roads

The figures below show variations in the cost per kilometer of asphalt and double bitumen surface treatment (DBST) roads for the period 2003–08. The data are disaggregated by International Competitive Bidding (ICB) and National Competitive Bidding (NCB).

At face value, figure 6.1 suggests that ICB costs for asphalt roads have approximately doubled between 2004/05 and 2007/08, while NCB costs more than quadrupled. This suggests that either national contractors became less competitive or their relatively low unit costs in 2004/05 were not sustainable.

Figure 6.2 shows a similar but more marked trend in the cost of DBST roads. During the same 2003–08 period, ICB costs increased by approximately 50 percent. During the same period, NCB costs more than quadrupled.

Figure 6.1   Trends in Unit Cost of Asphalt Roads in Ethiopia

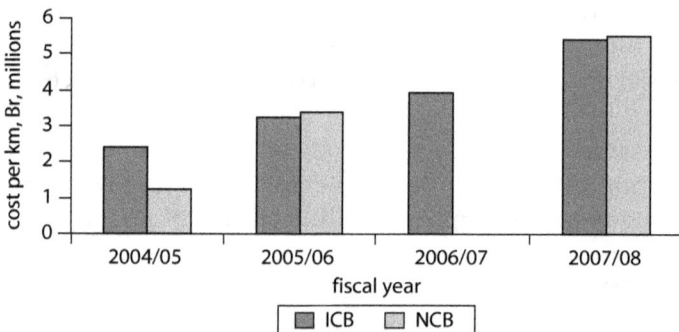

Source: Author's analysis of Ethiopian Roads Authority data.
Note: km = kilometer. ICB = International Competitive Bidding. NCB = National Competitive Bidding.

Figure 6.2   Trends in Unit Cost of DBST Roads in Ethiopia

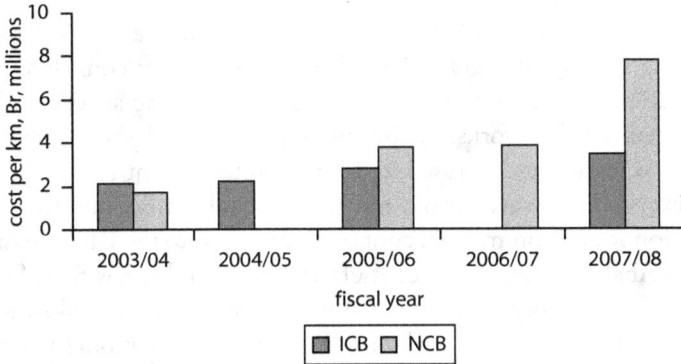

Source: Author's analysis of Ethiopian Roads Authority data.
Note: DBST = double bitumen surface treatment. km = kilometer. ICB = International Competitive Bidding. NCB = National Competitive Bidding.

Taken together, these results point to a possible lack of effective competition in the domestic market. At the same time, there have been marked increases in the unit costs associated with ICB contracts, the market for which is dominated by Chinese contractors that, in the light of widespread concerns in the sector, warrant special mention.

Role of Chinese Contractors in Ethiopia's Road Sector

As in other countries, the initial impact on Ethiopia's road sector of China's 2002 "Going Out" strategy coincided with a sharp reduction in unit costs.[10] One large state-owned enterprise (SOE) in Ethiopia was reported to have reduced its projected profit margins to as low as 3 percent (Leggett 2005), and several were understood initially to have suffered substantial losses as they struggled to adapt to the standards and quality called for. Few of the new entrants were familiar with International Federation of Consulting Engineers-style contracts, with the standard methods of preparing bids, or with claims procedures. As a result, some claims were not made to which the contractors would have been entitled had they maintained the relevant records.

Over time, most such companies adapted their performance to match the contract requirements. Several, including some now ranked as leading international contractors, are actively seeking to ensure compliance with international standards on corporate governance, health and safety, labor, quality control, and environmental protection. Both ERA and the World Bank report general improvement in the quality and speed of work by Chinese contractors, particularly those that are now well established in Ethiopia.

China's role in road construction in Ethiopia is controversial, generating sharply divergent views during stakeholder consultations. The participation of some Chinese contractors both in the survey and in the second stakeholder workshop of this study allowed the perspective of Chinese SOEs to be expressed and, to a limited extent in the time available, discussed. However, it did not prove possible to obtain the views of the economic and commercial counsellor attached to the Chinese Embassy in Addis Ababa despite significant efforts to do so.[11] It has therefore been assumed for the purpose of this study that the approach taken and role played in Ethiopia by the embassy, the China International Contractors Association (CHINCA), new entrants, and flagship Chinese companies in Ethiopia is broadly consistent with the general picture described in box 6.1. This picture is based primarily on international studies of Chinese contracting in Africa (including Ethiopia) and does not contradict the views expressed directly by stakeholders in Ethiopia.

As in other developing countries, some stakeholder groups within the road sector in Ethiopia have concerns about possible collusion among Chinese contractors to drive competitors out of the market by bidding below cost and later increasing prices to market rates. Competent authorities, including the World Bank, have studied the possibility of such collusion, but insufficient evidence has been found to support any specific allegations. In several cases, however, suspicions have been strong enough to warrant the suspension and relaunch of the procurement process.

Box 6.1

Market Entry Strategies for Chinese Construction Companies in Africa

The construction industry plays an important part in the implementation of China's Going Out strategy. The Chinese Ministry of Commerce (MOFCOMM) recognizes this and encourages construction firms to invest abroad through policy structures and financing systems (Chen and Orr 2009).

China's Africa focus is geared primarily toward resource-rich countries but also includes countries with strategic regional influence. The Chinese government regularly commissions SOEs for infrastructural aid projects in countries where it wishes to expand its influence.

(continued next page)

Box 6.1 *(continued)*

Winning a tender for a government-endorsed contract enables the Chinese company to secure low-cost capital from Chinese banks. Once established in a country, the company then draws on its knowledge and experience to identify more commercial opportunities. Where possible, it will register a local company to gain better access to the construction market.

The economic and commercial counsels attached to the Chinese embassies enjoy some autonomy but have as their primary responsibility the control and coordination of Chinese business activities in the host countries. They interpret their main role as being to provide information to Chinese companies. They also authenticate and translate official documents issued in China, such as company registrations and academic qualifications. The political support includes assistance to Chinese nationals with any administrative problems they may encounter with local authorities. MOFCOMM regulations require contractors to register with the Economic and Commercial Counsellor's Office upon entering a foreign country for the first time (Chen and Orr 2009).

MOFCOMM's Department of Foreign Economic Affairs does not restrict the number of Chinese contractors that participate in an overseas market bidding process, but it does require the China International Contractors Association (CHINCA) to take responsibility for coordinating the Chinese contractors before bidding commences. CHINCA is a nonprofit organization with corporate status, approved by MOFCOMM and a member of the International Chamber of Commerce (Chen and Orr 2009). Box figure 6.1.1 below provides a simple overview of the Chinese government's approach to organizing and controlling the Going Out national strategy through overseas construction.

Box Figure 6.1.1   Control of China's "Going Out" Strategy in African Infrastructure Provision

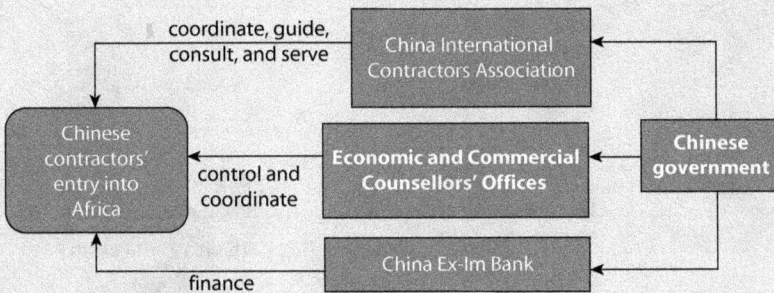

Sources: International studies of Chinese contracting in Africa, including Chen and Orr 2009.

Rural Roads

Any consideration of unit costs of rural roads is complicated by an unusual (compared with other countries in the region) arrangement whereby the bulk of experience still relates to "own force" activities rather than to private contractors. As a result, some client officials may retain the perception that they have the right to exercise direct control over private contractors rather than work through due contractual processes. A further distinction needs to be made between labor-based (LB) works (where the bulk of earthworks and finishing is carried out by manual labor) and equipment-based (EB) works (involving the use of heavy machinery such as dozers and graders).

The available primary data on rural roads in Ethiopia are limited and not always internally consistent. For the purposes of this study, secondary sources have therefore been used, including a recently completed study of unit costs based on an analysis of data from 100 road projects in Tigray and Oromiya, which include some relatively mountainous terrain (Taylor et al. 2008). Unless otherwise stated, all rural road costs relate to gravel (unsealed) roads.

As shown in figure 6.3, the average cost of LB gravel road construction in Ethiopia is higher than in Kenya, Uganda, and Zambia but lower than in Lesotho. This is plausible and broadly consistent with the degree to which mountainous terrain is likely to be encountered.

Figure 6.4 presents comparative data for costs of EB, low-volume gravel road construction in Ethiopia, Lesotho, and Uganda.[12] The first

Figure 6.3   Comparative Cost of Labor-Based Gravel Road Construction, Ethiopia and Selected Countries

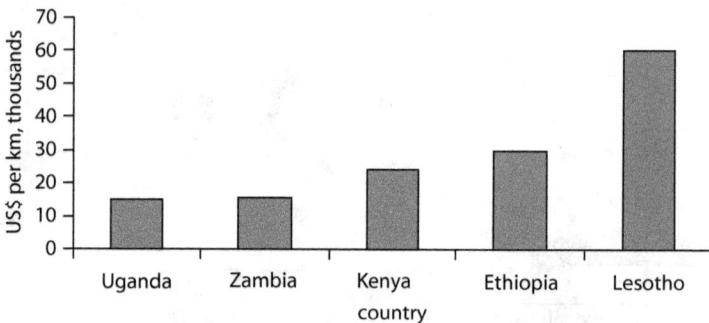

Source: Author's analysis of data from Taylor et al. 2008.
Note: km = kilometer.

Figure 6.4   Comparative Costs of Equipment-Based Gravel Road Construction, Ethiopia and Selected Countries

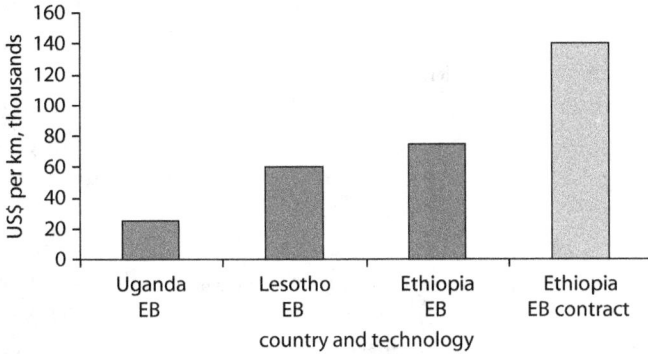

Source: Author's analysis of data from Taylor et al. 2008 and regional road authorities.
Note: EB = equipment-based. km = kilometer.

three (paler) bars present average costs per kilometer—showing that, at about US$75,000 per kilometer, such roads are relatively expensive in Ethiopia. The same figure shows, as a darker bar, the cost per kilometer of one of the few low-volume gravel roads being constructed contemporaneously under contract to an RRA in Ethiopia. At approximately US$140,000 per kilometer, this cost appears exceptionally high by international standards, suggesting the possibility of uncompetitive practices in the market. A site visit to the road in question did not reveal any evidence or allegations of corruption but did identify possible factors that may have contributed to the high cost.

None of the main technical factors that normally drive up costs was applicable in this case: existing and projected traffic levels were low, the terrain was flat or rolling, drainage structures accounted for only a small proportion of the contract cost, the site location was immediately adjacent to the sealed federal road network, and surfacing materials were in plentiful supply.

At face value, the road was costing approximately three times what could normally be justified on economic grounds—and double the normal cost for such a road. This inflated cost suggests either poor governance, corruption, or a combination of both. A more detailed study was neither possible nor appropriate in the circumstances. However, initial inquiries identified the following factors that may have contributed to the high costs:

- *High design standard.* Both the design standard of the road and the degree of quality control observed during an unannounced site visit exceeded what would normally have been expected under such circumstances in other countries.
- *Use of open tendering.* Bidding contractors may not have known whether they were competing against 2 other contractors or 10. As a result, they may not have invested in a proper site visit when preparing their bids. This may have led them to assume worse site conditions than those that existed.
- *Unfair contract terms.* The contract was described as assigning all risk to the contractor. As a result, bidding contractors would have made provision for all such risks in their prices.
- *Lack of confidence in procuring entity.* RRAs have relatively little experience as procuring entities as well as a reputation for refusing to honor some written contract provisions.[13] Again, these factors may have caused bidding contractors to increase their rates.
- *Lack of experience in pricing bids.* Some contractors in Ethiopia seem unaccustomed to pricing bids in the conventional manner, which entails building up projected unit rates for specified bill items. Instead, bids are apparently priced on the basis of rates used on previous contracts, irrespective of whether it may be possible to bid more competitively.

In discussing unit costs with staff from the RRA responsible, it was clear that the authorities were both aware of and deeply concerned about what they perceive to be excessively high bid prices for rural roads. They referred to another road project on which the bid evaluation had been completed, but they had decided not to award the contract because value for money was not being achieved.

The unit costs generally accepted by ERA for the nearest equivalent standard of unsealed federal road is understood to be approximately US$230,000 per kilometer. On this basis, the RRA gravel road cost of US$140,000 per kilometer appears more reasonable. However, international comparisons and comparisons with local costs built up from unit rates both suggest that road costs in Ethiopia are higher than would be expected in a truly competitive market.

Infrastructure Unit Costs in Sub-Saharan Africa

Concerns about high and rising unit costs in the road sector are not unique to Ethiopia. A comprehensive 2008 study, drawing on data from 24 countries including Ethiopia, looked specifically at the reasons for

increasing costs in the road sector (Africon 2008). Using data from current road projects, it tested three hypotheses: (a) rising input prices,
(b) tight construction markets, and (c) inadequate competition.

The study found that the single strongest explanatory factor for the
rising cost of roads was the absence of meaningful tender competition,
which affected 78 percent of projects. This finding, albeit tentative, is
consistent with the study finding that there are strong signs of a lack of
effective competition within Ethiopia's road sector.

Conclusions and Recommendations

On the basis of this preliminary study, operational-level corruption in
Ethiopia's construction sector appears to be relatively low by international
standards. However, the perception of higher-level corruption, whether
real or imagined, is already having a significant detrimental effect on confidence within the sector. Without corrective action, both the perception
and the reality of corruption in the sector are likely to increase, spurred
on by a combination of high spending levels, capacity constraints, and
increased exposure to corrupt practices commonly encountered more
widely within international construction.

Signs, Examples, Perceptions

Ethiopia's construction sector strongly displays both direct and indirect
warning signs of corruption risk. The direct warning signs include problems with the quality of construction, inflated costs, and delayed implementation. Indirect signs include unequal contractual relationships; poor
enforcement of professional standards; high multipliers between public
and private sector salaries; and a high level of government influence over
costs within, and access to, the construction market.

Specific examples of corruption have been reported (stripped of
identifying characteristics) at each stage of the value chain. The bulk
of these are related to tendering and procurement as well as construction and operations, but in most cases stakeholders consider them to
be the exception rather than the rule. As such, corruption risks are
broadly viewed as controllable by the stronger procuring entities such
as ERA.

At the higher level, however, stakeholders perceive that the opaque
nature of some aspects of policy making and regulation as well as planning and budgeting may be masking significant distortions of access to
construction markets. In the road sector, this perception is reinforced by

what many stakeholders view as a lack of effective competition, with Chinese contractors dominating the international market and a limited set of domestic contractors dominating the national market. A preliminary study of unit output costs in these two markets appears to confirm the possibility of restricted competition, though no specific evidence of related corrupt practices was identified.

Drivers of Corruption

The drivers of corruption in Ethiopia's construction sector are complex and interrelated but can be grouped into overlapping categories related to deficiencies in *accountability, capacity,* and *trust.*

Success on a project can be attributed to the combination of these factors:

- *Capacity* makes performance *possible* by ensuring the availability of sufficient resources, well-defined procedures for the management of those resources, and adequate training to ensure that proficiency is achieved through practice.
- *Accountability* makes performance *happen* by ensuring that there is adequate transparency to allow for objective assessment of performance against agreed-on performance standards.
- *Trust* makes performance *efficient* by giving contractors the confidence in the market that allows them to invest in increasing their own capacity.

Conversely, deficiencies in accountability, capacity, and trust can serve as drivers of corruption risks. A *lack of capacity* makes corruption possible, a *lack of accountability* makes corruption happen, and a *lack of trust* allows corruption to take root.

Figure 6.5 presents nine such drivers of corruption, as identified in this study.

The Ethiopian government is already actively engaged, to varying degrees, in addressing most of these drivers. The recent decision to join the pilot phase of the CoST initiative is potentially highly significant as an important, though in itself insufficient, step toward improved *accountability* in the sector. It will not fully address the growing risk of spreading corruption as spending levels continue to outstrip management capacity.

Figure 6.5   Drivers of Corruption Risks in Ethiopia's Construction Sector

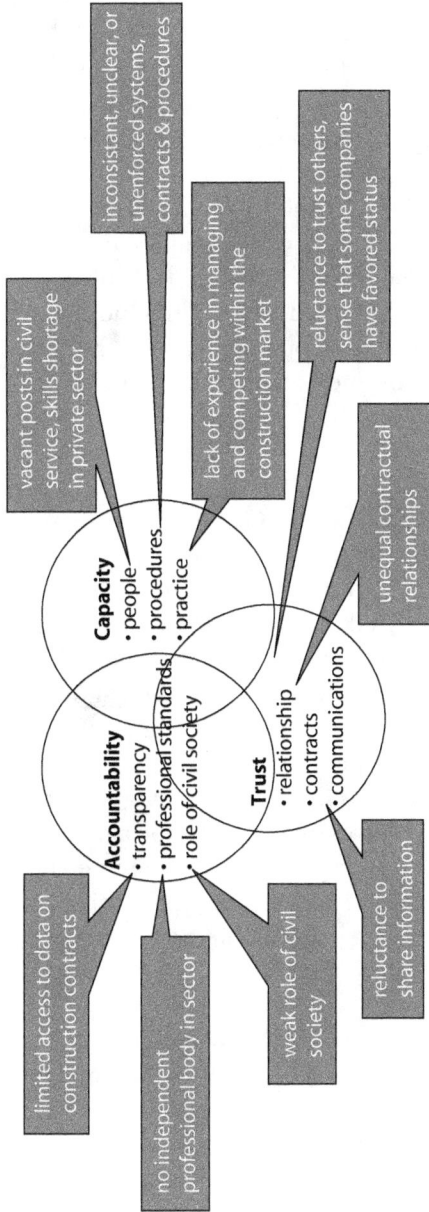

vacant posts in civil service, skills shortage in private sector

inconsistant, unclear, or unenforced systems, contracts & procedures

lack of experience in managing and competing within the construction market

reluctance to trust others, sense that some companies have favored status

Capacity
· people
· procedures
· practice

unequal contracctual relationships

Accountability
· transparency
· professional standards
· role of civil society

Trust
· relationship
· contracts
· communications

limited access to data on construction contracts

no independent professional body in sector

weak role of civil society

reluctance to share information

Source: Author's analysis.

Similarly, current initiatives to further strengthen project planning, procurement, and management procedures within ERA are important but could be undermined if the broader underlying issue of skills shortages (*capacity*) is not also addressed. Capacity should be strengthened not only through civil service reform (beyond the scope of this study) but also through the extended use of proven management systems and procedures and related training, as further detailed below.

By contrast, little emphasis has so far been placed on addressing the risks associated with *trust*, which significantly influence behavior in the sector. Trust should be restored through specific confidence-building measures (detailed below), including a fairer allocation of risk in contracts and more openness about the practical application of rules limiting the commercial interests of officials involved within the sector.

Recommendations

Validation of study results. Given the vast and diverse extent of Ethiopia's construction sector and the limited scale, scope, and depth of this study, it is important to recognize the tentative nature of its conclusions and related recommendations. Though the study findings have been broadly validated through stakeholder consultation, that consultation process was itself limited and should be extended before any major decisions are made to implement recommendations. Specifically, the Ethiopian government should have time to consider the findings and engage in ongoing dialogue with other stakeholders, including industry representatives, donor agencies, and civil society. A possible vehicle for such consultation may be the NMSG established under the CoST initiative. Such an approach could lead to constructive engagement on key issues, in turn allowing for early action in priority areas.

Areas requiring further study. Along with ongoing work in consolidating and validating the findings, there will in due course be a need to fill gaps in its scope—particularly those relating to cross-sectoral issues, the power sector, and large-scale community infrastructure initiatives. Within the roads sector, early follow-up studies are recommended to help the authorities identify and correct unequal contract relationships and to better understand why many companies have chosen to withdraw from (or not even enter) the construction market. Any such study should include consultation with international construction companies *not* currently working in Ethiopia.

To better understand the nature of competition in the sector, it is recommended that a study be conducted of unit costs, initially within the roads subsector. Such a study, which would look at both input costs and output costs, would seek a better understanding of the drivers of current high output costs and profit margins. Its scope should also include a review of the process by which decisions are made about the appropriate standards for new roads.

Other recommendations. Detailed stakeholder recommendations relating to each stage of the value chain are included in the tabulated summaries previously presented in tables 6.1–6.6. At a more strategic level, the following set of overlapping recommendations relate directly to the conclusions previously presented in figure 6.5.

Accountability

- *Improved transparency.* This recommendation should not be limited to Ethiopia's participation in the CoST initiative, significant as that is, but should also be a vehicle for broader transparency across the sector. Government, industry, donors, and civil society all have a role to play in promoting greater transparency and by demonstrating a willingness to share information that will result in greater clarity and accountability in the sector.

- *Independent professional body.* Consideration should be given to the benefits of establishing an independent body or bodies responsible for defining and upholding professional standards within Ethiopia's construction sector. This will in turn have a bearing on current discussions between industry and government about the most appropriate means of providing for the impartial and transparent classification, registration, and regulation of companies working in the sector. Its influence would ideally also extend to universities offering engineering degrees.

- *Strengthened role for civil society.* This is a cross-cutting issue that extends beyond the scope of the study. However, it is recommended that full advantage be taken of the opportunity presented by the CoST initiative to explore the benefits of increasing recognition of the role that civil society can play in improving accountability within the construction sector.

- *Better, more coordinated use of performance audits.* Due to capacity constraints, neither the PPA nor the Auditor General's Office nor some procuring entities themselves routinely undertake performance audits in the construction sector. Such audits—ideally including a combination of informed and random targeting—should form an integral part of any accountability system within the sector. To optimize their relevance and impact, financial and technical audits should ideally be combined.

- *Improved cost estimation.* Strengthening the approach to cost estimation and benchmarking of costs would provide a more robust basis for rejecting excessive prices and identifying and constraining possible collusive practices.

Capacity
- *Filling of vacant posts in procuring entities and addressing broader skills shortages in the private sector.* Though identified as a contributing factor to the risk of corruption, the detailed consideration of such capacity constraints falls beyond the scope of this study. It is nevertheless recommended that, as part of the preparation for major construction sector investment programs, capacity issues should routinely be considered. The scope of such consideration should necessarily extend beyond the inclusion of ad hoc, project-specific measures to enhance capacity and include a broader sectoral view of the need to match investment plans with anticipated capacity within the sector.

- *Clear and consistent enforcement of systems, contracts, and procedures.* The PPA should take the lead in this matter, specifically ensuring that contracts within the sector are both fair and equitably enforced. This effort will require an increase in capacity. Consideration should also be given to the possible need to strengthen the FEACC's capacity to prevent and investigate corruption within the sector by employing more experienced construction sector professionals who have a detailed understanding of corruption risks within the sector.

- *Experience of managing, and competing within, the construction market.* Because of the limited experience of some clients and construction companies, widespread misconceptions remain about the nature of the market—including the limits to the client's power and the fact that in any competition there will be losers as well as winners. It is recommended that, with possible donor support, the main professional associations within the construction sector organize a series of meetings at which these issues are discussed within the sector.

Trust

- *Increased confidence in the fairness of the market.* Government should set itself a specific objective of increasing levels of confidence and trust within the sector. This will in many cases be a by-product of other recommendations related to identifying and addressing areas where the construction market is perceived to be difficult to understand, difficult to enter, or difficult to work in. With increased confidence identified as an underlying objective, there is likely to be more clarity about the underlying purpose of related initiatives such as improved transparency and fairer contractual relationships.

- *Fairer contractual relationships.* Government should commission an independent study of the theory and practice of contractual relationships currently being entered into by the RRAs. The scope of such a study should include recommendations for an appropriate sharing of risk, an independent means of ultimate recourse in the event of a dispute, and related measures to raise awareness and capacity in understanding and applying contracts.

- *Increased willingness to share information.* Closely related to the issue of transparency are specific areas where a lack of information has given rise to perceptions, suspicions, and allegations that may be unfounded yet have not been refuted clearly and unambiguously. Specific information that could usefully be shared under this category includes: (a) details of planning and appraisal processes leading to investment decisions for rural roads; (b) details of the regulations limiting the involvement of party and government officials in construction companies; and (c) an accessible register of the declared commercial interests of such officials.

Notes

1. The "value chain" concept is based on a process view that identifies six distinct stages of project delivery—starting with the setting of policy and ending with the final payment of contractors.

2. The 2009 Ethiopia Country Profile on the Business Anti-Corruption Portal (www.business-anti-corruption.com) states, "The spread of corruption in the country has been noted by the African Development Bank 2003, which cites the customs service, land distribution, public housing, and utilities as areas characterised by institutionalised corrupt practices."

3. Phase 1, undertaken in mid-2008, resulted in grouping both the perceived risks and the related solutions under the interrelated categories of account-ability, capacity, and trust. It also identified issues, including an apparent lack of genuine competition in the market, that warranted further study. Phase 2, undertaken in mid-2009, looked more specifically at two such areas, both road-related: international contracting, where Chinese contractors have come to play a dominant role, and rural roads managed by the regional road author-ities (RRAs). In both cases, concerns had been raised because of recent marked increase in construction costs.

4. Twenty-six completed surveys were received in 2008 and another 24 in 2009.

5. For more information about the Global Infrastructure Anti-Corruption Centre, see www.giaccentre.org.

6. Although the reported occurrences were considered plausible by other stakeholders when discussed in a workshop setting, they are not necessarily indicative of the sector as a whole and should not be construed as describing common practices.

7. In one workshop, an experienced international contractor went so far as to describe working in Ethiopia as "a paradise compared with the corruption in other countries in Africa."

8. CoST is an international multistakeholder initiative to increase transparency and facilitate accountability in the construction sector through the public disclosure of information about the purpose, nature, timing, and cost of con-struction projects. Initiated by the U.K.'s Department for International Development and supported by the World Bank, the pilot phase started in 2008 in seven countries: Ethiopia, Malawi, the Philippines, Tanzania, the United Kingdom, Vietnam, and Zambia. For more information, see www.constructiontransparency.org.

9. The cost data in this section are derived from data provided by ERA to the World Bank and referred to in World Bank 2009.

10. The "Going Out" strategy refers to the Chinese government's encouragement of foreign investment by Chinese enterprises.

11. Approaches by e-mail and telephone, both through intermediaries and in person to the office in Addis Ababa, finally resulted in a recommendation, also acted upon, to contact the government in Beijing.

12. A low-volume road is generally one on which the average daily traffic level is under 50 vehicles per day.

13. These views were reported by stakeholders in interviews and validated in the stakeholder workshops.

References

Africon. 2008. "Unit Costs of Infrastructure Projects in Sub-Saharan Africa." World Bank Africa Infrastructure Country Diagnostic, Background Paper 11, June, World Bank, Washington, DC.

ASCE (American Society of Civil Engineers). 2005. "Combating Corruption." Policy Statement 510, drawing on data from Transparency International and adopted by the Board of Direction, ASCE, Reston, VA.

Campos, J. Edgardo, and Sanjay Pradhan. 2007. *The Many Faces of Corruption: Tracking Vulnerabilities at the Sector Level.* Washington, DC: World Bank.

Chen, Chuan, and Ryan Orr. 2009. "Chinese Contractors in Africa: Home Government Support, Coordination Mechanisms, and Market Entry Strategies." *Journal of Construction Engineering and Management* 135 (11): 1201–10.

Leggett, Karby. 2005. "China Forges Deep Alliances with War-Torn Nations in Africa." *The Wall Street Journal,* March 30.

Taylor, Gary, Getnet Alemu Zewdu, Beteseb Feleke, and Farhad Ahmed. 2008. "Comparative Study of the Impact of Labour-Based and Equipment-Based Methods of Roadworks in Ethiopia." Consultancy report, International Labour Office, Geneva.

World Bank. 2009. "Project Appraisal Document for Stage 4 of the Road Sector Development Project." Data provided by the Ethiopian Roads Authority to the World Bank, Washington, DC.

CHAPTER 7

Land Sector Corruption in Ethiopia

Tony Burns and Kate Dalrymple[1]

Introduction

The fundamental nature of land, both socially and economically, implies a unique and important role for the state. The land sector is particularly susceptible to corruption and rent seeking. Various global studies of perception of corruption highlight corruption in the land sector.

Land management and administration is typically implemented through a chain of activities:

- Policy formulation
- Translation of policy into laws, regulations, and directives
- Creation of institutions and capacity to implement policies and legislation
- Deployment of mechanisms to implement policy and legislation (processes, procedures, manuals, and so on)
- Implementation of systems for monitoring and evaluation, which ideally should feed back into policy formulation.

Although this chapter results from studies completed by January 2010, the process of checking, reviewing, and securing agreement for publication was finally brought to conclusion only in late 2011. The chapter is therefore put forward with the caveat that while it reflects the situation at the time of the study, some details will have understandably changed.

Although most corrupt activity in the land sector occurs at the implementation stage, the level of corruption is influenced strongly by the way policy and legislation are formulated and enforced. This influence can take many forms. For example, the capture of state assets by the elite can occur through the formulation of policy that favors the elite. Other examples are (a) inadequate provision of resources to institutions mandated to administer land under generally sound policies or (b) abuse of power where policy is weak or unclear.

Methodology
The data for analysis was gathered by conducting interviews with key stakeholders, reviewing key documents and information from the media and the Internet, and implementing an assessment of land governance using the Land Governance Assessment Framework (LGAF), which involved expert investigations, expert panels, and sampling (see box 7.2). This assessment has been undertaken quickly and draws heavily on the LGAF assessment, the Federal Ethics and Anti-Corruption Commission (FEACC) investigations of corruption in five subcities in Addis Ababa, and interviews with key stakeholders.

Overview of Findings
The key areas of corruption in the land sector in Ethiopia are these:

- *Capture of assets by the elite and senior officials.* Elite capture is facilitated by a weak policy and legal framework and poor systems to implement existing policies and laws.
- *Corruption in the implementation of land policy and laws,* particularly through the following:
  - *Institutionalization of informal fees.* The FEACC investigation of corruption in five subcities in Addis Ababa concluded that it was "nearly impossible to a get a plot of land without bribing city administration officials."
  - *Fraudulent actions of officials* to allocate land to themselves in both urban and rural areas and to housing associations and developers in urban areas.
  - *Willingness of officials to defraud or respond to bribes or nepotism* to overlook virtually all specified restrictions and requirements, particularly in Addis Ababa, which has seriously undermined the enforcement of land use plans, lease conditions, and building and construction codes in urban areas.

- ○ *Issuance of forged land documents* resulting from fraud, bribery, or nepotism, which has seriously eroded confidence in the land records system.

Overview of Recommendations

The fundamental recommendations arising from this study concern these aspects of land governance:

- Developing a comprehensive land policy and legal framework
- Improving institutions and systems in land sector agencies
- Building capacity and an environment for service delivery.

It is recognized, however, that the development of land policy will take time, and developing and implementing improved systems will also take time. Therefore, the immediate recommended actions to start addressing corruption in Ethiopia's land sector are these:

- Review implementation of improved systems to allocate land in the four subcities in Addis Ababa and the rollout of these procedures in the other subcities in Addis Ababa and other major urban centers in Ethiopia
- Improve systems to record rights in urban land and test pilot systems in Addis Ababa subcities
- Establish a supervisory body to address and investigate complaints by the public against the actions of officials in land sector agencies.

These three actions could be undertaken in the short term and make an immediate impact on the key areas of corruption this study identifies. Long-term activity to develop land policy and improve systems can then build on this initial momentum.

The FEACC investigation of corruption in five subcities in Addis Ababa has identified specific modes of corrupt activity and has resulted in improved procedures that are being trialed in four of the subcities. Further detailed investigations of land sector corruption in urban areas outside of Addis Ababa and in rural areas will help prioritize and focus efforts to reduce corruption.

Chapter Structure

The chapter begins with "Corruption in the Land Sector," about the extent and nature of corruption in the land sector globally. Further context is provided in "Corruption and Land Governance," after which the specific treatment of corruption risks in Ethiopia's land sector proceeds as follows:

- "The Land Sector in Ethiopia," which summarizes the policy and institutional arrangements for land administration in Ethiopia
- "Corruption in Ethiopia's Land Sector," which investigates the nature and extent of corruption
- "Mapping Corruption to the Value Chain," which uses a value chain model for corruption vulnerability in Ethiopia's land sector
- "Recommendations," which focuses on the five key areas of land sector corruption and a broader strategy to improve land governance and reduce vulnerabilities to corruption.

Corruption in the Land Sector

Land administration systems typically include processes to manage public land, record and register private interests in land, assess land value, determine property tax obligations, define land use, and support the development application and approval process. Box 7.1 sets out some simple definitions. Land administration is a basic tool that supports land management and operates within the framework established by a country's land policy and its legal, social, and environmental contexts.

The land sector globally is particularly susceptible to corruption and rent seeking. Land is an enormously valuable asset, typically accounting for 30–50 percent of national wealth in developing countries (Kunte et al. 1998). The value of land thus creates a significant opportunity for corruption on the part of those with the legal authority to assign, revoke, or restrict rights to it. In addition, externality concerns often necessitate the

---

Box 7.1

Land Administration and Management Defined

Land administration: the processes of determining, recording, and disseminating information about tenure, value, and use of land when implementing land management policies.

   Land management: the activities required to manage land as a resource from both environmental and economic perspectives toward sustainable development.

Source: UN-FIG 1999, 52.

delegation of authority to make case-by-case decisions, such as in the case of building permits or other restricted land uses, thus creating the scope for corrupt practices. The acquisition, management, and sale of state-owned land create further opportunities for bureaucrats to generate and collect rents. In land administration practice, corruption is often a serious problem.

Various studies of perceived corruption have highlighted the land sector. The 2008 Bribe Payers Index by Transparency International lists real estate and property development as the second-highest of 19 sectors for bribery of public officials (TI 2008). The 2009 *Global Corruption Barometer*, also prepared by Transparency International, lists the land services sector as the third-most-likely institution for the payment of petty bribes (TI 2009).

Among other studies, a global two-month desk review of land sector corruption reported in the media and on the Internet produced an extensive list of cases in both the developed and developing world (Van der Molen and Tuladhar 2006). Surveys indicating high customer perceptions of corruption were reported in countries including Bangladesh, India, Kenya, Lithuania, Nepal, Pakistan, Sri Lanka, and Vietnam. Specific cases of corruption, often involving senior politicians or bureaucrats, were reported in Australia, China, Ireland, Kenya, Malaysia, the Netherlands, Pakistan, and Uzbekistan. Still more reports cited investigations of corruption in countries such as Botswana and Cambodia. Clearly, the problem is widespread.

The Value Chain and Key Actors in the Land Sector

Land management and administration is typically implemented through a chain of activities including

- *Formulation of policy*
- *Translation of policy* into laws, regulations, and directives
- *Creation of institutions and capacity* to implement policies and legislation
- *Deployment of mechanisms* to implement policy and legislation (such as processes, procedures, and manuals)
- *Implementation of systems* for monitoring and evaluation, which ideally should feed back into policy formulation.

The typical key actors in the chain of activities in the land sector include

- *Policy makers*
- *Legislators*

- *Senior civil service agencies and officers* (civil service commission, treasury, and ministry or department heads)
- *Civil servants and officials* (in the land administration agency and other land-related agencies)
- *Local officials* (for example, city mayors, governors, and village leaders)
- *Private sector service providers* (for example, public notaries, lawyers, surveyors, valuers, brokers, and real estate agents)
- *Private sector investors* (for example, developers and building contractors,)
- *The general public.*

How the Value Chain Works

Land sector services are typically provided locally, usually through a special office such as a provincial or district land office or through an office or unit within an existing agency such as a local government authority or court. These services are typically provided either (a) *systematically*, where the government routinely provides particular services such as formalization of land rights village-by-village and conversion of records from a deeds registration to a title registration process; or (b) *sporadically*, as an individual process in response to an individual landholder's specific request.

In sum, land services are typically as follows:

- Undertaken as a set of clearly specified procedures or processes that implement policy
- Legally empowered by legislation (such as laws and regulations)
- Implemented through specified forms
- Specified in official instructions or directives, standard operating procedures, and manuals.

"Land sector services" also covers a wide range of topics, including land tenure and allocation; land management and land use planning; public land management; the recording and registration of rights in land and land records management; and land dispute resolution and conflict management. In turn, each of these topics requires many work procedures and processes to do the following:

- Formally recognize existing land and property rights through systematic, sporadic, or transaction-based approaches
- Allocate land through grants or leases to—or permit the extraction of resources (for example, logging of timber, extraction of gravel and sand) by—both domestic and foreign individuals or legal entities

- Certify existing land rights for a range of purposes, including transferring or selling rights, using the rights as security for a loan, accessing government and other services such as crop insurance
- Record or register changes in rights (including sale, exchange, gift, or inheritance) or encumber rights (including mortgage, easements, rights-of-way, liens, and caveats)
- Develop and implement land use plans and procedures to put into effect land management policies and legislation
- Make decisions related to applications to develop land and property
- Value the land and property for assessing land tax and collecting taxes
- Expropriate private rights in land and property for public or private purposes.

Weaknesses in the Chain

As noted above, the land sector is susceptible to corruption. This corruption can occur throughout the chain of activity, but is particularly prevalent in the downstream activity of implementation. The value chain, shown in table 7.1, sets out the conceptual framework for investigating corruption in the land sector.

Corruption in the land sector can have serious implications, including the loss of state assets and revenue; the undermining of systems to enforce restrictions on land use (which can affect the environment and degrade resources); and serious constraints on economic activity due to unwillingness or inability to invest in land and invest in land development as a result of uncertainty in rights and restrictions. More important, corruption in the land sector can undermine public trust in government in general and in the land administration system in particular.

There are at least five elements, or thematic areas, in assessing vulnerabilities for corruption and land governance:

- How property rights to land (for groups or individuals) are defined and enforced, and how these rights can be exchanged or transformed to support the wider objectives of economic growth and social equity
- How land is managed, how land use plans and regulations are prepared and implemented, and how land is taxed
- What is classed as state land and how it is managed, acquired, and allocated to private use
- What is the nature and quality of property ownership information available to the public and how easy it is to access or modify
- How land disputes are resolved and conflict over land is managed.

Table 7.1 Value Chain Analysis of Corruption Risks in the Land Sector

	Value chain stages	Potential forms of corruption
Upstream		

Policy and legislation	Policy formulation and legislation	• Capture of assets by the elite or narrow vested interests through a range of mechanisms, such as by
		  ○ influencing policy and legislation at the expense of society in general;
		  ○ failing to ensure adequate resources are available to implement and enforce policy and legislation; and
		  ○ exploiting a lack of clarity in policy and legislation.

Institutions	Budget formulation and allocation	• Funds or equipment for land offices not allocated to the land offices (for example, vehicles needed for field teams captured by head office staff) • Procurement staff colluding with suppliers (which can result in inappropriate or substandard equipment or supplies for land offices)
	Human resource management	• Nepotism, fraud, or bribery in appointments to key positions

Downstream	Land allocation	• Capture of assets by the elite
		• Illegal allocation of public land as a result of bribery, fraud, or nepotism, including
		  ○ allocation of land that should not be available for allocation because of the existing or proposed use of the land in question; or
		  ○ allocation of land to those either not eligible for the land being allocated or in preference to others with a clear or better right to the land in question.
		• Collusion with applicants to undervalue land being allocated
		• Solicitation of informal fees by officials

	Land certification and land records management	• Alteration of records through bribery, fraud, or nepotism • Incorrect certification of land rights (to deceive others such as potential purchasers or financers) to benefit self by fraud; benefit others as a result of bribery or nepotism; or extort money from others • Collusion with applicants to undervalue land being certified or transacted • Minimization or avoidance of fees and taxes through bribery, fraud, or nepotism

	• Payment of bribes to ignore or minimize any existing rights or conditions imposed on the land or restrictions imposed on transactions related to the land
	• Refusal to process applications in a timely manner without the payment of informal fees
Expropriation of private rights	• Collusion with landholders to overvalue land being expropriated
	• Misuse of the expropriation process to acquire or extinguish the rights of others through bribery, fraud, or nepotism
	• Solicitation of informal fees by officials
Land management and land use planning	• Manipulation of planning or land management processes to create wealth by altering rights over specific parcels of land through fraud, bribery, or nepotism
	• Disregard of land management and land use planning controls as a result of bribery, fraud, or nepotism
	• Solicitation of informal fees by officials
Land disputes and conflict management	• Adjudication of disputes or bias in decisions through bribery, fraud, or nepotism
	• Sale of judgments by judges, adjudicators, or other court officials
	• Payment of bribes to delay or influence the dispute resolution process
	• Payment of bribes to officials or witnesses giving evidence
	• Use of the dispute process to extort an advantage from another party
Monitoring and evaluation	
Oversight	• Alteration or destruction of land records as a result of bribery, fraud, or nepotism
	• Privileged or restricted access to land records as a result of bribery, fraud, or nepotism
	• Incorrect certification of land records as a result of bribery, fraud, or nepotism

Source: Author.

These five identified thematic areas are central to the Land Governance Assessment Framework (LGAF) that the World Bank recently developed (Deininger, Selod, and Burns 2011). The LGAF, described further in box 7.2, is a tool that has contributed to the assessment of corruption in the land sector in Ethiopia.

Box 7.2

Land Governance Assessment Framework

The LGAF is a diagnostic tool for the evaluation of the legal framework, policies, and practices relating to land policy, administration, use, and management. The LGAF groups the assessment into five thematic areas:

- Legal and Institutional Framework
- Land Use Planning, Management, and Taxation
- Management of Public Land
- Public Provision of Land Information
- Dispute Resolution and Conflict Management.

A coherent set of 21 indicators and 80 dimensions sets out objectives for land governance in the five thematic areas. For each indicator, a set of two to six dimensions describes key aspects in land governance that contribute to the indicator. In turn, for each dimension, a set of coherent statements describes four situations, graded from A to D. The methodology for LGAF implementation relies on

- expert analyses of more than half the dimensions;
- expert panels reaching consensus on various sets of dimensions (five panels with about 20 dimensions per panel); and
- sampling for a limited number of dimensions where further evidence is required.

An LGAF assessment highlights areas for legal, policy, or procedural reform to improve land governance. Using a comprehensive framework such as this provides an overarching illustration of issues and can be used over periodic intervals to reassess the status or compare interregionally.

Source: Deininger, Selod, and Burns 2011.

Corruption and Land Governance

Corruption occurs during implementation of the chain of activities set out above, through abuse by those responsible for making decisions. Investigations of corruption in the land sector often distinguish between two levels of corruption, both of which are significant:

- *State capture*, or the illegal conversion of state assets to private use where there are examples of corruption on a grand scale
- *Petty corruption or maladministration*, including officials' solicitation (either directly or through middlemen) of illegal or informal payments in return for processing routine work or overlooking often ill-defined restrictions or requirements.

Recent studies have shown that petty corruption can have significant financial cost. A study in India estimated that petty corruption in that country's land sector has a monetary value of about US$700 million per year (TI India 2005). In China, the loss of income from corrupt land transactions is estimated to be about US$1.25 billion per annum (*People's Daily Online* 2006). However, as both reports noted, petty corruption has a far wider impact than the purely monetary losses to government revenue: the widespread imposition of informal fees in the land sector undermines public trust in government and can be a serious barrier or disincentive to participation, particularly by the poor and disadvantaged.

The fundamental nature of land, both socially and economically, implies a unique and important role for the state and thus a particular set of concerns related to governance. The supply of land is fixed. Land is an important factor of production, particularly in agriculture. Establishing and protecting claims to land is an important concern of producers. Research in a variety of settings has shown that secure property rights can be provided more cost-effectively on a collective rather than private basis (De Meza and Gould 1992). In this sense, a secure property rights system has aspects of a public good and is thus appropriately provided by the state (Shavell 2003).

In addition to these economic justifications, security of tenure is important on social grounds. Protection from forced evictions is increasingly seen as a basic human right, acknowledged as part of the Millennium Development Goals. Ensuring equity of property rights protection is another important concern. In many cases, the poor, ethnic minorities, and women face particular obstacles in obtaining equally secure land rights.

The nature of land as an asset also implies the scope for significant externalities. Social, ecological, and aesthetic concerns mean that purely market-driven land use will be suboptimal. Property rights must thus be defined with these concerns in mind. Moreover, in practice, externality concerns are sufficient in many circumstances to necessitate state ownership of land, such as in the case of environmentally sensitive areas, national parks, roadways, and other public spaces.

The need for information services creates the scope for another public good the state can provide: the maintenance of accurate records and information about land rights and obligations. The transfer of land and its use as collateral for credit requires that information concerning the assignment and nature of land rights be available to all interested parties and the public in general. Because functioning land markets are important to ensure efficient allocation of resources, reducing associated transactional costs can have important benefits. In addition, publicly available information can help to better identify and inform decisions about externalities.

The Land Sector in Ethiopia

Land in Ethiopia, as in most developing countries, is a critical resource with a number of economic, social, political, and philosophical dimensions. Access to land was a key focus of the 1975 revolution that overthrew the imperial regime, after which the Derg regime nationalized all rural land and implemented a program to distribute land to the tillers. Under the federal constitution, all land is owned by the state and not subject to "sale or other means of exchange."

Land administration is delegated under the constitution to the regions (for rural land) and to city governments and municipalities (for urban land). Federal oversight of land administration is limited. The Ministry of Agriculture has put in place a framework law to enable the regions to develop policy and legislation for land administration, but until recently the ministry had no structure or resources that directly supported the land administration activities in the regions.

Rural Land

Only five of the nine regions have enacted laws to register rural land holdings: Amhara; Oromia; Tigray; the Southern Nations, Nationalities and Peoples Region (SNNPR); and, more recently, Gambella. In Amhara and Tigray, an Environment Protection, Land Administration and Use

Authority (EPLAUA) has been established. SNNPR formerly had established an EPLAUA, but this function was subsequently transferred to the Bureau of Agriculture and Rural Development. Oromia recently established a Lands and Environmental Protection Office that is mandated to administer both urban and rural land. In the other regions, land administration is undertaken by the Bureau of Agriculture and Natural Resources.

Amhara stands out as the region with the most capacity. Capacity in the other regions is limited, with many approved positions unfilled. First-stage certification of rural holdings is largely completed in Amhara and Tigray, and these regions are planning for second-stage certification, which will involve the survey and mapping of holdings (although there are issues concerning the reliability of the first-stage certification in Tigray). In mid-2008, first-stage certification was only about a third complete in both Oromia and SNNPR.

In the regions that have established a land administration system in rural areas, there is generally an oversight function at the regional and zonal levels. Land records are administered at the woreda level, based on adjudication by a kebele-level voluntary land administration committee elected by local kebele residents.[2]

In rural areas, peasants and farmers are entitled to a perpetual use right with protection against eviction except in accordance with the law. These holdings can be individual or community holdings. Rural land is also available for lease. Landholders have rights over immoveable property on the land.

In rural areas, individuals or groups of individuals have encroached on state land such as forests or parks. Most reports indicate that wildlife reserves and game parks exist on paper only. The Gambella National Park has virtually ceased to exist as a conservation area; Yabello Sanctuary has been taken over by a livestock project; Bale Mountains National Park has suffered from uncoordinated development in and near its boundaries; and encroachment of Nech Sar National Park near Arba Minich has been so severe that African Parks (an international park management company) terminated its contract and left the country. There is also significant pressure on forest land in some regions.

There are transfer restrictions, and most regions limit the amount of land that can be leased. Rural landholders cannot mortgage their holdings, although an investor who is leasing land can use the lease as collateral for a loan. There are no clear standards for the loss of rights due to environmental and conservation laws.

Urban Land

There is no common system to administer land in urban areas. In Addis Ababa, a Land Development and Management Authority (with about 46 staff members) reports to the city manager. There is also a land administration unit (with about 45 staff members) in each of the 10 subcities in Addis Ababa.

Large informal sector. Urban land is provided through (a) a lease system, with terms ranging up to 99 years; (b) a perpetual permit system for urban land outside the lease system; and (c) legislation for condominiums. However, the level of informality is high, with some estimates of the informal sector as high as 90 percent of housing units. In part, there is a historical basis for informality in Addis Ababa, which was developed under a feudal tenure system, but informal settlement has increased in recent years (including the recent phenomenon of land grabbing, or *Yechereka Bet*: building houses at night under lunar light).

Informal settlements do not house only those of low to moderate income; some estimate that 70–80 percent of informal settlement in Addis Ababa is occupied by those who are relatively well-off. A substantial part of the commercial building stock is also informal, and many large buildings in Addis Ababa have been built without lease rights or building permits. There is no process to regularize informal dwellings and little to discourage future informal settlement.

Context for measurable corruption risk. The legal framework has some serious gaps: a reliance on unpublished, easily changed directives and no real system to record rights and restrictions. The master plan plays little role in the development of Addis Ababa. This dysfunctional context has led to increasing corruption in the country's land sector. (However, Oromia recently announced the intention to form an independent land institution that will be responsible for land administration in both urban and rural areas in the region.)

The LGAF was a key tool in gathering data for this study. As previously documented in box 7.2, the LGAF is structured into five thematic areas, 21 indicators, and 80 dimensions and is implemented in three key steps:

- *Expert analysis,* which is undertaken in about half the 80 dimensions to gather existing data and information
- *Five expert panels* to review a subset of the 80 dimensions and rank the country into one of four precoded situations (ranking from A to D

based on the data captured in the expert analysis and personal experience)
- *Sampling* in a limited number of dimensions.

The results of the LGAF assessment in Ethiopia and results of the framework rankings are set out in the annex ("Country LGAF Scorecard for Ethiopia"), and the areas of weak land governance identified by the LGAF are set out in box 7.3.

Corruption in Ethiopia's Land Sector

Land has a very political nature in Ethiopia. There is ongoing debate on land tenure policy (Crewett and Korf 2008). As a political instrument,

---

Box 7.3

Areas of Weak Land Governance in Ethiopia

- Lack of federal policy and reliance on unpublished directives
- Lack of policy to formalize urban property and to discourage informal settlements
- Limited opportunities for tenure individualization
- Undefined extent of communal land and unregistered rights
- Serious limitations in the systems to record rights in urban areas
- Unclear administrative mandates, particularly in the resolution of disputes
- Limited participation in preparation of land use plans, unpublicized plans, and an urban planning process failing to cope with urban growth
- No clear process of valuation
- No inventory of public land and related systems, poor management of public land, expropriation of land for private purposes, and a lack of transparency in the allocation of public land
- Lack of a spatial framework for the registry, which (where it exists) does not record encumbrances and restrictions and is not kept up-to-date
- Financial unsustainability of the registry and very limited investment in land administration
- Multiple avenues for dispute resolution and forum shopping in light of an ineffective formal court system, and high costs and difficulty in accessing the appellate court system.

Source: Multi-Talent Consultancy 2010.

land is allocated and expropriated based on political and other considerations. Information about land is closely held and not transparent. In rural
areas, people distrust the government, and a key strategy to build community trust in the regions that have implemented registration programs
is the use of voluntary land administration committees whose members
are elected by the kebele community.

Corruption in the land sector in Ethiopia is frequently reported in the
media and on the Internet. The 2005 election in Ethiopia resulted in a
temporary power vacuum in the city of Addis Ababa. A substantial
amount of land was allocated based on political allegiances. City officials
in Addis Ababa used the transition to conspire with land speculators.
Using records on housing cooperatives that had approval for land allocation but had not been formed, these officials transformed the 24–36
approved housing cooperatives into about 300 housing cooperatives,
many fictitious, and applied to the municipal courts for legal recognition.[3] These housing cooperatives have been the vehicles for a massive
land grab. It is estimated that about 15,000 forged titles have been issued
in Addis Ababa in the past five years.[4]

The land sector has been a considerable focus of FEACC investigations in recent years. A household survey commissioned by the FEACC
indicated that the customs service is the most corrupt sector, followed
by land allocation, national housing, judges and the court system, and the
tax system.[5] In the 2007/08 FEACC Annual Report, 28 of the 63 cases
investigated during the year were in the land administration and development sector, and these cases involved about Br 476.5 million of the
Br 2.18 billion in undue advantage or lost revenue during the year.[6]
Eleven of the 55 work procedures and practices reviewed by the commission during the year were in the land sector (eight concerned with
land administration and three concerned with plots of land and construction).[7]

A key area where corruption occurs is in the allocation of land. In rural
areas, officials have distorted the definition of "public land" to mean "government land." Some officials also define "public purpose" in applying
expropriation, and some commentators are suggesting that this is leading
to landlessness. Some officials have engaged in land grabbing to grant land
to functionaries, which is not in accord with tradition. This is happening
at the woreda level and is being copied by the elected committee members at kebele level. There are no readily available mechanisms or rules
for accessing rural land, and investors have to apply through the Ethiopian
or regional investment agencies.

However, the situation is even more complex in urban areas, where land has been allocated as leases to influential, well-connected individuals but not put to use as required by existing regulations (as illustrated in box 7.4). There are three basic ways to obtain land in urban areas (as box 7.5 explains), but there are gaps and a lack of clarity in the policy and legal framework and no efficient, transparent system to implement policy. As a result, there is no vibrant land market and no conclusive means to assess land rights and land value, among other matters.

Nor is there any policy for land transactions: "Almost all transactions involving land most often incorporate corruption because there is no clear policy or transparent regulation concerning land" (*Reporter* 2008). The uncertainty in rights, the lack of clear rules, and the high levels of informality encourage corruption. The FEACC, in the July 2007 report of

Box 7.4

Urban Land Speculation in Ethiopia

Under the lease system that applies in urban areas, land is allocated to private individuals and organizations with the obligation that allocated land be developed according to the planned use within 18 months. Despite this clear requirement, there are numerous cases of allocated land being fenced off and remaining idle for long periods of time. Cases reported in the media include the following:

- The Bahir Dar Resort Hotel, sold by the Development Bank of Ethiopia more than three years ago as a largely completed development, today remains unopened.[8]
- The Hora Ras Hotel in Bishoftu, allocated more than 10 years ago to a developer who planned to build a five-star hotel, has not occurred to date.
- A modern resort hotel, planned for land acquired in Arbaminch town more than a decade ago, has not been built.
- A Sheraton hotel and a 50,000-seat stadium, both planned for land allocated in Adama, have not been built.[9]

In late 2008, the Oromia Investment Commission announced the results of a study that documented land held by inactive developers and was reported to be taking action against more than 60 investors who had submitted false bank statements to the commission.[10]

Box 7.5

Access to Land in Addis Ababa

There are three basic ways of accessing land in urban areas in Addis Ababa:

- Through the auction process for leases being offered by the municipality. Under a lease system introduced in 2002, the typical terms are a 20 percent down payment with the rest paid over 15–20 years and an obligation to undertake construction within 18 months of obtaining the lease. The offers for auction have been limited and infrequent. The bidding has therefore been very competitive.
- By negotiating with existing private holders of permits or leases, who typically require a down payment of 100 percent of the agreed-on amount and are expensive.
- By identifying a parcel of land and starting a process to negotiate a lease with the municipality. Because there are no guidelines for this process, there is a lot of corruption—"a very murky area," as one urban specialist in Addis Ababa described it.

The rules for access to land are not clear, and some people have better access than others, largely due to relationships or payment of bribes. The private sector usually cannot rely on or wait for the lease or auction process, so it usually looks to other means. A key method to illegally allocate municipal land was to allocate it to housing cooperatives controlled by developers who then sold off the land informally. The resulting buyers were usually unaware of the legal status of the land they were buying. The courts are not efficient in resolving disputes and can be aligned with the corrupt officials. Unless the occupier is a permit holder or a recipient of a lease from the municipality, the holding is insecure. The banks are not comfortable with lease land and typically will only lend money based on the amount invested and not on the land value.

Source: Author interview.

its investigation of corruption in five subcities in Addis Ababa, concluded, "It is getting nearly impossible to get a plot of land without bribing city administration officials" (*Reporter* 2007).

The land administration system is managed largely by directives in the municipalities and regions. The directives are not published and are easily changed. There has been little or no checking to ensure that regional regulations and directives comply with the requirements and objectives of overarching federal laws.

With limited systems in place to record rights, particularly in urban areas, and limited oversight, officials have plenty of opportunities to falsify documents. It is not uncommon for parcels of land to be allocated to many different parties, sometimes to as many as 10 different parties, from whom officials and intermediaries collect multiple transaction and service fees.[11]

In short, land is being allocated that should not be allocated. The master plan for Addis Ababa is being ignored, and most of the green areas and some of the roads in the master plan have been allocated for private use.[12] The uncertainty in land documents and the issuance of forged land documents creates opportunities for fraud, as box 7.6 explains.

In July 2007, the FEACC reported on an investigation of land sector corruption in five of the 10 subcities in Addis Ababa (FEACC 2008b, 2008c). The investigation report issued these key findings:

- The relevant laws, directives, and manuals for the allocation of land through the lease system were unclear, creating opportunities for corruption. In one cited case, a lease award to a successful bidder was canceled and the lease awarded to another by negotiation without reasonable cause. In some cases, bidders had submitted forged bank statements and paid bribes.
- There was frequently a conflict of interest for lease board members who often played a key role in the whole process, from identification

Box 7.6

Use of Forged Land Documents in the Finance Sector

A former local bank president cites a case in which the bank had lent Br10 million to someone who had produced a title deed. This person had not repaid the loan and had fled to Qatar. Another person then appeared with what he claimed to be the true title deed. The bank ended up writing off the debt. The banks do not trust title deeds and have all established informal systems to validate documents. These systems include interviews with neighbors and investigation of municipal tax records, among other means, which significantly increase the time and costs of acquiring loans and are an inefficient use of resources.

Source: Author.

of the land to awarding of the lease. Their involvement in the whole process conflicted with their roles as board members in overseeing the lease-award process.

- No process was in place to monitor compliance with the requirement that investors develop urban land within 18 months of being awarded the lease. Leased land was also being sold and put to uses not specified in the lease agreement.
- The mandates of the Addis Ababa city administration and the subcities were unclear, resulting in corruption whereby action at one level was being frustrated at another level. The investigation showed that at the stage when the successful winners of the 54th, 57th, and 58th rounds of auctions in Bolle subcity were identified, the land planned for allocation had already been allocated to other individuals through negotiation for unknown reasons.
- No system was in place to monitor lease payments and monitor compliance with lease conditions.
- No grievance process existed for people to resolve difficulties with the manner in which subcity officials implement and manage the lease system.

Based on the corruption evident in Ethiopia's land sector (as set out above), supported by the analysis of land governance in Ethiopia (as set out below), and using the value chain and vulnerability for corruption (shown previously in table 7.1), box 7.7 summarizes the key areas of land sector corruption.

Mapping Corruption to the Value Chain

This section looks at the assessment of corruption using the value chain (as previously shown in table 7.1), drawing on the information in the LGAF expert investigations, records of the panel deliberations, and interviews with key stakeholders.

Policy Formulation and the Legislative Framework

In rural areas, the policy in theory covers most of the population, but only five of the nine regions have enacted relevant laws. Communal land in rural areas has not been mapped, and communal rights are not registered. A more fundamental concern is lack of clear rules at the national level for dispute settlement and the system's numerous subjective limitations on rights—although some of the regional proclamations set out

Box 7.7

Key Areas of Land Sector Corruption in Ethiopia

The elite and senior officials are capturing assets. This land grabbing is facilitated by a weak policy and legal framework and poor systems to implement existing policies and laws. Corruption in the implementation of land policy and laws occurs particularly through the following:

- *Institutionalization of informal fees.* As mentioned previously, the FEACC investigation of corruption in five subcities in Addis Ababa concluded that it was "nearly impossible to a get a plot of land without bribing city administration officials."
- *Fraudulent actions of officials.* Officials have allocated land for themselves in both urban and rural areas and for housing associations and developers in urban areas.
- *Officials' willingness—fraudulently or in response to bribes or nepotism—to overlook virtually all specified restrictions and requirements,* particularly in Addis Ababa, which has seriously undermined the enforcement of land use plans, lease conditions, and building and construction codes in urban areas.
- *Issuance of forged land documents,* resulting from fraud, bribery, or nepotism, which has seriously eroded confidence in the land records system.

Source: Author.

dispute resolution procedures[13] and there are informal or traditional dispute resolution mechanisms.

There are no clear standards for the loss of rights due to environmental and conservation laws. Rural landholders cannot mortgage their holdings—although an investor leasing land can use the lease as collateral for a loan. There are also transfer restrictions, and most regions impose limits on the amount of land that can be leased.

Urban areas have fewer restrictions on rights and more active markets, but the legal framework for the recognition of land tenure in urban areas is weak, and most land issues—including those that need resolution at the federal level—are handled by ever-changing municipality directives that are generally not enforced.[14] One of the key obstacles for the legal recognition of urban tenure rights is the absence of clear, consistent, and systematic policy and procedures regarding informal holdings, either to prevent their occurrence or to formalize them when they occur. Municipalities put leasehold land out to tender. In Addis Ababa, small parcels have been put out to tender, and tender prices have often greatly exceeded benchmarks (an example quoted was a bid of Br 6,000 per square meter against a benchmark of Br 200 per square meter for a parcel with little or no infrastructure). The process is not transparent. The supply shortage is forcing those requiring land to explore other alternatives.

Rural land administration and land use laws are issued at the federal and regional levels, while the urban side is covered in the lease laws issued at federal, regional, and municipal levels. Despite the apparent decentralization of decision making, the policies and laws are developed by experts often hidden from the public eye, and the first time the public hears of a new policy is when it is presented to the legislative body. Even where consultation has occurred, it is by invitation only, as was the case with the development of the building code by the Ministry Urban Development and Construction. Although there is a trend of consulting the farmers in some rural areas, the academic community and other nonstate actors are routinely excluded from the consultation process.

The rural land laws mention orphans and women, and the urban land lease laws have provisions referring to women and persons who have disabilities or are physically challenged. However, the provision of land in urban areas has, to some extent, discriminated based on marital status and possibly encouraged simulated divorces.

Funding to implement policy is limited, as are monitoring and reporting on the progress of implementation.

Key policy and legislative issues that create opportunities for corruption include the following:

- The lack of a strong overarching policy framework, combined with the poor implementation and oversight of existing policy, creates opportunities for officials to abuse their authority.
- Limited public consultation in policy formulation leads to very limited public awareness of policy and public engagement with policy implementation. This creates a gap between policy and implementation that can be abused by officials.
- The imposition of subjective limitations on rights in rural areas without a strong policy framework creates opportunities for discretion by officials, particularly given the lack of an effective dispute resolution process.

- The reliance on ever-changing municipal directives in urban areas without a strong policy framework and clear oversight arrangements creates uncertainty among users and opportunities for abuse by decision makers, particularly given that the directives are generally not published
- The lack of a clear policy to address the issue of informal holdings in urban areas encourages informality and creates opportunities for officials to profit from abuse of their positions, particularly in an environment where there are high levels of informality and few adverse consequences to informal development.

Institutions and Capacity

In the relevant laws, the mandate or responsibility for the implementation of *rural* land policies and laws is given mainly to land administration authorities in each regional state, while the mandate to administer and manage *urban* land is given to land administration authorities or departments of municipalities or city governments. However, there are gaps in the laws, and the land policies are typically implemented through unpublished directives. These directives include serious rights issues; even fees are delegated to directives.

In addition to variations among localities, the directives are often changed. In rural areas, a federal proclamation provides some framework, although this proclamation was implemented after some regions had developed land administration policy and legislation, and this late engagement has resulted in some inconsistencies. There is no similar model proclamation for urban land, and the broad delegation has resulted in regional inconsistencies. There is also confusion about the role of the administration, which has both executive and adjudicatory powers. There are serious confusions between the mandate of the administration and the courts in resolving land conflicts. Another concern is the simultaneous membership of land administration committee and board members in municipal and regional councils.

Although urban centers and cities do not have registry offices, about 25 percent of the existing, individually held urban properties have been recorded in one way or another. The record keeping in urban areas lacks many of the essential elements of formal registration (such as accessibility, accuracy, and currency). In contrast, approximately 70 percent of rural households in the most populous regions with significant agrarian holdings have been registered and certified in an ongoing rural registration process, albeit with little emphasis on keeping these records up-to-date.

Problems can occur in compensating rural landholders where rural land is absorbed into a municipality. Although the laws provide for compensation, the party responsible for the payment of compensation is unclear. This lack of clarity has resulted in cases where rural people whose land has been absorbed into a city are not compensated

In rural areas, the land records that exist are predominantly manual and thus difficult to share. In urban areas, information on rights to land is available to interested institutions upon request by letter with no cost involved. However, because such information is not held in a systematic manner, it is usually difficult to access this information.

Key institutional and capacity issues that create opportunities for corruption include the following:

- The broad delegation to unpublished directives, in the absence of a strong overarching policy framework, creates opportunities for discretion by officials.
- The lack of a clear, unambiguous mandate for the resolution of disputes creates opportunities for forum shopping and fosters an environment where there is little consequence to illegal activity.
- The laws do not clearly provide for the appointment of independent lease board members, which creates conflicts of interest, reduces oversight of administrative activity, and creates opportunities for abuse of discretion.

Implementation of Processes, Procedures, Manuals

Public land management. State ownership of all land in Ethiopia under the constitution has the perverse outcome that the state has little incentive to manage public land because it is the residual owner. Nonetheless, the recording and demarcation of publicly held land in Addis Ababa and some regional states is substantial, especially in relation to protected forests and some of the national parks. Yet no consistent inventory (record or maps) of public land unambiguously identifies rights and responsibility for management across the different areas of public land, and this affects the efficient management of public land and creates opportunities for the illegal allocation of public land to private parties.

A substantial proportion of expropriated land is transferred to private interests. The expropriation and relocation of smallholders has been to the advantage of extensive commercial farming, including flower farms, biofuel, and other commodities.

Compensation for the expropriation of registered property involves the allocation of land as well as monetary compensation, but there is little if any compensation of secondary rights. Unregistered landholders typically are allocated the minimum area determined for residential purposes in compensation cases. However, there are problems in medium-size towns, especially in relation to timely compensation and resettlement issues. If land is expropriated for an investor, the investor is responsible for compensation, and this is typically paid in a timely manner. In urban areas, there are mechanisms to provide land for displaced informal settlers.

The relevant federal laws provide for the establishment of Land Clearance and Appeal Commissions—quasi-judicial tribunals accountable to the council at the municipal and regional levels, mainly through regional laws. One such commission is in Addis Ababa, but there is little activity in other municipalities and rural areas. The commission in Addis Ababa has a single location and is hampered by limited staff as well as jurisdictional disputes with the municipality courts.

In urban centers, most allocation of public land for residential, manufacturing, commerce, and construction purposes occurs through auctions. Allocation of rural land routinely occurs on a project basis through applications or proposals submitted by individual investors. The efficacy of auctions in ensuring optimum pricing is questionable because there have been inexplicable fluctuations in auction prices in Addis Ababa.

Little information is publicly available about the allocation of public land, the amount allocated, the mode of allocation, the parties involved, or the conditions of allocation.

Key public land management issues that create opportunities for corruption include the following:

- There is no inventory of public land, which affects the efficient management of public land and creates opportunities for the illegal allocation of public land to private parties.
- The process to allocate public land lacks transparency, which creates opportunities for corruption and the inappropriate allocation of public land.

Land use planning. In Ethiopia, the Ministry of Agriculture, with assistance from the Food and Agriculture Organization (of the United Nations), implemented in the 1980s a significant program to prepare rural land use plans. However, limited resources were devoted to maintaining and enforcing these plans. In recent times, there has been little planning in rural areas except for a recent initiative covering development corridors and areas around Addis Ababa.

In urban areas, there is little consultation in the preparation of land use plans and building codes. The real reasons behind the decisions relating to land use changes are not even discussed in many cases, except in academic circles. Urban land use plan changes are known only when the design has been completed, yet the completed plans are not well publicized.

The public does not capture benefits arising from infrastructure development in urban areas mainly because of outdated valuation benchmarks that limit the potential return through building and transfer taxes.

Although land use plans are in place in Addis Ababa, the development of the central and older parts of the city occurs in an ad hoc manner with infrastructure straining to catch up. In periurban areas, development almost invariably occurs well in advance of infrastructure. Although master plan preparation processes have been initiated in the major cities and urban centers, these plans have yet to be effective in controlling urban development.

Building permits are normally issued within a period much shorter than three months except where building permits are being used for purposes other than actual construction—for instance, as a means of establishing ownership or as evidence of rights in a dispute.

Key land use planning issues that create opportunities for corruption include the following:

- The lack of public consultation in preparing and changing land use plans and the fact that land use plans are not well publicized limits public awareness of the planning process as well as the plans themselves and therefore creates opportunities for abuse of authority by officials.
- Land use plans that exist are not implemented, which creates opportunities for officials to abuse their authority and leads to unsustainable and unplanned development (such as the substantial encroachment of the green area in the master plan for Addis Ababa).
- The weak or limited enforcement of land use plans is due in part to the weak link between the technical institutions responsible for planning and the judiciary. Courts often make decisions without reference to the relevant proclamations.

Valuation and taxation. In Ethiopia, the system to value land for taxation bears little or no relationship to market prices. The valuation of property for land rent and building taxes in urban areas, and land use fees in rural areas, is based on the following:

- *Urban land rent.* Benchmark prices are set for urban centers or areas within the larger towns and cities based mainly on infrastructure. This approach almost universally involves setting the value for the most accessible urban center or part of a town or city and calculating the benchmark for other locations as a percentage of the value.
- *Building taxes.* These urban taxes are calculated based on stated rates of rent for every single property.
- *Rural land taxes.* Valuation in rural areas for taxation purposes for smallholder farmers is normally set in terms of birr per hectare irrespective of location, the quality of land, or actual annual production.

Multiple valuation systems are applied by key institutions such as municipalities, courts, and banks, and there is no system to certify valuers in Ethiopia. In rural areas, land is not valued and tax is based on land area—not value, use, or production. There are no valuation rolls in urban areas. Nonetheless, the banks can usually gather information to value land when considering applications for finance.

In urban areas, notably Addis Ababa, exemptions from property taxes are granted to specific investment sectors or specific land uses while regions additionally exempt rural land below a minimum stated size. Residential and commercial houses exempted from property taxes in Addis Ababa include (a) more than 155,000 administered by the kebele (local administration); (b) more than 120,000 administered by the agency responsible for government-owned houses; (c) religious institutions and buildings for other uses exempted by law; and (d) government agencies under temporary exemptions pending the issuance of ownership certificates. There are significant regional and rural-urban variations, too, especially in relation to incentives.

The property listing in urban areas extends beyond those "liable to pay taxes." The preparation of the list is integrated with the land allocation process. Every plot of land allocated is listed in the tax rolls as a matter of procedure. There is also a misconception that a tax roll listing is a means of formalizing informal settlements despite stipulations to the contrary in the official tax forms. Similar misconceptions have also been identified in rural areas.

There is a high rate of collection (at least 80 percent) for assessed urban taxes for a number of reasons, including taxpayers' land rent payments at the finance offices instead of deployment of tax collectors, integration of property tax in the land allocation system, and unofficial incentives to pay taxes. It is more difficult to determine collection rates for rural land use fees and taxes.

The cost of collecting property taxes is minimal both in urban and rural areas mainly because of the simplicity in the tax legislation and concurrent collection of taxes. In rural areas, the land use fees are calculated per hectare and administered along with agricultural income taxes. Most important, the cost of identification and valuation, which accounts for most of the costs in other systems, is very low in Ethiopia.

Key valuation and taxation issues that create opportunities for corruption include the following:

- The lack of a standard valuation system and certified valuers can create opportunities for collusion in reducing tax liabilities and can lead to inequities in the compensation for expropriated property.

Public provision of land information. Rural areas have no maps of registered holdings, which will be undertaken under second-level registration. Second-level registration has been piloted only in selected sites in Amhara and Oromia, and there is no consensus at the federal level on the standards and specifications for second-level certification.

In urban areas, there is little mapping of registered property. Encumbrances and restrictions are not recorded in the registers, and the encumbrances, if registered, are listed in a separate document. Land use restrictions are not recorded in the register.

In the four regions that have established land administration systems, the overriding emphasis is on first-time registration, which is seen as a one-time activity. There is little emphasis on the recording of changes in holdings, and therefore the registers are not kept up to date.

The formal fees for registration are low. Two issues arise from this situation: (a) Registration systems are not financially sustainable because the only fee collected is a certificate fee in all regions except Amhara, where no fee is collected. Hence, capital investment in the rural registry system is low: dilapidated filing rooms with leaking roofs are typical. (b) Low official fees provide scope for petty corruption whereby informal fees have reportedly become "routine" in some urban contexts. In addition, "service payments" such as witnesses to formalize informal holdings or semilegal holding rights, significantly affect the overall cost of first-time registration without increasing official revenue.

Key public information issues that create opportunities for corruption include the following:

- The spatial location and extent of registered holdings has not been defined, which reduces the ability to validate records and makes issuing forged documents easier.
- Only about 25 percent of individually held urban properties have been recorded in one way or another, but the records are not reliable or conclusive—which reduces confidence in the records systems and creates opportunities for corrupt practices such as the issuance of forged documentation or the illegal alteration of records.
- About 70 percent of rural holdings have been registered, but the records are not being kept up to date, which reduces the usefulness of the records and fosters future disputes over land, particularly among family members.

Dispute resolution and conflict management. First Instance courts in Ethiopia are available at the woreda level, and social courts are available at the kebele level. However, in many places, even though formal institutions exist and personnel have been assigned, the institutions are not functional. In many rural areas, it can take a day or more to get to a woreda, so access can be difficult.

A more fundamental problem is the fact that the laws themselves are not accessible. Language barriers and the costs required for translation can also inhibit access in some localities. As a result, about half of the local communities lack access to First Instance conflict resolution but instead have the option to use informal institutions (arbitration by elders) that are recognized by the local community in most areas of the country. However, the decisions passed by local traditional elders may not always be equitable.

There are parallel avenues for dispute resolution in Addis Ababa and the regions. These alternative venues include land administration boards, land clearance appeals commissions, federal courts, municipal courts, regional courts, and other institutions with adjudication mandates. No mechanisms are in place for information sharing among institutions. Although those within the same institutional structure do meet, the collaboration and coordination across institutions is limited and often informal. As a result, three or four venues may entertain the same case at the same time, especially when one of the parties has resources. The practice in Addis Ababa involves initiating cases in two or more venues, such as the municipal courts and the land clearance commission or land administration board. Appellate courts, which are established at zonal and regional levels, are usually far away from the community, entail high costs, and can take a long time to issue decisions.

It is estimated that land disputes may constitute at least 50 percent of cases in the formal court system. Decisions at the First Instance court level tend to favor the government in land-issue litigation, which constitute a high percentage of longstanding cases. One judge reported that as many as 3,000 of the 4,000 cases in his court are land-related. Moreover, the judge reported that most crimes committed currently in the region, such as arson and homicide, are related to land disputes. In some areas, the rate of land disputes was escalating so rapidly that the authorities had stopped issuing land certificates.

Key dispute resolution and conflict management issues that create opportunities for corruption include the following:

• Given the existence of multiple dispute resolution options, little sharing of information, and opportunities for forum shopping, the formal system is ineffective in resolving land disputes, and there is a high cost in accessing appellate courts. This situation contributes to high case loads and forces people to consider alternative means of dispute resolution that may be less transparent and less equitable—or even to seek corrupt means of obtaining favorable judgments.

Monitoring and Evaluation

In rural areas, the register (other than in pilot areas) is usually recorded on a holding basis that limits the ability to search the register by parcel. Under normal circumstances, only the holder or the holder's legal representative can access records in urban areas. Commercial banks have access to the registers. Public records are routinely considered confidential personal records by the service providers. In rural areas, although the records system is relatively simple, poor records management systems can seriously delay accessing information.

In Addis Ababa, one can access some records (notably, authenticated copies of title deeds and transfer contracts) within one week. There are, however, difficulties in locating the relevant information in different institutions, and records are available only in manual format. This means that the process of accessing information is typically difficult and time-consuming, particularly with the high turnover of staff in many municipalities and towns.

Although some of the areas have meaningful service standards, these standards are seldom published, and little is understood by the service providers or the public. In most areas, either urban or rural, no service standards exist.

Key monitoring and evaluation issues that create opportunities for corruption include the following:

- Access to information in urban areas is difficult because of the lack of standards in records management and difficulties in locating information in different institutions, which creates opportunities for corruption such as the issuance of forged documents or the illegal alteration of records.
- Access to the registers at woreda level in rural areas is difficult, which reduces public access to the records and creates opportunities for corruption and the illegal alteration of records.

Recommendations

A number of factors can foster corruption or the abuse by decision makers in the land sector's value chain of activities:

- Lack of clarity in land policy
- Lack of public participation in policy formulation and legislative processes
- Failure of land policy and legislation to reflect how significant sections of the population recognize and deal with land issues
- Lack of public awareness of land policy, legislation, and procedures, compounded by
  - complicated procedures and forms;
  - unreasonable or conflicting restrictions or prerequisites for applications; and
  - complicated or nontransparent schedules of fees and charges.

Restricted access to land records can also reduce the ability of policy makers and the general population to exercise oversight over land management and administration systems, not to mention the officials responsible for these systems. There is no common solution to corruption in the land sector. To put forward a range of steps that could be undertaken in a country, one needs to understand the scope and extent of the problems and the underlying factors that foster corrupt practices.

Key Recommendations to Address Corruption in Ethiopia's Land Sector

The key areas of corruption in the land sector in Ethiopia, as identified in this analysis, are set out in box 7.7. Corruption in the key areas can be addressed with the following strategies:

- *Capture of assets by the elite and senior officials*: clear policy; improved record systems; public access to record systems; and improved oversight of the actions of these bodies, including establishment of an independent agency to investigate complaints
- *Corrupt practices in land management and administration (informal fees, fraudulent land allocation, disregard of specified restrictions and requirements, and forged land documents)*: clear policy to clarify and publicize restrictions and requirements as well as roles and responsibilities of officials; improved systems; better public awareness of policy and systems; development and implementation of service standards; improved oversight of systems and standards; improved dispute resolution systems; public access to records; and an independent agency to investigate complaints.

Based on these strategies, this study recommends the following three fundamental governance reforms (as covered in table 7.2 and further discussed below):

- Develop a comprehensive, clear land policy and legal framework.
- Improve institutions and systems in land sector agencies.
- Build capacity and an environment for service delivery.

Policy and legal framework. Implementing significant change to address the issues related to governance and corruption that exist in the land sector will require clear political will. Based on international experience, that political will is best demonstrated by the development and implementation of a national land policy. The scope of a land policy document can be broad, but based on the current situation in Ethiopia, it should at a minimum cover

- clear definition of the rights, responsibilities, and restrictions defining land tenure in both rural and urban areas;
- clear definition of transitional arrangements, particularly in urban areas (transition from permit to lease system and the process for formalizing informal development);

Table 7.2   Strategies and Recommendations for Governance Reforms in Ethiopia's Land Sector

	Develop comprehensive, clear land policy	Improve institutions and systems	Build capacity for service delivery
Capture of assets	Clarify, publicize restrictions and requirements	Improve record systems	• Public access to record systems • Improved oversight • Independent agency to investigate complaints
Corrupt land management and administration	Clarify officials' roles and responsibilities	Improve systems, improve public awareness of policy and systems	• Service standards • Improved oversight of systems and standards • Improved dispute resolution systems • Public access to records • Independent agency to investigate complaints

Source: Author.

- clear specification of institutional roles and responsibilities, including standards for the separation of responsibility for policy formulation, implementation, and the handling of disputes, as well as an agreement on appropriate oversight arrangements;
- clear guidance on the preparation of regulations and directives, including the need to ensure that regulations and directives have a legal basis and are accessible to the community;
- commitment to wide consultation in the implementation of policy;
- commitment to public access to records and the provision of services; and
- simplified framework for resolving disputes and managing conflict.

A clear land policy must be developed in a participatory manner, with wide consultation. The final land policy document should identify the legislative changes necessary to implement the policy, include a detailed action plan, set out appropriate monitoring arrangements, and be costed. Policy is not going to change things without the successful establishment of implementation processes. There should also be regular reporting to policy makers on implementation.

Improved institutions and systems. Improved land information systems that are readily accessible by the general public will be critical to building community trust in the land sector agencies. A new business process has been developed to administer the land allocation process and the management of the lease system in Addis Ababa (see box 7.8). This is a positive step, but the new process is only supported by a directive and has yet to be fully tested. Improved processes supported by comprehensive manuals and other materials are also required in a number of other areas, including the following:

- A participatory process for the preparation and implementation of land use plans
- A standardized process for property valuation, based on international standards
- Improved systems of land records and the management of records in both urban and rural areas, including information on public, private, and communal land
- Public provision of information, including the fees and rights of access
- A process to handle land disputes and manage conflict over land.

Box 7.8

New Process to Allocate Leases in Addis Ababa

A new business process has been developed to administer the land allocation process and the management of the lease system in Addis Ababa based on the ongoing business process reengineering initiative and the results of the recent FEACC investigations. This new system was implemented in January 2009 in four subcities (Bolle, Yeka, Utaki, and Wedati). A new directive has been prepared, and manuals have been produced and are being tested. The allocation of land by negotiation is being strongly discouraged, and each subcity is having one round of leases or auctions per month, with each round in a subcity offering 200–300 parcels per month. These allocations are being made on a block rather than parcel basis, and the level of demand has been less frantic than previously (in terms of the bid prices and the number of bidders per parcel).

Source: Author.

Building capacity and an environment for service delivery. Systemic changes need to occur to support the decentralized institutional environment providing normative frameworks at the woreda and municipal levels. Important steps in the reform process are (a) resolution of ambiguities in the administrative and management roles and mandates for local governance and (b) complementing this resolution with recurrent reporting and auditing of activities.

In addition, the reform of land institutions should place much greater emphasis on improving services and functionality. A large part of the effort involves ensuring sustainable financial and technical capacity within resource constraints. Reengineering processes and document management will have greater impact on curbing corrupt practices and generating behavioral shifts than a technically engineered solution of computerization. These steps need to be supported by significant financial and political support from the federal level. Moreover, informal systems and payments will continue to occur until the formal system offers a better service and cannot be undermined by corrupt practices.

These are the key steps in building capacity:

- Establishment of a supervisory body to deal with and investigate complaints made by the public
- Comprehensive public awareness campaigns, including systems to capture public feedback
- Definition and implementation of service delivery standards
- Agreement on fee schedules and funding for the development and ongoing operation of systems based on detailed financial models for anticipated service delivery
- Training of land sector staff in ethical conduct and the development and implementation of systems to monitor their conduct and handle any complaints from the public.

Phasing of Reform Activity

"It is important to note that there are no quick fixes to land tenure problems. Except in particularly favorable circumstances, improvements in this field can only be achieved in the long run." (Wachter and English 1992, 17)

As noted by Wachter and English in their 1992 review of World Bank experience with rural land administration projects, implementing change in the land sector is a long-term activity. The development of land policy will take time. Developing and implementing improved systems will also take time. However, some immediate actions can be taken to begin to address the problems with corruption in the land sector:

- A review of the experience in implementing improved systems to allocate land in the four subcities in Addis Ababa, possibly presented in a stakeholder workshop, and the rollout of these procedures in the other subcities and other major urban centers in Ethiopia
- Development of improved systems to record rights in urban land and the pilot testing of these systems in subcities in Addis Ababa. The effectiveness of this effort would be enhanced by a policy to make these records available for public inspection.
- Establishment of a supervisory body to address and investigate complaints by the public against the actions of officials in land sector agencies. The effectiveness of this new body would be enhanced if the other activities listed above for improved service delivery (comprehensive public awareness campaigns, the development and agreement on service standards, and the training of land sector staff in ethical conduct) were undertaken.

These three actions could be undertaken in the short term and make an immediate impact on key areas of corruption as identified in this study. The long-term activity in developing land policy and improved systems can then build on that initial momentum.

Further Study

The FEACC investigation of corruption in five subcities in Addis Ababa has identified specific modes of corrupt activity and has resulted in improved procedures that are being trialed in four of the subcities. Further detailed investigations of land sector corruption in urban areas outside of Addis Ababa as well as in rural areas will help prioritize and focus efforts to reduce corruption in the land sector in Ethiopia.

Annex 7.1 Country LGAF Scorecard for Ethiopia

Table 7A.1   LGAF Scorecard of Ethiopian Land Sector Governance, 2009

Score A: good governance	Score B: Progress toward good governance	Score C: Not quite meeting good governance criteria	Score D: No attempt to meet good governance criteria

(continued next page)

Table 7A.1   *(continued)*

LGI-Dim		Topic	A	B	C	D
Recognition of rights						
1	i	Land tenure rights recognition (rural)		√		
1	ii	Land tenure rights recognition (urban)		√		
1	iii	Rural group rights recognition		√		
1	iv	Urban group rights recognition in informal areas			√	
1	v	Opportunities for tenure individualization				√
Enforcement of rights						
2	i	Surveying/mapping and registration of claims on communal land				√
2	ii	Registration of individually held properties			√	
2	iii	Women's rights are recognized in practice by the formal system		√		
2	iv	Condominium regime provides appropriate management of CP	√			
2	v	Compensation due to land use changes [n.a.]				
Mechanisms for recognition						
3	i	Use of nondocumentary forms of evidence to recognize rights			√	
3	ii	Formal recognition of long-term, unchallenged possession			√	
3	iii	First-time registration on demand is not restricted by inability to pay formal fees		√		
3	iv	First-time registration does not entail significant informal fees		√		
3	v	Formalization of residential housing is feasible and affordable			√	
3	vi	Efficient and transparent process to formally recognize long-term unchallenged possession			√	
Restrictions on rights						
4	i	Restrictions regarding urban land use, ownership, and transferability		√		
4	ii	Restrictions regarding rural land use, ownership, and transferability		√		
Clarity of mandates						
5	i	Separation of institutional roles			√	
5	ii	Institutional overlap			√	
5	iii	Administrative overlap			√	
5	iv	Information sharing		√		
Equity and nondiscrimination						
6	i	Clear land policy developed in a participatory manner			√	
6	ii	Meaningful incorporation of equity goals			√	
6	iii	Policy for implementation is costed, matched with the benefits, and is adequately resourced			√	
6	iv	Regular and public reports indicating progress in policy implementation			√	

(continued next page)

Table 7A.1   *(continued)*

LGI-Dim		Topic	A	B	C	D
Transparency of land use						
7	i	Changes in land use based on public input				√
7	ii	Sufficient public notice of land use changes				√
7	iii	Public capture of benefits arising from changes in permitted land use				√
7	iv	Speed of land use change				√
Efficiency of land use planning						
8	i	Process for planned urban development in the largest city				√
8	ii	Process for planned urban development in the four largest cities				√
8	iii	Ability of urban planning to cope with urban growth			√	
8	iv	Plot size adherence [n.a.]				
8	v	Use plans for specific land classes are in line with use				√
Speed and predictability						
9	i	Applications for building permits for residential dwellings are affordable and processed in a nondiscretionary manner.	√			
9	ii	Time required to obtain a building permit for a residential dwelling	√			
Transparency of valuation						
10	i	Clear process of property valuation				√
10	ii	Public availability of valuation rolls [n.a.]				
Tax collection efficiency						
11	i	Exemptions from property taxes are justified			√	
11	ii	Property holders liable to pay property tax are listed on the tax roll		√		
11	iii	Assessed property taxes are collected		√		
11	iv	Property taxes' correspondence to costs of collection		√		
Identification of public land						
12	i	Public land ownership is justified and implemented at the appropriate level of government			√	
12	ii	Complete recording of publicly held land			√	
12	iii	Assignment of management responsibility for public land			√	
12	iv	Resources available to comply with responsibilities			√	
12	v	Inventory of public land is accessible to the public				
12	vi	Key information on land concessions is accessible to the public.		√		
Incidence of expropriation						
13	i	Transfer of expropriated land to private interests				√
13	ii	Speed of use of expropriated land			√	
Transparency of procedures						
14	i	Compensation for expropriation of ownership			√	
14	ii	Compensation for expropriation of all rights				√
14	iii	Promptness of compensation			√	

(continued next page)

Table 7A.1   *(continued)*

			Score			
LGI- Dim		Topic	A	B	C	D
14	iv	Independent and accessible avenues for appeal against expropriation			√	
14	v	Appealing expropriation is time-bounded				√
Transparent processes						
15	i	Openness of public land transactions				√
15	ii	Collection of payments for public leases			√	
15	iii	Modalities of lease or sale of public land				√
Completeness of registry						
16	i	Mapping of registry records				√
16	ii	Economically relevant private encumbrances				√
16	iii	Economically relevant public restrictions or charges				√
16	iv	Searchability of the registry (or organization with information on land rights)		√		
16	v	Accessibility of records in the registry (or organization with information on land rights)			√	
16	vi	Timely response to a request for access to records in the registry (or organization with information on land rights)			√	
Reliability of records						
17	i	Focus on customer satisfaction in the registry			√	
17	ii	Registry/cadastre information is up-to-date				√
Cost-effective and sustainable						
18	i	Cost of registering a property transfer	√			
18	ii	Financial sustainability of the registry				√
18	iii	Capital investment				√
Transparency						
19	i	Schedule of fees is available publicly			√	
19	ii	Informal payments discouraged			√	
Assignment of responsibility						
20	i	Accessibility of conflict resolution mechanisms		√		
20	ii	Informal or community-based dispute resolution				√
20	iii	Forum shopping				√
20	iv	Possibility of appeals			√	
Low level of pending conflicts						
21	i	Conflict resolution in the formal legal system			√	
21	ii	Speed of conflict resolution in the formal system				√
21	iii	Long-standing conflicts (unresolved cases older than five years)				√

Source: Multi-Talent Consultancy 2010.
Note: LGAF = Land Governance Assessment Framework (World Bank). LGI-Dim = Land Governance Indicator dimension.

Notes

1. With support from Imeru Tamrat of Multi-Talent Consultancy PLC.

2. Woredas are administrative districts in Ethiopia, each of which comprises a number of kebeles. The kebele is Ethiopia's smallest administrative unit (in Amharic, literally "neighborhood").

3. Author interview with FEACC Commissioner Ato Ali Sulaiman.

4. This estimate was provided by an interviewee who had more than 12 years' experience in land administration in Addis Ababa municipality. The members of the opposition interviewed stated they wanted to establish an independent body to investigate the 20,000–25,000 properties that they believe politicians and the elite have grabbed. These numbers are subjective and subject to political bias.

5. FEACC Web page, "Toward Consolidating Anti-Corruption Efforts." http://www.feac.gov.et/web_collection/publication_and_spots_English_starter.htm.

6. FEACC 2008a, Appendix 7.

7. FEACC 2008a, Appendix 1.

8. FEACC, "Toward Consolidating Anti-Corruption Efforts." http://www.feac.gov.et/web_collection/publication_and_spots_English_starter.htm.

9. FEACC 2008a, Appendix 7.

10. FEACC 2008a, Appendix 1.

11. Author interview with Amare Aregawi, editor of *The Reporter*, Addis Ababa.

12. The FEACC commissioner described the encroachment on the green areas in the Addis Ababa Master Plan as endemic and a key outcome of corruption in the land sector (interview with Ato Ali Sulaiman, June 2009). The Office for the Revision of the Addis Ababa Master Plan states that one of its key environmental objectives is protecting endangered green areas.

13. For example, the Amhara land law (proclamation 133/2006) sets out a dispute resolution process in article 29.

14. One of the expert panels cited the example of recent attempts to formalize possession in Addis Ababa, Dire Dawa, and Hawassa municipalities by using unpublished municipal directives. The formalization activities were conducted with little consistency and transparency and were discontinued for unexplained reasons before benefiting all eligible informal holders.

References

Crewett, Wibke, and Benedikt Korf. 2008. "Land Tenure in Ethiopia: Path Dependence, Shifting Rulers and the Quest for State Control." *Review of African Political Economy* 35 (2): 203–20.

Deininger, Klaus, Harris Selod, and Anthony Burns. 2011. *The Land Governance Assessment Framework: Identifying and Monitoring Good Practice in the Land Sector.* Agriculture and Rural Development Series. Washington, DC: World Bank.

De Meza, D., and J. Gould. 1992. "The Social Efficiency of Private Decisions to Enforce Property Rights." *Journal of Political Economy* 100 (3): 561–80.

FEACC (Federal Ethics and Anti-Corruption Commission). 2008a. FEACC Annual Report 2007/08. FEACC, Addis Ababa. http://www.feac.gov.et/web_collection/Com_report_english.htm.

———. 2008b. "Report on the Investigation for Improving the Working Procedures to Prevent Corrupt and Bad Practices in Five Subcities of the Addis City Administration: Yeka, Bole, Nifas-Silk/Lafto, and Kolfe/Keranio." Unpublished report, Amharic version, FEACC, Addis Ababa.

———. 2008c. "Report on the Investigation for Improving the Working Procedures to Prevent Corrupt and Bad Practices Regarding Procedures in Allocating Land, Monitoring, and Control for Real Estate in the Addis Ababa City Administration Land Development and Administration Authority." Unpublished report, Amharic version, FEACC, Addis Ababa.

Kunte, Arundhati, Kirk Hamilton, John Dixon, and Michael Clemens. 1998. "Estimating National Wealth: Methodology and Results." Departmental Working paper, World Bank, Washington, DC.

Multi-Talent Consultancy. 2010. "Improving Land Governance in Ethiopia: Implementation of the Land Governance Assessment Framework." Final report, Multi-Talent Consultancy, Addis Ababa.

People's Daily Online. 2006. "Land Transactions, Hotbed for Corruption in China: Expert." November 22.

The Reporter. 2007. "Ethiopia: Chronic Corruption in Land Administration." July 7. http://allafrica.com/stories/printable/200707090232.html.

———. 2008. "Oromia to Take Strong Measures against Inactive Land Developers." October 4. http://en.ethiopianreporter.com/index.php?option=com_content&task=view&id=22&Itemid=26.

Shavell, Steven. 2003. "Economic Analysis of Property Law." Working Paper 9695, National Bureau of Economic Research, Cambridge, MA.

TI (Transparency International). 2008. "TI Report: Emerging Economic Giants Show High Levels of Corporate Bribery Overseas." Press release, December 9. http://www.transparency.org/news_room/latest_news/press_releases/2008/bpi_2008_en.

———. 2009. *Global Corruption Barometer.* Berlin: TI.

TI India (Transparency International India). 2005. "India Corruption Study 2005." Annual publication, TI India and the Centre for Media Studies, New Delhi.

http://www.transparency.org/regional_pages/asia_pacific/newsroom/news_archive2/india_corruption_study_2005.

UN-FIG (United Nations-Fédération Internationale de Géomètres). 1999. "United Nations-FIG Declaration on Land Administration for Sustainable Development." Prepared at the International Workshop on Cadastral Infrastructures for Sustainable Developmentin Bathurst, New South Wales, Australia, October 18–22.

Van der Molen, P., and A. M. Tuladhar. 2006. "Corruption and Land Administration." Paper TS50.02 presented at the XXIII FIG (Fédération Internationale de Géomètres) Congress, Munich, October 8–13.

Wachter, D., and J. English. 1992. "The World Bank's Experience with Land Titling." Divisional paper 1992-35, Policy and Research Division, Environment Department, World Bank, Washington, DC.

CHAPTER 8

Corruption in the Telecommunications Sector in Ethiopia: A Preliminary Overview

Introduction

Although service delivery remains low compared with neighboring Sub-Saharan African countries, the telecommunications sector in Ethiopia is now expanding rapidly. Sector investment in the past 10 years has exceeded US$14 billion and is currently sustained at about 10 percent of gross domestic product (GDP). This investment is taking place under the auspices of a state-owned monopoly: the Ethiopian Telecommunications Corporation (ETC) is the sole provider of telecommunications services in Ethiopia (including fixed-line, mobile, Internet, and data communications); telecoms equipment is provided and installed by international suppliers.

The telecommunications sector in Ethiopia is characterized by paradox and controversy. Despite the country's exceptionally heavy recent investment in its telecoms infrastructure, it has the second lowest

---

This chapter draws on fieldwork conducted by Neill Stansbury in 2009 and is supplemented by additional internal research.

Although this chapter results from studies completed by January 2010, the process of checking, reviewing, and securing agreement for publication was finally brought to conclusion only in late 2011. The chapter is therefore put forward with the caveat that while it reflects the situation at the time of the study, some details will have understandably changed.

telephone penetration rate in Africa. It once led the regional field in the laying of fiber-optic cable, yet suffers from severe bandwidth and reliability problems. And it boasted the first privately owned public telecoms service in Africa, yet is now the only nation on the continent still permitting a state-owned company to maintain a monopoly on all telecoms services.

Amid its low service delivery, an apparent lack of accountability, and multiple court cases, some aspects of the sector are perceived by both domestic and international observers to be deeply affected by corruption. To date, however, no exposition of the scope and nature of this perceived corruption has been developed for public understanding. This chapter attempts to contribute to such an understanding, while offering recommendations aimed at rebuilding confidence in the sector.

The resulting risk map provides an overview of typical corruption risks in the sector, together with an assessment of the perceived prevalence of these practices in Ethiopia.

Methodology

The approach adopted is diagnostic and intended neither as an audit nor as a political economy assessment, though the latter may be warranted. By mapping areas seen to be at high, and low, risk of corruption, attention is then focused on those that warrant further study.

Using information obtained from document analysis, stakeholder interviews, and consensus building workshops, key risks are unpacked for seven defined areas of activity within the sector:

- Licensing
- Design
- Appointment of equipment suppliers
- Delivery and installation of equipment
- Construction of facilities
- Theft
- Public interface of service delivery.

Chapter Structure

The next section provides an international overview of corruption risk in the telecommunications sector and briefly assesses why it is considered to be particularly prone to corruption. The chapter then proceeds as follows:

- "The Context: The Ethiopian Telecoms Sector" describes how the sector developed; the large investments to bring Ethiopia's telecoms

industry up to international standards; sector performance; the institutional landscape; and the general regulatory, policy, and legal framework within which ETC operates.

- "Corruption in the Ethiopian Telecoms Sector" includes the corruption
  risk map to depict the various types of corruption that take place in any
  country's telecoms sector. The section also explores the risk of these
  practices occurring in Ethiopia and maps the high and low points in the
  functional areas of the sector, highlighting areas for further study. Using
  information obtained from document analysis, stakeholder interviews,
  and consensus building workshops, it unpacks perceived corrupt practices in each of seven value chain areas.

- "Procurement of Equipment Suppliers: The 2006 Vendor Financing
  and Supply Agreement" focuses on one area of risk frequently referred
  to during the study, presenting the findings of the primary area of risk—
  that of equipment supply. The section details a specific, controversial
  procurement involving both equipment supply and related financing.

- "Current Anticorruption Mechanisms for Ethiopia's Telecoms Sector"
  provides an overview of existing anticorruption controls and their
  implementation in telecommunications in Ethiopia.

- The chapter concludes with a set of concrete recommendations for the
  consideration of the government of Ethiopia and the principal telecoms
  stakeholders. Although not comprehensive, these recommendations
  represent the minimum that the telecoms sector must take on if corruption risks are to be quickly and effectively curbed in the face of
  rapid sector growth.

Corruption in the International Telecommunications Sector

Internationally, the telecoms sector is considered particularly susceptible
to corruption. Transparency International's Bribe Payers' Index ranks telecoms as perceived to be the 11th most corrupt sector out of 19 sectors
surveyed in terms of bribes paid, and the 10th most corrupt in terms of
state capture (TI 2008).

To understand the sector, it is useful to consider who is involved and
how the sector's unique characteristics make it prone to corruption.[1]

Stakeholders in the Telecommunications Sector
Stakeholder roles and functions in the telecoms sector are generally similar
to those in other utilities such as urban water supply, electricity, and gas.

A range of stakeholders are involved (figure 8.1). *The government* establishes regulatory policy for the sector, and an *independent regulator* oversees the adherence to these regulations and grants licenses. In competitive environments, the government (or the independent regulator) will grant a license to one or more *telecoms network operators* (which can be either a government or private sector organization or company) to own or operate all or part of the network. The network operator will typically purchase equipment and services from *telecoms suppliers*. The telecoms suppliers are normally major international companies that design, manufacture, supply, and install their own specialist equipment. This equipment and the services may include transmission and receiving equipment, mobile telephone masts, software, cables, satellite services, and telephone handsets. The network operator arranges for *contractors* to carry out the necessary civil and building works, such as foundations for mobile phone masts, access roads and buildings, and the laying of cables. Once the network infrastructure is in place, the operator then sells telecoms services such as telephone and Internet services to *business, individual, or business consumers*.

Corruption Risks in Any Telecoms Sector

In common with some other industries or utilities, the telecoms sector in many countries is regulated by government, requires major investment in infrastructure, and generates significant revenues. As such, the following factors make it prone to corruption risks:

- *High revenues.* Telecommunications is a high-volume, high-value business. A well-run telecoms network can be exceptionally profitable, producing large revenue streams for many years. A bribe of millions of dollars for a license or reduced regulatory controls may be only a fraction of the profit achieved by a private sector network operator if it can, as a result, obtain market entry or improve its market share.

- *High research and development costs.* Telecoms equipment suppliers invest millions in research and development of new products in the expectation of recovering that investment by winning high-value contracts. Therefore, they are under considerable pressure to win such contracts, which may induce some to engage in corrupt practices.

- *High costs and significant risks of market entry.* The installation of the basic infrastructure needed for a telecoms network can represent a significant investment—most notably in the case of satellites and cables (particularly undersea)[2] as well as with secondary mast-based

Figure 8.1 Typical Telecoms Sector Stakeholders

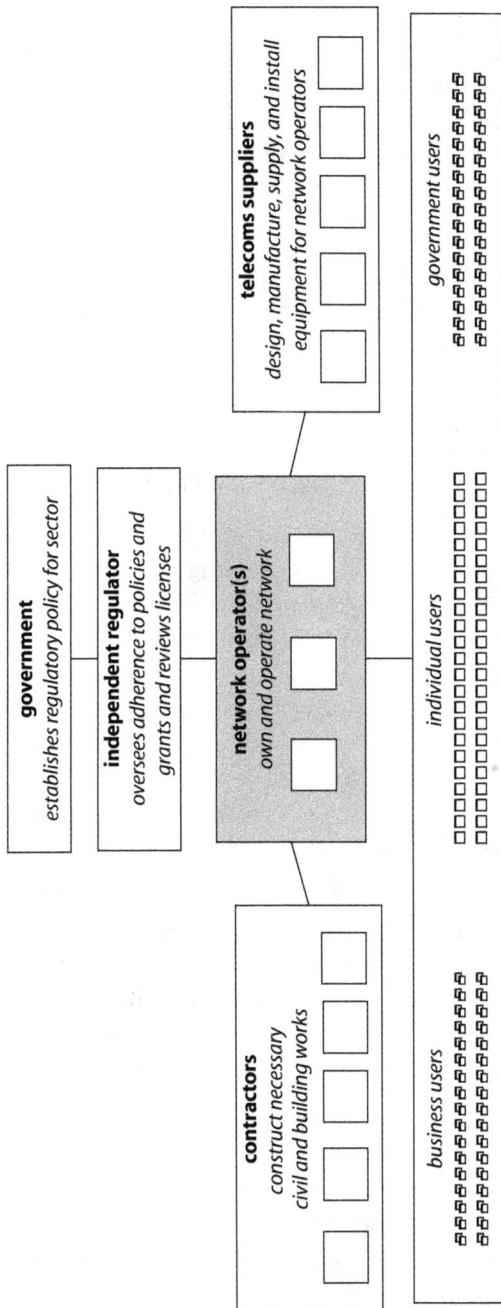

government
establishes regulatory policy for sector

independent regulator
oversees adherence to policies and grants and reviews licenses

contractors
construct necessary civil and building works

network operator(s)
own and operate network

telecoms suppliers
design, manufacture, supply, and install equipment for network operators

business users

individual users

government users

Source: Authors.

networks in large countries with predominantly rural populations. In any case, there is a risk that the investment may not be recouped. Risk factors include lower-than-expected demand, higher-than-expected costs, technical difficulties, unplanned obsolescence, and unexpected competition in the market. Unpredictable government behavior also creates risks, ranging from punitive increases in the license charges or conditions to worst-case scenarios such as nationalization.

- *Difficulty in valuing telecoms concessions and operations.* Numerous factors affect the value of a network operator's concession, including the cost of installing and operating the network; the level of consumer demand; the number of competitors; the prices charged for telecoms services; and the license fees, taxes, and other costs paid to the government. Each of these factors can fluctuate significantly from year to year, making it difficult to determine objectively whether a contract with a telecoms supplier has been placed at a fair market value.

- *Extent of government control.* Most countries control their telecoms concessions through regulation and licensing. Typically, a license is required for the initial concession, and permits are needed in connection with various construction, safety, and environmental protection issues. This gives considerable discretionary power to officials. Unless the law and regulations are extremely clear and unless the officials have integrity and are properly monitored and controlled, this power can be abused and result in corruption. Such risks are particularly high in countries where telecoms services are delivered by a state-owned monopoly that is not accountable to a strong and effective regulator.

- *Interface with the construction sector.* The construction industry is known to be a particularly high-risk sector from a corruption perspective.[3] Given that construction companies deliver much of the infrastructure used by the telecoms industry—including buildings, the erection of mobile phone masts, and the laying of cables—there are clear and significant indirect risks affecting the telecoms sector.

- *Lack of transparency.* Few countries actively disclose the details of telecoms network licensing or enable the public (including the media) readily to determine the competitiveness of a telecoms license awarded to a private sector operator. Similarly, few governments disclose the revenue they receive from telecoms licenses and network operations or account publicly for how they are used. Private operators must report revenue to tax authorities and their shareholders, but they often have no obligation to make financial information available to the public. Such a lack of transparency can contribute to a lack of accountability and an associated risk of corruption.

The Context: The Ethiopian Telecoms Sector

Historical Overview

Ethiopia boasts the oldest functioning telephone system in Africa. In 1894, just 17 years after the invention of the telephone, work began on the provision of telephone and telegram communication between Addis Ababa and Harar, a distance of some 477 kilometers. This open-wire system was then extended to link the capital with all of the major administrative centers in the country.

The private company responsible for this development was placed under palace control at the beginning of the 20th century, in time falling under the auspices of the Ministry of Post and Communications. Severe damage to the network was sustained during the period of Italian occupation. In 1952, telecommunications services were separated from the postal administration and structured under the Ministry of Transport and Communication (MTC). Supported by a combination of domestic finance and World Bank loans, the resulting Imperial Board of Telecommunications of Ethiopia (IBTE) had financial and administrative autonomy in fulfilling its mandate of expanding and maintaining telecommunications facilities in Ethiopia. In 1981, the IBTE became the Ethiopian Telecommunications Authority (ETA), maintaining responsibility for both the regulation and the operation of telecoms services.

With the regime change marking the end of the Derg era in 1991, the government included telecommunications in its efforts to update Ethiopia's legislative environment. This resulted in a fundamental revision to the laws and procedures relating to the telecoms sector, intended at the time to pave the way for an eventual opening of the market to outside investors. It also marked the beginnings of a renewed expansion of the network. In 1996, the functions of regulation and operation were separated through the establishment of the Ethiopian Telecommunications Agency (ETA) as regulator and the setting up, by the Council of Ministers, of the ETC as a government-owned telecoms operator. The ETA became operational in 1997 with the appointment of its general manager.

In the 10 years that followed its establishment, the ETC invested some US$14 billion in infrastructure development. The government is currently investing about 10 percent of GDP in the sector, an unusually high level of investment by international standards. Investments are currently directed into fixed wireless and mobile network infrastructure, including third-generation (3G) mobile technology as well as a national fiber-optic backbone.

Current Institutional Setting

The ETC is the sole provider of telecoms services in Ethiopia, providing fixed-line, mobile, Internet, and data communications services as well as related training services. As a state-owned company,[4] the ETC has management autonomy, a separate legal personality, a supervising authority, and a management board. It must maintain accounts that are audited annually by the government-owned Audit Services Corporation (ASC). The ETC's liability is limited to its assets.[5] Provision of telecoms services is to some extent regulated by the ETA. In providing such services, ETC is responsible for

- Design of the telecoms network
- Procurement of telecoms equipment
- Construction, installation, and maintenance of the equipment
- Provision of telecoms services to the public.

Although the ETC's monopoly rights are reported as having been granted under a license issued by the ETA in 2002, some uncertainty surrounds the details and current status of that license, including whether the ETC ever entered into a related agreement over mandatory performance standards. The ETC enjoys privileged access to foreign exchange but is deemed to be independent of government funding and to generate its own funding through services provision.

The ETA regulates the telecoms sector. It is responsible for ensuring that "effective, reliable and affordable telecommunications services are equitably distributed to the entire people in Ethiopia in compliance with the industry standards, and consumer protection is ensured." Its stated responsibilities include the supervision of the ETC, the regulation of tariffs, and the specification and coordination of technical standards and procedures. Under Ethiopian law, no person may operate any telecommunications service without obtaining a license from the agency. In 2002, the ETA licensed the ETC as the sole national operator of telecoms services. The provision of terminal equipment is liberalized, subject to ETA approval. About 20 entities, including Ethiopian Airlines and the World

Bank, have been granted special authorizations to operate independent communication links supplied by the ETC.

Figure 8.2 provides an overview of the institutional setting in which ETC currently operates. As indicated, major influence channels include the following:[6]

- *MTC to the ETC*. The ministry receives targets, goals, and plan objectives from the Council of Ministers and relays these to the ETC. In theory, the ETC could lose its license as an operator if it fails to meet targets set by the ministry.
- *MTC to the ETA*. The ministry controls the appointment of the ETA director and must approve the ETA's annual report. The ministry sends general policy initiative frameworks to the ETA for drafting.
- *Council of Ministers to the ETA*. The Council of Ministers controls the ETA's budget and reviews annual ETA performance.
- *The ETA to the ETC*. The ETA regulates the ETC and has the right to adjudicate in disputes between the ETC and its customers. The ETA's licensing procedures are intended to hold the ETC to international standards of efficiency and service quality.

Technical Performance of the ETC

Ethiopia has in recent years experienced strong annual subscriber growth, particularly in the mobile sector, which has experienced a compound annual growth rate of almost 90 percent since its inception in 1999 and more than 100 percent in the past six years (figure 8.3).

Despite this high and sustained recent growth, which has seen mobile penetration reach close to 4 percent in 2009, Ethiopia still performs poorly in comparison with its neighbors in terms of overall telephone penetration rate (figure 8.4). It has the second-lowest such rate in Africa and ranks at the bottom in a regional assessment (BuddeComm 2009a). This is in part a reflection of Ethiopia's low per capita GDP (the second lowest in the region) and the extremely dispersed nature of its population, of which only 16 percent live in urban areas. However, most international commentators suggest that such poor performance can be attributed, at least in part, to underlying weaknesses in the structure of Ethiopia's telecoms market.

Financial Performance of the ETC

Available data, as reported in ETC 200x, are incomplete. However, the available data suggest strong growth in income, coupled with high reported gross profits (figure 8.5).

Figure 8.2   Current Institutional Setting of the Ethiopian Telecommunications Corporation

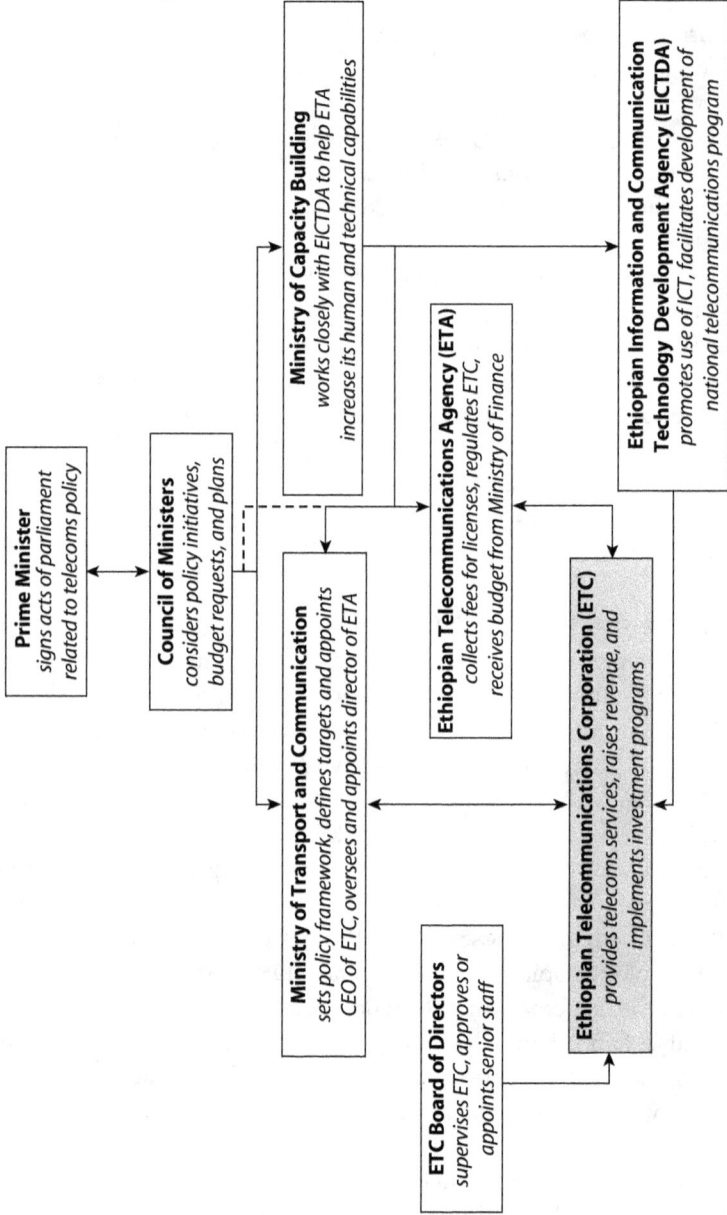

Prime Minister
signs acts of parliament related to telecoms policy

Council of Ministers
considers policy initiatives, budget requests, and plans

Ministry of Capacity Building
works closely with EICTDA to help ETA increase its human and technical capabilities

Ethiopian Information and Communication Technology Development Agency (EICTDA)
promotes use of ICT, facilitates development of national telecommunications program

Ministry of Transport and Communication
sets policy framework, defines targets and appoints CEO of ETC, oversees and appoints director of ETA

Ethiopian Telecommunications Agency (ETA)
collects fees for licenses, regulates ETC, receives budget from Ministry of Finance

Ethiopian Telecommunications Corporation (ETC)
provides telecoms services, raises revenue, and implements investment programs

ETC Board of Directors
supervises ETC, approves or appoints senior staff

Source: Adapted from Hartley and Murphree 2006.

Note: ICT = information and communication technology; CEO = chief executive officer.

336

Figure 8.3   Growth in Mobile Telephone Subscribers in Ethiopia, 1999–2008

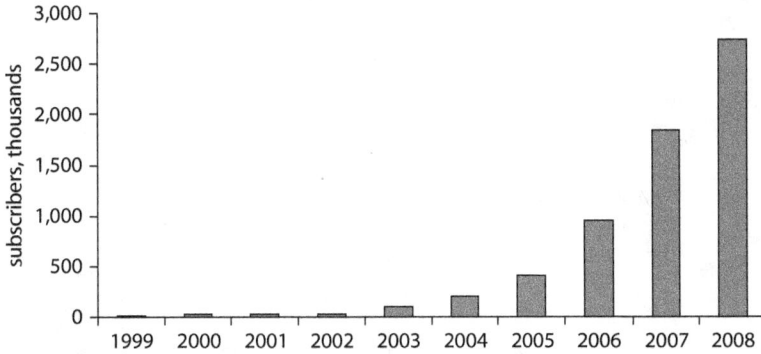

Source: BuddeComm 2009a.[7]

Figure 8.4   Regional Comparison of Telephone Penetration Rates, Ethiopia and Selected Countries, 2009

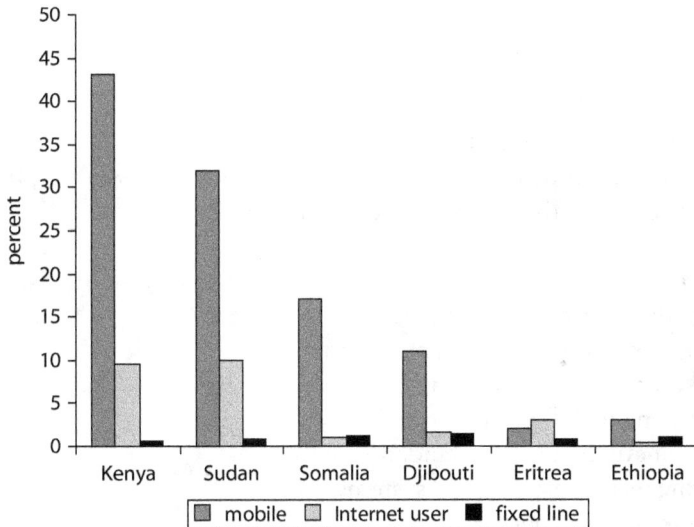

Source: BuddeComm 2009b.

The reported data do not include details of loan repayments associated with recent infrastructure investments. Such annual repayments, set to start three years after the start of the 2006 supply contract, are estimated to be of the same order as current total annual income. The ETC has historically experienced severe problems in revenue collection for its fixed-line services (BuddeComm 2009a).

Figure 8.5   Ethiopian Telecommunications Corporation Reported Income and Expenditure, 2001–08

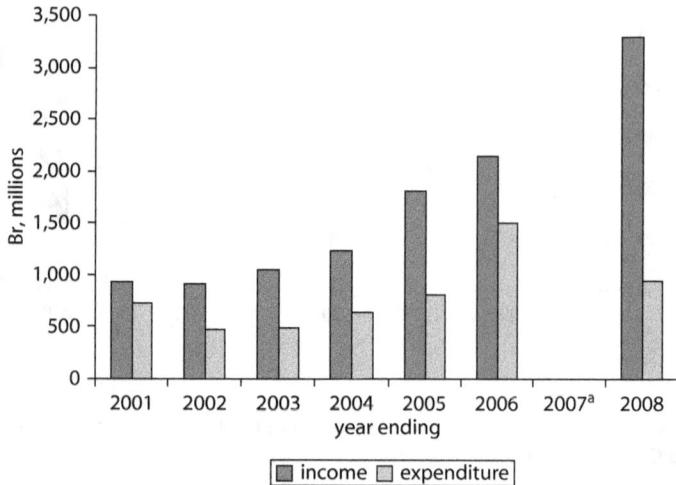

a. Data not available.

Customer Perceptions of the ETC

Despite recent improvements, from the consumer's perspective, the ETC has over the past five years earned a reputation for

- not meeting the demand for fixed-line, mobile, and Internet services;
- providing slow and unreliable Internet access;
- charging high rates as means of curtailing demand;
- seeking to curtail and control communication;
- managing its billing system poorly;
- coordinating technical standards poorly;
- having weak procurement systems; and
- hesitating over market liberalization.

Not all of these widely quoted perceptions are borne out by the evidence, particularly when account is taken of recent developments.[8] The ETC noted the following:

- *Not meeting demand.* Waiting lists for some services remain high but are falling. According to ETC data, the waiting list for fixed-line services fell from 157,000 in 2004 to 19,000 in 2008.

- *Providing slow, unreliable Internet access.* This continues to be reported as a problem.

- *Charging high rates.* Although premium communication services in Ethiopia are indeed costly, some basic domestic services are not. A 2006 comparative study of the cost of international bandwidth in Africa found that costs in Ethiopia were approximately double those in neighboring Kenya, broadly comparable to Cameroon and Malawi, and less than in Ghana (Balancing Act Africa 2006).

- *Seeking to curtail and control communication services.* Following the disputed 2005 elections, the short message service (SMS) was disabled. Internet cafés were not formally permitted until 2005, and (relatively cheap) Internet telephony is still banned. In 2006, the ETC created a new organization, the Network Operation Centre, to fight illegal Internet telephony. Although part of the underlying reason for this focus may have been to protect revenue streams, the perception articulated repeatedly was that telecoms services had been used to limit communications in the period following the election.

- *Managing the billing system poorly.* Major problems were experienced with a new billing system installed in 2004. In 2006, the system failed completely, resulting in a revenue loss of US$6.3 million. The entire customer database was lost and there was no backup, even though the equipment for such a backup had reportedly been procured (Budde-Comm 2009b).

- *Coordinating technical standards poorly.* Several cases have been reported in the media of major investments in the sector apparently being wasted as a result of incompatibilities between equipment provided by different suppliers (Balancing Act Africa 2009).

- *Having weak procurement systems.* Several cases have been reported in the media of follow-on contracts being awarded to nonperforming suppliers and of stipulated procurement procedures being manipulated, bypassed, or simply ignored. The Federal Ethics and Anti-Corruption Commission (FEACC) is currently investigating several such cases, one of which is examined in more detail in the "Procurement of Equipment Suppliers" section below. Some domestic and international observers of Ethiopia's telecoms sector have expressed concern at possible market distortions arising from Ethiopia's increasingly close political relationship with China.[9]

- *Hesitating over market liberalization.* Although the ETC has been unable to keep pace with demand, there are no firm plans to allow another operator to enter the market.

Market Liberalization

The slow rate of progress in liberalizing Ethiopia's telecoms sector remains a source of considerable contention. In recent years, the hesitation has led the World Bank to reduce its Poverty Reduction Support Credit to Ethiopia (World Bank 2008) and may constitute an obstacle to Ethiopia's entry into the World Trade Organization (WTO).

No firm schedule has yet been set for liberalization. The ETC continues to control all telecommunications services in Ethiopia except for the sale of customer premises equipment, which is still subject to ETA authorization, even for private use. No licenses have been granted to private operators to sell or resell telecoms services. The authorities tolerate Internet cafés, although Internet telephony and call-back services are illegal.

The government has, since 1996, been planning the partial privatization of the ETC as a means of bringing to bear new funding, management techniques, and skills into the sector. In 1998, the Investment Proclamation was amended, providing for the possibility of private companies, national or foreign, to invest in the telecoms sector in partnership with the government.

In 2002, the Ethiopian Privatization Agency invited international investors to acquire a 30 percent stake plus management control in the ETC. The intention was that the company would be granted exclusivity periods of between 5 and 25 years for the provision of fixed, mobile, Internet, and data services. Though several companies expressed interest in acquiring a stake, no progress was made until mid-2005, when the government announced a new plan that entailed selling 49 percent of the ETC. This plan was taken off the agenda when the chief executive officer (CEO) was replaced in 2005. Although there are reports that the privatization of the ETC will take place after the current phase of infrastructure investment results in rural areas being fully connected, the ETC notes that this is not an official position of the government of Ethiopia (ETC 2010).

Organizational Structure of the ETC

Since its creation, ETC has been restructured many times, sometimes more than once in a single year. Following the latest, most definitive, reorganization in May 2006, the ETC been structured around operations, technical services, and internal supply services (figure 8.6). In the absence of a permanent post holder, there is an acting chief of internal audit.

The Graduate School of Telecommunications and Information Technology in Ethiopia is closely associated with the ETC. It provides training, research, and education in the specialized fields of telecommunications and information technology, offering both graduate and master's in business administration programs. The possibility has been raised that the name of this key Ethiopian facility may be changed to reflect the generosity of a major Chinese supplier in providing free equipment to be used for training purposes (Belay 2008).

Policy, Regulatory, and Legal Frameworks

Policy framework. Key milestones in the evolution of Ethiopia's telecommunications policy include the 1996 separation of regulatory and operating functions and the 2003 establishment of the Ethiopian Information and Communication Technology Development Authority (EICTDA). In 2006, EICTDA developed and published an information and communication technology (ICT) policy and related 577-page ICT action plan for 2006–10.

Figure 8.6   Organizational Chart of the Ethiopian Telecommunications Corporation

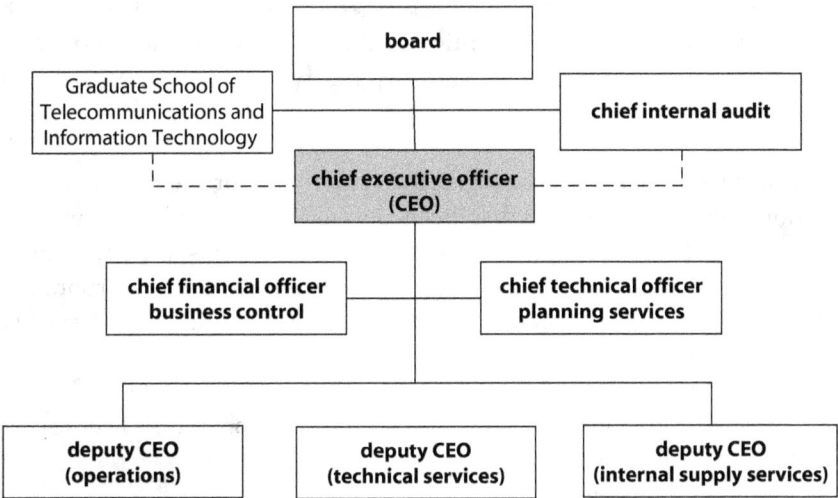

Source: The ETC's Web-based organizational chart, effective May 2006.

The underlying policy objective is to "improve the social and economic well-being of the peoples of Ethiopia through the exploitation of the opportunities created by ICT for achieving rapid and sustainable socio-economic development, and for sustaining a robust democratic system and good governance." The primary guiding principle for achieving this objective is that the government will provide strategic leadership—suggesting the maintenance, at least in the short term, of a public monopoly to deliver ICT.

Regulatory framework. Regulatory functions in the sector are the ETA's responsibility, as set out above. As yet, however, the ETA remains closely associated with the MTC and possesses neither the capacity nor the powers to enforce quality of service targets, set tariffs, or carry out other significant regulatory functions that would be expected of a strong regulator.

As part of a broader study of selected African countries, a telecommunications regulatory environment perception survey was carried out in Ethiopia in late 2006 (Adam 2007). Although the unique political and institutional context in Ethiopia posed methodological challenges for some aspects of the study, the tentative conclusion was nevertheless that Ethiopia's regulatory environment was perceived to be "highly ineffective" in promoting market entry, quality of service, and regulation of anticompetitive practices. In comparison with regulatory perception surveys—which did not simply assess the regulator but also the entire telecommunications regulatory environment, including the policy framework and regulatory effectiveness—Ethiopia fared badly, with the third-most-negative perception of the 10 countries surveyed. Only two countries, Côte d'Ivoire and Nigeria, were viewed positively in that survey.

Legislative framework. The legislative framework for the telecommunications sector in Ethiopia has been developed since 1992. Laws and regulations (such as telecommunication proclamations, a public enterprises proclamation, the Ethiopian Telecommunications Corporation establishment, and telecommunications services regulations)[10] specify the following:

- Procedures to apply for, grant, and terminate an operator's license
- Contents of the license
- Duties of the licensee
- Duration of a license
- Fees for a license

- Pricing principles for providing telecommunications services to the public
- Technical standards.

A significant implementation blockage emerges in relation to procurement. By law, public sector bodies in Ethiopia are governed by the public procurement law, which specifies how procurement should be controlled and addresses various offenses that might be committed by a person appointed or employed by a procuring entity.[11] In particular, it is an offense to participate in bribery or to breach procurement procedures (resulting, if convicted, in imprisonment for a term of not less than 10 years). In addition, any person who commits theft or intentional destruction of telecommunications networks—which threatens the national security and economy of the country—can be sentenced to between 5 and 20 years' imprisonment.[12] However, because the ETC is a public enterprise established under the Public Enterprises Proclamation, it is not subject to the public procurement law.

In 2004, ETC published its own Procurement Policy Directives and Procurement Procedure Manual governing ETC procurement, which the next section examines in more detail.

Corruption in the Ethiopian Telecoms Sector

Risk Factors Identified in Initial Document Analysis

In the light of the overview of typical corruption risks in any country's telecoms sector (as identified in the initial document analysis), some features of Ethiopia's telecoms sector give cause for concern:

- The combination of exceptionally high investment costs and poor service delivery
- The ETC's apparent lack of accountability as the sole service provider
- The study suggesting that anticompetitive practices may be occurring within the market
- Media reports suggesting serious mismanagement within the sector
- Recent and current corruption investigations being conducted by the FEACC.

None of these "red flags" necessarily means there is corruption within the sector because each may, at least in part, be the result of acknowledged past weaknesses in institutional capacity. Such a conclusion is unsatisfactory, however, both because it disregards strong anecdotal evidence of recent corruption and because it does not lead to corrective action. Neither does it allay the concerns of those affected stakeholders who remain convinced that corruption is a real issue in the sector that urgently needs to be addressed. The remainder of this chapter therefore seeks to start the process of improving understanding of these issues in an objective, structured, participatory, and constructive manner that draws on the views of all parties and leads to clear recommendations.

Approach to Remainder of Diagnostic Study

Following the initial document analysis, further information was obtained in the following ways: [13]

- *Expert interviews* with senior representatives from the relevant bodies including the Ministry of Transport and Communication, the ETC, the FEACC, and private sector telecoms companies. The public was not included in this study.
- *A multistakeholder consensus-building workshop* that included senior representatives from the MTC, the ETC, the FEACC, private sector telecoms companies, and the Oromia Ethics and Anti-Corruption Commission.

In the interviews and workshop, representatives provided their views on the occurrence of corruption in the telecoms sector in Ethiopia, the major areas of corruption risk, how the risk is being handled, and how risk prevention could be improved.

To structure the consultation and related analysis, as previously noted, key risks were considered in connection with seven defined activities within the sector: licensing, design, appointment of equipment suppliers, delivery and installation of equipment, construction of facilities, theft, and public interface of service delivery.

The Map of Corruption in Ethiopia's Telecommunications Sector

The results of the consultation are presented in the seven-part table 8.1.[14] For each of the seven risk areas, examples and a rating are provided of typical international experience of corruption, followed by a description and comparative rating of perceived risks in Ethiopia. Both the assessments and the ratings draw on the review of documentation, the expert interviews, and the stakeholder perceptions as expressed in the consensus-building workshops.

The ratings (ranging from low to very high) are assessed based on the *value* of the perceived corruption, which does not necessarily correlate with *prevalence* or *frequency*. In cases where a high incidence of low-value corruption results in a low overall risk rating, the narrative draws attention to this.

Summary of Comparative Assessment of Corruption Risks

In most developing countries, a risk analysis will show that the areas of telecommunications most prone to corruption are those where large sums of money are involved or where there is a lack of accountability. High-risk areas tend to include the issuing of network operating licenses and appointment of equipment suppliers, followed by awarding and execution of equipment supply contracts and construction of telecoms facilities and infrastructure. Corruption in the design of the telecoms network is subject to higher risk of state capture, but lesser risk in relation to other corrupt practices. Corruption in other areas, such as theft of equipment and provision of telecoms services to the public, may occur more frequently but are more likely to involve small-scale or petty corruption.

There is a considerable inherent challenge in attempting to compare telecoms sector corruption risks in Ethiopia with those in other countries. Not only is the nature of Ethiopia's government unique, but so too is the institutional nature of its telecoms sector, which is characterized by a combination of monopolistic service provision and apparently weak accountability mechanisms.

Nevertheless, some comparison is possible, albeit on a tentative basis, as figure 8.7 illustrates.

All the factors that make the international telecoms sector prone to corruption are largely present in the Ethiopian telecoms sector as well. As

Figure 8.7   Indicative Comparative Assessment of Corruption Risks in Ethiopia

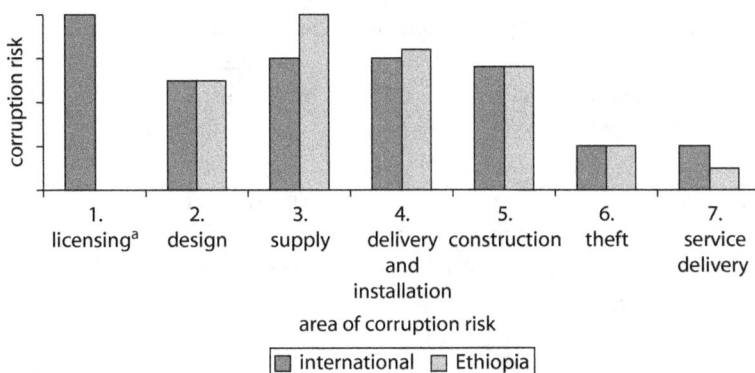

a. Risk level in Ethiopia assessed as "none."

a result, telecoms can be considered in general to be a moderately high-risk sector. However, the apparent mismatch between de jure and de facto processes and safeguards in the procurement of high-value telecoms equipment results in the supply of equipment being perceived to be the area of highest risk.

The large sums involved render the overall perceived corruption risk in Ethiopia's telecoms sector to be particularly high by international standards. By contrast, the low levels of petty corruption reported in the sector's day-to-day interaction with the public results in that area of corruption risk being relatively low.

To gain a better understanding of the nature of the major corruption risk identified, a more detailed analysis was undertaken of a particularly high-value, and controversial, contract for the supply of telecoms equipment. The next section describes this analysis.

Procurement of Equipment Suppliers: The 2006 Vendor Financing and Supply Agreement

The vendor financing contract entered into by the ETC in 2006 appears to be highly unusual. This section studies it to cast light on broader corruption risks related to the ETC's procurement of equipment suppliers. This brief study should not be seen as an investigation or interpreted as alleging in itself that corruption has necessarily occurred. However, the circumstances as perceived both by stakeholders and by independent observers do raise serious questions about the control of corruption risks in this sector.

The 2006 agreement is of high value and grants one supplier the right to supply all telecoms equipment to the ETC over a three-year period. In contrast with normal ETC practice,[15] no evidence is immediately apparent in this case that there was a commercial justification for the award of such a large contract to one supplier, that a competitive tender took place, or that there was an effective contractual mechanism for price protection and technical compliance. The following preliminary analysis seeks to understand this in more detail.

In 2006, the ETC placed a contract with an international supplier to provide financing for, supply, and install telecoms equipment up to a value of US$1.5 billion. The agreement as signed provided for a 13-year loan period, with the first three years being interest-free. The ETC agreed, for a period of three years, to place all telecoms contracts with the supplier. Specifically, the agreement required the ETC to place nine pre-specified equipment packages with the supplier.

How the Agreement Works

A framework agreement between the ETC and the supplier specified the commercial terms and conditions under which the nine contracts would be placed. The supplier committed, under this agreement, that all technology supplied would be state of the art and all its prices internationally competitive. For each of the nine equipment packages, the ETC provides technical specifications, in response to which the supplier submits a technical proposal to meet those specifications. The proposals for each package are then agreed on, and the supplier provides the ETC with its price for the supply and installation of compliant equipment. The contract for that package is then signed, incorporating the terms of the financing agreement and framework agreement. The contract grants the ETC 30 days from the date of signature to verify whether there are any "big problems with the technical proposal" and whether the supplier's prices "far exceed reasonable industry prices." If any such problems are identified, the supplier is required to adjust the technical proposal or price accordingly. During the 30-day verification period, the ETC (with the help of its consultants) assesses the supplier's prices by comparing them with market prices of comparable equipment.

When agreed-on milestones are reached during execution of the equipment package contracts, the ETC pays the supplier by issuing a promissory note that states the amount payable. The promissory note records a debt due from the ETC to the supplier. The ETC then pays the capital plus interest due on the promissory note to the supplier under the terms of the financing agreement.

Key Elements of the Contracting Process

The procurement process for the vendor finance contract was initiated by the ETC through a request to several suppliers.[16] The equipment to be supplied under the proposed financing was not specified in detail at that time, and the process was kept informal for the most part. Interviewees suggested that some losing bidders may not have been given a genuine opportunity to compete for the financing package, though this cannot be fully substantiated and is challenged by the ETC. A number of stakeholders, however, noted the following:

- The ETC's financial requirements were not provided in detail to those suppliers (other than possibly the winning supplier) that had been approached to consider providing such financing.

- There is no evidence of a formal tender procedure for the finance package. The supplier selected by the ETC to supply the finance package was the only company that offered a financing package that suited the ETC's purposes.
- As described above, the equipment supply element of the vendor financing contract was not put out to competitive tender.

This analysis does not comment on the fairness or suitability of the financing package, equipment prices, and quality because consideration of such issues is not within the scope of this study. However, several aspects of this contract point toward equipment supply as an area at particularly high risk of corruption. The current structure, policy, and regulation of the sector do not appear to be adequately guarding against that risk. The aspects of concern in this case are the following:

- *No competitive tender.* This contract was given to one supplier, apparently on a direct procurement basis, with no proper competitive tender for either the financing element or the equipment supply. International best practice would suggest that a project of this size and nature would normally involve full, competitive, separate tenders for provision of finance (for example, from banks) and for supply of equipment (from equipment suppliers) and possibly also combined competitive tenders for financing and supply of equipment from suppliers willing to provide financing as well. This absence of competitive tender means that there is a considerable risk of overpricing and unfavorable contract terms for the ETC. The competiveness, or otherwise, of the agreement could readily be determined through an independent unit cost study.

- *No competitive tenders on subcontracts.* The ETC committed to purchase all telecoms equipment over a three-year period from one supplier. Such a wide-ranging commitment without competitive tender is highly unusual. There does not appear to be any commercial necessity to place the whole US$1.5 billion contract with one supplier. The nine different equipment packages being sought (for example, mobile, customer data center, and Internet) could have been placed with different suppliers and still have resulted in a compatible and efficient network. This sole-sourcing commitment means that there is a considerable risk of overpricing and unfavorable contract terms for the ETC in relation to each supply contract.

- *Inappropriate and unclear procedures for ensuring technical quality and competitive pricing.* The technical and commercial verification processes as described above introduce significant additional risks of corruption because additional approvals are required and because of the judgment to be exercised in interpreting what constitutes a "big" technical problem and whether prices "far exceed" "reasonable industry prices." These tests are vague, not least because it is difficult to make like-for-like comparisons in the absence of detailed bids from competitors. As such, the supplier seems to have no incentive to provide a competitive price. The contract was awarded before agreement on either the specification or price—and without a sufficient contractual price protection mechanism.

- *Difficulty in measuring technical compliance.* By appointing one supplier without competitive tender, the ETC has no opportunity to assess the degree of technical compliance of the supplier's equipment. Although the supplier has agreed that all technology supplied would be state of the art, there is no clarity on how this will be assured or verified.

- *Contract not in accordance with the ETC's procurement procedure.* It appears that this contract was not awarded in accordance with the ETC's Procurement Policy Directives and Procedure Manual. The manual specifies comprehensive and detailed procurement procedures to ensure that the equipment to be provided by a supplier is in accordance with the specification and that the overall price, quality, and program offered by the supplier are evaluated as the best out of a range of competitors. There is no evidence that such an exercise was carried out in this case. It appears that there were no competitive bids for the equipment supply and the specification, price, quality, and program were only agreed upon after the contract had been placed with the supplier. This contract was therefore a "direct procurement." Though the Procurement Act does provide for direct procurement in some limited circumstance, the applicable factors were not present in this instance.

It is a matter of public record in Ethiopia that there are problems with the management of ETC equipment supply contracts. In 2008, the FEACC undertook a review of the ETC's procurement procedures and issued a report to the ETC. The report states that procurement is considered to be the highest-risk area for corruption and identifies a number of concerns, including the following:[17]

- A significant amount of equipment appears to become obsolete soon after procurement.
- In some cases, decisions appear to be made quickly on the basis that the matter is urgent. As a result, the procurement procedures are by passed—thus, for example, allowing sole-source purchasing instead of competitive tendering.
- Some contracts are placed and then terminated shortly afterward.
- In some cases, the ETC purchases new equipment when it already has the necessary equipment in the warehouse.
- The ETC's procurement procedures allow for the debarment of poorly performing suppliers, but the ETC does not appear to exercise this right.
- Some prequalifications and tenders allow too much room for subjective assessment, potentially causing some suppliers to be inappropriately eliminated from the tender list.
- There should be greater use of more objective tender criteria.
- Some suppliers offering home country visits during a tender can improperly influence tender evaluation.
- The ETC's staff lacks capacity, which increases the corruption risk.

Press reports cite three cases of alleged corruption between July 2007 and August 2008:

- In July 2007, the ETC allegedly dismissed 16 high-level employees for corruption as a result of an audit report that suggested irregularities in purchases from international suppliers. The contracts in question allegedly were worth US$54 million.
- In January 2008, the FEACC brought charges against a former ETC CEO and 26 former ETC executives for allegedly "procuring low-quality equipment from companies that were supposed to be rejected on the basis of procurement regulations." The contracts in question allegedly were worth US$154 million.
- In August 2008, the FEACC arrested a senior ETC manager after receiving an audio recording and transcript from an anonymous source in which the manager is allegedly recorded soliciting a bribe from an international supplier. The case is yet to be resolved.

Differing Stakeholder Perceptions

During the interviews and the stakeholder workshop, the views expressed tended to coalesce into three broad groups as follows:

- *Minority Group A.* This group acknowledged weaknesses within the sector but attributed those weaknesses primarily to a lack of capacity rather than corruption.
- *Minority Group B.* This group acknowledged serious breaches of procedure and other "dubious practices" but considered these mainly to be well-intentioned attempts to act in the best interests of Ethiopia's telecoms sector, even if that meant having to bypass some unduly cumbersome administrative procedures.
- *Majority Group C.* This group considered the sector to be deeply affected by corruption that goes well beyond what can reasonably be attributed to lack of capacity or genuine efforts to bypass cumbersome procedures.

Box 8.1 sets out further details of each group's perspectives.

Box 8.1

Stakeholder Perceptions of Corruption in the Ethiopian Telecoms Sector

In the course of interviews and workshops, a range of stakeholder perceptions were obtained about corruption in the telecoms sector, particularly in relation to the appointment of equipment suppliers. These views are summarized below.

Minority View A: "Low capacity but not corruption"
- Because many ETC senior managers are involved in key decisions and so many controls are in place, any corruption would need to involve too many people to be plausible.
- Some contracts are placed where all procedures had been properly followed.
- There is a capacity problem, evident both in a shortage of properly qualified ETC staff and in flaws in the ETC procedures.
- The high technology and quickly advancing nature of telecoms equipment results in poor decisions that could be mistaken for corruption.
- The high levels of changing technology create an asymmetrical relationship between ETC staff and international suppliers.

(continued next page)

Box 8.1 *(continued)*

Minority View B: "Dubious practices but not corruption"

- The ETC procurement procedures are cumbersome and not suitable for high-technology purchases, so equipment can be obsolete by the time it is received. It is therefore necessary to bypass the procurement procedures to speed up the processes.
- The ETC tender evaluation points system can allow a supplier to win a bid even if it is not technically compliant.
- There is too much bureaucracy at the ETC that is further increased by the fear of being accused of corruption. Consequently, approval for decisions is often sought from the top of the ETC or from government.
- The ETC mistakenly purchased the wrong equipment, which it then could not use.
- International suppliers use high-pressure sales techniques, which put ETC staff under pressure to award contracts.
- Western telecoms companies have in the past had a reputation for corruption, so a direct agreement with an alternative understanding and trusted supplier may have been seen as a means of reducing that risk.

Majority View C: "Very high risk of corruption in the sector"

Most of the stakeholders viewed telecoms as carrying very high corruption risks, particularly in relation to the ETC's placement of equipment supply contracts with some international suppliers. Some stakeholders (both public and private) cited the following examples that led them to suspect corruption in the sector:

- The US$1.5 billion vendor finance contract was apparently placed in breach of the ETC's procurement procedures.
- Contracts for the civil works for the new mobile phone masts were apparently placed in breach of the ETC's procurement procedures.
- Current or previous ETC employees are believed to have an interest in some of the companies building the mast foundations.
- There was a suspected breach of procurement procedures in an open tender where it is believed one of the tenderers should have been eliminated after assessment of its technical bid. Instead, its technical bid was approved, and other, better-qualified bidders were eliminated. The unqualified bidder went on to win the award.

(continued next page)

Box 8.1 *(continued)*

- Surplus or unnecessary materials and equipment were bought from suppliers. In one reported case, materials were purchased in excess of the ETC's requirements, and in another case, it was reported that equipment was ordered when suitable equipment was already contained in the ETC's warehouse.
- Some international suppliers have offered unsuitable or overpriced products to the ETC, taking advantage of unskilled ETC staff.
- Some international suppliers fraudulently and grossly overcharge in the case of negotiations for a direct supply.
- In one case, it was claimed that a supplier requested US$12 million but then reduced the price to US$9 million as a final price. The ETC did not purchase from the supplier and instead put the contract out to tender. In that tender, the same supplier allegedly offered the same scope for just US$2 million.
- Allegedly, functioning equipment is being disconnected and being replaced by new equipment unnecessarily.
- Some suppliers have apparently invited ETC managers on overseas tours with excessive per diems and hospitality.
- A recorded conversation, allegedly between a contractor and a public official in which corrupt arrangements are discussed, has been reported in the press and is currently being investigated by the authorities.
- The FEACC Annual Report of 2008 reports details of "another big corruption case at ETC." The details of this case are not yet public knowledge (FEACC 2008).

Current Anticorruption Mechanisms for Ethiopia's Telecoms Sector

Overview of Anticorruption Mechanisms

In most countries, corruption risks within the telecoms sector are, with varying degrees of effectiveness, addressed through a range of mechanisms, as listed below with the relevant Ethiopian application then shown in parentheses:

- Adherence to defined internal processes and procedures of the procuring entity (the ETC)
- Oversight by the regulating agency responsible for ensuring cost-effective service delivery (the ETA)
- Compliance with the national regulatory environment, typically a Public Procurement Act as overseen by the relevant national body

(Public Procurement Proclamation overseen by the Public Procurement Agency)

- Scrutiny from the national auditor (Office of the Federal Auditor General and the ASC)
- Compliance with anticorruption programs of companies working in the sector (private companies from Europe and the United States and publicly owned corporations from China)
- Scrutiny by national civil society organizations (Transparency Ethiopia)
- Investigation by national authorities (the FEACC and the police).

Necessary as they are, laws and regulations are not in themselves sufficient to neutralize the risk of corruption. Indeed, they can even in some circumstances generate additional incentives either to bypass procedures seen to be unduly cumbersome or for corrupt public officials to engage in rent-seeking activities. As has been observed down the ages, "A corrupt society has many laws."[18]

Ethiopia is unique in Africa in terms of its political history, its highly centralized political power, the weak voice of its civil society, and the monopolistic arrangements in its telecoms sector. These factors can have the effect of undermining most of the above mechanisms, specifically the following:

- *Oversight by the ETA.* In view of the monopoly status currently accorded to the ETC, the low capacity of the ETA, and its lack of independence from government in the form of the MTC and the Ministry of Capacity Building, the ETA does not have a truly independent role in identifying or addressing corruption risks in the sector. In practice, its only function in this regard appears to be in helping to combat the risk of illegal Internet telephony.

- *Compliance with the Public Procurement Act.* As a public enterprise, the ETC is not bound by the Public Procurement Proclamation regulating other government agencies. Even if it were, the Public Procurement Agency is understaffed and suffers from capacity constraints.

- *Scrutiny from the Office of the Federal Auditor General and the ASC.* The role of the Auditor General is to report on federal government receipts and expenditures, assets and liabilities, financial statistical data, and the performance of the offices and organizations of the federal government. Though some aspects of the ETC's finances (including the US$1.5 billion financing agreement) appear to extend beyond the bounds of its financial autonomy, it does not appear that the Auditor General would have the mandate to conduct a financial audit of the ETC or the capacity to conduct a performance audit, should that be required. The entity responsible for auditing state-owned enterprises in Ethiopia is the ASC, itself a government-owned corporation. No attempt was made in this study to obtain access to those audits.

- *Compliance with corporate anticorruption compliance programs.* Over the past decade in general, and since 2005 in particular, major international corporations have significantly changed their commercial behavior. Whereas in the past companies from many Organisation for Economic Co-operation and Development (OECD) countries could expect tax incentives from their governments to win lucrative international contracts, such practices are now illegal and subject to punitive fines, potential debarment, and possible imprisonment of senior managers. As a result, most responsible companies working from OECD countries have now established, or are establishing, internal safeguards and procedures to guard against, in particular, the risk of bribes being paid to foreign public officials. This enhanced level of awareness of the need to avoid both the real and the perceived risk of corruption does not yet extend to some companies from non-OECD countries, particularly those countries that have only recently acceded to the WTO.

- *Scrutiny by civil society organizations (CSOs).* Civil society in Ethiopia is relatively weak compared with other countries in Africa. Where CSOs do exist, they are more subject to government influence.

- *Investigation by the FEACC.* The FEACC has undoubtedly achieved a great deal, both by raising awareness of corruption risks and by undertaking specific investigations related to the ETC. There is, however, a sense of mismatch between the underlying substance of the investigations and the eventual action being taken against key responsible officials. This has led some observers, albeit those with underlying political agendas of their own, to question the degree to which the FEACC is indeed independent of the government. The FEACC has a full-time ethics officer within the ETC, primarily as part of its awareness-raising and training function but also having some whistle-blowing and investigative powers.

Therefore, the primary line of defense against corruption risks in Ethiopia's telecoms sector lies in the ETC's internal processes and procedures.

The ETC's Internal Safeguards against Corruption

There are two aspects to the ETC's control of corruption in Ethiopia's telecoms sector: (a) its de jure controls, which describe the theoretical procedures and regulations, and (b) the de facto implementation of those controls. These are examined in turn below, broken down into the seven areas of risk previously identified in table 8.1. Some project management provisions cut across more than one of these risk areas. These are described in box 8.2.

Table 8.1   Corruption Risks in Ethiopia's Telecommunications Sector

Risk Area 1: Issuance of Operating Licenses	
International experience	*Typical international risk: Very high*

Internationally, this is one of the areas where the risk of corruption is greatest because the receipt of such licenses can lead to lucrative long-term revenues for network operators. Typical areas of such risk include the following:

1a. Misappropriation of license fee by senior government officers or license-issuing officials
The fee paid by the network operator may not be properly accounted for by the recipient body. Instead, it may be diverted into personal or party accounts, with or without the knowledge of the operator.

1b. Bribery of senior government officers or officials to issue license
A network operator may agree to give a government official's relative a free share in the telecoms project if it is granted a license on beneficial terms to the network operator; an official may refuse to grant a license, or may delay the granting of a license, unless the network operator pays him a bribe or facilitation payment.[19]

1c. Senior government officers or officials issuing licenses to companies or joint ventures in which they or their family have a commercial interest
A government official may require the network operator to make a large donation to a charity. Although the charity may appear to be genuine, it may in fact be a front for a political party or for the official's personal or family gain.

When large sums are involved in such corruption, it generally entails a conspiracy orchestrated by senior government or party officials rather than by junior public officials seeking personal advantage.

In Ethiopia	*Current risk in Ethiopia: None*

The ETC, as a state-owned enterprise, has been awarded the exclusive license by the government to be the network operator in Ethiopia. There is, therefore, currently no conventional corruption risk specific to the actual license award process, though a lack of transparency is noted over the accountability mechanisms, if any, associated with that license.
1a, 1b, 1c. The government has, over the years, prepared for the possible eventual partial privatization of the ETC. If and when this occurs, and licenses are issued to private sector operators, this is likely to become a very high risk area, in each of the three typical risk areas identified above.

(continued next page)

Table 8.1 *(continued)*

Risk Area 2: Design of the Telecoms Network

International experience	*Typical international risk: High*

Internationally, this is an area of high risk. Bribery can occur in the appointment of the designer, but this normally involves significantly lower-value contracts. Alternatively, the specification may be written to give preference to a particular, preferred supplier from whom the official preparing or approving the specification receives a kickback. Typical areas of such risk include the following:

2a. Bribery of network operator's employees by consultants tendering for design contracts

2b. Award of design contracts to consultants in whom network operator's employees or senior government officers have an interest
Corruption could take place in relation to the appointment of the designer in the same way that it could take place in the appointment of a supplier (see below).

2c. Elimination of competition through design specifications with associated bribery by potential supplier of person writing a specification or of senior government officials approving it
An official responsible for a specification may propose that certain equipment be supplied only by a named supplier, thus creating a monopoly position for that supplier. Bribes may be paid to the manager of the network operator, or to an independent consulting firm appointed by the network operator, so that only the supplier paying the bribe could win the tender because only that supplier will be technically compliant.

In Ethiopia	*Current risk in Ethiopia: Medium*

In the Ethiopian telecommunications sector, corruption in this area was not perceived to be widespread. The risk in relation to network design was assessed as medium, although the following examples were given of such corruption having taken place:[20]

2c. Elimination of competition through design specifications
A recent ETC specification listed an item to be procured by competitive tender. The item was listed with the supplier's name and a photograph of the item. Competitive tendering for this item was therefore impossible. There was also a perception that problems in design occurred partly because the ETC was short of staff with the suitable technical skills to write the necessary technical specifications.

In the Ethiopian context, a significant risk in relation to network design is considered by some stakeholders to be state capture, in terms of the following:

- Restrictions placed on the design as a means of providing preferential opportunities to companies more likely to be sympathetic to government or party interests
- Policy capture that may be well intentioned but that can nevertheless result in similar opportunities for corruption.

Risk Area 3: Appointment of Equipment Suppliers

International experience	*Typical international risk: High*

Internationally, this is an area of high risk. Typical areas of such risk include the following:

3a. Procurement procedures bypassed by network operator's employees
This is typically on the pretext of urgency, allowing sole-source purchasing instead of competitive tendering.

(continued next page)

Table 8.1   *(continued)*

Risk Area 3: Appointment of Equipment Suppliers

| **International experience** | *Typical international risk: High* |

3b. Bribery by the supplier of the network operator's employees or of senior government officials
(i) to award the contract to the supplier;

An international supplier appoints a local agent who is paid a percentage of the sale price if the contract is won. The agent then approaches a senior official of the network operator, or a government minister, and offers a share of the commission if the supplier is awarded the contract. The tender procedures or result is manipulated accordingly.

(ii) to agree on an inflated price;

The international supplier enters into a subcontract with a local contractor. The subcontract price is significantly higher than the value of the work involved. The local contractor offers a bribe to an official or minister on the basis that, if the international supplier wins the order, the local contractor will receive a subcontract and pay the bribe out of the surplus in its subcontract price.

(iii) to agree on supply of excess, unnecessary, unsuitable, or defective equipment;

(iv) to replace working equipment with new equipment;

(v)   to award contracts without proper equipment specification and pricing;

(vi) to award numerous contracts to one supplier with no commercial justification; and

(vii) to bypass requirements of tender.

3c. Wrongful elimination of tenderers by network operator's employees to fix the contract award

3d. Failure by network operator to debar poorly performing suppliers

3e. Appointment by network operator's employees of suppliers in whom they or senior government or party officials or financial supporters have a commercial interest.

| **In Ethiopia** | *Current risk in Ethiopia: Very high* |

3a, 3b, 3c, 3d, 3e. This is the highest area of perceived risk in Ethiopia, with reports of all five of the typical risks listed above. In particular, procurement procedures are understood at times to be manipulated or bypassed along the lines currently being investigated by the FEACC. Many former ETC officials are currently facing corruption charges.

The risk is especially high in Ethiopia because of the extraordinarily high costs of supplies involved, which means that significant corrupt gains can potentially be made on the basis of relatively few transactions. In addition, the bulk of telecoms equipment is supplied by major international companies that have the financial capability to offer large bribes and to pay these bribes outside the country, thereby making illicit payments difficult to trace. This potential for major incentives increases the possibility of intervention by senior government officials who may request that procurement procedures and anticorruption safeguards be bypassed.

Particular concerns are expressed in media reports, expert interviews, and in study workshops about a US$1.5 billion vendor financing contract that appears to have been placed without competitive tender and in breach of the ETC's own procurement procedures. By comparison with

(continued next page)

Table 8.1   *(continued)*

Risk Area 3: Appointment of Equipment Suppliers	
International experience	*Typical international risk: High*

experience elsewhere, this 2006 vendor financing contract appears to be highly unusual and of extremely high value, granting one supplier the right to supply all telecoms equipment to the ETC over a three-year period. Although the ETC claims it invited eight vendors on equal footing, this is disputed. There appears to be no clear commercial justification for the award, no proper competitive tender, and no effective contractual mechanism for price protection or technical compliance. This preliminary analysis does not itself constitute an allegation that corruption has taken place but does raise serious concerns that are expressed and addressed in more detail in the "Procurement of Equipment Suppliers" section in this chapter.

Risk Area 4: Delivery and Installation of Equipment	
International experience	*Typical international risk: High*

Internationally, this is an area of high risk. Fulfillment of the original contract, subsequent contract variations requiring additional equipment, undisclosed arrangements, and inadequate monitoring each may provide the context for price manipulation, fraud, and bribery. Certifying officers may be bribed so that they order or approve these fraudulent variations.

Corruption risks in this area increase significantly when the original contract itself was a product of corruption. Government officials and contractors who collude to award a contract unfairly are likely to continue with corrupt activity during the execution of the contract, particularly where there is little prospect that this activity will be detected, reported, or prosecuted. Typical areas of such risk include the following:

4a. Delivery by supplier of less equipment than required under contract
The supplier should supply 200 kilometers (km) of cable but supplies only 180km. It bribes an employee of the network operator to overlook the short delivery or relies on the shortfall going unnoticed as a result of inefficiencies in the network operator's organization.

4b. Delivery by supplier of equipment that is defective or not in accordance with the specification
The network operator corruptly refuses to pay the supplier for all or part of the equipment, claiming either that the equipment was not delivered or that it was defective. This claim could either be because the network operator wants to negotiate an additional price reduction from the supplier or because an official of the network operator wishes to receive a bribe from the supplier to withdraw the claim.

4c. Bribery (by supplier) of network operator employee to approve delivery of defective or inferior equipment or equipment that is less than required under the contract

4d. Bribery (by supplier) of network operator employee or of senior government officer to order further unnecessary equipment at inflated prices as a variation to the contract

4e. Extortion by network operator employee or government officials against suppliers seeking payments due

4f. Illegal sale by supplier of equipment imported free of customs and import duties.

(continued next page)

Table 8.1   *(continued)*

Risk Area 4: Delivery and Installation of Equipment

In Ethiopia	*Current risk in Ethiopia: High*

This is a high area of perceived risk in Ethiopia. Examples were identified of the following:

4a. Short delivery of equipment

4b. Delivery of inferior or defective equipment
A supplier supplied defective cable, and some ETC managers allegedly ordered it to be quickly installed even though defective, apparently to cover up its defective nature. Another case, widely reported in the media, involved the installation in 2006 of a major new billing system that failed to work properly and eventually had to be replaced (BuddeComm 2009a).

Each of these examples carries associated risks of **4c, 4d, 4e,** and **4f**.

In addition, examples were identified of the following: *working equipment being replaced by new equipment and new equipment being delivered but not installed.* Stakeholders perceived some of these difficulties to have potentially been caused by factors other than corruption. These factors could include poor coordination at project handover from the ETC's procurement to project management functions; lack of capacity in some ETC staff; frequent changes of project manager; and failure to properly order and document contract variations. It was, however, agreed that these difficulties could equally have been caused by corruption.

In the course of the study, contract documents for a major contract were briefly examined. This was a contract with a major international supplier, placed in 2004 but not yet finalized. From the contract documents reviewed, it appeared that appropriate management procedures were in place. There were progress reports, invoices, packing lists, takeover certificates, and correspondence between the ETC and the supplier disputing certain items. The records were logically filed. However, a detailed assessment was not undertaken as to whether the contract was effectively managed or implemented from the perspective of either the ETC or the supplier.

Risk Area 5: Construction of Telecoms Facilities

International experience	*Typical international risk: High*

Internationally, this is an area of high risk. Typical areas of such risk include the following:

5a. Bypassing of procurement procedures
Often on the pretext of urgency, sole-source purchasing is used instead of competitive tendering.

5b. Bribery of network operator employees or senior government officers
Contractors pay bribes as an inducement to award the contract improperly, to agree to an inflated price, to agree on construction of excess or unsuitable facilities, or to award numerous contracts to one contractor with no commercial justification.

5c. Wrongful elimination (by network operator employees) of tenderers from tender list

5d. Failure by network operator to debar poorly performing contractors

(continued next page)

Table 8.1   *(continued)*

Risk Area 5: Construction of Telecoms Facilities	
International experience	*Typical international risk: High*

5e. Appointment of contractors in which senior government or party officials have an interest

5f. Network operator withholding sums due to contractors to extort bribes
A network operator corruptly refuses to pay the contractor for the work undertaken by the contractor and raises a false counterclaim against the contractor alleging defects in its work as justification for nonpayment.

5g. Contractors not carrying out works to specification, making inflated claims, or carrying out defective works

5h. Bribery of network operator employees by contractors to have fraudulent claims approved.

In Ethiopia	*Current risk in Ethiopia: High*

This is an area of perceived high risk in Ethiopia. Examples were identified of the following:
5a. ETC procurement procedures being deliberately bypassed
The justification is based on urgency or because of previous good performance of specific contractors.

5d. Failure to debar poorly performing contractors
Media reports refer to several cases of poor performance followed by further contracts.

5e. Appointment of contractors in which key decision makers have a commercial interest
Some interviewees reported that ETC staff have a commercial interest in some contractors.

5g. Contractors not carrying out works to specification
Some interviewees report that some regional ETC buildings have not been constructed to specification.

The examples cited carry associated risks of **5b, 5c, 5f,** and **5h**. Stakeholders expressed particular concern about the apparently favorable treatment accorded to some, apparently well-connected, contractors.

Additional information on construction sector risks is provided and analyzed in chapter 6 of this volume, titled "Construction Sector Corruption in Ethiopia."

Risk Area 6: Theft of Equipment	
International experience	*Typical international risk: High*

Internationally, this is an area of low risk in terms of the total value of stolen equipment. Typical areas of such risk include the following:

6a. Theft of equipment from warehouse or other facility
A small, high-value product is hidden on the person of an employee who has access to the warehouse; or equipment is stolen at night by truck, with the thieves bribing the security guards not to stop them.

(continued next page)

Table 8.1   *(continued)*

Risk Area 6: Theft of Equipment

International experience	*Typical international risk: High*

6b. False entries in accounts to conceal theft by public officials

An employee responsible for warehouse records falsifies store records to conceal theft by the employee, the employee's accomplices, or influential officials.

In Ethiopia	*Current risk in Ethiopia: Low*

This is a low area of perceived risk in Ethiopia in terms of the total value of stolen equipment, although it is a high-risk area in terms of the number of individual incidents.

6a. Theft of equipment from warehouse or other facility

An FEACC report states that theft of equipment is a high risk, particularly from the ETC's warehouse. The report recommends that improvements be made to the stock control system to ensure that the correct equipment is delivered and that equipment does not go missing.

6b. False entries in accounts to conceal theft

The same FEACC report comments that there is a high figure in the ETC's accounts for "goods in transit" and considers that, in reality, some of these goods may have gone missing. It also comments that there was previously a problem with theft of subscriber identity module (SIM) cards but that this has now been solved by activating the cards only once they are legally purchased.

Interviewees noted the following:

- The risk of theft depended on the commodity. Much of the high-value equipment purchased by the ETC is specialist equipment that could be used only in establishing a network. This is not considered to be at high risk. The risk of theft rises according to how easily resellable the items are. For example, a theft of 15 computers from the ETC's warehouse was reported.
- Apparent theft may, in some cases, be the result of inadequate control and documentation rather than corruption involving public officials.

Risk Area 7: Providing Telecoms Services to the Public

International experience	*Typical international risk: Low*

Internationally, this is an area of low risk in terms of total value. Typical areas of such risk include the following:

7a. Extortion against members of the public by network operator's employees to supply telecoms services such as Internet broadband lines or SIM cards

A technician working for the network operator may refuse to provide the physical connection to a fixed line in the house of a member of the public, or may refuse to repair a defective connection, unless he or she receives a bribe or a facilitation payment.

7b. Bribery by members of the public of network operator's employees to use the network operator's internal test password to make free calls

7c. Bribery by members of the public of network operator's employees to give other illegal or preferential access to telecoms services

(continued next page)

Table 8.1   *(continued)*

Risk Area 7: Providing Telecoms Services to the Public	
In Ethiopia	*Current risk in Ethiopia: Low*

This is an area of low perceived risk in Ethiopia, not only in terms of total value but also in terms of incidence. Though there is a general perception that some such corruption is likely to be occurring, driven in part by low salaries, none of the interviewees was aware of any specific recent example of a bribe being paid to grant any member of the public access to telecoms services.

This finding suggests that the incidence of such minor corruption is less prevalent in Ethiopia than in many other countries. It is all the more remarkable in view of the fact that the ETC is a monopoly and that demand for telecoms services in Ethiopia has for a prolonged period greatly exceeded supply.

There were, however, examples of corruption in this area in the recent past:

7c. Bribery by members of the public to obtain preferential access to telecoms services
At a time when there was a shortage of SIM cards, it was reported that some ETC managers had made SIM cards available to preferred customers in return for a bribe.

In addition, there have been several cases of illegal provision of telecommunications services in Ethiopia, considered to be corruption in view of potential lost revenue to the ETC. *In November 2008, the FEACC arrested eight individuals, including a foreigner, for allegedly providing international telecoms services using banned devices. Press reports indicated that some of those arrested were ETC officials and that the sums allegedly involved were high, totaling some US$450,000.*

Box 8.2

General ETC Safeguards Applicable to All Projects

In relation to all ETC projects, the general measures described below apply.

Overall management of the project is undertaken by the ETC's project department. It is overseen by ETC's project steering committee, made up of approximately seven members who meet weekly. Major decisions in relation to a project are taken by the ETC's management committee. The ETC's board receives a monthly report on each project.

To guard against fraudulent issue and pricing of variations, the ETC manages changes to the scope of work during contract execution (variations) by the following method:

- A committee is established comprising at least one representative from the project department, one from operations, and one from planning. The committee

(continued next page)

Box 8.2 *(continued)*

will assess and agree on the technical necessity for the variation as well as the resulting price and program changes.

- Where changes are to quantities and the contract has a specified schedule of rates, modest changes can be calculated by measuring the new quantities, comparing them against contract quantities, and amending the price accordingly.
- Major decisions in relation to a variation are made by the ETC's management committee, which includes among its members the ETC's CEO, chief technical officer, and relevant project manager.

Further general provisions applicable to all ETC projects include the following:

- The payment terms depend on the contract but would normally be based on stage payments at key milestones, the final payment being upon expiry of warranty period.
- The ETC's internal audit department undertakes random audits on the project execution process.
- Upon conclusion of every contract, the ETC undertakes a review of the performance of suppliers, consultants, and contractors to identify poor performers and, if necessary, debar them from future contracts until appropriate corrective action has been taken.

1. ETC Safeguards in Relation to Licensing

As a state-owned enterprise, the ETC has been awarded the exclusive license by the government to be the network operator in Ethiopia. There is, therefore, currently no conventional corruption risk specific to the actual license award process. There is, however, a clear risk associated with the apparent lack of transparency over applicable accountability mechanisms, if any, associated with that license.

2. ETC Safeguards in Relation to Design

Corruption in relation to slanting a design to favor a particular supplier is addressed in considerable detail by the ETC's Procurement Policy Directives and Procurement Procedure Manual. This provides that technical specifications should be defined in a manner that results in fair and open competition.

3. ETC Safeguards in Relation to Suppliers

ETC procedures include comprehensive safeguards in connection with supply contracts. These include a general presumption in favor of competitive bidding; decision making by committees rather than by individuals; a division of responsibilities between those committees; and provision for regular internal audits to safeguard against any breach of procedures, failure to ensure value for money, or perceived conflicts of interest. Provision is also made for external audits where these are deemed necessary.

4. ETC Safeguards in Relation to Delivery and Installation

The ETC has a range of controls in place to prevent or detect corruption in relation to delivery and installation. These include detailed checks on quality and compliance to be carried out by the ETC's project, operations, and internal audit departments.

5. ETC Safeguards in Relation to Construction

In relation to the construction of telecoms facilities, the ETC is required to comply with established best practice in terms of the use of qualified contractors, inspection of the works, testing of materials, and sanctioning of poorly performing contractors.

6. ETC Safeguards in Relation to Theft

In relation to theft of equipment, ETC procedures reduce the risk by strict signing in and out of all items, the employment of guards at storage facilities, and internal audits. Any discrepancies should be reported to the board of the ETC and suspicions of theft should be reported to the police.

7. ETC Safeguards in Relation to Public Interface of Service Delivery

The ETC's website specifies the documentation that members of the public need to submit to the ETC to apply for telecommunications services. The procedures appear to be reasonably simple and quick. A telephone SIM card, for example, could be purchased in a few minutes upon payment of a fixed fee and production of an identity document.

Departmental Responsibilities

In addition to the above procedural safeguards, the ETC has the following departments, which, if operating properly and effectively, should act as a check that the safeguards are being followed:

- *A procurement department*, which manages the procurement phase
- *A project department*, which takes over responsibility on award of contract
- *A finance department*, which is responsible for financial management and control
- *An internal audit department*, which undertakes random financial and performance audits
- *A legal department*, which handles legal negotiations and documentation
- *An ethics department*, which provides ethical training and guidance to staff, operates the internal ethics reporting line, investigates potential corruption, and reports any suspected cases to the FEACC.

An audit of these functions falls beyond the scope of this study. However, it does appear that in most cases the theoretical controls are generally reasonably well written and comprehensive. Where scope exists for some areas to be enhanced, appropriate recommendations are made in the next section. Even as they stand, however, these procedures would, if followed, greatly reduce the risk of corruption.

Practical Implementation of the ETC's Safeguards against Corruption

Even if procedures are comprehensive, they can be bypassed, which can result from an official mandate from an influential person to ignore the procedures, collusion between senior officials responsible for implementing the procedures, or negligence or inefficiency. As described above, strong indications arose from interviews and document analysis that the ETC has, in some cases, not followed its own procedures. The fundamental problem appears to lie not in the lack of adequate procedures but in a failure to effectively follow these procedures.

Two other factors affecting anticorruption controls have been highlighted by this chapter:

- First, to be effective, anticorruption endeavors require oversight that enjoys a widespread degree of trust and confidence. Few stakeholders in Ethiopia considered such trust and confidence to be present. Despite significant improvement in its record, even the FEACC is still considered by many telecommunications stakeholders to be unduly influenced by the government, limiting its investigations to certain areas that do not unduly embarrass the political executive.

- Second, and most disturbing, the study identified among respondents a marked sense of fear that is not observed in other countries. Such a fear promotes a lack of openness and reporting. Many interviewees suggested that if a person were to report actual or potential corrupt practices, there was a perceived danger that he or she would be victimized through dismissal or a lack of promotion. In some cases, a whistleblower could, it was believed, be in physical danger. Whether or not there is a basis in fact for such fears, the fact that they exist at all highlights the urgent need for confidence-building measures among stakeholders in the sector.

Recommendations

The findings of this diagnostic study highlight specific areas of concern in Ethiopia's telecommunications sector, centered on the appointment of equipment suppliers, delivery and installation of equipment, and related construction of facilities. The recommendations that arise fall into two categories:

- Additional study in demonstrated areas of highest risk
- Corrective actions that can be taken immediately and have proven effect in reducing the risks—whether perceived or real—of corruption.

The key to rebuilding sector confidence will be to target known areas of high perceived risk through the introduction of improved transparency and accountability. Over time this will serve to both facilitate and underpin the reforms needed to reduce corruption risks and increase stakeholder confidence in the sector.

Recommendation 1: *Launch an independent audit and public inquiry into the 2006 vendor financing and equipment supply contract and related equipment supply processes.*

A full independent audit and public inquiry, conducted in accordance with international best practice, should examine the ETC's equipment supply processes, including in particular the award and execution of the 2006 vendor financing and equipment supply contract. The scope of the audit and inquiry should include an examination of the following issues:

- Whether and, if so, why the 2006 financing and equipment supply contract was placed
  o without an effective competitive tender for the financing component;
  o without a competitive tender for the equipment supply; and
  o as a single large contract.

- Whether the current equipment supplier has supplied or is supplying the equipment to the ETC at genuinely competitive prices. In this regard, comparable prices of other suppliers should be examined as well as the actual prices at which the supplier is supplying the same equipment to other customers.
- Whether the supplier has supplied or is supplying equipment of suitable quality to the ETC. In this regard, comparable quality of other suppliers should be examined as well as the actual quality that the supplier is supplying to other customers.
- Whether there is any evidence of irregularities in the procurement, terms, or execution of the contract. Any possible suspicions should be referred to the FEACC and to the anticorruption authorities in the supplier's home country. In particular, the reported audio recording that allegedly relates to a corrupt act should be investigated by the FEACC and by the anticorruption authorities in the supplier's home country.

The method and results of the audit and inquiry should be made fully available to the public. If any wrongdoing is established, it can be appropriately dealt with. If no wrongdoing is established, and if the audit and inquiry are genuinely independent and public, the perceptions of corruption and wrongdoing that surround this contract will be removed and a significant contribution made toward restoring public and stakeholder confidence.

Recommendation 2: *Apply, develop, and build confidence in ETC procurement processes.*

- *Enforce minimum standards of procurement, consistent with the Public Procurement Proclamation.* The ETC is reportedly not subject to the Public Procurement Proclamation, under which it is a criminal offense not to follow the procurement procedures contained in the proclamation.

However, because the ETC is a publicly owned enterprise and is acting in a monopoly position, it should be subject to similar levels of accountability. If it is permitted to continue to define its own procedures, they should be consistent with the minimum standards laid down in the proclamation, and any failure to follow the procurement procedures should be construed as being as serious as a breach of the proclamation.

- *Establish a working group to validate the appropriateness of procurement procedures.* Some ETC managers interviewed expressed the view that the procurement procedures are too cumbersome for a high-technology industry requiring quick methods of procurement. It is important to understand this position and either address the problem or remove it as a possible reason for bypassing procedures. A working group should consider:
  - whether the procedures, as written, are fit for purpose;
  - if not, how the procedures can be genuinely improved in accordance with best practice; and
  - whether the procedures are being implemented in an unduly slow and bureaucratic way, and, if so, what aspects could be addressed through management.

- *Appoint an independent assessor to monitor procurement.* For all contracts over a specified minimum value (for example, US$250,000), the ETC should appoint an independent assessor to monitor the procurement and execution of the contract for any signs of corruption, either by the government; by the ETC; or by the designer, supplier, or contractor.[21] The assessor should be engaged on an intermittent part-time basis in relation to lower-value contracts and on a full-time basis for higher-value contracts, ensuring, so far as possible, that
  - stipulated designs and specifications are fair, objective, and reasonable and do not give an unfair advantage to any one bidder;
  - the prequalification (if any) and tender processes are handled in accordance with the ETC's procedures and do not give an unfair advantage to any one bidder;
  - the selected designer, supplier, or contractor is properly chosen after a fair, objective, and reasonable evaluation process;
  - the execution of the contract is carried out in accordance with the ETC's procedures and the contract; and
  - specific suspicions or allegations of corruption, including reports received through a whistle-blower reporting mechanism, are investigated in an appropriate manner.

In keeping with the disclosure recommendation above, reports of the independent assessor should be published on the ETC's website. The process of selecting, appointing, and remunerating the independent assessor will require particular care to ensure that he or she is suitably experienced and independent and enjoys the full respect of all stakeholder groups.

Recommendation 3: *Ensure greater transparency through disclosure agreements.*

The ETC's Procurement Policy Directives and Procedure Manual requires that the ETC maintain procurement records and documents for 10 years. However, there are only limited rights for anyone to view this information. At present, competitors in the bidding process can view only some of the records and documents relating to their bids within one month after contract award. The public is not entitled to view these records and documents. As an anticorruption measure, the problems associated with the very limited disclosure of information in the sector should be addressed by an effort aimed at improving transparency and access to information. It is recommended that disclosure should be materially increased, as follows:

- *Establish the scope and nature of documentation for disclosure.* There should be full public disclosure on the ETC website of all relevant documents associated with telecommunications services. This disclosure should include the following information, presented in a clear and consistent manner:
  - consultants' advice regarding the type of network and equipment that should be introduced;
  - outline designs of the network and equipment;
  - prequalification and tender documents relating to the design, supply, construction, and installation of telecommunications equipment and services;
  - prequalifications and tenders submitted by designers, suppliers, and contractors in relation to the telecommunications network;
  - reports evaluating which designer, supplier, or contractor should be selected;
  - full details of the price, program, specification, contract conditions, and payments in relation to contracts awarded to designers, suppliers, and contractors and of any variations to these contracts—with details of price covering both the initial contract price and the final actual cost of the contract, together with the price of major variations;

o any enforcement action taken by the ETC against any designers, suppliers, and contractors;

o any enforcement action taken by the authorities for corruption against any designers, suppliers, and contractors;

o the outcome of such enforcement action;

o compensation paid to land occupiers in relation to the construction or erection of telecommunications facilities;

o details of conflicts of interests declared; and

o relevant asset declarations.

There should be very limited exceptions to full disclosure in relation to technical data that are genuinely confidential to the designer, supplier, and contractor. Disclosure of tenders should not be made until the contract in relation to those tenders has been awarded.

- *Establish a range of cost-efficient, easily accessible methods of disclosure.* Disclosure should be made as soon as possible (within a specified number of days) after the ETC produces or receives the relevant documents. Subject to appropriate consent agreements being in place, disclosure should be of all future contracts placed by the ETC. The ETC should make the public aware of the methods of disclosure and how and where further information can be viewed. Disclosure can be both on the Internet and at the relevant federal, regional, or city registry. The management of this disclosure should be relatively simple and cheap because virtually all the above documents will be available in electronic form, so they can readily be uploaded onto a well-managed website.

- *Establish the legal framework for disclosure.* The Public Procurement Proclamation does not currently provide for this level of disclosure. In the short term, the most effective way to provide a legal basis for enhanced disclosure may therefore be through the ETC's procurement procedures. A provision requiring the designers', suppliers', and contractors' consent to full disclosure should be inserted into all new design, supply, and construction contracts.

Recommendation 4: *Strengthen internal auditing.*

The internal audit function within the ETC does not appear to have sufficient resources, expertise, or authority to be able to act as effectively as is necessary. Random checks by internal auditors for compliance with procedures and contract provisions, compliance with specification and quality, and any evidence of corruption is vital, both to deter corrupt acts and to help uncover corruption. It is recommended that the function be strengthened in the following ways:

- The number of auditors in the internal audit department should be increased to allow a wider-reaching, more frequent audit.
- Auditors should receive specific anticorruption training that highlights likely areas of corruption risk.
- The internal audit function should be able to select, on its own, which projects and which departments it audits, and at what time. It should not need approval from the ETC board in this regard and should resist and report any attempts by any director or manager of the ETC to prevent it from looking at any particular issue.
- The internal audit department should report any findings of possible corruption or wrongdoing simultaneously to four parties: the ETC's board, the ETC's ethics officer, the FEACC, and the ASC.
- The internal audit department should follow up on any request by the ETC's ethics officer to investigate a particular issue, project, or department.

Recommendation 5: *Create an ETC-supplier forum.*

This chapter has exposed a degree of discontent on the part of both the ETC and private sector stakeholders about the performance of the other party. Although this is to some degree inevitable in any commercial arrangement, relationships could be improved and efficiency increased if the ETC and suppliers were to meet in a regular open forum where they could discuss any issues and propose solutions. Participation should be open to the ETC staff, to current and potential suppliers and contractors, and to relevant industry associations.

Concluding Remarks

This chapter is not intended to be definitive or to provide a financial or technical audit. Rather, it is a compilation of research, document analysis, and sector expert views that is intended to catalyze improved understanding of processes and practices in the sector. In undertaking this analysis, presenting the findings, and making recommendations, the authors are aware of the limited nature of the analysis as well as the polarized views of state and nonstate stakeholders. The chapter has therefore only taken small steps: mapping corruption risks within

Ethiopia's telecommunications sector, attempting to explain whether current perceptions of corruption are warranted; what type of corruption is taking place; and, if so, in which parts of the telecommunications sector and in which parts of the process. Based on stakeholder perceptions and analysis of available documents, the conclusion here is that there are indeed significant corruption risks in three specific areas. Detailed recommendations have been made about how these risks, and the associated lack of confidence in the sector, can be addressed.

Notes

1. In this analysis, "corruption" is interpreted widely to include bribery, extortion, fraud, deception, collusion, cartels, abuse of power, embezzlement, trading in influence, money laundering, and similar unlawful actions.

2. A recently completed international fiber-optic cable, one of several potentially indirectly serving Ethiopia, required an investment of US$650 million.

3. Transparency International listed public works and construction as the most corrupt sector out of 19 international sectors surveyed (TI 2008). http://www.transparency.org/policy_research/surveys_indices/bpi.

4. Ethiopian Telecommunications Corporation (ETC) Establishment Council of Ministers Regulation No. 10/1996.

5. Public Enterprises Proclamation No. 25/1992

6. This section and figure 8.2 draw on a range of sources, including Hartley and Murphree 2006.

7. Source data for figures are drawn from the BuddeComm telecommunications research site, in turn compiled from various sources (BuddeComm 2009a, 2009b).

8. The ETC response to the draft of this chapter strongly challenged a number of these perceptions (ETC 2010).

9. The ETC strongly challenged this perception (ETC 2010).

10. Federal Democratic Republic of Ethiopia (FDRE): Definition of Powers and Duties of the Executive Organs of the Federal Democratic Republic of Ethiopia Proclamation No. 471/2005; Telecommunication Proclamation No. 49/1996; Telecommunications (Amendment) Proclamation No. 281/2002; Public Enterprises Proclamation No. 25/1992 ; Ethiopian Telecommunication Corporation Establishment Council of Ministers Regulations No. 10/1996; Telecommunication Services Council of Ministers Regulations No. 47/1999; Telecommunication Services Council of Ministers Regulations No. 47/1999.

11. FDRE: Determining Procedures of Public Procurement and Establishing its Supervisory Agency Proclamation No. 430/2005.

12. FDRE: Protection of Telecommunications and Electric Power Networks Proclamation No. 464/2005.

13. Discussions with sector representatives revealed some willingness to discuss their perceptions verbally but a strong reluctance to commit them to writing. A confidential survey of the sector was distributed to all organizations consulted, but only two completed surveys were returned.

14. This section reports on the research conducted by Neill Stansbury.

15. The diagnostics noted that the ETC did follow proper procurement procedures in some instances. For example, a contract with a major international supplier placed in 2004, which is not yet finalized, was also briefly assessed. As far as could be told from the contract documents, this contract was publicly advertised before tender, involved several major international competitors in a competitive tender, and there was a public bid opening.

16. The ETC indicates that it invited eight international vendors: Nokia, Ericsson, ZTE, Siemens, Alcatel, Wouhawe, Midock, and CITCC (ETC 2010).

17. At the time of conducting this diagnostic, the FEACC was not aware of whether these areas have been appropriately dealt with by the ETC.

18. This saying, initially by a late Roman sage, is now commonly attributed to Dr. Samuel Johnson, who referred to it in "The Idler," No. 85, December 1 1759.

19. Though both bribes and facilitation payments are illegal, there is an important distinction between them. A bribe is intended to induce an official to behave *improperly*, such as by overlooking breaches of procedure. By contrast, a facilitation payment is intended to induce an official to behave *properly*, when all the necessary documentation is in order and due process has been followed. The distinction between the two becomes blurred when the sums involved become significant in relation to the recipient's salary.

20. In the response to the draft of this chapter, the ETC did not agree with all examples provided in the following risk areas (ETC 2010).

21. Internationally, the concept of an "independent assessor" is most commonly encountered in connection with integrity pacts in the construction and defense sectors. The same concept can, however, be applied to any situation where there is a need for an experienced independent assessor who carries the respect of all stakeholder groups.

References

Adam, Lishan. 2007. "2007 Ethiopia Telecommunications Sector Performance Review: A Supply Side Analysis of Policy Outcomes." Country Profile Series, Research ICT Africa!, Cape Town.

Balancing Act Africa. 2006. "Africa Satellite Markets." Report on satellite provision, Balancing Act Africa, London.

———. 2009. "Ethiopia's ETC: The Elephant in the Room Slows Down ICT Development." *Balancing Act Africa News*, 437 (January 16). http://www2 .balancingact-africa.com/news/en/issue-no-437/top-story/ethiopia-s-etc- the-e/en.

Belay, Teshager. 2008. "Chinazation of the Ethiopian Telecommunications Corporation." November 9. http://www.docstor.com/docs/51312783/ Chinazation-of-the-Ethiopian-Tel.

BuddeComm. 2009a. "Ethiopia: Telecoms Market Overview, Statistics & Forecasts." Market research report, Paul Budde Communication Pty Ltd., Bucketty, Australia.

———. 2009b. "Ethiopia: Telecoms, Mobile, Broadband and Forecasts." Market research report, Paul Budde Communication Pty Ltd., Bucketty, Australia.

ETC (Ethiopian Telecommunications Corporation). 2008. "Annual Statistical Bulletin 2007/08," ETC, Addis Ababa.

———. 2010. "Remarks on 'Corruption in the Telecommunications Sector in Ethiopia.'" Response to report draft, June 25, ETC, Addis Ababa.

FEACC (Federal Ethics and Anti-Corruption Commission.) 2008. "Annual Report." FEACC, Addis Ababa.

Hartley, Lynn, and Michael Murphree. 2006. "Influences on the Partial Liberalization of Internet Service Provision in Ethiopia." *Critique* (Fall 2006): 87–115.

TI (Transparency International). 2008. "TI Bribe Payers Index 2008." Periodic survey report, TI, Berlin. http://www.transparency.org/policy_research/ surveys_indices/bpi.

World Bank. 2008. "Country Assistance Strategy for Ethiopia." World Bank, Washington, DC.

CHAPTER 9

Corruption in the Mining Sector: Preliminary Overview

Introduction

The mining sector in Ethiopia is relatively undeveloped and does not form a significant part of Ethiopia's economy. However, the country is rich with mineral resources, and both the Ethiopian government and national and international mining companies wish to see a major expansion. Mining is a relatively high-risk sector for corruption, and thus any increase of activity inevitably carries with it both an increased risk of corruption and an increase in the amounts potentially lost to corruption. It is therefore vital for Ethiopia's future prosperity that mining activity be increased in a manner that minimizes the opportunities for corruption. This analysis of the mining sector in Ethiopia was commissioned to assess the current level of corruption in the sector and to recommend improvements in management controls and other preventive measures that could minimize corruption in the future.

This chapter draws on fieldwork conducted by Neill Stansbury in 2009 and is supplemented by additional internal research.

Although this chapter results from studies completed by January 2010, the process of checking, reviewing, and securing agreement for publication was finally brought to conclusion only in late 2011. The chapter is therefore put forward with the caveat that while it reflects the situation at the time of the study, some details will have understandably changed.

Methodology

This risk analysis is supported by a number of sources, including the perceptions and experiences of senior government and private sector representatives in Ethiopia who gave their views in interviews, a workshop, and a survey. Sources included the following:

- *Documentation*, including laws, regulations, license conditions, and other documentation about processes.
- *Interviews* of senior representatives from the Ethiopian government, the Ministry of Mines (MOM), Oromia Mineral and Energy Resource Development Agency (the regional licensing authority for Oromia Region), Addis Ababa City Government Environmental Protection Authority (the city licensing authority for Addis Ababa City), the Federal Ethics and Anti-Corruption Commission (FEACC), and private sector mining companies.
- *A multistakeholder workshop* involving senior representatives from the above organizations and the Oromia Ethics and Anti-Corruption Commission.
- *A confidential survey of the sector stakeholders* through a detailed questionnaire sent to senior representatives of the above organizations and the Tigray Water Resource, Mines and Energy Bureau. Approximately 120 survey forms were sent out, and 19 were returned: 12 from private sector mining companies and 7 from government sources. (Although the survey returns are small in number, they were provided by senior and experienced people, so should be regarded as credible.)

In the interviews, workshop, and survey, representatives were asked for their views on the occurrence of corruption in the mining sector in Ethiopia, the major areas of corruption risk, how the risk was currently being dealt with, and how risk prevention could be improved.

Overview of Findings and Recommendations

The extent of corruption in the mining sector appears to be lower, in both occurrence and value, than in other Ethiopian sectors such as construction and telecommunications. In fact, most of the people interviewed had not encountered corruption in the sector. However, approximately one-third of interviewees had witnessed or heard of actual corruption. All interviewees perceived a significant risk of corruption throughout the mining cycle and believe effective anticorruption controls to be important.

The three major areas of corruption risk in the Ethiopian mining sector have been analyzed and mapped:

- *License issuing.* Licensing authority officials may extort or be offered bribes by mining companies in return for issuing licenses, for issuing licenses more quickly, or for specifying less-onerous license conditions.
- *License operation.* Mining companies may deliberately breach mining conditions (for example, environmental, health, and safety regulations, as well as the extent or area of mining permitted).
- *Mining revenue.* Mining companies may deliberately understate output and profit and overstate costs to reduce royalties and profit taxes.

If the license operation and mining revenue breaches are discovered, the mining company may also bribe inspectors to overlook the breaches. In addition, there are corruption risks in relation to

- The interface between mining companies and local inhabitants (for example, theft of compensation payments by local officials or illegal mining by local inhabitants in a mining company's license area)
- The contractors and suppliers to the mining operation
- Falsification of the quality of the product
- Theft of the product.

In general, some effective anticorruption measures govern the Ethiopian mining sector. The laws and regulations as well as the documentation and processes for issuing and operating licenses are clear and simple, therefore minimizing the complexity in procedure and discretion of officials that can facilitate corruption. There are some committed and well-qualified licensing officials and inspectors. A new computer database is being developed to improve access to license information, and the Ethiopian government is implementing business process reengineering (BPR) to speed up the license issuing process. These all play an important part in reducing the risk of corruption.

However, further steps are recommended to enhance existing anticorruption controls, particularly regarding the licensing and regulation processes. A key problem lies in the shortage of well-trained licensing authority staff. In license issuing, there is a shortage of officials to deal with the increasing number of license applications and the complex issues that arise in relation to license conditions. In license operation and revenue calculation, there are too few inspectors and auditors to inspect mining operations, monitor compliance with license conditions, and ensure that mines are correctly declaring output and profit for royalties and taxes. There are no detailed guidelines in relation to the environmental, health and safety, and social conditions that should be attached to licenses. The lack of guidelines causes uncertainty during both license issuing and inspection, which can lead to corruption.

Chapter Structure

This chapter first provides an overview of corruption in the Ethiopian mining sector, beginning with a look at the structure of the international mining sector, whether the sector is perceived as corrupt, and, if so, why. International factors affect the Ethiopian mining sector because many of the mining companies operating in Ethiopia are international companies and because the Ethiopian sector operates similarly to the mining sectors of other countries in many ways.

Following the next section, "Corruption in the International Mining Sector," the analysis proceeds as follows:

- "Overview of the Ethiopian Mining Sector" examines the size and nature of the Ethiopian sector in particular.
- "The Legislative and Institutional Framework for Mining in Ethiopia" presents the legislative framework and institutional arrangements that govern the Ethiopian sector.
- "Corruption Risk in the Ethiopian Mining Sector" is the heart of the analysis—identifying the seven main corruption risk areas, examining the levels of corruption in these areas, presenting hypothetical examples of corruption in each area, and specifying recommendations to improve anticorruption procedures in each area.
- The chapter concludes with a number of general anticorruption recommendations.

Corruption in the International Mining Sector

Any interface between two people that involves money or other advantage creates a corruption risk—a risk that increases as the complexity of transactions and the amounts at stake increase. The international mining sector requires large sums to explore, develop, and operate mines, but the potential returns on a successful mine are also extremely high.

Transparency International's Bribe Payers' Index 2008 listed mining as the fifth most corrupt sector out of 19 international sectors surveyed

(TI 2008). Despite the known limitations of such indices, the high instance of perceived corruption in international mining does suggest that the sector needs to be carefully controlled to minimize the corruption risk.

Mining Sector Stakeholders

The mining sector involves a broad range of stakeholders:

- *The government* owns the mineral rights and grants licenses to use land for exploration and mining.
- *Mining companies* explore for and mine the minerals.
- *Contractors and suppliers* are appointed by the mining company to undertake one or more of the following on a subcontract basis: (a) geological surveys; (b) construction of the mine infrastructure (access roads, mine buildings, housing for the miners, schools and clinics for the mine staff and families, and so on); (c) excavation services (for example, earthworks, boring, or drilling); (d) transportation of minerals from the mine to their destinations (by road, rail, or sea); (e) provision of consumables, food, and so forth; and (f) provision of mining equipment (such as excavation equipment, crushers, lifts, conveyors, trucks, and drills).
- *Local inhabitants* may have arrangements with the mining company to use their land, pay them compensation, and provide them with services.
- *Utility companies* provide services to the mining companies such as power, water, and telephone. In practice, however, most mines are in remote areas, so mining companies usually provide their own electricity generators and water pumps and use mobile phones.
- *Employees* of the mining companies work at the mine and provide administrative and support services.
- *Purchasers* buy the minerals from the mining companies.

A Sector Prone to Corruption

Globally, the mining sector is prone to corruption for several reasons:

- *Significant values are at stake.* A successful mine can produce extremely large quantities of minerals for many years. The high values at stake make mining vulnerable to corruption. On the supply side, the mining company could realize significant long-term profits if granted a mining license on advantageous terms. A bribe of many millions of dollars may represent only a fraction of the company's potential profit. On the demand side, officials realize the value of the license to the mining company. Corrupt officials may therefore extort large bribes from a mining company in return for a license or in return for imposing less-onerous environmental or other controls.

- *Mining is a high-risk enterprise.* Success in a mining enterprise is not certain. Considerable sums of money can be invested in a mining enterprise that then fails for any number of reasons: (a) the minerals may not be present in the quality or quantity estimated; (b) the cost of extracting the minerals may be higher than expected; (c) the market price for the minerals may be lower than expected; (d) the government may increase the license charges, royalties, or taxes to a point where the mine becomes uneconomic; or (e) the government may nationalize the mine with inadequate or no compensation. It can be just as important to a mining company to avoid a large loss as to make a profit, and therefore it may be beneficial to the mining company to bribe an official to avert or minimize a loss. Similarly, realizing the risk of loss to the mining company, an official could extort large bribes with the threat that, if the company does not pay, it will incur a loss far greater than the amount of the bribe.

- *There are uncertainties in valuation.* Numerous factors affect the value of a mining concession (upon initial award or assignment), including the estimated or actual
  - Costs of exploring and evaluating a concession, developing the mine and related infrastructure, extracting and processing the minerals, and transporting them to the end user
  - Output of the mine
  - Sale price of the minerals
  - Premiums, royalties, and taxes paid by the mining company to the government.

Each one of these factors is difficult to establish. Comparative data from other mines do not normally help to establish what these costs should be because differences in the mine's location and the mineral's quality and quantity can vary significantly among different mines, affecting the costs. Mines are often in remote locations, making it difficult for inspectors and auditors to verify production quantities and costs. As a result, it is difficult to value a concession and to calculate what the mining company should reasonably pay the government by way of an up-front premium. It is also difficult for government inspectors or auditors to ensure that the mining company is declaring the correct output of minerals for royalty purposes and the correct net profit for tax purposes. This difficulty in calculation and comparison makes it easier for corruption to take place.

- *The government exercises considerable control over the sector.* Mining concessions are normally controlled by governments through regulation and licensing. It is normally necessary to obtain a license for both the initial exploration and the mining concession, and permits are normally needed for issues such as environmental controls, safety, building regulations, and explosives. Thus, officials have considerable discretionary power. Unless the officials have integrity and are properly trained and monitored and unless the law and regulations are extremely clear, this power can corrupt. Officials may refuse to issue licenses or permits, or they may delay in issuing them unless they receive bribes.

- *Stock market perceptions affect the sector.* Many mining companies are listed on a stock exchange. Smaller exploration companies are often a high-risk stock whose share price can fluctuate significantly according to the stock market's perception of their likely success. An announcement of a new license or a possible mineral find can cause sudden, large surges in their share prices. Because mining company managers are often paid in stock options and can become enormously wealthy if the share price rises, they have an incentive for corruption (for example, to pay bribes to secure licenses or to exaggerate the likely benefit of a mining license) to increase their personal wealth.

- *The mining sector has a significant interface with the construction sector.* Construction companies normally perform mine excavation and build the mine buildings and related infrastructure (roads, power, water supplies, and so on). From a corruption perspective, the construction industry is perceived as a high-risk industry and any interface between the two sectors could affect the mine project.[1]

- *Transparency in mining is very limited.* Financial data and other details on mining projects are not normally available to the public. As a result, it is impossible for the public to determine whether a mining concession was fairly awarded for a fair price, what the mining conditions are, and whether the government is properly accounting for and using revenues from the mine.

- *Mining has a major, and potentially adverse, impact on local inhabitants.* Mining can take place over large areas of land and cause major environmental degradation. This can affect the local inhabitants by requiring them to be resettled and by polluting the air, land, and water. There can be considerable corruption surrounding the calculation and payment of compensation to inhabitants and in assessing, imposing, and policing the necessary environmental controls.

Overview of the Ethiopian Mining Sector

Current mining activities in Ethiopia include the production of gold, tantalite, soda ash, kaolin, limestone, marble, basalt, granite, gemstones, salt, and other products. The Ethiopian government retains title to all these minerals and the land that holds them. All mines were once publicly owned. However, since 1993, Ethiopian mines have been privatized; only three currently remain under public ownership.

Therefore, all new mining licenses are being issued to privately owned mining companies. Foreign mining companies are entitled to obtain licenses on the same terms as Ethiopian companies. Mining licenses can be issued either to foreign or Ethiopian companies acting individually or to joint ventures involving foreign or Ethiopian companies.

The Ethiopian mining sector is currently relatively small but growing. The Ministry of Mines and Energy's "National Report on Mining" (submitted to the United Nations Commission on Sustainable Development in November 2009) reveals the following (MOME 2009):

- The contribution of the mining sector to the Ethiopian economy is currently 6 percent of gross domestic product (GDP), compared with less than 1 percent before 1990.
- The federal government has collected royalties of more than US$4 million from large-scale production of gold every year between 2006 and 2009.
- Regional and city administrations have also collected royalties of an estimated US$3 million per year from small-scale and artisanal production of precious minerals and industrial and construction materials.
- The total private sector investment is estimated at US$1.1 billion, of which 95 percent comes from direct foreign investment for the mining of precious and industrial minerals.
- Foreign currency earnings total US$135 million per year from the export of minerals such as gold, tantalite, concentrate platinum,

decorative dimension stones, and gemstones. These exports contribute 7–10 percent of Ethiopia's total export foreign currency earnings.

As of 2010, 13 licensing authorities (one federal, nine regional, and three city) were responsible for issuing prospecting, exploration, and mining licenses. They are also responsible for inspecting licensed mines to ensure that the companies are complying with license conditions and that all mining revenues are being paid.

The sector is undergoing a rapid expansion. In 1998, only three exploration licenses and one mining license were issued. By early 2009, however, the federal Ministry of Mines and Energy[2] had issued 160 licenses[3] involving 99 foreign companies, 50 joint ventures (of foreign and Ethiopian companies), and 11 Ethiopian companies. Just over a year later, in April 2010, another six exploration and two mining licenses had been issued. This growth means that the amount of money at stake in the sector will increase and, with it, the corruption risk in monetary terms. In addition, the government will need to significantly increase resources to manage this growth. Inadequate management, in terms of both number of staff and ability of staff, can lead to increased corruption.

The Legislative and Institutional Framework for Mining in Ethiopia

Legislative Framework

The Ethiopian mining sector has a well-defined process for controlling mine licensing and operations. Detailed mining laws and regulations govern license issuing, license conditions, mining operations, mining revenues, and the functions of the licensing authorities, as follows:[4]

- *License issuing.* Under Ethiopian law, a license is required to prospect, explore, or mine in Ethiopia (although Ethiopian nationals do not need prospecting licenses). The license types include discovery certificates, prospecting licenses, exploration licenses, and mining licenses. There are three types of mining license: artisanal, small-scale, and large scale. People who satisfy the license requirements have the right to acquire a license provided they are suitably qualified and possess the required financial resources, technical competence, and professional skill and experience necessary to fulfill the license obligations.

- *License conditions.* The licenses specify the conditions with which the licensee must comply in prospecting, exploring, or mining. In particular, the conditions specify the license area; the type of mineral that can be mined; the equipment and resources that the mining company must use; the work program; and any applicable environmental, health and safety, or social conditions.

- *Mining revenues.* A mining company operating in Ethiopia must pay royalties and taxes to the relevant licensing authority. Royalties are calculated on the mineral output of the mine—currently 5 percent of sale price for precious metals and 3 percent for other minerals. Income tax of 35 percent is calculated on the mine's net profits. Artisanal mining is exempted from income tax. A tax of 10 percent is payable on dividends distributed from taxable income after deduction of income tax.

- *Compensation.* The mining company is legally obligated to compensate the people whose land or homes are lost or affected because of the mining operation. The companies are not currently required in Ethiopia to submit and comply with a social management plan. However, the federal Ministry of Mines (as it is currently named, or MOM) now encourages mining companies to consider a social management plan, which may become a legal requirement in due course. Such a plan could include housing, schools, hospitals, water, food, and so on for the mine workers, their families, and the local community.

- *Government permits* may be needed for planning permission, building approvals, safety and environmental issues, import and export clearances, payment approvals, and currency exchange, among other matters.

- *Customs duties.* Mining equipment may be imported. Licensees are exempt from custom duties and import taxes on the equipment, machinery, vehicles, and spare parts necessary for mineral operations. There are restrictions on sale of this equipment in Ethiopia.

Institutional Arrangements

Responsibility for controlling the mining sector in Ethiopia is divided among federal, regional, and city licensing authorities who are responsible for issuing all licenses; determining the conditions imposed at the time of license issuance; monitoring mine operations to ensure that mining companies comply with laws, regulations, and license conditions; and monitoring output and profit to ensure that the correct amounts of royalty and tax are paid. The authorities' respective responsibilities break down as follows:

- *Federal licensing authority.* MOM acts as the federal licensing authority, with responsibility for large-scale mining by domestic investors and all operations by foreign investors
- *Regional and city licensing authorities.* The relevant regional or city licensing authorities act as the licensing authorities in their respective areas for artisanal mining, prospecting, exploration, small-scale mining, and small- and large-scale mining of construction minerals, provided that only domestic investors are undertaking these activities.

In view of the division of responsibility among licensing authorities, the licensing process often requires liaison between authorities to determine whether licenses have already been issued in a particular area. This territorial overlap can result in delay and uncertainty.

To assist the licensing process, MOM operates a computer database that shows the status of federal licenses (for example, type of license, identity of license holder, nationality of license holder, location of license, type of mineral) and the location of federal licenses on a map. Most regional and city licensing authorities currently hold data in paper-based systems or separate computer systems. The Ethiopian government is currently developing a new computer database that will show all federal, regional, and city licenses in the mining sector. This consolidated system will enable applicants for new licenses (federal, regional, or city) to find out immediately whether the areas that interest them are available and, if so, to obtain immediate priority.

The Ethiopian government is also currently implementing BPR in relation to the mining sector, affecting MOM and regional and city licensing authorities. One objective of the BPR is to shorten significantly the time frame for issuing licenses. In particular, the BPR aims to issue exploration licenses within two days after application submission and to issue mining licenses within 19 days after application submission.

Figure 9.1 illustrates the licensing process, from prospecting to issue of a mining license. An Ethiopian national can reserve rights over discovered minerals by way of a discovery certificate, which in turn provides the right to apply for an exploration license, which in turn provides the right to apply for a mining license (if, in each case, the national satisfies the

Figure 9.1   The Licensing Process in the Ethiopian Mining Sector

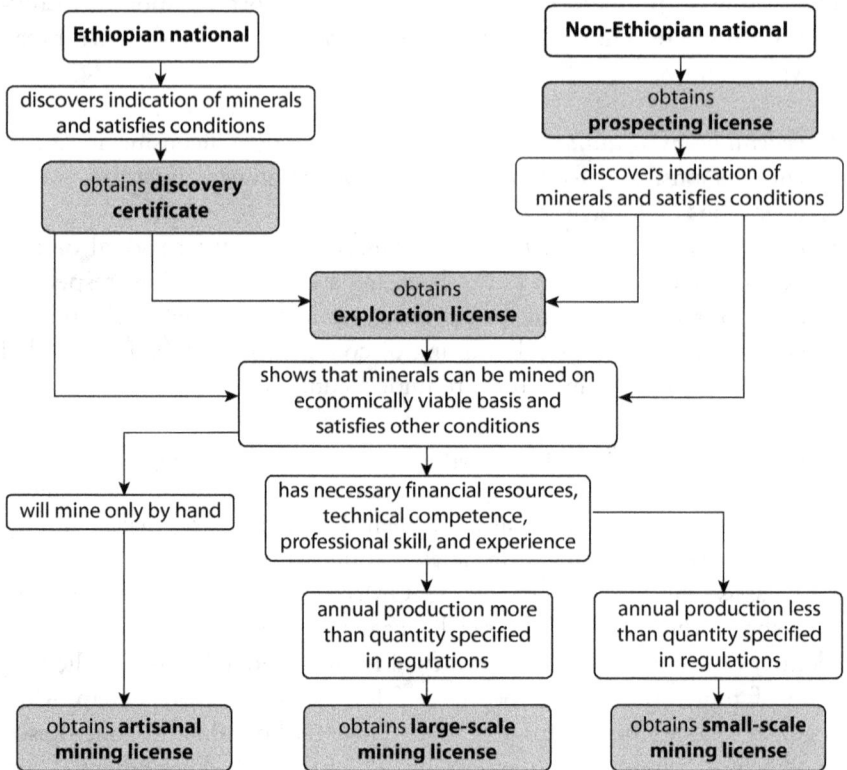

Note: Possession of a discovery certificate or prospecting license gives a preferential right to an exploration or mining license for the particular area. Similarly, possession of an exploration license gives a preferential right to a mining license.

relevant technical and financial conditions). Alternatively, an Ethiopian national can skip the discovery certificate and exploration license and apply directly for a mining license. The type of mining license depends on the method of mining and size of the reserve.

Non-Ethiopian nationals have the same rights and follow the same procedures as Ethiopian nationals except that they cannot search for minerals without a prospecting license and cannot apply for an artisanal license (the right to mine by hand).

Figure 9.2 illustrates how an application for a large-scale mining license is processed at the federal level. This procedure tries to balance the potentially conflicting rights of the federal, regional, and city governments (because, for example, a regional license may already have been granted over an area sought by a mining company for a federal license).

Figure 9.2   Application Process for Large-Scale Federal Mining License in Ethiopia

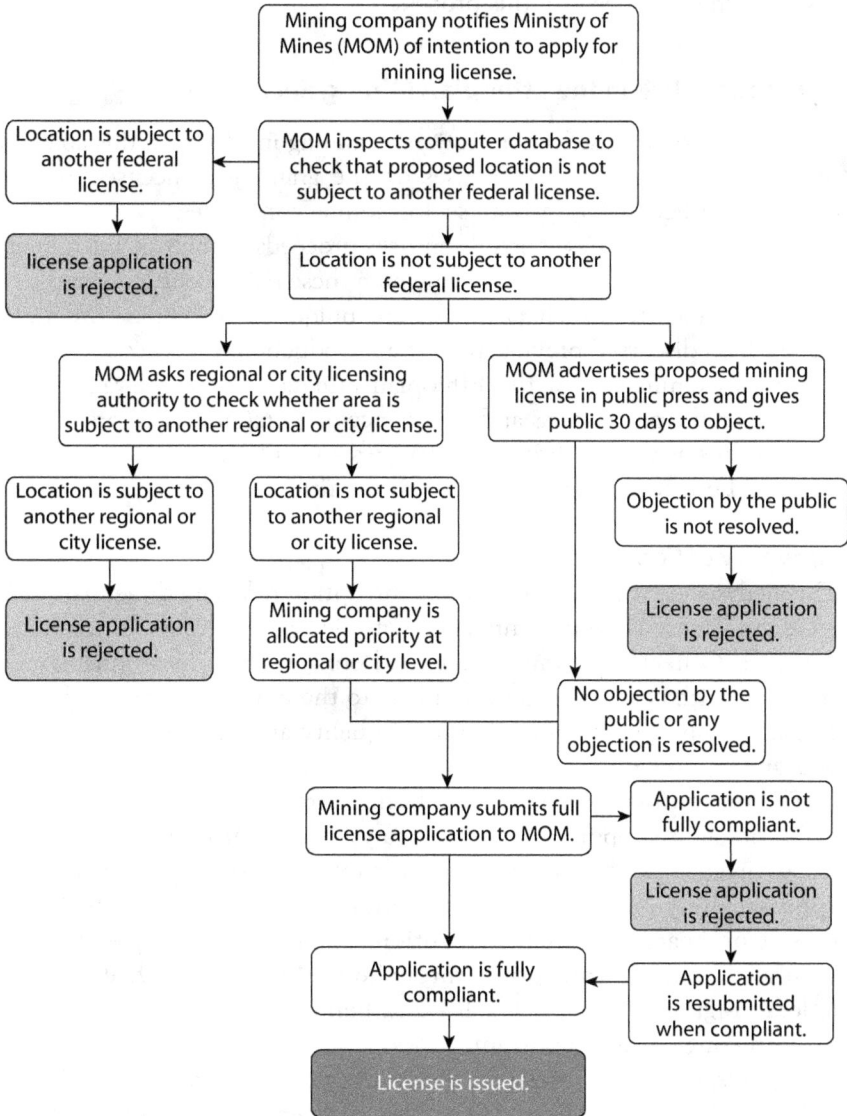

Note: The Ministry of Mines was previously the Ministry of Mines and Energy during 2005–09. The length of time this process takes will depend on many factors, such as whether or not there are any objections, the correctness of the mining company's application, and the length of time the relevant licensing authorities take to review the applications.

The 2009 introduction of the BPR and a new consolidated computer system aimed to speed up this process.

Corruption Risk in the Ethiopian Mining Sector

In view of the increased privatization of mining in Ethiopia, this analysis of corruption in the sector focuses on the granting of licenses to, and operation of licenses by, private sector mining companies.

The mapping of these corruption risks proceeds as follows: Each main risk area is identified. The extent to which these risks occur in Ethiopia—and the extent to which any risks are unique to Ethiopia—are then assessed. As discussed previously in the introduction, the assessments are based on examination of the Ethiopian mining process, relevant documents, and the perceptions and experiences of corruption and preventive mechanisms as shared through interviews and surveys of senior government and private sector participants in the Ethiopian mining sector.

Summary of Corruption Risks

The analysis identifies seven areas of corruption risk. The three main risk areas are license issuing, compliance with license conditions, and mining revenues. Others are compensation and obligations to local inhabitants, contracts with contractors and suppliers to the mining companies, falsification by mining companies of product quality, and theft of mining products and equipment.

The perceptions of corruption obtained from the survey, interviews, and workshop supported this risk analysis. Most of those interviewed or surveyed had not encountered corruption in the sector. However, approximately one-third of people interviewed or surveyed had witnessed or heard of actual corruption. All interviewees perceived a significant risk of corruption throughout the mining cycle—at the federal, regional, and city levels—and believed that effective anticorruption controls are important.

The respondents expressed a range of perceptions about the size of bribes paid in the issuing and operation of licenses. In the survey, 4 out of 19 respondents were aware of the value of the bribes: two were aware of bribes of above Br 500; one was aware of bribes of Br 5,000–Br 10,000; and one was aware of bribes in excess of Br 100,000.

The respondents shared a general perception that the Ethiopian mining sector was less corrupt than the mining sectors in other African countries.

In the survey, 9 out of 15 respondents thought that corruption in the min-ing sector in Ethiopia was much less frequent than in other countries in Africa, 4 out of 15 thought it was less frequent, and 2 out of 15 thought it was the same. No one believed that it was more frequent.

In relation to *issuing of licenses*, the main corruption risks surround officials who either extort or accept bribes from mining companies to (a) issue licenses, (b) issue licenses more quickly, or (c) impose less-onerous license conditions. There is also a risk that officials may secretly have ownership stakes in companies to which licenses are granted; acquire land for which a license application has been made; demand a share in mining companies or in their profits; and manipulate license registration to give themselves or their associates prior registration. This latter type of corruption was seen as facilitated by the territorial over-lap between licensing authorities. In the survey, 32 percent of respon-dents were aware of corruption in this area—with 32 percent aware of it at the regional level, 26 percent at the federal level, and 11 percent at the city level.

In relation to *compliance with license conditions*, there is a major risk that nonethical companies might operate without a valid license or delib-erately fail to comply with license conditions and thereafter conceal those breaches and bribe officials to overlook them. There is also a risk of inspectors demanding bribes to not report breaches and of officials requiring mining companies to take actions that will personally benefit the officials. In the survey, 37 percent of respondents were aware of cor-ruption in this area—with 37 percent aware of it at the regional level, 32 percent at the federal level, and 11 percent at the city level.

In relation to *mining revenues*, the main revenue-related corruption risks concern mining companies that make false declarations about cost, output, and profits to reduce the royalties and taxes payable to the gov-ernment or that bribe government auditors and inspectors to approve the false declarations. There is also the risk of illegal sale of mining products. In the survey, 24 percent of respondents were aware of corruption in this area—with 18 percent aware of it at the federal and city levels, and 12 percent at the regional level.

In relation to *compensation and obligations to local inhabitants*, officials or community leaders may steal compensation that should have gone to local inhabitants; mining companies may bribe officials to set compensation below a proper rate; and local inhabitants may, to claim compensation, falsely claim that they occupy land subject to a license application. In the survey, 25 percent of respondents were aware of corruption in this area—with 6 percent aware of it at the federal level, 25 percent at the regional level, and 13 percent at the city level.

In relation to *contracts with contractors and suppliers* (contracts for the supply of work, services, and materials for the excavation and operation of mines and the construction of mine buildings and related infrastructure such as roads, power, and water supplies), the major risks are in tendering, submission of claims, and concealment or approval of defective works. Eleven percent of respondents had witnessed or heard of corruption in this area.

In relation to *falsification of quality*, mining companies may commit fraud by making false declarations about the identity and quality of minerals or by bribing certifiers to approve false declarations. A major, ongoing investigation into corruption of this type is under way in Ethiopia. Twenty-four percent of respondents were aware of corruption in this area.

In relation to *theft of mineral product and mining equipment*, workers, local inhabitants, or gangs may steal mineral products or mining equipment, and 19 percent of respondents were aware of corruption in this area.

Detailed Overview of Risk Areas

To diagnose corruption in the Ethiopian mining sector, the mining cycle has been divided into the seven areas of risk identified above. In relation to each area, the analyses summarize the key corruption risks, present hypothetical examples of corruption, consider the respondents' perceptions of corruption, assess current anticorruption controls, rate the degree of risk, and, where appropriate, recommend further anticorruption measures.

Risk 1: Issuing of licenses

Potential risks in sector

The key potential corruption risks concerning issuing of licenses in the Ethiopian mining sector include the following:

- *Bribes are paid or extorted to issue licenses.*
  - A mining company could be required to pay a large premium in return for a mining license. Senior officials and the mining company could keep this premium secret, and the officials could receive payment in offshore bank accounts. (This example is not currently an issue in Ethiopia because payment of premiums is not required.)

- *Bribes are paid or extorted to speed up license issuance.*
  - An official may require the mining company to make a large donation to a charity if it wants the license to be issued more quickly. Although the charity may appear to be genuine, it may in fact be a front for a political party or for the official's personal or family gain.
- *Bribes are paid or extorted to impose less-onerous license conditions.*
  - The mining company may submit a health and safety plan for a mining license in accordance with good practice, but an official may tell the company that unless it pays a bribe, he or she will impose additional and unnecessarily onerous health and safety conditions.
  - The mining company may submit an environmental management plan for a mining license that will inadequately control the leaching of poisonous chemicals into the water supply. Proper controls would, for example, cost US$50,000 per year more than the mining company's proposed controls, so inadequate controls could save the mining company US$1 million over the 20-year mine operation. The mining company may pay the official responsible for approving the license a bribe of US$20,000 to approve the deficient conditions.
- *Officials demand a share in the profits of a mining company.*
  - A mining company may agree to give an official's relative a free share in the profits of the mining project if it receives a license on beneficial terms.
- *Officials grant licenses to companies secretly owned by them.*
- *Officials secretly acquire land that is subject to a license application.*
  - An official who is aware that mining may take place on an area of land may lease the land in advance of the mine licensing. Once the license is granted, the value of the land may materially increase. The official thereby profits from his or her inside knowledge by selling or licensing his or her rights to the land to the mining company.
- *Companies illegally on-sell licenses granted to them.*
- *Officials manipulate license registration.*
  - An official in the department that issues mining licenses may hear that a mining company wishes to apply for a license. The official may alert a business person with whom he or she has connections, and the business person may quickly apply for a license over the same area. The official grants the license to the business person. The mining company then has to purchase the license from the business person, and the business person shares the profit with the official.
  - A prospector may discover minerals, mark the area, and contact the relevant licensing authority to receive a discovery certificate. A corrupt

official may not register the discovery in that person's name but instead notify a business colleague and register the discovery in the colleague's name. The corrupt official may then falsely inform the discoverer that someone else had previously discovered the minerals.

- *Officials collude with mining companies to grant subcontracts to relatives.*
  ○ The licensing authority could, as a condition of the license award or social development plan, require the mining company to undertake a large amount of additional infrastructure works at the mining company's own cost. For example, the mining company may be obliged to build or refurbish a road, a school, or a hospital. A government official could then require the mining company to award one or more of these infrastructure projects to a contractor secretly owned by a member of the official's family.

Existing licensing procedures

Ethiopia has generally good procedures to help to minimize corruption risk in the license issuing process, including the following:

- Mining laws and regulations are reasonably well written, clear, and simple. There is a clear process for the issuing of licenses. Application forms, mining licenses, and mining agreements are in standard format and are reasonably well written. The regulations specify the documents and information that a mining company has to provide when applying for a license. Guidelines help the applicant understand the requirements for prospecting, exploration, and mining programs as well as the environmental impact assessment. There are also guidelines that state the minimum amount and type of equipment a licensee must provide for different types of licenses. All of these factors help to minimize uncertainty in procedures.

- MOM requires all license applicants to produce evidence showing which licensed professional had assisted them in developing the exploration or mining works program and to confirm that the professional has no link to the ministry.

- The risk of delay is reduced by the introduction of faster procedures under the BPR previously mentioned.

- Officials have limited discretion to determine license entitlement. The law grants the licensee the right to receive a license as long as the licensee complies with the specified licensing requirements. Although some element of discretion still remains (namely, as to whether the licensee *has* complied with the requirements), that discretion has been largely minimized by the clarity of the regulations.

- The risk of registration date manipulation (caused by MOM needing to obtain clearance from the regional or city licensing authority that a license area is available) is likely to be minimized by the introduction of the new computer database that will show all federal, regional, and city licenses. The federal mining minister also receives a status report of all federal license applications every two weeks.

- Separation in functions is achieved at the federal level (a) because officials from different MOM departments assess which mining, environmental, and social conditions to apply to the issuing of a license, and (b) because of the separation in function between the department issuing the license and the department administering the license. This separation of functions reduces the chance of corruption in license issuing because if corruption results, for example, in unduly weak license conditions, the license administration department may spot this deficiency and query it.

- Access to information at the federal level is good because the MOM computer shows the current status of all federal license applications, including the status of federal licenses (for example, type of license, identity of license holder, nationality of license holder, location of license, type of mineral) and the location of federal licenses on a map. This database helps to identify trends and comparisons that may reveal corruption (for example, if one company receives an unusually high number of licenses).

- Officials at MOM and at the Oromia Regional and Addis Ababa City licensing authorities appeared to be knowledgeable about their areas as well as enthusiastic, intelligent, and determined to ensure that the system worked well. Some mining companies spoke highly of the capability of some licensing officials.

- The risk of conflict of interest at the federal level has been reduced by the Ethiopian Environmental Protection Authority's (EPA) requirement that the mining company prepare the environmental impact assessment independently of government. No official is permitted to help prepare the assessment. The mining company is required to sign a statement that no member of the government or the EPA has helped it prepare the assessment.

Despite the above measures, however, the interviews, workshop, and surveys showed a perception of some corruption in connection with the issuing of licenses.

The interviews and workshop revealed the following perceptions:

- Most people interviewed believed that the risk of corruption in the issuing of federal licenses was generally low. Some mining companies commented that they had never come across any corruption in relation to license issuing.
- However, comments from some people indicated areas of corruption that need to be addressed:
  - Some regional mining licenses have allegedly been given to companies that did not have the necessary technical and financial capability.
  - On some occasions, there had allegedly been long delays in the issuing of licenses.
  - It was felt that the federal, regional, and city licensing authorities lack sufficient staff and systems to check whether licenses have expired.
  - Some mining companies thought that there was no effective mechanism for addressing their complaints if they believed they had been unfairly treated.
- A lack of clarity was perceived about which health and safety and environmental conditions should be imposed on a mining company at the time of license issue.

The survey revealed the following perceptions:

- Out of the 19 people who completed the survey, seven (37 percent) were aware of bribery in relation to the issue of prospecting, exploration, or mining licenses.
- One survey respondent (5 percent) was aware of bribery in relation to obtaining less-onerous license conditions at the time of license issue.
- Two survey respondents were aware of bribery from their own experiences, two from their organizations' experiences, and three from rumors.
- Six survey respondents believed that such bribery took place at the federal government level, seven at the regional level, and two at the city level.

These results suggest that corruption is occurring, although not throughout the licensing function. The continued and improved implementation of anticorruption action is therefore imperative, particularly as the mining sector grows in size and wealth.

The territorial overlap between MOM's responsibilities to issue federal licenses and the regional and city licensing authorities' responsibility to issue regional and city licenses was seen as causing a specific corruption risk. So, for example, if an applicant applies to MOM for a federal license, the ministry will check its own records to ensure that no federal license has been issued for that area. It then needs to check with the relevant regional or city licensing authority to ensure that it has *not* already issued a license for that area. A corrupt official at the regional or city licensing authority could therefore be alerted to the interest in that area and could alert a business person with whom the official has connections. The business person could quickly apply for a license over the same area. The official could then grant it and notify MOM that the area is already taken. The mining company will then have to purchase the license from the business person. The introduction of the new computer system (previously mentioned in the licensing process section) will help reduce this risk.

Some areas were specifically identified as needing improvement. All officials interviewed complained of a significant shortage of staff in their departments to deal with both the complex issues and the increasing number of license applications. They also expressed the view that more training would help staff to deal with the many complex issues. They believed that the mining companies normally had better resources and expertise than the government. This disparity in resources and expertise can lead a mining company to try to corrupt government officials. In addition, there are no detailed health and safety or environmental guidelines to assist officials and mining companies to know what conditions should be applied to a license. This makes it more likely that health and safety and environmental controls proposed by mining companies may not be up to international standards or that an official may corruptly abuse discretion in approving a health and safety or environmental management plan.

Risk rating: Low[5]
Although the *potential* risk in license issuance is high, the *actual* risk in Ethiopia at the federal licensing level is considered to be low because of the generally good federal procedures in Ethiopia and the apparently effective implementation of these procedures.

Recommendations to mitigate risks
- Increase staff to levels adequate to handle the increasing number of license applications and the complex issues that arise.
- Increase training of staff to deal with the complex issues.
- Ensure that comprehensive guidelines exist to help officials and mining companies know which conditions to apply to a license—particularly detailed environmental and health and safety guidelines that comply with international best practice.
- Increase local community involvement in determining the applicable license conditions.

Risk 2: Compliance with license conditions
Potential risks in sector
In the second key area of risk—compliance with license conditions—the potential corruption risks in the Ethiopian mining sector include the following:

- *Mining companies deliberately breach license conditions (which constitutes fraud).*
  - The environmental management plan for a mining license requires the mining company to treat wastewater before releasing it into the water course. The mining company may deliberately not do so, thereby saving considerable cost. Although the mining company might not have paid a bribe to any official, a deliberate breach of a license condition to make an additional profit is likely to defraud the government.
  - A condition of the mining company's social development plan requires the company to build an access road to the mine site to a minimum specification designed to also benefit the local inhabitants. To save cost, the mining company may build the road to a cheaper specification. The road breaks up, depriving the area of the good transport link it had expected, resulting in loss to the local community.
  - A license condition requires the mining company to ensure that the conditions for the mine workers are safe. To save cost, the mining company may deliberately not comply, the result of which may be that a worker is killed.
  - A license condition requires the mining company to use a specified amount of equipment to maximize the mine output. The company may not wish to mine the product but may obtain the license

speculatively with the hope of selling it to another mining company for a profit. It therefore may not comply with the condition.

- *Mining companies offer bribes to overlook breaches.*
  - The environmental management plan for an exploration license requires trial trenches to be infilled after testing is complete and for vegetation to be replanted. The mining company may not do so and may offer a bribe to the licensing authority inspector to overlook the breach.
- *Inspectors request bribes to overlook breaches of license conditions.*
  - The environmental management plan for a quarry requires the access area (which is next to houses) to be watered to reduce dust. The mining company might decide at any time during mine operation not to water the area, as a result saving considerable staffing and water costs over the duration of the license. The licensing authority inspector arrives at the quarry and notices that no watering is taking place. He threatens enforcement action against the mining company and requests a bribe from the mining company to overlook the breach.
- *Officials require the mining company to*
  - undertake work for the official's benefit;
  - use land or facilities that the official owns or has an interest in; or
  - donate to charities for the official's secret benefit.
- *Mining companies operate with no license or an expired license.*
- *Mining companies illegally sell mining equipment that has been imported into Ethiopia free of customs duties and taxes.*

Existing license compliance procedures

In Ethiopia, the licensing authorities attempt to reduce the risk of mining companies' noncompliance with license conditions by inspecting the mines. However, this procedure is hampered by two factors: the current lack of inspectors and the lack of clear license conditions in some cases.

As an example of the shortage of inspectors, at the time of this writing,

- MOM has only 13 staff members in its general inspection unit and three environmental inspectors to handle 160 federal licenses across the country, many of them in remote areas.
- The Oromia regional licensing authority has only three inspectors to monitor approximately 570 active regional licenses.

In contrast, the Addis Ababa city bureau is in a better position because it has seven inspectors for approximately 400 licenses. Because Addis Ababa is a relatively small area, it is also much easier to inspect mines there. The maximum distance from the licensing authority headquarters to a mine is 25 kilometers. Many of the mines are clustered in the same outlying areas of the city. Five of the seven inspectors are located at sub-city level to be closer to the mines that they need to inspect. Their target is to inspect each mine four times per year.

A shortage of properly trained and equipped inspectors can result in inadequate numbers of inspections, inadequate time given to each inspection, and failure to detect breaches of license conditions if the inspector lacks adequate skill, time, or the appropriate instruments.

The lack of detailed health and safety and environmental conditions attached to the license means the inspector has insufficient detail against which to measure the mining company's performance. This lack can either weaken the inspector's ability to assess the mining company's performance or increase the inspector's discretion in interpreting the requirements, in turn more easily allowing the inspector to extort or accept a bribe from the mining company in return for interpreting lesser requirements.

Some aspects of license or social development conditions may be enforced by other government departments. For example, if the mining company is required to build an access road, the obligation to inspect the road would fall to the relevant federal or regional road authority, not to MOM.

The interviews and workshop revealed the following perceptions:

- Interviewees perceived a high risk of corruption by some mining companies that might be deliberately breaching their license requirements.
- Many interviewees perceived a high risk that mining companies were deliberately not fulfilling their environmental obligations, both during the exploration or mining operation and at completion.
- Respondents believed that the licensing authorities were so under-staffed that they did not have enough inspectors to properly supervise the mining companies' compliance with mining conditions. It was believed that, in the absence of effective inspection and enforcement, the companies had little incentive to comply.
- They also believed that the corruption risk would increase materially as the number of mines in operation increased.

- No one interviewed was personally aware of any official being bribed to overlook a license breach. However, the respondents acknowledged it as a clear possibility.

The survey revealed the following perceptions:

- Out of the 19 people who completed the survey, six (32 percent) were aware of bribery or fraud in relation to the operation of licenses.
- Two were aware of bribery or fraud from their own experiences, three from their organizations' experiences, and four from rumor.
- Five believed that such bribery or fraud took place at the federal government level, six at the regional level, and two at the city level.

These results suggest that current preventive mechanisms are not adequate.

Risk rating: High
The actual risk in Ethiopia that mining companies may be breaching mining conditions at the federal license level is considered to be high.

Recommendations to mitigate risks
- The number of inspectors should be materially increased.
- Training of inspectors should be increased.
- The number of inspector visits to each license area should be increased substantially. The more frequent the visits, the more difficult it will be for mining companies to breach mining conditions on a routine basis. The number of visits should depend on the importance of the mine in terms of revenue and environmental and social impact. A small, low-value and low-impact mine would justify fewer inspector visits than a large, high-value, high-impact mine. On some very large mines, a full-time government inspector stationed at the mine may be appropriate. Expert advice could be sought from a government with high experience of mine control in inaccessible locations (for example, Australia or Canada) regarding a suitable inspection regime.
- The inspector visits to each license area should be long enough to properly inspect as much of the mine area as is practicable.
- Consideration should be given to basing inspectors close to where a number of licenses are located. This would reduce travel time between visits and make more visits possible.

- Inspections of license areas should be unannounced to prevent the mining company from complying with requirements only when the inspector is expected or from having sufficient warning to conceal breaches.
- The risk of an individual inspector receiving or demanding bribes can be reduced in the following ways:
  - Conduct inspections using a team of at least two inspectors: one responsible for environmental issues and the other to verify compliance with other license conditions. However, they should both be aware of the other's responsibilities and should discuss their observations with each other. This team approach would increase the chance that one inspector would notice if the other inspector overlooks a major issue.
  - Rotate the inspection team so that consecutive inspections are never undertaken by the same team.
- Detailed guidelines should be prepared on what to look for during an inspection and what actions to take if license conditions are breached.
- The local community should also be involved in policing compliance with conditions.
- Permanent installation of environmental monitoring equipment at major sites should be considered.

Risk 3: Mining revenues
Potential risks in sector
In the third key area of risk—mining revenues—the potential corruption risks in the Ethiopian mining sector include the following:

- *Premiums are misappropriated* (although this is currently not an issue because mining companies in Ethiopia do not pay premiums in exchange for licenses).
- *Mining companies fraudulently understate output or profit or overstate costs.*
  - A mining company may operate two sets of accounts: (a) one that correctly states the mine's annual production and is used for the mine's internal accounts, and (b) another set that understates annual production figures. The mining company sends the accounts with the lower figure to the licensing authority to reduce the amount of royalty it pays.
  - A mining company may, in its accounts, falsely increase the mine's capital or operating costs or falsely decrease the mine's revenues from

mineral sales—thus reducing the mine's reported net profit, in turn reducing the income tax paid to the licensing authority.

- *Inspectors and auditors solicit or accept bribes to agree with false declarations.*
- *Mining is conducted without a license, and output is not declared.*
- *Mining is conducted outside the scope of the license, and output is not declared.*
  - While carrying out its mining operation, the mining company may uncover a mineral for which it does not have a license. Instead of applying for the license, it may mine the additional mineral illegally and transport it off-site for sale without declaring it to the licensing authority and without paying royalty or profit tax on it.
- *Mining companies illegally export mining products.*
  - A mining company may reduce its royalties and income tax payable to the licensing authority by illegally exporting part of its production out of the country. It may pay a bribe to an official to assist it in this purpose.
- *Mining products are sold illegally within Ethiopia.*

Existing mining revenue procedures
Collection of royalties and income tax apparently depends almost entirely on the mining companies' self-certification of output and profit because of the lack of resources at the Ethiopian federal, regional, and city licensing authority levels. It would, therefore, be relatively easy for the mining companies to exaggerate their capital and operating costs and understate their output and profit.

In addition, artisanal mines currently appear to be an almost impossible problem to monitor—bearing in mind the large number of artisanal mines, the number of illegal mines, the small scale of the operations, the high labor element of the mining, the lack of records kept by artisanal mines, and the fact that the miners often personally keep and sell their own share of the output. The shortage of inspectors makes it difficult to find out about and monitor these mines, and it is also possible that local officials may extort bribes from artisanal miners in exchange for not reporting their illegal mining activities.

The risk of large-scale corruption in the payment of up-front premiums to the government is eliminated by the fact that the Ethiopian government does not currently require such payments. In some other countries, this premium can be the largest single source of corruption. However, the Ethiopian government *does* currently receive up-front premiums (in the form of signature bonuses) on the award of some petroleum concessions, so these could be introduced in the future in the mining sector, with the resultant corruption risk.

The interviews and workshop revealed a perceived high risk of the following:

- Mining companies not correctly declaring their output or profit, thereby denying royalty and income tax to the licensing authority
- Artisanal miners mining gold and selling it to illegal intermediaries who smuggle it out of the country
- Artisanal miners illegally digging in a seam that a major mining company has been exploring or excavating.

The survey revealed the following perceptions in relation to corruption in mining revenues:

- Out of the 17 people who completed this section of the survey, four (24 percent) were aware of bribery or fraud in relation to mining revenue.
- Two were aware of bribery or fraud from their organizations' experiences and four from rumor.
- Three believed that such bribery or fraud took place at the federal level, two at the regional level, and three at the city level.

These results suggest that current preventive mechanisms are not adequate.

Risk rating: High
The actual risk in Ethiopia of mining companies falsifying mining revenue at the federal license level is considered to be high.

Recommendations to mitigate risks
- The number of trained inspectors and auditors should be materially increased.
- At large mines that have a very high-value output, an official could be permanently stationed at the mine to monitor output.
- At smaller mines, officials could make periodic but frequent visits to monitor average output.
- These officials could be periodically rotated to decrease the risk of corruption.

- Auditors with experience in the mining sector and its costs could audit the annual accounts of mines. They will be able to query and check any unusual figures.
- Mining companies should be required to fully disclose to the auditors all their documents, production records, and accounts.
- Comparative analysis of the data from different but comparable mines should as far as possible be assessed to try to identify trends and discrepancies.
- The estimated mine output at time of license should be checked against the actual declared output, and the mining company should be asked to explain the reason for differences (although the mining company may have deliberately understated estimated production at the time of license application).
- The land shape at time of commencement of mine operation could be checked against the current shape (the difference being the amount excavated). However, several factors make this an inexact method:
  - Dependence on the sophistication and accuracy of
    - the ground contour data possessed by the licensing authority
    - the equipment used by the inspector
    - the inspector
    - the methods used to compare the data.
  - The amount of inappropriate material or wastage that is excavated but not exported
  - The fact that gold mines in particular export only a fraction of the product excavated.

Risk 4: Compensation and obligations to local inhabitants
Potential risks in sector
When a mining company applies for a license, it must negotiate compensation and land use rights with the local zones, woredas, and inhabitants. It may also have to agree to mining conditions that benefit the local inhabitants. In the fourth key area of risk—compensation and obligations to local inhabitants—the potential corruption risks in the Ethiopian mining sector include the following:

- *Officials or community leaders steal compensation.*
  - A fund may be set up to compensate all affected residents, the value of which may be a fair market value. However, local officials may expropriate all or part of the fund before the affected residents receive it.

- *Officials demand or accept bribes to set low compensation and impose less-onerous social conditions.*
  - Residents who are unwilling to move may have the site compulsorily purchased from them. However, the compensation from the mining company may be significantly below market value (particularly if the company has bribed the relevant official to approve a price that is below market value).
- *Local inhabitants disrupt mine operations to extract more compensation.*
  - Local inhabitants may block the road to the mine, preventing the minerals from being exported, and continue to do this until the mining company pays them additional compensation.
- *Local inhabitants wrongly claim that they occupy the land in order to claim compensation.*
  - When local inhabitants hear that an area is to be mined, they may immediately plant crops on the land to claim compensation. It may be difficult for the mining company to prove that the land was previously unoccupied.
- *Local inhabitants steal the mining company's property.*
- *Local gangs extort money by threatening personal injury or damage to property.*
- *Corruption may occur in relation to the social conditions imposed on the mining company that are designed to benefit or protect the local community.*
  - In some cases, the mining company will need to lease some land outside the license area (for example, for mine buildings). Where there are several possible sites, an official may ensure that a site is chosen that is owned by him or his family or where his own community may benefit from the exploration or development (such as by the building of roads or schools or by the provision of jobs).
  - The manager responsible for providing facilities to the community (for example, free health care) may corruptly require the community to pay him for the use of these services even though they are meant to be provided free of charge.
  - The mining company may not provide the service or may provide a subquality service and then bribe the relevant inspector to overlook the breach. Alternatively, the inspector may have insufficient expertise or time to detect the breach.
  - The mining company may deliberately breach the license requirements not to damage the surrounding area during mining operations and therefore may damage the local inhabitants' agricultural or grazing

ground. The breach may never be spotted for lack of effective inspection, or the mining company may bribe an inspector to ensure that the breach is overlooked.

Existing procedures for compensation and obligations to local inhabitants
Because a wide variety of federal, regional, city, and local administrations control compensation and social conditions, no analysis was undertaken of the control mechanisms in place. MOM does not itself have powers to ensure enforcement of compensation requirements.
    The interviews and workshop revealed the following perceptions:

- Most of the interviewees were not aware of any corruption in relation to local inhabitants, but they believed that this was a risk.
- Some interviewees were aware of corruption in this area, including
    ◦ local inhabitants planting land once they had heard of a possible license to get additional compensation; and
    ◦ compensation being stolen by officials.
    The survey revealed the following perceptions:
- Out of the 16 people who completed this section of the survey, four (25 percent) were aware of bribery or fraud in relation to local inhabitants.
- One was aware of bribery or fraud from an organization's experience, and four from rumor.
- One believed that such bribery or fraud took place at the federal level, four at the regional level, and two at the city level.

Risk rating: Medium
The actual risk in Ethiopia of corruption in relation to compensation and obligations to local inhabitants at the federal license level is considered to be medium.

Recommendations to mitigate risks
- Clear procedures should be in place so that mining companies and local inhabitants know in advance the companies' obligations in relation to compensation and social requirements and so that the discretion of all relevant officials is reduced.
- The mining company should be required to publish—both on the Internet and at a local office—details of the social conditions with which it must comply and the compensation it has agreed to pay. Any local inhabitant can then see what he or she should receive.

- A local committee including residents, local officials, and religious leaders should oversee the administration of compensation to reduce the risk of the money being stolen.
- Some mining companies reported difficulties with local inhabitants who, when they hear about a license being issued, plant crops on areas over which a license has been granted. The compensation arrangements could be changed to account for the length of time a farmer has occupied the land. This would help prevent this type of speculative planting.
- The inhabitants should know how they can complain if the mining company breaches its mining conditions or compensation obligations.
- Greater collaboration between the mining company and local inhabitants should be encouraged. If the local inhabitants are aware of the benefits the mine can bring to the community as well as the importance of ensuring that the company complies with its mining conditions, the inhabitants could both support and monitor the mining operation.
- Some mining companies complained of confusion and overlap in some cases between the different responsibilities of (a) the federal, regional, and city governments; and (b) the administrations of the zones, woredas, and kebeles. Confusion and uncertainty can increase the risk of corruption because the power and discretion of officials increase under such conditions. These responsibilities should be clarified and published.

Risk 5: Contracts with contractors and suppliers
Potential risks in sector

In the fifth key area of risk—contracts with contractors and suppliers—the potential corruption risks identified in the Ethiopian mining sector include the following:

- *Tenderers pay bribes to win contracts.*
  - The contractor could pay a bribe to the procurement manager of the mining company in exchange for the contractor being appointed.
  - The procurement manager of the mining company may be required to purchase mining equipment from overseas. Several different suppliers may be able to provide the equipment. In return for a bribe paid by one of the suppliers, the procurement manager may write the specification for the equipment in such a way that only the supplier that paid the bribe could win the tender.

- *Procurement officials give contracts to contractors in which they have an interest.*
  - ○ The procurement manager of the mining company may appoint a contractor that he or his family secretly owns.
- *Contractors claim payment for work that was not done or materials that were not delivered.*
  - ○ The earthworks contractor may claim payment from the mining company for more loads of excavation than it actually carried.
  - ○ The contractor appointed to construct the mine buildings may have an obligation to excavate down to minus 2 meters for the foundations of the mine buildings. However, it may only dig down to minus 1 meter, and therefore save all related excavation, steel, and concrete costs. It may pay a bribe to the construction supervisor so that the supervisor falsely certifies that the foundations were excavated to minus 2 meters.
- *Contractors conceal defective works.*
- *Contractors pay bribes to have fraudulent claims and defective works approved.*
- *Officials require mining companies to give work to a company owned by the official or in which he has an interest.*
- *Mining companies fraudulently refuse to pay contractors.*
  - ○ The mining company could corruptly refuse to pay the contractor for the work properly undertaken by the contractor and raise a false counterclaim against the contractor alleging defects in its work as justification for nonpayment.

Existing procedures for contracts with contractors and suppliers
This risk of corruption does not appear to be controlled in any way by the federal, regional, or city licensing authorities. It would be difficult for the authorities to control this risk because these activities are normally between private sector mining companies and private sector contractors and suppliers. MOM does not itself have powers to ensure enforcement of contract conditions between mining companies and contractors and suppliers. Many mining companies are international companies and likely have procedures to help control these risks.

The interviews and workshop revealed no personal knowledge of these types of corruption.

Two out of the five people to respond to this section of the *survey* indicated experience of this type of corruption.

Risk rating: Low to medium
The actual risk in Ethiopia of corruption in relation to contracts with contractors and suppliers at the federal license level is considered to be low to medium.

Recommendations to mitigate risks
It is difficult for licensing authorities to exercise any direct control over private-sector-to-private-sector corruption because no government interface is involved. However, the licensing authorities could take several indirect steps at the federal, regional, and city levels:

- Mining companies could be required, as a license condition, to implement anticorruption controls.
- The FEACC could provide anticorruption training to mining companies.
- The remit of the FEACC and the regional ethics and anticorruption commissions could be extended to include private-sector-to-private-sector corruption.

Risk 6: Postextraction falsification of quality
Potential risks in sector
In the sixth key area of risk—postextraction falsification of quality—the potential corruption risks identified in the Ethiopian mining sector include the following:

- *Mining companies make false declarations as to the identity of the mineral.*
- *Mining companies make false declarations as to the quality of the mineral.*
  - Gold bars may be sold that are not solid gold but instead are a cheaper metal plated in gold. These bars may be accompanied by falsified certificates of quality.
  - A mineral may be sold accompanied by a certificate that exaggerates its quality, therefore resulting in a higher sale price.
- *Mining companies may bribe certifiers to certify false declarations.*

The interviews and workshop revealed no personal knowledge of these types of corruption. Purchasers of the product are in most cases likely to exercise their own controls to ensure that they are buying products of the correct quality.

Two out of the four people who completed this section of the *survey* believed that this type of corruption was common or fairly common.

The FEACC is currently dealing with a specific case of falsification of gold quality, as box 9.1 explains.

Risk rating: low to medium
The actual risk in Ethiopia of corruption in relation to falsification of quality at federal license level is considered to be low to medium.

Recommendations to mitigate risks
Falsification of quality will normally require a fraudulent certificate of quality to be issued by the relevant testing laboratory or a fake certificate to be issued. Controls therefore need to be in place to ensure that, as far as possible:

- the sample being tested is from the correct batch;
- the testers in the laboratories are well trained and honest; and
- additional random tests are undertaken to cross-check the accuracy of the testing system.

Box 9.1

Falsification of Quality: Corruption Investigation by the FEACC

The FEACC Annual Performance Report for 2008 states as follows:

"The budget year also saw a huge scandal at the National Bank of Ethiopia (NBE). It was dubbed by many as 'the huge scandal of the year.' Here is the trick. The NBE is by law entrusted with procuring and reserving gold. Some business-men, who were allowed to supply gold to the NBE, supplied many kilograms of gilded iron, instead of gold. Some employees of the Bank, business people, man-agers and other government employees were allegedly involved in this disastrous and disgracing scandal. The government lost nearly 16 million USD to this par-ticular gold scam. The FEACC is spearheading the investigations and prosecutions of the above cases. Dozens of suspects have already been arrested and the cases are in due process of law. As to the restraining of properties obtained through corruption in connection with the above cases, nearly 4.6 million USD and 81 kg of gold, among others, was restrained on court order."

Source: FEACC 2008.

Risk 7: Theft of product and equipment

Potential risks in sector

In the seventh key area of risk—theft of product and equipment—the potential corruption risks identified in the sector include the following:

- *Workers, local inhabitants, or gangs steal mineral product and mining equipment.*
  - A small, high-value product can be hidden on the worker's person.
  - A larger, low-value product may be shipped out at night by truck, with the thieves having bribed the security guards not to stop them.
  - Local inhabitants may break into the mine and steal the mining product or equipment.
- *Artisanal miners dig illegally in a mining company's license area.*

The interviews and workshop revealed no personal knowledge of these types of corruption.

Two out of the four people who completed this section of *the survey* believed that this type of corruption was common or fairly common.

Risk rating: Medium

The actual risk in Ethiopia of corruption in relation to theft of the product and equipment at federal license level is considered to be medium.

Recommendations to mitigate risks

Theft prevention is primarily a question of adequate resources: for example, (a) security fences around the mine that prevent people from entering or leaving the mine except through the main gate; (b) well-trained, honest security guards; and (c) the searching of staff and vehicles that leave the mine to check for stolen equipment or product.

General Recommendations

A number of recommendations apply to all corruption risk areas. Because there are separate licensing authorities at the federal, regional, and city levels, these recommendations are kept as broad as possible.

Recommendation 1: *Increase the number and capacity of high-caliber officials.*

Efforts should increase to enhance the number and capacity of licensing authority staff by appointing the best available people and giving them appropriate training. Although the caliber of some staff members at licensing authorities is high, there is generally a shortage of appropriately qualified and experienced staff. Corruption can be reduced by having staff of high integrity and ability. Staff members with integrity will not become involved in corruption and will report any corruption they see that affects their employer.

Recommendation 2: *Enhance transparency by improving disclosure requirements.*

One of the best ways to help reduce corruption is to increase transparency. Corruption thrives in secrecy. It is significantly more difficult to conceal corrupt license awards, corrupt conditions of mining, and corrupt payments if all details are made available to the public. There is currently only limited disclosure of license details. It is recommended that this disclosure be materially increased, particularly in the following ways:

- Full public disclosure of all relevant documents associated with mining licenses and mine operation, including all license applications, agreements, and conditions; royalties, profit taxes, and any other payments made by the mining company to the licensing authorities; inspection guidelines and reports; any enforcement action taken by the authorities against the mining company; and compensation required to be paid to local inhabitants
- Very limited exceptions to full disclosure in relation to technical data that are genuinely confidential to the mining company
- Disclosure as soon as possible after the licensing authority produces or receives the relevant documents
- Disclosure of all federal, regional, and city prospecting, exploration, and mining licenses awarded within the last six years as well as all future licenses
- Disclosure available both on the Internet and at the relevant federal, regional, or city registries
- Relatively simple, cheap management of disclosure by making virtually all the above documents available in electronic form for easy downloading onto a website
- A simple amendment both to the law and to the model license agreement to provide for the above disclosure management.

The Extractive Industries Transparency Initiative (EITI)[6] is an international initiative to improve transparency and accountability by the full publication and verification of company payments and government revenues in extractive industries (including mining). In 2009, Ethiopia announced its commitment to join the initiative. Ethiopia's commitment is welcome, and its EITI membership will assist in its moves toward greater transparency. However, EITI currently only requires relatively limited disclosure of information, and corruption prevention would be best assisted if Ethiopia adopted the wider disclosure requirements recommended above. In particular, it is imperative that Ethiopia does not treat its EITI membership as a complete solution to corruption in the sector. Transparency is a vital part of corruption prevention, but it is only one of many actions that need to be implemented, and all the recommended actions in this chapter should be adopted.

Recommendation 3: *Strengthen internal audit procedures by introducing random checks and improving capacity.*

Random checks by internal auditors for compliance with procedures and for any evidence of corruption can both deter corrupt acts and uncover corruption that has taken place. All federal, regional, and city licensing authorities should have an internal audit department that functions as follows:

- The internal audit department should have enough auditors to allow a wide-reaching and frequent audit.
- The auditors should receive specific anticorruption training that highlights the areas of corruption risk they should be looking for.
- The internal audit function should be entirely independent and able to choose on its own which licenses and which departments it audits and at what time.
- The internal audit department should report any findings of possible corruption or wrongdoing simultaneously to the board of the relevant licensing authority; to the ethics officer of the relevant licensing authority; to whichever is appropriate of the FEACC, the regional ethics and anticorruption commission, or the police; and to the Office of the Auditor General.

Recommendation 4: *Enhance the role and status of the ethics officer.*

MOM currently has a temporary ethics officer who is responsible for examining procurement by MOM. There should be a major increase in the scope of that officer's work and resources. The ethics officer should be responsible for organizing anticorruption training for MOM staff, advising MOM staff on ethical issues, receiving reports of corruption from MOM staff or the public, and investigating those reports (in collaboration, if appropriate, with the internal audit department). The ethics officer also should be a senior-level appointment and have adequate staff to support him or her in carrying out the ethics function. The ethics officer and relevant support staff should receive specific anticorruption training that highlights the areas of corruption risk they should be looking for. In addition, the ethics officer should be independent and should report corruption on the same basis as described above in relation to the internal audit function. Ethics officers should also be appointed on the same basis as described above at all regional and city licensing authorities.

Recommendation 5: *Improve the appeals and complaints procedures.*

Appeals and complaints procedures need to be in place at each licensing authority for mining companies that are unhappy with any aspect of the licensing and operations procedures of the licensing authorities and for local inhabitants who believe they have been undercompensated. At the federal level, complaints can be made to MOM's ethics officer or by completing a complaints form. However, the perception of some mining companies interviewed was that these mechanisms may not always be effective.

Recommendation 6: *Encourage reporting of corruption.*

Staff of the federal, regional, and city licensing authorities; staff of mining companies; and members of the public should be strongly encouraged to report any suspicions of corruption. Reporting can be to the appropriate ethics officer or to whichever is appropriate of the FEACC, the regional ethics and anticorruption commission, or the police. People need to be assured that they may report anonymously if they wish and that staff will suffer no prejudice in their employment if they do report (unless the report is made maliciously). Reporting could be encouraged by a publicity campaign on television and in the press. A system for anonymous reporting could be established by providing an address to which people can write with their complaints and by informing people that they do not need to include their name and address on the letter.

Recommendation 7: *Establish a licensing authority and mining company forum.*

A forum should be established made up of senior members of MOM, the regional and city licensing authorities, the FEACC, and mining companies. This forum should meet periodically (such as once every quarter) to discuss how to improve license issuing, license management, and anticorruption mechanisms.

The Ethiopian mining sector is currently a relatively small part of Ethiopia's economy. Therefore, the extent of corruption in the mining sector appears to be lower—both in occurrence and in value—than in other Ethiopian sectors such as construction and telecommunications. However, the sector's rapid expansion will increase both the risk of corruption and the amounts potentially lost to corruption. Effective anticorruption action is imperative. The implementation of effective actions not only reduces the extent of corruption but also reduces the perception that corruption is occurring.

Notes

1. For further information on corruption in the construction sector, see chapter 6 of this volume—"Construction Sector Corruption in Ethiopia"—as well as the Global Infrastructure Anti-Corruption Centre's free online resource, http://www.giaccentre.org.
2. The Ministry of Mines and Energy was reorganized and renamed the Ministry of Mines in 2010.
3. Five licenses were issued for prospecting, 109 for exploration, 19 for small-scale mining, and 27 for large-scale mining
4. Federal Democratic Republic of Ethiopia (FDRE) Mining Proclamation No.52/1993; Mining (Amendment) Proclamation No.22/1996; Mining (Amendment) Proclamation No.118/1998; Mining Operations Council of Ministers Regulations No. 182/1994; Mining Operations Council of Minister (Amendment) Regulations No. 27/1998; Mining Income Tax Proclamation No.53/1993; Mining Income Tax (Amendment) Proclamation No. 23/1996.
5. An attempt has been made in relation to each risk area to rate the potential degree of corruption risk at the federal mining license level (for example, low, medium, or high). Obviously, the rating is subjective without hard data on which to base this assessment. No attempt has been made to rate the risk at the city and regional levels because there are likely to be major discrepancies in the degree of effective control between the different cities and regions. However, it is likely that the risk level will be higher at the city and regional

levels than at the federal level primarily because of the more limited resources and lower capacity at the city and regional levels.

6. http://eiti.org/.

References

FEACC (Federal Ethics and Anti-Corruption Commission). 2008. "Annual Report." FEACC, Addis Ababa.

TI (Transparency International). 2008. TI Bribe Payers Index 2008. Periodic survey report, TI, Berlin. http://archive.transparency.org/policy_research/surveys_indices/bpi/bpi_2008.

MOME (Ministry of Mines and Energy). 2009. "National Report on Mining." Report to the United Nations Commission on Sustainable Development, Addis Ababa.

www.ingramcontent.com/pod-product-compliance
Lightning Source LLC
Chambersburg PA
CBHW071827270326
41929CB00013B/1921

9780821395318